Landscapes of Relations and Belonging

SERIES:
Person, Space and Memory in the Contemporary Pacific

Series editor: **Prof. Jürg Wassmann**, University of Heidelberg, Institute of Anthropology
Assistant editor: **Katharina Stockhaus-White**, M.A., University of Heidelberg, Institute of Anthropology
Advisory board: **Prof. Pierre R. Dasen**, University of Geneva, Department of Anthropology of Education and Cross-Cultural Psychology), **Dr. Verena Keck**, University of Heidelberg, Institute of Anthropology, **Prof. Donald H. Rubinstei**n, University of Guam, Director of the Micronesian Area Research Center, **Prof. Robert Tonkinson**, The University of Western Australia, Department of Anthropology, **Prof. Peter Meusburge**r, University of Heidelberg, Department of Economic and Social Geography, **Prof. Joachim Funke**, University of Heidelberg, Department of Psychology

The many different localities of the Pacific region have a long history of transformation, under both pre- and post-colonial conditions. More recently, rates of local transformation have increased tremendously under post-colonial regimes. Yet, until now, research has concentrated on the macro- or culturally specific aspects of globalization, while neglecting actual actors and their perspectives of social change. This series supplements earlier work through the integration of cultural research with psychological methodologies, linguistics, geography and cognitive science.

Volume 1
Experiencing New Worlds
Jürg Wassmann and Katharina Stockhaus

Volume 2
Person and Place:
Ideas, Ideals and the Practice of Sociality on Vanua Lava, Vanuatu
Sabine C. Hess

Volume 3
Landscapes of Relations and Belonging:
Body, Place and Politics in Wogeo, Papua New Guinea
Astrid Anderson

Landscapes of Relations and Belonging

Body, Place and Politics in Wogeo,
Papua New Guinea

Astrid Anderson

Berghahn Books
New York • Oxford

Published in 2011 by

Berghahn Books

www.berghahnbooks.com

©2011 Astrid Anderson

Library of Congress Cataloging-in-Publication Data

Anderson, Astrid.
  Landscapes of relations and belonging : body, place and politics in Wogeo,
Papua New Guinea / Astrid Anderson. – 1st ed.
    p. cm. – (Person, space and memory in the contemporary Pacific ; v. 3)
  Includes bibliographical references and index.
  ISBN 978-1-84545-775-4 (hardback : alk. paper) – ISBN 978-0-85745-034-0
  (ebook)
  1. Ethnology–Papua New Guinea–Vokeo Island. 2. Ethnopsychology–Papua
New Guinea–Vokeo Island. 3. Ethnicity–Papua New Guinea–Vokeo Island. 4.
Geographical perception–Papua New Guinea–Vokeo Island. 5. Vokeo Island
(Papua New Guinea)–Politics and government. 6. Vokeo Island (Papua New
Guinea)–Social life and customs. I. Title.
  GN671.N5A64 2011

                                                           305.800957'5–dc22

British Library Cataloguing in Publication Data
A catalogue record for this book is available from the British Library
Printed in the United States on acid-free paper.

ISBN: 978-1-84545-775-4 (hardback)
E-ISBN 978-0-85745-034-0

Contents

List of Illustrations

Acknowledgements

Since I first read Ian Hogbin's books about Wogeo 17 years ago and started to plan my first fieldwork on the island, many people have helped and inspired me in my work. The Norwegian Research Council, Lumholz-fondet and Nordic Institute of Asian Studies funded my research in 1993–94, 1998 and 1999, and the research was carried out under the auspices of the Institute of Papua New Guinea Studies and the National Research Institute in Port Moresby. The Institute of Comparative Cultural Research in Oslo should be thanked for facilitating the cooperation with linguist Mats Exter by funding his research in Wogeo in 1999 and 2000. For all the periods of fieldwork I was affiliated to the Department of Social Anthropology at the University of Oslo. I am grateful to the department and the funding institutions for giving me the opportunity to go to Wogeo. Thanks are also due to Nancy Frank and Frøydis Haugane for the best library service possible, and to Nancy Frank also for improving my English.

This book is based on my doctoral dissertation accepted at the University of Oslo in 2003. Several people have read and commented on my texts during the various stages of the work leading up to this book and should be thanked: Rune Paulsen, Tone Sommerfelt, Heidi Fjeld, Benedicte Lindskog, Trude Bell, Dag Tuastad, Thorgeir Kolshus, Arne Røkkum, David Lipset, and in particular Arve Sørum, Edvard Hviding, Sidsel Roalkvam and Ingjerd Hoëm. I would also like to thank Signe Howell for important encouragement. I am particularly gratified that in 2003 I got the chance to meet Donald Tuzin and was able to discuss the Wogeo ethnography with him before he died. His generous and inspiring comments on my work have been of immense value.

I am indebted to Jürg Wassmann who gave me the opportunity to publish my book in this series, and I thank him and Verena Keck for inviting me to their seminar in Heidelberg in 2006. Katharina Stockhaus should also be mentioned in this regard, and Don Gardner should be thanked for commenting on my manuscript. Joshua Bell has reviewed this manuscript on behalf of Berghahn Books, and his detailed and conscientious comments have been most helpful in preparing this book, although I have not been able to incorporate all of his suggestions. For all shortcomings I am solely responsible.

Mats Exter, at the time a master student of linguistics at the University of Cologne, joined me for six months of fieldwork in Wogeo in 1999 – a cooperation made possible by Ingjerd Hoëm and Even Hovdhaugen of the Oceania group at the Department of Linguistics, University of Oslo. Mats has made the Wogeo language more intelligible for me, and he has transcribed and translated most of the songs and myths presented in this text. I greatly appreciate all his help – and for eating the food I served him when I tried to be a proper Wogeo woman. In Papua

New Guinea, Ralph Stüttgen should be thanked for providing accommodation and assistance in various ways during field breaks in Wewak.

I also wish to thank my life companion, Rune Paulsen. He introduced me to Papua New Guinea when I first went there in 1993, and we spent one year in our respective field sites, he in May River and I in Wogeo. For his encouragement and company I am eternally grateful. With him I have also been so lucky as to become the mother to two wonderful boys, Eirik and Askil, who make sure everything is kept in a proper perspective.

But I am, of course, most of all indebted to the people of Wogeo Island. Not all of the Wogeos who have helped me in my work can be mentioned by name, but some of them have to be: Niabula, Sanganie, Kanemoeka, Gris, Boarinya, Matarena, Saramoin, Sanum, Bo, Jeda, Kumi, Guria, Min, Ima, Soufa, Kaite, Saboakai, Boanga, Iakena, Marajina, Nunu, Ialoma, Gamuia, Koan, Libaliba, Fein, Bagim, Sako, Tangom, Kenang, Boakie, Jagamoin, Makanga, Sidaia, Jabat, Main, Kamagun, Iangeine, Ganem, Oaiari, Bujon, Sesare, Tamoin, Malo, Gouso, Bareoa, Jangara, Talbul, Munjal, Lala, Mango, Tangarua, Kaiaga, Salam, Singi, Nyem, Gulegule, Kenai and Majebra. My friends, Medo, Tangina and Saea, have to be mentioned in particular, as should Sarakamot, my young friend and companion in 1999. Bernard Gagin Dale and Tom Fandim lived on the mainland while I was in Wogeo, but we have had many interesting discussions about Wogeo customs – with Gagin also in letters. Marifa and Kulbobo took upon themselves the role as my teacher in Wogeo and told me numerous important stories. Both of them are now sadly dead, but hopefully their voices remain in this text in ways they would have appreciated. In Dab, Maria Sua and Tarere adopted me as a daughter, and I lived with them and their children, Roger, Kijua, Sheila Ia, Boeka and their niece, Moatakia, during all my stays on the island. Parts of the time *bum* Moita also stayed with us. Their patience with me and all my inquiries was admirable and I thank them for their hospitality and the way they included me in their family during the months I spent in Dab.

To all my Wogeo friends who allowed me to take part in their lives – *Kalingó tuka!*

Note on Orthography

The Wogeo language is spoken by Wogeos and the people of the neighbouring island Koil – according to the 2000 census, 1,624 people. The Wogeos call their language Oageva – the same as the local name of the island. When I started to do research in Wogeo, the Wogeo language was still undocumented. In order to start the work of documenting the language, linguist Mats Exter accompanied me to Wogeo in 1999 as part of his MA project (Exter 2003).

The orthography he developed differs from the one Hogbin used in his texts, and also from the rather unsystematic way Wogeos themselves wrote in the 1990s. In this book I use the orthography suggested by him (Exter 2003; Anderson and Exter 2005). The phoneme inventory of Wogeo is as follows:

	t		k		i		u
b	d	j	g		e		o
f	s					a	
m	n	ñ	ŋ				
	l						
	r						
v							

For those familiar with Ian Hogbin's work from Wogeo, some changes in orthography should be noted. The most conspicuous change is that *w* is replaced with *o*: for instance, what Hogbin wrote as *warabwa* (food festival) is in this text *oaraboa*. Hogbin's *y* is in most cases changed to *i*, so that *yata* (up) becomes *iata* and *Yamwi* (name) becomes *Iamoe*. In the present text, *y* is only used after *n* – as in *nyonyo* (mother) – a sound that according to linguistic convention (and in the phoneme inventory above) is written as *ñ*. Here *ny* is used. Similarly *ng* is used rather than *ŋ*. What Hogbin wrote as *p* is here written as *b* – for instance *Dab* instead of *Dap*. The *r* (as for instance in *ruma*) is pronounced as a mix of *r* and *l* (to be more accurate, as a 'voiced retroflex flap in prevocalic postition (Anderson and Exter 2005: 16) and as a 'voiced retroflex approximant' (ibid.) elsewhere). After vowels, *d* is pronounced as a 'trill': the village *Dab* is pronounced *Dab*, whereas the mountain *Ilodab* (the mountain 'inside of Dab') is pronounced *Ilorab*. Elsewhere it is pronounced as an English *d*. For a further elaboration on the orthography and the Wogeo language, see Exter (2003) and Anderson and Exter (2005).

In this book I have written all native terms in italics. I have also written the Tok Pisin (Papua New Guinean Pidgin English) terms I use in italics, but always with an indication that the term is in Tok Pisin.

Maps of Wogeo and the Coast
of East Sepik Province

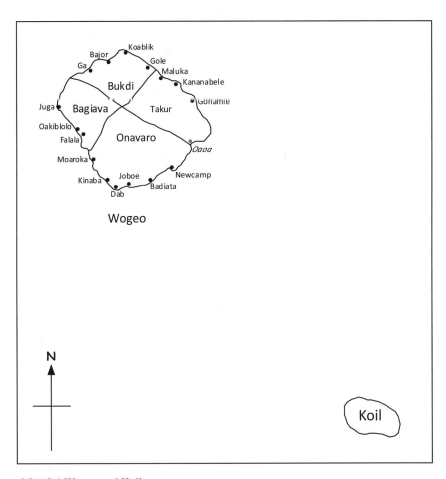

Map 0.1 Wogeo and Koil

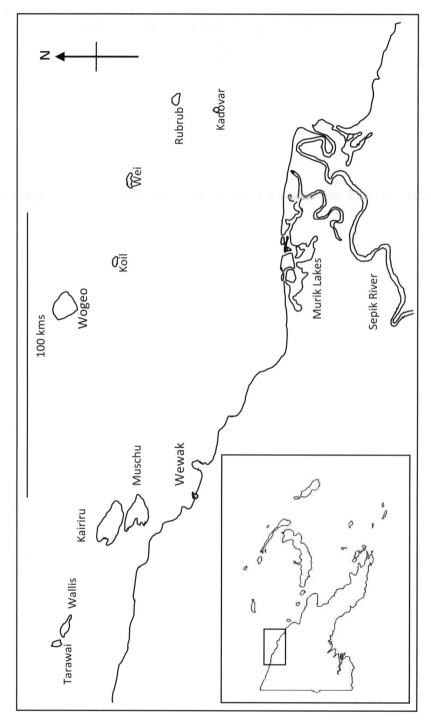

Map 0.2 The coast of East Sepik Province

Introduction

Standing on the beach of Wewak, the provincial capital of East Sepik Province on the north coast of Papua New Guinea, the silhouette of Wogeo Island can be seen on the horizon on clear days. It takes a 2-3 hour ride in a dinghy with outboard motor to get from Wewak to the island, often in rough seas and strong currents. After hours at sea, continuously being washed by salty waves, the beautiful stony beaches of Wogeo are a welcome relief. Big trees lean out over the blue sea, providing a much appreciated shade from the baking sun. Then, trying to come to terms with the fact that the ground is not swaying, you are most likely presented with a fresh coconut to drink. Later, if you are lucky, your Wogeo friends will rub your salty, tired skin with pleasant smelling herbs dipped in water.

The Wogeos do this in order to wash away contamination accumulated in your body as a result of having stayed in foreign places, leaving your body fresh and with the smell of Wogeo. The welcoming ritual places your body on the island cleansed and prepared for wanderings through the Wogeo landscape. The wanderings presented in this text start in the village of Dab, a place of great importance. The stories of many people, alive and dead, are infused into this place, stories of people's origins and their movement within and between places. It is these stories that will form the core of this text.

The purpose of this book is to show how the bodily experiences of dwelling in, and moving through, the landscape of places and people on the island shape the manner in which Wogeos conceptualize and give meaning to their world. My aim is, however, not to present an exclusively phenomenological perspective on the Wogeo 'being-in-the-world'. It will be complemented with a semiotic analysis of the ways these experiences are made manifest in the physical world: in bodies, houses, pathways and places. Phenomenology has been called 'a science of beginnings' (Csordas 1999: 183) and, as such, it is the beginning-point for the analyses of this book.

A house in the forest and paths leading through it is an image used by philosopher and phenomenologist Martin Heidegger (1993[1954]) to describe the salience of 'dwelling' as the basis for how we experience and give meaning to the phenomenal world and, thus, to life in general. We may envisage that we have just moved to a house in a forest. The forest is unfamiliar and may be, lest there are already well-worn paths in it, difficult to manoeuvre in. It is to us nothing more than a forest filled with trees. We need to find landmarks in order to get a sense of direction and to mark out routes that are good to walk. The trees that make up the forest are merely trees, but soon we will start to pay attention to particular trees. If this forest is situated in Norway, we might notice that in an old, near-dead pine a woodpecker has carved out its hole. A birch marks out the point where we should take a turn to the left in order to avoid ending up at a precipice. In the spring we may become aware that a certain alder is the first tree to sprout. As time passes we look for signs of whether or not the woodpecker has returned after the winter to lay eggs in the hole in the old pine. We wonder if the dead branch on the birch has fallen down since last time and measure the growth of leaves after the early sprouting alder. We might even think about these trees when sitting in the kitchen planning a walk in the forest. When we first moved to the house, the forest became a part of our life. As time passes, the particular trees we have endowed with meaning and histories also become parts of our life as separate entities within that forest and, as time goes by, more and more entities in the forest will be made meaningful. Places can be seen as created in such a manner. By moving through the phenomenal world we attach our experiences and histories to certain sites and, thus, transform these sites into places. Through our movement and experience in it, the indistinct forest becomes a meaningful landscape of places and pathways, and the pathways we follow gather our experience into meaningful life-worlds.

As an analogy we can say that we create relations with people in a similar manner in some contexts. When first joining an unfamiliar social setting – like that of an introductory class at university – the people present are merely an anonymous mass of fellow students. As time passes one notices some of them more than others – one because he dresses in a particular manner, another because she asked the lecturer an interesting question or a third because she asked for a light for her cigarette during a break. These may be the people one starts to talk to, and after a while one has established what we can call a social network. It is impossible to establish meaningful relations with all the fellow students, and one chooses some in favour of others for some reason or another. A social landscape emerges, based on relations to more or less significant others. Through time, the network of relations becomes increasingly complex, and some relations become more solid than others.

Taking these experiential foundations for 'being-in-the-world' to Wogeo, I believe useful insights can be gained. The experienced landscapes are centred in places along the coastline of the island with pathways between them, to the gardens in the nearby bush and onto the reef. The interior of the island and the sea are the horizons for these loci of experience at the same time as pathways lead across the island and over the sea to other places and people, turning horizons into experienced landscapes for those who travel along them. Through time, continuous and repeated movements in these landscapes make every part of them meaningful to the people living there.

But these landscapes are not only filled with people's own subjective experiences: histories of people and events from the past are also imbued in them. Through generations, people's histories have been attached to the places, and some of these are more or less collectively remembered. To the Wogeos, the meaningful landscapes constitute much more than merely being the result of everyday human experience or the equivalent to history books. The histories infused in the landscape tell people where and with whom they should belong, where they should cultivate their crops and with whom they should maintain particular relations. Wogeos order their social life according to this landscape of history and experience.

Such geographical and social landscapes are not created separately from categorizations and knowledge already present in mind. Due to knowledge we already had when we started to walk in the forest we knew that there existed a bird called a woodpecker that makes holes in trees. We knew that it was dangerous to climb down steep precipices and we knew that eventually all the trees would bear leaves in the spring. We started to talk to the guy who dressed in a certain manner because his clothing signalled that we might share certain likes and dislikes. We knew that it was good to have company while smoking outside during the breaks, and there was a reason why we found the girl's questions to the lecturer particularly interesting.

As Wogeos move in their geographical and social landscape, various categorizations are made relevant. Children accompany their parents to their gardens and learn to whom the trees and gardens belong, from underneath which trees they may pick the nuts they know they like to eat and that some paths are better to follow than others to get to the family's gardens. In the village they learn not to play under the house because it is dirty since the pigs sleep there, they learn to which house they may go to get something to eat, and when visiting other villages they soon know to which houses they may go and rest. In the constitution of social networks, social categorizations are made relevant. Wogeos reckon all people on the island as kin. 'That is why we don't have a word for "friend"', they say. The categorization 'kin' versus 'non-kin' is thus not relevant within the island and 'friendship' based exclusively on mutual sympathy is not conceptualized as a separate category of relationship. Close kin and distant kin are relevant, but not predominant, categorizations since people living in villages close to each other are usually close kin in one way or the other. Categories based in matrilineal descent are relevant in certain contexts, but in daily interaction it is those who share meaningful landscapes (or histories) who are the more relevant 'others': those who follow the same pathways, who belong to places connected by the same pathways and who regard the same histories as significant. The geographical and the social landscapes are constitutive of each other. Places are constituted by histories of people and events, and, at the same time, they provide the means for establishing belonging and relations that continue these histories. People's movements in the landscape constitute pathways between places that become conduits for future movement, creating and maintaining relations and the memory of relations between people.

Heidegger's concept of 'dwelling' signifies the way we are in the world and 'involves a lack of distance between people and things' (Bender 1993: 28). To dwell is in the nature of being – we are 'dwellers' (Heidegger 1993[1954]: 350). To Heidegger, cognition is not 'opposed to reality, but is wholly given over in the total social fact of dwelling, serving to link place, praxis, cosmology and nurture' (Tilley 1994: 13). Merleau-Ponty's phenomenology (1962), on the other hand, emphasizes the sensing body as 'the existential ground of culture' (Csordas 1990: 5). Bodily movement is essential to how meaningful landscapes are constituted; pathways, as manifestations of bodily movement through time, channel people's social relations in the landscapes of places where Wogeos dwell and belong (cf. Roalkvam 1997: 61). From this perspective, space becomes a product of movement.

However, as Richard Eves has argued in his analysis of bodily movement and space among the Lelet of New Ireland,

> [A]ny full conceptualization of space must be coupled with an analysis of, and be grounded in, a concept of space as social space. The movement of the body, which Merleau-Ponty sees as important to the constitution of space, does not exist outside of people's symbolic construction of socially inhabited space and also of the body (Eves 1997: 178).

My phenomenological starting point will, accordingly, lead to an analysis of how Wogeos give meaning to and represent their world, inspired by important theorists in Melanesian anthropology, mainly Roy Wagner and Marilyn Strathern. The contributions of these two anthropologists elicit what Sandra Bamford has called 'the forward-going momentum' (1998: 159) of New Guinea cultures: 'The "work" of most New Guinea cultures is not centred around reproducing a formalized model of "society" as such, but rather is geared toward creating particular kinds of social relationships' (ibid.).

Alfred Gell (1999: 32) has described Strathern's perspective in her most important work *Gender of the Gift* (1988) as 'idealist semiotics'. As such, the social world she calls Melanesia is comprised not of entities that have external relations to each other and to the interpreter but of internal relations of terms that constitute and give meaning to the entities in the world (ibid.: 33). Even man becomes a sign to Strathern – in the sense that a person can stand for something else than him- or herself, for instance the relation between his or her parents. But rather than seeing entities, such as a person or other singular things or beings, as the primary focus for her semiotics, Strathern places *relations* as the main constituents of her Melanesia (ibid.: 35).[1] As the term 'father' only makes sense in relation to the fact that a man has a child, all aspects of people's social lives are cast in relations to significant others.

James Weiner has argued that in worlds that are relationally based, 'the task confronting humans is not to sustain human relationships but to "place a limit on relationships"' (J. Weiner 2001: 76; see also Roalkvam 1997: 200; 2003; Strathern 1996: 529). In the Wogeo relationally based world, people make various types of relations relevant in different situations rather than finding their place in a predetermined social landscape of groups into which people are recruited on the basis of unambiguous criteria such as unilineal descent and marriage. Strathern (1996) has pointed out that without overarching, indisputable principles that set limits for relationships, social networks in such worlds appear to have a potential for endless expansion. This book is also about how Wogeos place limits on relationships; how they channel flows of sociality by cutting certain connections and facilitating others; how networks are cut or expanded.

People's movements in the landscape and the continuous work of creating and maintaining certain relations create an image of Wogeo sociality as fluid and contextual, but to the Wogeos the landscape also provides a template for the structuring of social relations – or placing limits on relations, to use Weiner's words – that is conceived of as permanent and enduring and in which people need to find their proper place. This is most of all made apparent in the way Wogeos build and inhabit houses and imbue them with meaning. In every house of significance on the island, the rafters in the ceiling are named and associated with certain pieces of land, names and histories of the people associated with the names and the land. The rafters are fastended in the ceiling corresponding to which part of the village the associated land is located and to which the people having rights in the rafter belong. The villages are conceptualised in both social and spatial terms as being divided in complementary sides or halves, often explained with the image of an eagle with its wings spread out to both sides, and the spatial composition of the house and the rafters replicates this spatial and social organization of the village. Further, the sides of the village are associated with offices of leadership, and the houses with certain matrilineages.

Wogeo named houses are powerful, polysemic and totalizing images: as icons of containment, as microcosms of the geographical and social composition of the villages, as well as images of overarching diagrams of sides and directions. But at the same time they are also part of the realm of concrete experience: they are the place where people dwell. Heidegger (1993[1954]) made the point that in the same manner as building is related to dwelling, thinking is related to dwelling. Our experience of dwelling is the basis for our thinking in the same manner as dwelling is the foundation for building: 'We do not dwell because we have built, but we build and have built because we dwell' (ibid.: 350). It is the concreteness and immediacy of houses – the continuous experienced presence of the complex and meaning-loaded image – that gives the house its evocative power, not primarily as it is presented and interpreted by means of language. As Kulbobo, one of my most important teachers of Wogeo *kastom*, stressed, experience is essential to understanding. Hearing words does not properly elicit meaning.

Wagner has written extensively about symbols and the dynamics of meaning formation in Melanesia. Rather than seeing signs as mediators of an arbitrary relation between abstract coding and 'natural percept' (1986b: 24), he argues that meaning is formed in a perceived or experienced macrocosm where signs and signified belong to a single relation (analogy), and that a microcosm of symbols (coding) is formed through abstraction from this macrocosm. There is an ongoing dialectic process of abstraction into such a microcosm and concretization into the macrocosm – the lived and experienced world (ibid.: 14). By naming beings or entities, we abstract a microcosm of symbols (or names, 'if names are symbols and symbols names' (Wagner 1986b: 16)).

> If we treat names as merely names, points of reference, then symbolism becomes a matter of reference: a microcosm of names is counterposed to a macrocosm of referents. But if we treat 'name' as a relationship, the microcosm of names is no longer a microcosm; it becomes immersed in a macrocosm of analogic constructions (ibid.: 15).

Meaning is not constituted in the abstracted microcosm: meaning is created in the perception of the relation between name and referent, Wagner states. Meaning is perception, he says (ibid.: 19), and this happens in the experienced and concrete macrocosmic world. The restriction of a symbol to represent a specific entity (the abstracting half of the dialectic process) cuts the macrocosm 'into manageable pieces' (ibid.) for social purposes, allowing us to communicate with symbols in relations to other symbols. But in the other half of the dialectic process, when we focus on the relation between name and referent, the symbolization is concretized in a larger macrocosm of other such analogical constructions. All analogical relations between names and referents are again analogous to each other (for instance by the fact that they are 'named'). This macrocosm of analogies 'mediates the microcosmic points of reference by allowing us to 'see' resemblances among them' (ibid.). It is this flow of analogies that makes meaningful metaphors possible, and metaphors are the means of expanding mere reference into meaningful constructions of specific 'cultural' worlds. This is how 'side' may come to refer to a set of people rather than merely 'half of the village' or 'half of the house', 'pathway' to a history of relations, or a male cult house to a female birth hut.

> A metaphor is meditative, inserting an unconventional element 'in the way of' conventional reference, so that the new relations comes to supplant, to 'anticipate and dispose of' conventional effect. And by constituting 'its own' relation in the process, becoming an 'icon' of itself, a symbol that shows its own meaning, the trope renders itself 'apparent' (Wagner 1978: 31–32).

A house is like a container (*jiraboa*), my Wogeo friend Kulbobo said, and showed me his water bottle. It is like the shell of a hermit crab: without it the crab becomes vulnerable and dies. When saying that the house is 'like the shell of a hermit crab', the original and conventional referent (house as concrete structure) is obviated – 'anticipated and disposed of' – and the image of the hermit crab shell is evoked. Other analogies are also evoked in the process: for instance that a person without a house somehow is like a hermit crab without its shell, vulnerable without the shell to protect its soft body. It is due to the analogical relation between the two images in a macrocosmic realm – 'house' as built structure and 'shell' as the shell with or without its inhabitant – that makes it possible to obviate conventional reference and create a new symbolization. Kulbobo used this metaphor to explain to me something about the quite concrete and experienced house. Obviously the metaphor would have been meaningless unless the relation between the name 'house' and the actual house was the prime focus, evoking the sensual feeling of being inside a house. And someone who had never actually experienced seeing and sympathizing with a helpless hermit crab without its shell would not have perceived the effect Kulbobo wanted to evoke. In fact, his message may have been made just as well without words by bringing a hermit crab to the veranda of his house and tricking it out of its shell. Such an act may, however, well be likened to communication with speech (cf. e.g. Wagner 1981: 42; J. Weiner 1991: 31) and the image (analogy) used would still belong to a microcosmic as much as a macrocosmic realm. Had we not been able to abstract macrocosmic analogies into a microcosm of which language is a part, our communication about meaning would indeed have been made difficult. We need the macrocosm of experience and meaning to be cut up into 'manageable pieces' in order to communicate – whether the symbols used are verbalized or not.

Just as houses most of the time remain unelicited by words and maintain their powerful potential through the 'total social fact' of dwelling, the meaningfulness of people's actions is not necessarily communicated in speech. In Wogeo, a girl's first menstruation is celebrated with extensive rituals consisting of visits to other villages, ceremonial exchanges of food, and various cleansings and other rituals, but hardly any parts of the rituals are explained or interpreted to the girls or the other participants in the events. It was the experience of the wanderings from place to place, the ritual cleansings, the socializing with other women, and the exchanges of food that rendered the events meaningful (cf. Barth 1975). Similarly, while Wogeo mourners can be seen as embodying a deceased person during funeral rituals as they wander through the landscape that the dead has filled with his or her life, this is not an explicitly stated function of their wanderings. People merely said that they had to make the dead 'sit down'. But the places they went to during the rituals were the same places as those who would have contributed with food for a ceremonial exchange in the deceased's name belonged to, and the paths were the same as the deceased him- or herself would have followed in life: the paths that a girl would have followed at a her first menstruation rituals. The mourners were, quite physically, doing for a last time (or 'undoing' in the sense of 'finishing') acts the deceased had done through his or her life, and, at the same time, embedding his or her relations in the landscape as pathways for others to follow.

Paths are the result of people's movement in time and become, in this sense, images of the history of movement and relations between places. At the same time people actually walk upon them and, thus, inscribe their own movement and history on them. To follow a path may refer to a range of 'movements'. The evocativeness of path as a metaphor for how a person has received rights in a place is evident: a path always leads to a particular place. If a child gets rights to a piece of land through adoption, which is common in Wogeo, the image becomes even more concrete: in an ideal adoption the adopted child should be carried along the pathway to its new place hidden in a basket – like food and other items are continuously carried along pathways around the island. 'Adoptions follow many kinds of pathways', Wogeos say. One man referred to path as a 'logical reason', implying a relation or history that is indisputable or clear – like a path as opposed to unmarked trails in the forest (cf. Hviding 2003: 99). In the more overarching construction of the Wogeo landscape, the experienced movement of the sun and the stars as well as the flow of the water of the Sepik River past the island, create a 'bad' downwards path and a 'good' upwards path. Accordingly, good things should move upwards and bad things, downwards.

Such analogical capabilities of paths make them 'the perfect "shifter", or hinge element, between the microcosm of restricted, value-coding sensory range, and the *realization* of that microcosm in the larger world of contrastingly fuller sensory range', Wagner (1986b: 21, original emphasis) points out for the Australian Walbiri's use of paths in their art (drawing on Munn's (1973) ethnography (see also Roalkvam 1997: 170)). In this process, paths appear as referring to something other than themselves – e.g. the movement of people in time – but may also, since paths are concretizations of these movements, take the position as signified: they are the concrete outcome of movement. 'If symbols can be shown to function both as signifier and signified, to embody one or both of these functions, then any particular arbitration of the "innate" versus the "artificial" is obviated' (Wagner 1978: 27). Paths are particularly apt illustrations of such processes of obviating differences between micro- and macrocosmic realms, and clearly show how a definite division between a microcosm of 'cultural' representations and a more 'natural' and experienced world becomes superfluous.

The use of the concept 'obviation' – to 'anticipate and dispose of conventional effect' and, in the process, 'to render apparent' (ibid.: 31) – to describe what goes on when metaphors are created, is central in Wagner's theory (see also Sørum 1991), not only in analysing single metaphors, but also in interpreting more encompassing imagery, such as myths, rituals or construction of houses.

> The transformation that takes place in a myth is as surely an instance of obviation as the transformation that occurs in metaphor, and the meaning elicited as unitary. Though we may not be used to considering an entire 'work' on the same terms as a single word, this is one of the implications of the concept obviation (ibid.: 32).

Myths and rituals, or house building, can be seen as successions or collections of metaphors and the 'entire works' accumulates or condensates meaning (cf. Turner 1967). In such 'narratives', a succession of metaphors substitute one another (obviate the latter in creating a new) until the dialectics return to their beginning point (Wagner 1986b: xi). When Wogeos follow taboos, build a house or follow pathways in exchange, these 'works' (Wogeos themselves label rituals and exchanges 'work': *manif*) channel their experience in certain directions, and, at the same time, invent (or reinvent) the imagery that make meaning appear. When a house is built, it is not only a dwelling that is constructed: the social composition of the village is also elicited and made manifest in the process. The house as a mere construction is obviated and the parts of the house successively come to stand for the offices of leadership, the sides of the village, the matrilineages and the landholders. When the house has been completed and the final food exchange has been held – when the obviation sequence is completed – the house again comes to evoke the conventional effect: that of dwelling (although, due to its enduring and concrete presence, it still contains the images created in the process in the shapes of named parts of the house, and their meanings can still be evoked).

As the mourners at a funeral go through their cleansing rituals, they first take upon themselves to carry with them the deceased by touching the corpse. By temporarily cutting the connections with their ordinary social network, they come to represent the deceased, obviating their own composite personhood. When they wash themselves, the mere cleansing of the body is obviated and the connection to the deceased is evoked in terms of disconnection. Eventually the exchanges of food in the deceased's name dissolve the compositeness of the deceased and the mourners re-enter their own social network: the obviation sequence is completed.

Repeated 'inventions' of such images or obviation sequences conventionalize the images that are evoked. Convention, what makes 'because it is tradition' the common answer to my interrogations into the meaning of Wogeo customs, 'exists at the level of the image, not that of its verbalized gloss', Wagner (1986a: xv) has written. And all potential glosses of the metaphors do not have to be evoked as long as the image contains them all. The first-time menstruating girl may not be aware of all the potential meanings of the rituals at the time they were performed, but the experience itself (and the continued experience of following the same pathways later in life) provides her with the imagery from which meaning may (or may not) be elicited whenever she is ready. Besides, as important as the girl's own experience during the rituals are the experiences of the other participants – for instance those who gave her food when she visited a place, or her mother who remained in the village and cooked food for the visitors. In the way her immanent sociality is made evident through these rituals (Strathern 1993: 46), the roles of her relevant others are as crucial a part of the rituals as her own. In the same manner as the rituals elicited her own relevant loci of belonging, relations and accompanying obligations, they also elicited these relations for those she is related to. Most of them would also have participated in similar rituals from different positions previously, experiencing the rituals from different angles. According to their experience and knowledge, the various participants would gloss the rituals differently and to different degrees: '[A]ll that is necessary is to retain the image itself' (Wagner 1986a: XV). All that is necessary is to keep on following the pathways, so to speak.

Place, Landscape and Gendered Bodies

Based on research on Makira Island, in the Solomon Islands, Michael W. Scott (2007b) criticizes the generalizations of the relational and fluid character of Melanesian sociality in the work of, among others, Wagner (1977a; 1986a) and Strathern (1988) – what in recent literature has come to be known as The New Melanesian Ethnography (e.g. Scott 2007a). He uses the concepts of mono-ontology and poly-ontology to describe the foundations for different social arrangements found in Melanesia: the first for the world seen as a fluid an undifferentiated whole that needs to be differentiated and where people are relationally (and cognatically) conceived, and the latter for where humanity is seen to have multiple origins, manifested for instance in unilineal descent groups that each have their own origin stories, rituals and knowledge and where people are seen to have an essence beyond their relational and dividual sociality (e.g. Harrison 1989; 1990). Scott (e.g. 2007b: 27) criticizes The New Melanesian Ethnography for ignoring poly-ontologies that also prevail in Melanesia. Without denying that the Strathernian model of sociality may accurately be used to describe many Melanesian societies, Scott writes about the Arosi from Makira: 'at the core of each Arosi person stands an unchanging matrilineal essence concretely imaged as an unbroken umbilical cord' (ibid.). Whereas a 'New Melanesian Ethnographer' would perhaps interpret this as a part of the composite person that is 'elicited only situationally' (ibid.), Scott argues that the social categories based on matrilineal descent have a real and permanent existence for the Arosi.

In Wogeo matrilineally transferred essence is also important in the constitution of persons, associated with knowledge and the named houses, and by adding matrilineal essence to the emphasis on places and houses as loci for continuity,

Wogeo appears to having some similarities to Scott's ethnography from Makira. Wogeo conceptualizations of their world also seem to be founded on unique and enduring social categories, and the salience of these are, as in Makira, kept hidden from public discourse. Although agreeing with Scott's caution to not generalize a mono-ontology as the foundation of Melanesian sociality, I do, however, believe that there is not necessarily a contradiction between the presence of several ontologically primordial categories and the relational and fluid emphasis of Strathern and Wagner's perspectives. Even though a matrilineage exists as a lasting social categorization for the Wogeos, and an unchangeable essence is at the core of each person, it does not create one exclusive pathway to follow for a person, but constitutes one among a multitude of alternatives pointing in various directions, and always in relation to other aspects of a person's identity and history.

Whereas matrilineal identity is undisputable, people are not predetermined to belong to one particular place. They are defined as belonging to a certain place according to the history that is chosen to be the most significant. The pathways into a place are found on the background of combined images of history and relationships based on filiation, descent, adoption and alliance that are embedded in the landscape. Places and houses in this way become concrete manifestations of histories of relations at the same time as they provide the conduits for the establishment of relations.

At Reite on the Rai Coast near Madang, James Leach has described a similar emphasis on place. Rather than regarding land as something relations work upon to order people and their activities, Leach argues that the constitution of persons and places among the Nekgini speakers in Reite are aspects of the same process: 'kinship is geography, or landscape' (Leach 2003: 31; see also Bamford 2007). Nekgini notions of kinship relations are based on the idea that human beings are grown: kinship is not an expression of growth (an indisputable genealogical connection based in conception), but is the result of being grown on the same land. '[T]he role of the [father] is not to pass on some component of substance to [his son], but – through his work – to establish the conditions for the latter's growth on the land' (Leach 2003: 30; 2009: 188). Shared substance refers not to genealogy but to shared histories of belonging and growth, and knowledge of the histories, names and land associated with the places that create sameness is essential in this – in fact, becomes essence, Leach (2009: 188) argues. Places and people are not only analogies of one another but are consubstantially constituted (ibid.: 214).

In the case of Wogeo, persons and landscape are inseparably constituted but still the landscape seems to have a different significance from Reite in the way Wogeos use images of the landscape to create a social order that transcends the living people. They divide the villages and the island in sides that are the main loci for belonging, and they follow pathways to find their place in the landscape and to maintain relationships and alliances. The aim is to fill the proper places with the right people according to the history of the places and in that way to maintain the sociogeographical map, a map that appears to represent an enduring social structure.

The Wogeo matrilineages are different. They are unchangeable, embodied and often tacit parts of each person, made explicit only in certain contexts. The notion of shared matrilineal substance has to be seen in relation to ideas of gendered fertility and growth. The salience of female reproductive powers in Wogeo is manifested in many ways – in terms of kinship, as matrilineages. All Wogeos belong to one of two nominally exogamic matrilateral moieties known as Kilbong (flying fox) and Taregá (eagle). A moiety is called *tiná*, which means 'mother'. The Wogeo people further belong to several named matrilineages also called *tiná*, but these cannot merely be seen as subdivisions of the moieties. Some matrilineages are said to have come from the outside, where as others are said to be of Wogeo origin, and the moiety division arrange the lineages in relation to marriage and othe ritual relations. The people belonging to the same matrilineage are said to be of 'one skin' (*kus ta*), a term often used synonymously with 'one body'. The matrilineages should not be spoken about openly: they are something that should be kept hidden, mainly because of collective ownership of sorcery. Such hiddenness is possible because the matrilineages are not groups that have to be socially made or manifested, but can be seen as embodied parts of every person born. Since all the members of a matrilineage are 'one skin', the actions of one person represent the lineage to which he or she belongs. The matrilineages are not localized in the sense that determine residence, but they are connected to places since they own the named houses on the island. The named houses exist independently of the built structures and are associated with corpi of knowledge and titles. They can be seen as embodiments of the matrilineages but, as built structures, houses do not have to contain the people of the matrilineages that own them in order to endure. Ideally people fill the houses primarily according to the history of the places and not because of their matrilineal belonging.

Accordingly belonging to matrilineages and belonging to places are in many ways opposing aspects of Wogeo social organization. The histories of the places told in public tend to (over)emphasize patrifilial relations, whereas matrilineal relations are frequently elicited as significant in 'backstage' versions of the same stories. Many conflicts concerning land rights, sorcery or moral conduct in general are connected to these seemingly discordant aspects of people's identity. Great effort is put into maintaining a balance between the two. The hiddenness of the matrilineages must be seen in the light of this 'work', and an understanding of this effort is essential in any attempt to describe Wogeo kinship and residence, and will be important in this book.[2]

Eric Silverman has pointed out that idioms of gendered reproductive powers are a necessary focus in studies of social formations and ideologies in the region (see also Lipset 1997; Lutkehaus 1995b). He argues that for the Eastern Iatmul of the Sepik River there is 'a symbolic homology between the gendered human body, the body politic and the cosmos' (1996: 30), and a similar statement can be made in the case of Wogeo. The anthropologist Ian Hogbin conducted research on Wogeo in the 1930s and 40s and wrote the book *The Island of Menstruating Men* (1970b) about gender and ritual life in Wogeo. An important focus in the book is the male cult. He stated that its underlying theme in the cult was 'the gulf, physical and social, between men and women. The people sum up the situation in the saying, "Men play flutes, women bear infants"' (1970b; see also Silverman 1996: 36). This theme is not merely underlying the male cult, but is central to the constitution of Wogeo sociality as such – similar to what Lipset (1997) has called a 'maternal schema' for the Murik or to the Iatmul gendered homology. 'Mother carries the place' (*tiná vanua ebaj*) goes another saying in Wogeo.

Most rituals concerned with transforming the status of people's bodies in Wogeo evolve around the themes of unmediated fertility and controlled growth. The experience of the unequal qualities of male and female bodies clearly shape the manner in which Wogeos construct their world, but at the same time these inequalities are seen as evoked by human agency in a mythical past. Wagner has argued that Papuans conceptualize the living beings of the world as essentially similar and that the potential for differentiation – the social order – flows 'more or less spontaneously in the world' (1977b: 397). It is man's task to differentiate when necessary and 'keep differentiating against a countervailing pull of similitude' (Bamford 1998: 159). Wagner uses notions like 'flow of analogies' or 'strain of similarities' to describe this process. Human sociality is the flow 'in the first instance' (1977b: 397). Differentiation is 'immanent in man, other creatures and in the cosmos itself' (ibid.), and it is man's responsibility to invoke and restrain it. The flow in the 'second instance' is 'fertility, spiritual power and the "knowledge" of the diviner or shaman' (ibid.: 398). In Wogeo one man said to me 'Men and women's bodies are the same. Only when women give birth they change.' An important function of ritual life is about differentiation but also about marking out similarities. This is most clearly seen in the wide array of taboo and cleansing rituals on the island that will be an important focus in this book.

Wagner notes that expressions of art – such as music, poetry and painting – may seem to be opposed to 'natural' perception as a more 'artificial' one (1986b: 26). But there is no such distinction between the perception of art and 'everyday' images, he argues. Rather, the perception and creation of art are meaningful acts of 'greater concentration, organization, and force ... within the same semiotic focus' (ibid: 27). Without probing deeper into Wagner's complex language of obviation, this volume will present some important gendered images that have been salient in how Wogeos have represented their world to me – images that may well, like art, be said to be of 'greater concentration, organization and force' than everyday experience.

As rainforest gardeners, trees are a central part of the Wogeo lived landscape and tree symbolism is played upon in many contexts (cf. e.g. Rival 1998; J. Weiner 2001). For instance are the distribution of the offices of leadership and the sections of knowledge they are responsible for, imaged as Cordyline plants (*moanuboa*) standing on the beach, in the village and in the forest. A common image is innate fertility represented as roots that trees grow from and, further, are released from but without which they cannot exist – like flutes played to instigate male growth, rafters that represent the land of the village, poles that a new leader in the village should climb while men of knowledge evoked the power of motherhood to hold them steady, or the tree that the mythical archetypal husband cut down in order to get hold of the girl (his future wife) who had climbed up into it. Trees can, in this sense, be seen as gendered images of a sort: roots represent female values of nurture and innate fertility, and trunks, cut-off trunks in particular, male values of controlled growth. [3] One particularly powerful spell presents an image of the village as a tree rooted in the ground with its branches held steady by vines and lianas, and this becomes a totalizing image of sociality: the roots representing motherhood and 'rootedness' or 'groundedness'; the trunk and the branches representing growth and prosperity, and the vines, relations to people 'rooted' in other places, including those of exchange.

The experienced difference between male and female bodies is central in Wogeo imagery. *Look around you*, Kulbobo said:

> *Everything has a mother. If it were not for mothers none of us would have been here. And if it were not for the ground we would not have been here. Pigs, birds, and men, even fish: all of these have mothers! And from where do they get their food? When you leave your mother, from where do you get your food? The ground! And when I say mother I mean all women: black, white, yellow and green. Even you, even though you haven't had a baby yet. Like Queen Elizabeth carries her crown. This is really important in the world: women carry the ground, mother is the ground.*

Motherhood is associated with the fertile soil, with nurture, peace and safety. 'When you die, you return to mother, to the ground', Kulbobo said. Like the mythical hero called Nat Kadamoanga who, as a foetus, was nurtured in the ground on the sap from the roots of a breadfruit tree, people return to the ground 'mother' when they are buried, and the souls of the dead are made to 'sit down' at the roots of old trees. The island is cleansed like a menstruating woman at the New Year celebration. Houses are also like mothers: they provide safety and containment, and in a good house no one can harm you. Women have good thoughts of peace and harmony that are located in the stomach whereas men have thoughts of conflict and fight located in the head. That is why men do not carry anything on their heads like women do, Wogeos say. 'What will happen when Queen Elizabeth dies and Charles will stand up in her place?' two of my oldest male informants wondered.

Several myths will be presented in this book, and the heroes in these stories are mostly male: the great heroes Onka (Goleiangaianga) and Mafofo gave Wogeos the ability to produce an abundance of food and other goods (through overseas exchange), and to put on great exchanges that gave male leaders the means of achieving renown and manifesting their power. Nat Kadamoanga, already mentioned above, was not all that heroic. He made a foolish mistake and stole the magical flutes that represented the original unhindered flow of fertility. By doing this, he attempted to take control over powers that were not his to take. On the other hand, had Nat Kadamoanga not taken the flutes, 'it might have been us men who would have had the hard work of cooking', Wogeo men speculated. The flow of fertility was cut and, thereby, Nat Kadamoanga inadvertently instigated gendered incompleteness as a prerequisite for reproduction. The potential for differentiation, was, however, already present – there were men and there were women. Rather, it was a gendered interdependence and incompleteness that was the result of the theft: analogous beings were differentiated by making evident (abstracting in order to communicate) their 'names' (man and woman) and, thus, restricting their reference to individual bodies – half of a whole became one of a pair (Strathern 1993).

But there are also several heroines in Wogeo mythology. One story tells how the heroine, Jari, dismantled her house and carried it with her in her vulva, together with pots and pans for cooking, before she met another mythical being, married him and rebuilt the house (cf. Hogbin 1970b: 35). Houses as icons of containment, nurture and safety, follow female lines of descent and can be given as dowry. Another myth tells how a house was made from the body of a woman (Anderson and Exter 2005: 55–58). She tricked her son into killing her and the son then fell asleep. Then she summoned birds to make a house from her body, and, when the son woke up, he found himself inside the house. Later he lured two sisters to the house and married them. The relation between the son and his mother was cut short by her death before he married and started his own family (the analogy man as son was obviated and man as husband evoked), but the house as an embodiment of motherhood remained and contained him. A son does not continue his mother's blood and he cannot use his matrilineal identity to openly argue for what he sees as his rightful position in the world, but affiliation to houses as embodiments of the matrilineages still makes matrilineal belonging a salient constituent of the social landscape.

It is in the sense of dwelling that the above aspects of houses become evident, something we might call 'enhousement' as James Weiner does when making the distinction between 'an "inside" of vision and viewing opposed to external space of sound and movement' (2001: 120). But the named houses do not only contain people: they also contain the rafters that represent the land of the village and the histories of the people who have looked after the land. These histories should ideally be based on patrifiliation: 'The side of father is the side of land, the side of mother is the side of blood', Wogeos say. When a named house is built, the rafters that are usually held and controlled by men due to their platial[4] belonging and may be seen as images representing male continuity, are brought together with the female house: 'mother carries the place'. As such, houses can be seen as images or signs of both female and male continuity; they become 'androgynous' in that they contain within them 'the potentiality for emerging in particular contexts as predominantly male or female gendered' (Howell 2002: 160). We can say that a relation between male and female, between maleness and femaleness, is contained or nested in the house (ibid.). When seeing houses in this manner, the conventional effect (dwelling) is obviated and the house comes to stand for something new: the relation between male and female. Furthermore, the relation between sign and one of the relational components (e.g. the male) may be temporarily emphasized and 'eclipse' (Strathern 1988: 155; see also Howell 2002) the relation to the other relational component (the female), making it appear dominant to the other.

With this analytical focus, the semiotic perspectives of Wagner and Strathern have been found to be of great value in understanding the complexities in Wogeo efforts to create, maintain and balance a proper and gendered sociogeographical landscape, even though it may be poly-ontologically constituted. The inherent and apparently opposing aspects of the social person – place and matrilineage – cannot be properly understood without taking into account the relational character of Wogeo sociality, in spite of the presence of enduring, transcending social categories.

Wogeo and Ian Hogbin

The above-presented perspectives on place and sociality, on experience and meaning formation, constitute the analytical framework of this book. The aim is to explore how meaning is constituted in a dialogical relation between experience and representation. But in addition to presenting Wogeo life from certain analytical perspectives, the book also adds to an already existing body of ethnography from the island. In anthropology, Wogeo is known through the work of the Australian anthropologist Ian Hogbin (1904–1989) who conducted anthropological research in Wogeo in 1934 and 1948.

Herbert Ian Priestly Hogbin, as was his full name,[5] was born in England but moved to Australia in 1914 as a child (Hogbin and McGrath 1983). He graduated from the University of Sydney, and assisted Radcliffe Brown in expeditions to Rennell Island and Ontong Java in the late 1920s before he completed his Ph.D. at the London School of Economics in 1931 (Hogbin 1961; Beckett 1989). He returned to Australia and was employed at the University of Sydney until he retired in 1971 – apart from the period of fieldwork in the early 1930s. Hogbin also played a role in shaping the Australian policies in Papua New Guinea (PNG) after the Second World War through his work with the Australian Army's Directorate of Research (Westmark 2001: 48). He conducted research in Malaita and Guadalcanal, and in 1934 he went to Wogeo for the first time. He stayed for nearly a year, and returned for a shorter visit in 1948. In the following years he wrote numerous articles about Wogeo on a wide range of topics[6] – most of them published in the journal *Oceania* – but the best known of them, the monograph *The Island of Menstruating Men* about religious beliefs, taboos and notions of pollution, was not published until 1970. Eight years later came the book *The Leaders and the Led* (1978) on leadership and politics on the island, and this book also contained a report from a short visit Hogbin made to Wogeo in 1974.

As I was planning research in the Schouten Islands to which Wogeo belongs, I felt inclined not to choose Wogeo in order to avoid having to measure my own work against Hogbin's extremely detailed and conscientious ethnographic descriptions. But the more I read about Wogeo, the more I became intrigued by Hogbin's vivid descriptions and felt irresistibly drawn to the island. Based on *The Island of Menstruating Men*, I wrote a research proposal about continuity and change in local conceptualizations of gender and pollution, and went to Wogeo for the first time in 1993. I was not sure to what degree the Wogeos would remember the young Australian who had lived there for a year before the Second World War and for some weeks after it. But when I arrived in Wogeo, I found that the reminiscences of Hogbin were overwhelmingly present. During the first weeks on the island, most conversations I had with people were about Hogbin: about his immense knowledge of Wogeo and his doings on the island. As Hogbin (1978) himself noted from his revisit to the island in 1974, he had become a heroic, almost mythical figure to the islanders. People were disappointed to find out that I was not related to Hogbin (initially some thought that I was his granddaughter), but I have nonetheless come to develop a feeling of kinship with the old distinguished anthropologist (cf. Lutkehaus 1995b: 16). My cast of informants were the descendants of his; I was named after his best informant's wife; his texts have been crucial to most of my understandings of Wogeo culture, and the stories about him are entangled, crucial and enriching parts of my own Wogeo experience. In the late 1970s, Nancy Lutkehaus did a restudy of Manam, the eastern most of the Schouten Islands, where Camilla Wedgewood did research at the same time as Hogbin was in Wogeo. She has noted that '[i]n a restudy the other anthropologist is something more than a text to be dealt with, he or she is another social or personal, as well as intellectual, relationship' (1995b: 17). It should be noted, though, that it has been impossible for me, within the confines of this book, to constantly relate my writings to his. In this I take a different approach from Lutkehaus (ibid.) who had an ongoing dialogue with Wedgewood throughout her monograph. In order to let my own data 'speak', I have in many places chosen not to discuss discrepancies between the 1990s Wogeo representations of their world and history and what Hogbin wrote. What has actually changed or been forgotten and what is due to Hogbin's and my different interpretations would, in many cases, be mere speculation. However, his work still constitutes an important part of the ethnographic basis for this text, and also, to use the words that Lutkehaus (ibid.) borrows from Bakhtin, as a more or less silent dialogue partner.

As it was for Hogbin, the point of departure for this book is the village of Dab. Before going to PNG, I had, among other things, written a letter to the Catholic Mission in Wewak, the provincial capital, in order to get in touch with people on the island, but I did not receive any reply. When I arrived in Wewak, I was not sure if I could go ahead with my plans at all, but by a peculiar coincidence, one of the first Papua New Guinean men I spoke to turned out to be from Wogeo (Tom Fandim) – I even knew his grandfather from Hogbin's writings. He was most happy to send a message to the island about my arrival. As it turned out, the councillor from the district that Dab belongs to had actually received the letter I had sent to the mission many months earlier, and people there had agreed that I was welcome to do my research. It had been decided (I am not sure by whom) that I was to follow in Hogbin's footsteps and live in the same place as he did,[7] and when I arrived Wogeo I was given a room of my own in the house of Hogbin's main informant's granddaughter. I spent approximately seventeen months in Dab spread over three periods between 1993 and 1999 – the latter two periods conducting doctoral research after completing my masters thesis in 1996 (Anderson 1996). Before continuing to the main chapters of this book, I will give a short introduction to the island, its landscape and its inhabitants, as I know it.

Wogeo Island

Wogeo is a relatively small volcanic island of twenty-five to thirty kilometres in circumference, about seventy kilometres off the coast of East Sepik Province.[8] The island is entirely covered by rainforest, all the way down to the narrow strip of flat land along the coastline. Travelling around Wogeo by boat, freshly cleaned gardens can be seen on the slopes descending to the coastline. The secondary forest, resulting from centuries of gardening, is clearly distinguishable from the darker green forest covering the mountains that culminate in three peaks five to six hundred metres high. Along the beaches, coconut palms are planted in between the large trees leaning out over the sea. All of the twenty or so villages are situated along the coastline, providing homes to a thousand islanders.[9]

Most of my arrivals on Wogeo were at the beach of Dab that has one of the best anchorages for boats. From the beach of Dab, pathways lead up to the village. Upon entering the village, a large space opens up, edged by coconut palms and mango trees. Behind them the mountainside rises, covered with rainforest. The ten to twelve houses in Dab are built around this open place, most of them on poles, from bush material with walls and roof thatch from the sago palm. The ground of the village space is covered with pebbles that prevent vegetation from growing. The pebbles are always swept clean of leaves and garbage and make a neat and tidy impression, and flowers are planted around the houses and on the graves in the village. In Dab all the houses have verandas facing the village place, and this was where people spent most of their time in the village. Only when the sun went down and the pebbles were no longer baking hot, did people move down on the ground to the fireplaces.

Photo 0.1: Dab village in 1999

As you enter a Wogeo village, people usually shout to you from their veranda and ask you to come over. Then you are offered a betel nut from someone's basket or you give one away from your own, and nothing much is said before the betel mixture is chewed red. If a pot is on the fire, you will soon be offered food and, if people have them, coffee or tea or perhaps a fresh coconut. At the side of each village a pathway leads through the forest to the next village, and anyone going from one village to another follows this path. In the next village the procedure starts all over again. To refuse such hospitality is unthinkable, and so it can take hours to get from one village to another.

This harmonic scenario from Wogeo adheres to ideals and values Wogeos emphasize when speaking about their island. In Wogeo you will never go hungry, you do not need money, and you can always find a place to sleep. Collectiveness in work and village life is highly valued, and people who stick too much to themselves are regarded with suspicion and are prone to be gossiped about. When I asked the old man Marifa what he regarded as the most important aspect of Wogeo culture, he answered the large food festivals of the past (*oaraboa*). 'Then we were all together, and nobody sat on their verandas gossiping about each other' (see also Hogbin 1978: 176).[10]

This emphasis on hospitality and communality also relates to a very different side of Wogeo life. Death occurs frequently, and funerals are among the most common social events on the island. Malaria and tuberculosis kill many people, but even though such diagnoses are acknowledged, almost every death, including those that are medically diagnosed, are explained by human agency – by sorcery, poison or breaches of taboos (cf. Hogbin 1978: 46). Breaches of taboos frequently result in tuberculosis, and sorcery often causes symptoms similar to malaria, and, as one man explained, 'Even though it is the malaria mosquito that gives malaria, there is something that causes the mosquito to sting' (cf. Evans-Pritchard 1937). After only two hours on the island in 1993 I found myself attending a funeral, and during the last month of my last visit in 1999, I participated in as many as three funerals of people whom I knew quite well. People always fear for their lives, and it is dangerous to be alone – it is when you are alone in the bush or in your house at night that sorcerers strike. And even if you are not alone, you cannot be sure of what the people around you have done lately that would be dangerous and polluting to anyone in their vicinity.[11]

There are many precautions that can be taken in order to protect oneself from these dangers. Among others one should, of course, not be alone; one should not eat food cooked by people suspected of having ill intentions; there are certain places one should not go; one should not accept food from menstruating women or other people regarded as being in impure states; one should be very careful in one's dealings with dead bodies and those who have touched dead bodies; and one should conduct all the necessary cleansing rituals following encounters with dangerous substances, people and places. Many Wogeos, particularly the elderly but also younger people, complained that people no longer observe the taboos. They also claimed that sorcery had been out of control since the male cult vanished some thirty to forty years ago – 'now people kill for no reason' (see also Hogbin 1978: 12). '*Kastom* (Tok Pisin[12] for custom, tradition) is dying,' was a phrase I often heard, and people seemed to feel that their island was in a critical state.

All Wogeos have been Christians since the 1950s and 60s – most of them Catholics – and in some ways Christianity is conceived as a solution to the problems of sorcery and lack of proper conduct regarding taboos and cleansing rituals. 'Before, we were in the dark', I often heard. There appears to be an immanent contradiction in such statements: Christianity is both seen as what initiated the perceived decline of *kastom* as well as having provided a positive alternative to more disruptive customs of the past. As newly converted Christians, Wogeos were taught that many of their traditional customs were the work of Satan, and according to Hogbin (1978: 11), the first converts were as eager as the missionaries in discouraging the traditional customs and rituals. After his brief visit to Wogeo in 1974, Hogbin described his impressions of a changed island:

> The religious system had collapsed, and my book *The Island of Menstruating Men* (1970) might as well have been written about a people living in the Middle Ages. No young man had been initiated and no older one hacked his penis in ritual purification until the blood flowed, and the sacred flutes and masks had rotten away or been burned. … The only surviving relics of earlier beliefs were vague notions about pollution in respect to females and the dead (Hogbin 1978: 11–12).

The Catholic Church has since then revised its politics. In some respects they encourage the maintenance of traditional customs and, for instance, integrate traditional songs and dances in church services. In the case of the Wogeo male cult and initiation rites, however, the change of mind came too late.

In spite of the changes that worried Hogbin when he revisited Wogeo, I found that it was not difficult to recognise life on the island from what I had read in his texts. In the early seventies many changes were recent and dramatic, and the emphasis on things lost, by Hogbin as well as the islanders, was to be expected. In the 1990s Wogeos still struggled to come to terms with these changes, and in conversations people often disregarded enduring traditions and emphasized those that had been lost – particularly the conspicuous rituals associated with male initiation, the male cult, and the great food festivals. But what Hogbin described as the only surviving relics of earlier beliefs – 'vague notions of pollution' – were during my stays on the island not at all vague notions but influenced many aspects of life on the island. I do not believe that this was due to a revitalization of tradition that had taken place since Hogbin's visit in the 1970s but, rather, that the way these beliefs were made manifest had taken on less conspicuous forms compared to how it was in the 1930s and 40s. I found that the ideas associated with the customs described by Hogbin remain crucial to the understanding of Wogeo life. Joel Robbins (2007) criticizes anthropologists studying newly Christianized societies for ignoring the radical changes that have taken place and over-emphasizing continuity. I do not wish to underestimate the changes that have taken place since Wogeos converted to Christianity, but I believe Wogeos exaggerate their pessimism on behalf of what they regard as *kastom* – in particular in dialogue with anthropology, that is, with Hogbin (both in person and as an icon of the value of tradition) and with me. The idea of loss can also be seen as a cultural notion that has a longer history in Wogeo than worries about recent changes, as will be discussed in chapter 2.

The difference in time and in anthropological theory between Hogbin's and my own research in Wogeo opens up for interesting comparisons, but it also raises issues of positioning and interpretation: the view of a male anthropologist in the 1930s is surely different from that of a female one in the 1990s. As a result of the cumulative knowledge gained through field research, anthropologists induce or imagine cultures (in Roy Wagner's words (1981: 26)) for the people they study –

whether it be on an island in the Pacific or among skaters in Oslo. This imagination is not necessarily recognized by the informants as a proper representation, nor would the next anthropologist imagine the same culture for the same people. If the aim is not to present some distinguishable, authentic, and observable 'culture' but rather examples of ways of thinking or speaking about the world common to some people, this does not pose a problem. But in the eyes of the Wogeos, however, my work is about a distinguishable and authentic Wogeo culture or what they usually refer to as *kastom*. My work should, according to them, be to talk to all the elder people in Wogeo in order to obtain information about disappearing customs, to collect as many myths as possible from the rich oral traditions on the island, and to participate in as many *kastom* activities as I could, in order to help save or, at least, document *kastom*.

It has not been easy to decide how I should relate to the expectations of what 'my book' should contain. The concept of *kastom* has been analysed as having been invented in opposition to colonial powers, missionaries and the accompanying rapid change (cf. e.g. Keesing 1993b). People 'invent' a distinct tradition (*kastom*) for themselves in order to avoid being engulfed by new ways and customs. As Biersack describes this position, tradition 'developed in the present and as a political instrument in colonial and post-colonial contexts – is contrasted to "culture", which – because it is not "objectified", "externalized", "reified", or "substantivized" ... – is not an ideological source' (Biersack 1991: 14–15). I do not believe that such a contrast between 'invented tradition' and 'culture' suites to describe the situation in Wogeo, whether it is the Wogeos or I who take on the role of the 'inventor' (cf. Biersack ibid.). As David Akin states: 'with our attention so focused on objectification of culture as *kastom*, we have neglected the concurrent subjectivization of *kastom* as culture' (2004: 302). Culture and tradition can both be seen as inventive processes, and both the anthropologist and his or her informants can be thought of as field workers of a sort 'controlling the culture shock of daily experience through all kinds of imagined and constructed "rules", traditions, and facts' (Wagner 1981: 35). To take a position where 'tradition' or objectified *kastom* is dichotomized against the 'cultural' present – either as something invented opposed to 'real' life or as 'before' against 'nowadays' – leaves us no more capable of grasping the cultural than an identification of culture with tradition.[13] Anthropological conceptions of culture can better be put to use if we see them as 'tentative bridges to meaning', as 'part of our understanding, not its object. ... [W]e treat them as "real" at the peril of turning anthropology into a wax museum of curiosities, reconstructed fossils, and great moments from imaginary histories' (Wagner 1981: 27). As such, the dichotomization of 'tradition' against 'culture' becomes meaningless since tradition or *kastom* (and discourses about it) are no less a part of 'culture' than that which is not 'objectified' or 'externalized'.

Hogbin provided a thorough documentation of life in Wogeo as it was in the 1930s and 40s, and this was still of great value to the islanders in the 1990s. Although few Wogeos by the late 1990s had actually read them, Hogbin's books remained as manifestations of the importance of remembering and as symbols of the value of *kastom*. When I left Wogeo in 1994, after my first fieldwork, one of the councillors of Wogeo thanked me for coming to Wogeo in order to 'write the history of Wogeo'. Since the islanders regarded me as 'following in the footsteps of Hogbin', they also expected that my work first and foremost would, by filling the gaps in Hogbin's writings, serve as a documentation of Wogeo *kastom*: for the Wogeos themselves as well as for the rest of the world. As Keesing has commented upon the Kwaio's (of the Solomon Islands) wish for him to write a book about customary law: 'The book they have hoped for is a book I do not know how to write' (Keesing 1992: 14). The work of preserving what Wogeos talk about as *kastom* is not my task, but I still hope that this book will be of some value to the Wogeos in their work of not forgetting the *kastom* ways. But, more importantly, notions of *kastom* are important in this text because, as Andrew Strathern has argued, 'People's attempts to construct history, both contemporaneously and in retrospect, are attempts to construct sets of meanings for the course of events in which they are involved' (A. Strathern 1991: 206). It is as such that Wogeo conceptualizations of *kastom* will be central for the argument of the book.

The People of Dab

I once discussed with a Wogeo man the possibility of anonymizing or using pseudonyms when writing my book. I had had this discussion on several occasions before, both with him and other people, but nobody really seemed to understand what I meant. To them it was impossible to separate a documentation of Wogeo life from the history of real, named people. To change or take away people's names would render the book inauthentic and meaningless to them. On this particular occasion, I tried to use concrete examples of disagreements and conflicts regarding land rights – a central topic in the last part of this book – to make the man see what I meant. He understood my difficulties, and eventually he said 'Okay, if they make this much trouble out of it, you should take away their names!' But what he meant was not what I had intended. To him 'to take away someone's name' was to take away that person's importance and renown.

It is impossible to write this book in a manner that would not, in one way or another, evoke disapproval from Wogeos. The use of pseudonyms would not meet the Wogeos' expectations of what the book should contain, as would not using names at all. The latter would also render the examples I use difficult, if not impossible, to read. To represent only the most commonly agreed upon stories would not demonstrate what really goes on. Besides, stories have a tendency to change through time – what was agreed upon in 1999 might be quite different five years later – so this would not solve the dilemma. In certain sensitive cases I will therefore take care not to make it obvious whose versions of events and whose truths I am presenting, but in the case of land rights in chapter 9 I have instead chosen to use the whole spectre of stories, not only to demonstrate complexity and flexibility but also so that people should find at least one version they agree with. As Shryock (1997: 9) writes in the introduction to his book about writing history in Jordan, 'Had I decided to respect the sensitivities of everyone involved (a relativistic stance that merely accomplishes a more subtle form of insult), this book could not possibly have been written'.

The people who taught me to live in accordance with Wogeo *kastom* and took care of my well-being were all the descendants of Hogbin's friends and informants. All my three periods of fieldwork were based in Dab village, and I participated in day-to-day life, trying the best I could to blend in and behave as a proper woman as the Wogeos define it. When I first arrived in Wogeo, Maria,[14] the granddaughter of Hogbin's main informant Moarigum, adopted me. During the ten months on the island in 1993–94, I lived in the house Singero together with Maria and her family, and participated in their daily activities as an adopted daughter. When I returned for two months in 1998, the construction of my own house close to Singero was planned, and I had my own house for the last months of the third period of fieldwork in 1999. I also had a small garden on my adoptive mother's land, I cooked my own food and I took part in food exchanges as a grown up woman. Most of the knowledge I have of Wogeo life has been gained through such participation.

Dab is divided into three parts, and the house Singero belongs to the middle part, called Lukaluka. This was also the place were the male cult house used to be built, and Lukaluka in Dab was an important place in Wogeo. Singero was often referred to as one of the two most important houses on the island and, by inhabiting this powerful house and possessing rights to land associated with a powerful position in Dab, Maria was a woman of importance in Wogeo.

Her father was Dale, the son of Moarigum and his favourite wife Iamoe. In 1934 Dale had worked as Hogbin's assistant. After Hogbin's fieldwork, Dale married two women. The one spoken of as his 'first wife', Namboak, came from the neighbouring island of Koil. Namboak was the daughter of a leading man in Koil, and the marriage was meant to strengthen an alliance between the two places. It was due to her chiefly rank that she was said to be the 'first wife' – Dale had already, at the age of twenty-nine (Hogbin 1978: 21), married Moita, a woman from Gole on the back of the island. She was originally supposed to marry Gabis in Dab, but then Moita and Dale fell in love. Old Moita had Dale's name tattooed on her lower arm and often told me that she had been the only true love in Dale's life.

Namboak did not give birth to any children, and when Moita had her first child – a son called Gagin – Namboak adopted him and took care of him.[15] Gagin was given the rights to land and house in the western part of Dab, called Kajenamoa, since Saoang, the leading man there, did not have any male children. Gagin was in the 1990s regarded as the leading chief (*koakoale*) in Dab. Moita then gave birth to a daughter, Sanum, and adopted her to Tafalti, Moarigum's eldest son who also did not have any children of his own. Sanum was later to marry Kulbobo who is a prominent figure in this text, and through this marriage, Sanum followed the same story or pathway that Moita originally was meant to follow with the planned marriage to Gabis.

In 1958 Dale became terminally ill while he was undergoing treatment for leprosy near Murik Lakes on the mainland. Moita was with him and was again pregnant. While in Murik, Dale died, and during the same night, Moita gave birth to Maria. Some people say that Dale had told his companions before his death that no matter what the gender of the unborn child, it should take over his land and house in Lukaluka. If the child were a girl, her future husband would have to follow his wife 'like a woman'. Others claim that Maria's position was decided later by the leading men in Wogeo in order to commemorate Dale, having been born at the moment of his death. Whether it was Dale or others who decided, Maria took her father's place in Lukaluka.

Since Moita, according to herself, was in too much grief following Dale's death to take care of her daughter and her house, Maria was taken care of by an elderly couple that moved into Singero in order to look after this important house. Moita later remarried and lived with her new husband in Badiata, while Maria remained in Singero and has lived there ever since.

During my visits to the island, the family inhabiting Singero consisted of Maria, her husband Tarere (from Badiata village) and their son Roger, whom they had adopted from Maria's sister Sanum, their two daughters Kijua and Boeka, and Maria's brother's daughter Moatakia. Maria and Tarere also had two other adoptive children, but they both lived with their biological parents. In order to properly include me into the history of Dab, I was given the name Iamoe after Moarigum's wife (Yam in Hogbin's writings), and most people in Wogeo addressed me by that name.

In 1999 there were twelve houses in Dab. The number of inhabitants varied since people would come to stay for weeks at the time and others would go and stay in other places for periods of time, but there were approximately forty people living in Dab at that time. Close to Singero lived Kulbobo and Maria's sister Sanum with their daughter, and on the other side of Singero my friend Tangina and her husband Kenang with their daughters and Tangina's sister. In Kajenamoa was the house of the young chief Kumi and his wife Guria from Koil and their baby daughter, with Kumi's mother and another widow in the neighbouring house. In the other side of the village, in Moarmoar, Boarinya and Matarena and their children lived, opposite to the widow Nunu with her many children – among them, Gamuia who had a baby of her own. Also her cousin Ialoma lived with them. Just outside of Dab, beyond Kajenamoa, Saboakai and his family had built their house. In addition there were guests living there for a while, for instance the girl Sarakamot who used to accompany me to the garden or on visits to other villages, and there were Dab villagers who stayed in other villages – like Saea and Koan with their children who stayed in Joboe most of the time in 1999.

Moarigum's youngest son Marifa and his wife Kanemoeka, as well as Tangina's father Niabula, should not be forgotten. They were important sources of information during my 1993–94 fieldwork – Marifa in particular. At that time Kulbobo was hospitalized on the mainland, and Marifa took it upon himself to be my teacher with great enthusiasm and humour. When I returned in 1998, the two old men had sadly died, and Kanemoeka died during Christmas 1998.

These people made up the main social scene of Wogeo life, as I knew it. They inevitably made me see Wogeo from a Dab point of view, and my relations beyond the village mostly followed the same pathways as those of my Dab family and friends. These paths led me to invaluable sources of information, but were also limited by the social relations that made them, since they necessarily excluded other and different pathways. In daily life I was in regular contact also with people from the other four villages in Onevaro district to which Dab belongs. I have also visited the other districts on the island several times, but I mostly conducted more formal interviews in these places.

This was especially true for the last fieldwork when the German linguist Mats Exter, who was to start the work of documenting the Wogeo language, accompanied me. Together with Mats, I travelled around the island in order to collect myths, songs and stories from all the villages as part of our joint project of publishing a text collection in the Wogeo language (Anderson and Exter 2005).

In addition, I had two important informants who did not live in Wogeo at the time of my research; during the Christmas holidays in 1993 I had many interesting discussions with Maria's brother Gagin, the grandson of Moarigum and the chief in Dab, and he has later commented upon my writings in letters. Tom Fandim, the grandson of Ian Hogbin's best friend in the village of Gole, worked for the local government in Wewak, and I have met him several times in Wewak. As a young man Tom had visited Hogbin in Sydney, and for a period he had been in charge of approving research proposals in East Sepik. As a result he had good knowledge of anthropological questions, and he has shed light on important aspects of life on Wogeo during our conversations. With their more intellectual point of views, these two men have given me invaluable information about life in Wogeo as seen from a distance.

My fieldwork language was mainly Tok Pisin (Melanesian Pidgin English). I learnt Tok Pisin while I was on Wogeo, and it was therefore a Wogeo version of Tok Pisin that included local words and phrases. As time passed I could understand quite a lot of the local vernacular, but I continued to use Tok Pisin as my spoken language. Since all Wogeos are fluent in Tok Pisin and use it about as much as they use the Wogeo language, this was convenient. The cooperation with Exter during the last six months of fieldwork was most helpful in eliciting etymology and metaphors, and the work of transcribing and translating the myths and stories of the text collection has contributed greatly to the understanding of the issues dealt with in this book.

*   *   *

On rainy nights during my last fieldwork, I usually sat on the roofed veranda of my house. The village space would be deserted. People were huddling up in front of their indoor fires, and from the house next to mine I would probably see that my linguist companion had lit his lamp and was working with his notes. I would enjoy the solitude and listen to the rain. Sometimes the light from a torch would appear in the door opening, and Tangina, my friend from the neighbouring house, would climb up the ladder. She would most likely ask for a smoke, and we would sit for a while, smoking our cigarettes in peace.

Moments like these had been rare during my first year in Wogeo. I had, to my great disappointment, problems in establishing friendships with the young women in the village. Most of them seemed shy when I was around, and I believe they found the role I had taken in the village difficult to handle. I spent a lot of time talking to the older men who came to see me, and the women seemed to think that the questions I asked were not for them to answer. As time went by, my need for companionship increased, but probably my expectations of how a friendship with a woman of my own age should be became more of a hindrance than a help in establishing such relations. I had expected that my gender would open up quite different fields of exploration to those that Hogbin had the chance to investigate, but instead I ended up sitting on verandas talking to men much of the time. The exceptions were when I was accompanying Maria as a daughter in women's spheres where I was treated more like a helpless child.

During the last fieldwork, however, when I was in charge of my own household, I was doing pretty much the same things as the other women. In this manner I made a better companion for the young women, and I also became more independent of the relations I had through my Wogeo parents. I could, thus, establish relations independent of their presence. Tangina became one of my closest friends in Wogeo, in addition to Medo from Moaroka, and Saea and Gamuia from Dab. Such nights on my veranda we talked about nothing and everything without my role as anthropologist and outsider continuously demanding attention and concentration. We would lie on the veranda floor gossiping and giggling about people and recent events in the village, and we often had good laughs over my shortcomings as a novice in Wogeo work-life. These relationships became important sources of information to me, providing a quite different type of information to the more formalized conversations I had with men. Most of all it gave a feeling of belonging and being able to contribute to (rather than disturb) social life as a relevant social person. It also, I believe, added significantly to the gendered difference between my own and Hogbin's research.

My neighbour and mentor Kulbobo plays, as already mentioned, a significant part in my research and in this text. His expectations and demands often troubled me while I was in Wogeo. I returned to the island in 1998 with the idea that my research this time should be less dependent on my Wogeo parents and that I would get wider and more representative interpretations of Wogeo life than I did the first time. In many ways I felt that Kulbobo, with his undivided attention to my work and me, was an obstacle in this respect. He was generally regarded as the most knowledgeable man in matters regarding *kastom* in Wogeo, and it was unthinkable to object to his self-appointed role as my teacher. I eventually accepted the situation and became his obedient student, and he gave me invaluable data regarding so many aspects of life in Wogeo. As I sat down with him under the mango tree behind Singero, he would say: 'Alright, Iamoe, today I will tell you about diseases.' Or 'today I will tell you the names of the parts of a house' and so forth. Then he would give me a lecture on the topic, and as he was a master of oratory and history his lectures were brilliant and always informative. I always tried the best I could to crosscheck his stories, but often I was met with the response that 'you should listen to Kulbobo, he is the one who knows these things'. And if people disagreed with what he said, they would not necessarily provide any alternative versions of the stories or customs in question. This touches the issue of the status of knowledge in Wogeo, a classical theme in Melanesian ethnography that will be discussed in Part III of the book.

As far as Kulbobo's role in my work is concerned, he has unavoidably channelled my attention in certain directions. As 'expert' images of Wogeo culture, Kulbobo's representations will be an important dialogical partner (cf. Csordas 1999: 184) to the experiential foundations of Wogeo culture that I will try to elicit. His point of view must, however, also be seen in relation to his own political agenda; it will be presented as such – not as a more 'true' or 'authentic' version of a Wogeo culture than those of other people.

Kulbobo no longer sits on his veranda overlooking the village life. He died on 28 November 2000, and did not get the chance to see 'my book' as he wanted to so much. I hope this book in some ways will fulfil his expectations concerning my work and prove worthy of his confidence that I would manage to preserve some of the knowledge he feared would be lost with him. He wanted 'everybody to be startled'[16] when they read my book. I know he had the satisfaction of feeling that he had given me the 'full story', as he said when he presented me with a pair of boar's tusks, as a symbol of my belonging in Dab, on the morning of my departure in 1999. For me not to try to present 'the full story' as he told it to me would be an act of deceit. I will, however, elaborate on his stories, deconstruct them, and even contradict them, but, in honour of Kulbobo and the expectations of the people of Wogeo in general, I will attempt to present most of his lessons as they were told – images of a Wogeo culture as a 'dialogical partner' to the lived and experienced landscape of people and places.

The Chapters

Part I of the book will give the relevant background information for the next parts. It starts with an account of a myth that is regarded as the first and most important one in Wogeo. The myth introduces some salient features in Wogeo life, most importantly the value of food in abundance, but also the significance of origin places in the Wogeo landscape. Chapter 1 describes the Wogeo geographical landscape, and gives an introduction to Wogeo daily life in general – among other things, the important place producing, exchanging or talking about food has in people's lives. It also gives an introduction to the important role of the Catholic Church on the island. The second chapter in Part I is devoted to the legacy of Ian Hogbin and the local culture heroes. The myths about the heroes present further important themes in Wogeo life, as well as eliciting notions about change and continuity on the island. In some respects, these stories also become intertwined with histories about Hogbin, and a discussion of Hogbin's position on the island is also included, as it is key to understanding the circumstances in which my own research has taken place..

Leaving this introductory part, Part II concerns what Wogeos regard as being of great importance in their lives: to 'look after' their bodies. In chapter 3 I describe ideas of pollution and the taboos and cleansing rituals associated with them – in particular those related to life cycle rituals, menstruation and childbirth. Gender and differentiation will be central in the discussions of these. In chapter 4 I will argue that taboos and avoidance are central in the constitution of social persons. By observing taboos and avoidance, people create, cut and channel connections to what and whom they encounter in the phenomenal world. Among other topics, I will present notions of what Wogeos call 'diseases of the place' – diseases that, in one way or another, are the result of human agency. By this, I aim to show how Wogeos, by looking after their bodies, also look after the network of relations they at all times are immersed in. Chapter 5 takes this argument further by presenting the rituals following the death of an old man in Dab. By temporarily cutting the ties to their own social network, the people who touched the dead body take upon themselves to carry the spirit of the dead on their bodies and make him 'sit down' in the landscape in which he led his life. The final exchange of food following a death finally finishes the deceased's productive life, and his place in the village is now vacant for his heir to fill.

The social and geographical landscape as mutually constituted is the topic for Part III. As people look after their bodies, they also look after their island, and chapter 6 starts with an account of cleansing rituals, intended to secure the well-being of the island, that take place each year. These rituals follow the movement of the Pleiades across the night sky, and this movement also creates notions of sides and directions – diagrams that are salient features in how Wogeos organize their social landscape. Sides become central loci for belonging, and pathways constitute conduits for relationships beyond the place of belonging. Chapter 7 describes how offices of leadership and the associated knowledge are embedded in this landscape of sides and directions, and I discuss the status of knowledge in Wogeo. Leadership is also associated with matrilineal descent, and the balancing of platial and matrilineal belonging is crucial in how men attain power in Wogeo.

These notions are also the topic for the last part of the book that I have called the Politics of Belonging. Chapter 8 starts with a short review of some important contributions in recent discussions about kinship and group formation in the region, followed by a presentation of how Wogeos define their belonging in terms of kinship, place and history. Adoption is common in Wogeo, and a discussion of this practice as a way of 'following history', securing continuity as well as balancing platial and matrilineal belonging will conclude this chapter. Chapter 9 presents how Wogeos follow histories or pathways in the constitution of their social landscapes. The main part of the chapter concerns histories about the inheritance of the land belonging to Dab as they were made manifest in the construction of an important house in Dab in 1998. These histories are further elaborated by comparing Hogbin's and my own data, as well as a map made of the village by a leading man of Dab. It will be made evident that, in the constitution of belonging and social identity, representations of kinship and continuity appear as arguments in ongoing discussions about how to fill places with the proper people. It is such histories about places and people that become the central focus for Wogeo politics, and, at the same time, these histories elicit the 'compositeness' of Wogeo persons and places.

The conclusion picks up the threads from the different parts of the book and sums up the discussions of experience and representation and how people through life are continuously engaged in the constitution and maintenance of one's own and others' compositeness. As people wander through the Wogeo landscape, they create, cut and channel connections to people and their physical surroundings. By securing beneficial connections or flows with whatever and whomever they encounter, they look after their bodies as well as their relations. The experienced landscapes of houses, places and pathways are crucial in this work of relating: as loci for dwelling and movement and as images used to order and create a meaningful world.

Notes

1. Gell (1999: 37) stated that in Strathern's 'system M' (M for Marilyn or Melanesia), these relations are between terms in a 'ghostly landscape of semiotic idealism'. Even though the relations may be between 'terms', I am not convinced that Strathern's Melanesia is a ghostly landscape – rather it appears similar to Wagner's quite real and perceived macrocosm.

2. In order to come to terms with the ideas causing this 'cognatic dilemma', the local traditional conception beliefs may be expected to provide an explanation, but neither Hogbin nor I found an unanimous answer to how children are seen to be composed in terms of substances. In the light of the five or six versions I have recorded, it is clear that the 'cognatic dilemma' is not merely a dilemma to anthropologists with a preference for descent theories, as will be discussed later in this book.

3. Fox (1995) and Hoëm (2003) note how 'roots' is a common metaphor for origins in the Austronesian world. Similarly Roalkvam (1997) has shown that ideas of female fixity andmale mobility in Onotoa (Kiribati) are fundamental for Onotoan sociality, and McKinnon (1991) writes of similar ideas in Tanimbar, Indonesia.

4. The neologism 'platial' has the last decade been used as an adjective to denote thing related to place or of place as opposed to spatial in relation to space, particularly by human geographers (see e.g. Mels 2005). Stuart Elden (2002: 36) translates Heidegger's 'örtlich' with 'platial'.

5. His birth name was Herbert William Hogbin (McCarthy 1993).

6. Hogbin 1935a, 1935b, 1935c, 1935/36, 1936, 1938, 1938/39, 1939, 1940, 1943, 1945a, 1945b, 1946a, 1946b, 1952/53, 1964, 1970a, 1971.

7. I never asked who made the actual decision about this, but probably it was the councillor together with the people of Dab.

8. Its coordinates are 3°S, 144°E. In old sources the island is called Roissy, the name given to the island by Le Maire and Schouten who were the first Europeans to see the island, on 7 July 1616 (Hogbin 1970b: 7). On present day official maps it is called Vokeo ('for which there is no excuse', according to Hogbin (Hogbin and McGrath 1983)), but I have chosen to stick with Hogbin's spelling which is closer to the native 'Oageva'. Wogeos themselves say it does not matter which way I choose to write it.

9. According to the 2000 census, 194 households consisting of 561 males and 439 females.

10. See Smith (1994: 68) for similar comments about the importance of communality and festivities on the neighbouring island Kairiru.

11. From Kairiru, Smith describes this way of viewing the world, as governed by 'animate and conscious beings and forces' (Smith 1994: 44), a 'personalistic view' as opposed to 'a view in which blind, impersonal forces dominate' (ibid.). The continuous fear for one's life and suspicions of people's ill intentions are the 'dark side' of this worldview (ibid.: 62) (see also Hogbin 1935a: 312).

12. Tok Pisin is the Papua New Guinea version of Melanesian Pidgin English and Lingua Franca in the country. I have chosen to use 'Tok Pisin' instead of 'Pidgin' in order to keep the distinction from, for instance, Solomon Islands Tok Pijin or Vanuatu Bislama.

13. Cf. Berkaak 1991.

14. Wogeos have both a Catholic name and a Wogeo name. In this text I have mostly used Wogeo names, except for those cases where the Catholic name is the most commonly used name.

15. Namboak died sometime in the period between my two fieldworks. In 1993 she lived in Koil, but I met her when she came to Wogeo to celebrate Dale's granddaughter's first menstruation.

16. *Gerap nogut* in Tok Pisin.

⇥ Part I ⇤
Wogeo Island – Place and People

Prelude

The following story, as told here by Joe Kosman from Gole, the headmaster of the Wogeo primary school to Exter in 2000 (told in Wogeo language and translated by Exter), is reckoned as the most important story about the origins of Wogeo *kastom* (see also Anderson and Exter 2005: 31–34):

The story of Goleiangaianga

The story that I am going to tell is the story of Goleiangaianga, a nanaranga *of ours, the people of Gole where he used to stand in the past and hold* oaraboa; *hold* kolova,[1] *where he used to give food to the people.*

Goleiangaianga … descended upon a mountain they call Vanasoro. He descended upon the top of Vanasoro. He descended like this: he descended inside a cocoon. Inside a cocoon, as a caterpillar, he descended. He descended. He descended, then he changed; he changed himself. He descended till he stood on the ground on the top of Vanasoro and became a human being. He stood there, saw the place and descended all the way to Gole.[2] He came to stay in the village of Gole; he stayed there as a human being.

He stood there, and everything was in his hands only: the production of food, the raising of pigs. Everything that he thought of in his mind, he created and it appeared. He stayed, then he held oaraboa; *he gave* oaraboa, *he gave food to one side and the other side. He gave to the people of Takur; he gave to the people of Bukdi. He stayed and he placed platforms there. He placed platforms there and he threw food on top of them. He erected* boaboaur *[ceremonial poles]; he hung up pigs on the* boaboaur. *Then he gave the pigs to the people. When he came and held* oaraboa, *the food was indeed abundant. The pigs that he bred and gave to the people, in the whole village you would step on them, even today you would step on them. He continued to stay; he stayed only a little longer, then he held a* kolova, *he held another* oaraboa. *He stayed only a little while longer, then he held another* kolova, *he held another* oaraboa. *When he stayed in Gole he did only good work. What was this work? He held* oaraboa *and he held* kolova. *He distributed food to people on one side and the other side. His name returned to the top. He rose over all other people.[3] Everything that he created came into being in his hands; he talked, he said spells, he stood there and everything appeared. It was not like today, in our time, that food appears in any manner, no: at that time he merely spoke and it came into being.*

Well, he stayed for a while longer and he only made good work; everything that he created he gave to one side and the other side. He erected boaboaur, *held* oaraboa, *got pigs; gave taros and bananas to the people. Some time passed again and once one man, his name was Gule, talked very badly; he said, 'When we go to Gole, we stay really hungry!' Goleiangaianga heard it and he ordered an* oaraboa. *When he ordered the* oaraboa, *they [Gule and his companions] came. Goleiangaianga had already instructed all the households: 'When he comes, call for him!' One house should call him, then another house should call him; they should have an eye on him. When they came for the* oaraboa, *one woman called for him, 'Gule, come and eat!' Gule entered the house and went to eat. When he came out again, another woman called for him, 'Gule, come, come and eat!' He ate and came out again, then another called for him, 'Gule, come out again and eat!' And the food they gave him did not fill his stomach. And he finished the food in all the houses. When he entered the last house, the very last house, and ate, his stomach was full. He came down again and Goleiangaianga said: 'A small bunch of bananas*[4] *is lying there, carry it with you!' Gule saw the bananas and said: 'This bunch of bananas is very small!' His stomach was already full; he was very happy. He jumped up and carried the bananas with him. From the ridge he came down, on the path that comes down from the ridge, at Odauta. He came down, stood at Simot, and then he walked on. He came to Takur. When they came to Oaoa, Gule's stomach already caused him trouble, it was uneasy. He stumbled over a stone – the stone was not big, it was a small one – and he started staggering and fell down. When he fell down, his stomach burst and he died. And so, when you walk to Oaoa today, some stones that lie there they say are from when Gule's stomach burst. That is the story of Gule, the one who spread rumours about Gole; the one who said, 'When I go to Gole, I stay really hungry!' Then they marked him; his stomach burst and he died.*[5]

[…][6] *When Goleiangaianga stayed in Gole, he only made good work. Everything that he created, he left behind; it remains in Gole. All that Goleiangaianga created by coming down to the place and working there; all that remains. The place of the platforms, the places of the* boaboaur; *what they make today is a mark of what Goleiangaianga placed there. Our leader, our* koakoale, *what is he like? He is a reflection of Goleiangaianga. So when Goleiangaianga stayed in Gole, he made only good, absolutely only good, work. He stood there, he gave* kolova; *whatever he did; he stayed and worked, called for food, called for foodstuff: that was how Goleiangaianga was. He did not do one bad work.*

He stayed and stayed in Gole, and then he came down. He descended, he came down to Bagiava, and then he came down all the way to Onevaro. I guess my story only goes so far; I would tell only of how Goleiangaianga stayed in Gole and gave oaraboa, *gave* kolova, *and gave food to the women and men. He was a very good man when he stayed in Gole. I guess my story is finished.*

Goleiangaianga is seen as an initiator of *kastom* on the island: he is the leading character among the mythical heroes who are said to have laid the foundations for the way of living in Wogeo. Above all, Goleiangaianga introduced the great food distributions (*oaraboa*) that Wogeos regard as the most important custom on the island – even though they do not take place on the same scale today as in the past. Food is a key symbol in Wogeo: exchange and sharing of food is central in most events on the island, manifesting and maintaining relations between people and places, and abundance of food is a mark of wealth and proper conduct. The production of food occupies most of people's working hours, and food is what people most often talk about around the fires at night. Food is a prerequisite for bodily well-being, it is an important medium for pollution and magic, and abundance of food is the Wogeos greatest pride. The production, distribution, exchange and display of food are also intrinsically tied to platial belonging and the landscape of sides and directions.

With these aspects of Wogeo culture as a point of departure, this part of the book will give a general introduction to life in Wogeo: to the landscape of places and people, to life as it is presented in accordance to *kastom* and as it was in the 1990s. Further, it will present in more detail the place of the culture heroes on the island, such as Goleiangaianga. Hogbin has written extensively about many aspects of Wogeo life, including the heroes, and to Wogeos he himself has become somewhat of a mythical figure. I have therefore found it appropriate to present his legacy on the island together with accounts of the most important Wogeo culture heroes as the second chapter in this part of the book.

Notes

1. A food distribution for men held on the beach, e.g. for the initiation of a new *koakoale*.
2. He was said to have landed upon a big stone called *boro* ('pig') – in one version of the story the stone was the first pig that he created.
3. Lit. 'made them come down'.
4. *Titi* – a yellow banana that makes the urine yellow. Men use it to purify their bodies.
5. This part of the story has given Wogeos the magic to improve people's appetites – magic that is often used when people are ill and do not eat.
6. I have omitted a part of the story that is not significant here. The full version is presented in Anderson and Exter 2005: 31–34.

⊰ Chapter 1 ⊱
Life in Wogeo

Wogeos often describe their island as a canoe. The bow is to the east where the sun rises, and the stern is to the west where the sun sets. The bow is regarded as up and the stern as down. The side of the canoe, where the outrigger should be, is spoken of as the front of the island (*baga varo*, lit. 'mainland front'). This is the side facing the mainland, and the smaller island Koil situated in this direction is sometimes spoken of as the outrigger. The back is where nothing else than the open ocean can be seen. A tour around the island as it was in the 1990s, starting in Dab, the middle place on the front side of the island, will suit to introduce the Wogeo landscape and its villages as it is experienced in terms of sides and directions.

When leaving the tidy open space of Dab village to the east, a narrow pathway led towards Joboe. The vegetation along the path was neatly trimmed, and hibiscus plants framed the path with red and pink flowers. Small bridges had been built across a few narrow streams and muddy stretches, and in some places fences surrounding gardens could be seen close to the path. The soil on Wogeo is extremely fertile: even the sticks used to fasten the solid fences around the gardens soon grow leaves when the fence has been made. Marifa claimed that every tree in their forest could be used for something - that is every tree apart from one, he said, and referred to the story from the Bible about the Garden of Eden. Rainfall is plentiful, and, even though there is only one stream on the island that never runs dry, wells on the beaches always provide a sufficient supply of fresh water. When El Niño was giving people on the north coast of PNG a hard time in 1997, Wogeos were never short of food or water. Walking along the path, the lushness was overwhelming.

After about fifteen minutes walk on the pathway, one reached the village of Joboe that was made up of several clusters of houses and, like Dab, had an open and tidy space in the middle, covered with pebbles. Most houses in the 1990s were built with bush material, but in all the villages there were a couple of houses with corrugated iron roofs. In Joboe there was also a small trade store, but it only had goods to sell on the infrequent times when its owner had the means to restock. On the distant horizon the silhouettes of the islands Koil and Wei could be seen – as all along the coast on the front on clear days.

Past Joboe the path went through a stretch of rockier ground and the hillside rose close to the path before the landscape widened out and the path passed through an area with coconut and cocoa groves for cash cropping. The approximately one thousand Wogeos are first and foremost gardeners, their main crops being taro, sweet potatoes, bananas and green leafy vegetables.[1] Several different kinds of nut are important to the Wogeos: of course the coconut, but a special place is given to the *kangar* (Canarium almond)[2] that traditionally had been, and still was, the most important item in overseas exchange with the inherited trading partners (*lo*). 'Originally there were only these four that were important in Wogeo: taro, banana, *kangar* and pig,' people said. '*Kangar* and pig were the meat (*kanyik*) of the taro and bananas.' The vegetables are spoken of as *monyako*, a term that can be translated as 'food', whereas meat, fish, *kangar* and greens are spoken of as *kanyik* – which Hogbin (e.g. 1938/39: 312) translated as 'relish'. Hogbin (ibid.: 129) noted that taro and bananas were the staples whereas sweet potatoes were rare, but since then a series of diseases affecting the taro have resulted in sweet potatoes becoming the most common crop. As cash crops, coconuts for copra and cocoa were the most common crops in the 1990s.

At the entrance to Badiata the path crossed a deep riverbed on a single slippery log. The houses in Badiata were spread along a wide path rather than a large open space, but here also the village space was covered with pebbles and an abundance of flowers were planted on graves and around the houses. Domesticated pigs walked around freely in Badiata as in most villages. Pigs are of vital importance on the island as a means of exchange, for paying compensations and fines, as well as being an important element in feasting and rituals. In Badiata was the house of Lala, the elected overall leader of the island, often referred to as *hanbruk* (TP), since half of his right arm had been cut off in a fishing accident.

Men fish from canoes and dive off the reef, while women gather shells and fish with bamboo rods on the reefs. But whereas everyone participates in gardening, fishing is more a matter of choice and personal preference. If a village has a lot of young boys who enjoyed the friendly competitive aspects of fishing, there will always be fish for dinner. If there are no young boys in a village, fish is more of a luxury not enjoyed every day (cf. Hogbin 1935a: 311; 1938/39: 135). Larger fish are usually smoked on platforms over the fireplace and can, in that manner, be kept for several days – although they eventually become rubber-like and hard to eat. The Wogeos are first and foremost gardeners.

After leaving the last house of Badiata, the pathway passed a few large gardens and some cocoa groves, and after quite a while a side-path led off from the main path to Newcamp, a Seventh-Day Adventist (SDA) village. Newcamp was situated right on the beach with a good view of Koil and Wei on clear days. The SDAs distanced themselves spatially from the rest of the islanders and did not take part in many of the more traditional sides of island life. They also had their own church in Newcamp. Because of their strict adherence to the laws from the Old Testament, there were no pigs in their villages and none of the familiar red stains from betel nut spit on the ground. Depending on the context, people pointed this out as either one of the good sides or the bad sides of being SDA.

From this point the surroundings changed character. The bush seemed wilder, the trees were larger and the light dimmed as you walked along. A bit further, the main path crossed Koarug Creek, the largest riverbed on Wogeo. It appeared as a wide channel coiling through the forest, bedded with large, smooth rocks, and water ran in it only during heavy rain. This was the border of Onevaro, and beyond this point the forest bore no signs of recent cultivation until where the

Map 1.1: Villages and districts of Wogeo Island

pathway leads down to the beach of Jelalab Bay. A long time ago there used to be a village called Oaoa here. It was one of the largest villages on the island, but then most of the inhabitants were killed and the village burned down in a conflict with the other districts on the island.[3] Since then, people from nearby villages had only seldom cultivated the gardening land surrounding Jelalab Bay. The story of Oaoa and what happened there is still important in political life on the island, and I will return to these events in chapter 8.

Jelalab was the upper end of the island: the bow of the canoe, the good direction where the sun rises and from where good things come (see chapter 6). The bay had a beautiful long beach with small black stones. The islanders took pride in the fact that the airstrip in one of the towns on the mainland was made with pebbles from this beach. It was a great place for picnics, and sailing boats with tourists had sometimes anchored in this bay. Diving was great off the reef and the tourists had enjoyed the peacefulness and solitude of the place. But in the late 1990s there had not been any tourists there for many years.

At the northern end of the beach the pathway ascended up the steep hillside. After a while, the path opened up to a lawn with green grass and a marvellous view over the sea. This was the previous site of the SDA mission on the island. SDA missionaries arrived in the 1950s, but there had not been any resident missionaries in Wogeo since the 1970s or early 1980s.

From here the path again descended towards the shore. This was, according to the official map, the eastern most point of the island. There were no beaches, only cliffs, and the hillside rose steeply and much closer to the path than in Onevaro.

After quite a long walk, gardens could be seen on the hillside, and eventually the path reached Gonamie, the other SDA village in Wogeo. At this point Koil or Wei could no longer be seen, only the vast ocean: we were on the back of the island (Seo 1991).

In between the cliffs there were beaches that were covered with coral and sand – not pebbles as in Onevaro. This was the district of Takur. Dab people had few close relatives in this area, and whenever we met people along the path in this area, the tone was polite and we seldom met anyone that I could recognize from Sunday mass or as guests in Dab. The villages looked similar to those in Onevaro, but the village spaces were covered with coral sand, and the houses were built closer to each other. In one place there were hot springs on the beaches. In other places, springs with drinking water trickled out onto the sand.

The pathway now passed through the village of Maluka before reaching Goleiangaianga's village: Gole in Bukdi district, regarded as the first and oldest village in Wogeo. Hogbin had a house in Gole and stayed here for periods during his fieldwork. Here the hillside ended in sharp cliffs where the sea broke. The repetitive sound from the breaking waves was a continuous background sound to life in Gole. There were no good places to go ashore from a boat. Only people from Gole knew how to properly steer boats to the shore – 'We are afraid of their cliffs', people from Onevaro said. 'We are used to flat land and good beaches. The back is ok for a visit, but we would not like to live there.'

In the distant past the Wogeo villages were often built on narrow ridges on the mountainsides. In that way they were easier to defend, but since then all the villages have relocated close to the beach.[4] Gole, the last village to move down to the beach, did so just after the Second World War. The people living in the villages on the side facing the mainland have lived on the beach for as long as anyone could remember. The only reminders left of the old settlements on the mountain ridges were pebbles from the beach that normally covered the village sites and stones said to be the marks of the culture heroes who were the first people to inhabit the island in the mythical past. No one could say when people on the front moved down from the mountains. Probably it was in the time of the culture heroes, they reckoned. The people on the back (*kalet*) had 'just moved down', the people from the front (*varo*) would say, implicitly stating that the *kalet*-people were somewhat backward compared to the people from the front.[5]

Traditionally it was the people from the front that had the most frequent contact with outsiders, mainly through the extensive network of trade relations between the Schouten Islands and the villages along the coast of East Sepik Province.[6] This fact is also used to point out the difference between people from the back and the front. 'The back is like our warehouse,' people from the front would say, 'and we do all the trading' – even though fertile land is scarcer on the back in comparison to the front. In the past the people on the back would bring their goods to specific partners (*bag*) on the front for them to exchange on their behalf with their trading partners (*lo*) on the mainland. The people on the front also said that the people on the back are better at preserving customary traditions, something the people from the back also took pride in.

On the narrow ridge on which Gole had been situated until the Second World War, a couple of old house posts could still be seen in the bush covering the village site. Here was also the big stone that the important culture hero Goleiangaianga first stepped on when he descended from the sky. Marks from another well-known story in Wogeo, referred to as 'Kurita',[7] could also be found near Gole. The story was the property of the neighbouring village of Koablik, but the marks left in the landscape by the characters in the story – a rock and some impressions in stones on the beach – were situated close to Gole. Gole is 'the middle place' on this side of the island, conceptualized as being situated exactly opposite of Dab, like the head and the tail of an eagle with its wings spread out on each side (see chapter 6).

As the path continued through the district of Bukdi, the land flattened out and eventually opened up to a large cleaned area where the Catholic church on this side of the island had been built. Only the concrete foundation of the original building was left and a roof structure raised next to it functioned as a church in the 1990s. The congregation had not managed to raise enough money to rebuild the church after the old building had broken down due to corrosion from saltwater. Leaving Koablik, the village next to the church, the path climbed up the hillside and continued along slippery rocks descending steeply down into the waves.

After this dangerous passage is the village of Bajor. Here the beach looked similar to the beaches of Onevaro. The sea was calmer, and the broken-down, diesel-driven community boat used to anchor here. Bajor was the most populous village on the island in the 1990s (93 people according to the 2000 census). Here Dab people had several relatives, and on several occasions I stayed for a few days in the house of Nyem from Dab who was married to Singi, a man from Bajor. Just outside of Bajor was the only stream on the island that always contained water.

The next village was the village of Ga. It used to be a large village and a district on its own (see e.g. Hogbin 1970b: 10), but was now included in the district of Bukdi. Ga was situated next to the small mountain called Iamoe that marked the border between Bukdi and Bagiava and was regarded as the lowest point of the island and the stern of the canoe. The mountain was famous for its bat cave, only accessible along sharp rocks when the tide was low. It was swarming with bats and tiny swallows, and on the top of the guano that covered the cave floor, the Ga people kept a couple of big, old, beautifully carved outrigger canoes. The canoes were for catching flying fish (*gag*),[8] a task that people from this side of the island were said to be particularly capable of doing due to powerful knowledge passed down through generations and that belonged to the place. The droppings from the swallows and bats that covered the canoes were said to ensure a good catch.

The pathway climbed over the mountain, and from the top there was a great view. Again it was possible to see the island of Kairiru near Wewak before descending down the hillside into the district of Bagiava and the front side. As in Takur, most Dab people did not have many relatives in Bagiava – apart from in Falala and Oakiblolo.[9] The path now went through an area with flat land, huge trees and less of the typical rain forest vegetation under the trees. There were several coconut groves and a little hut that was used to dry copra. Before the village of Juga there were a couple of small camps with only two or three houses. Juga was situated on flat land close to the seashore, and the village site was covered with white coral sand. Near Juga the water was willow for some 100 metres out from the beach, and it was a good place for women to collect shells and fish with their bamboo rods.

Juga was situated on a cape and, rounding this cape, the mainland could again be seen. The view started to look similar to the one from Dab, but Koil was not yet visible. After Juga there were the more densely populated villages of Oakiblolo and Falala that had almost grown into one, big village. Moarigum's first wife was from Falala, and one of her daughters had married back in this village and given birth to many children. Maria thus had many relatives here that we visited at times. Kenai, *koakoale* of Falala, was a great storyteller, and I had several interesting conversations with him. After Falala the pathway continued towards Taro, the mission station. It was quite a long walk through land with many gardens and the mountainside now ascended a couple of hundred metres inland.

The mission station was established in Taro in the 1950s, since the site was near one of the two best anchoring spots for larger boats on the island and also had a good fresh water supply from a well on the beach and a river closer to Falala. Here were the island's Catholic church and the primary school. Only the teachers lived permanently in Taro. During weekdays, schoolchildren from Takur and Bukdi, who lived too far away from the school to walk back and forth every day, also stayed with them. Father Schultz, who was the parish priest of the Schouten Island parish from 1957 to 1987, built a house in Taro. It was a two-story building, supplied with electricity from a generator that sometimes worked. During my stays in Wogeo, the house was only used when the parish priest, stationed in Kairiru, came for Sunday mass once every second or even third month.

Between Taro and Moaroka was a river that usually contained at least a little water. After Moaroka was the small camp of Karajala where the Wogeo representative in the local government in Wewak in 1999 (Toby Samek) lived with his family when not in Wewak. The pathway then led through coconut groves and gardening land before reaching Kinaba, and from Kinaba it was only a ten-minute walk to Dab: the tour is complete.

This tour followed what is spoken of as the good direction: the ideal way to round the island (see chapter 6). This way of moving around the island channels the experience along the pathway and the village places, emphasizing the directions up and down and the sides of the villages. Central to the experienced landscapes are also the gardens and the beaches, the reef and what can be called the seascape. A closer introduction to Dab village will also present these aspects of the Wogeo sociogeographical landscape.

Dab Village

Dab was said to be one of the largest villages (*vanua*) on the island. In the beginning of my research this view puzzled me, since I had seen several other villages that had a lot more people and houses than Dab. But, as time passed, I understood that the size of a village was not reckoned on the basis of how many people and houses were actually present at a given time. A village is made up of houses and people that have their place (*maleka*) there: people who possess rights to build a house and cultivate the land of the village; who have been given a name that belongs to the village; who follow a history associated with the place. The houses are not necessarily present as built structures, and people belonging to the village could live in other places but still be conceptualized as a part of the village. As I learnt more and more histories of the people and houses of Dab, I started to see the village as crowded with people and houses – both those present and those absent. Seen in this manner, Dab is a big village. Dab is also a village of great importance: it is like the capital of Wogeo, people said, and the people of Dab and Gole are spoken as *taregá ramata* – eagle people – people above the others.

In the 1990s, Dab did not have many inhabitants or houses physically present. Bajor was the largest in terms of people actually living there and houses that were built, and both Moaroka and Joboe had more houses than Dab.[10] Still Dab had a certain atmosphere and appearance that (at least in my mind) distinguished it from other villages. The large open village space was neat and tidy, and the houses were placed around it in a manner that gathered the village into a clearly defined community of houses. The impression was strengthened by the fact that the village space (*malala*) was edged with trees all the way around, closing the village off from its surroundings. Towards the beach there were coconut groves; towards the mountains was the bush. All around the village enormous mango trees created shade for people to rest under when the sun was overhead. Towards Joboe a great jacaranda tree rose behind Matarena's house. The sea was visible only behind the house Ruma Bua in the part of the village called Moarmoar, towards the old site of Hogbin's residence (Ambola),[11] since the coconut grove here was less dense. In the past there used to be fences around the villages.

Three rectangular, upright stones, said to represent Dab's culture heroes, marked off the different parts of Dab: the stone Kalet Moarmoar in Moarmoar to the east, Mafofo in Lukaluka, the middle, and Tavara in Kajenamoa to the west. There were other such stones as well, but these three were regarded as the most important. In front of the stone Mafofo there were three small stones in a row marking the grave of Moarigum – placed right in the middle of Dab, in front of Singero – the house he had the right to live in through his marriage to Iamoe. In the past people were

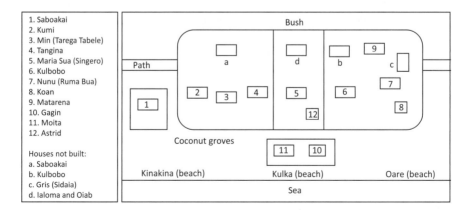

Figure 1.1: The houses of Dab in 1999

buried under their houses, and Singero used to stand where Moarigum's grave is. Only important people had their graves marked with stones like this.

In addition to the main pathway leading to the neighbouring villages of Kinaba to the west and Joboe to the east, several pathways (*jala*) led from the village space into the bush and down to the beach. The garden land belonging to Dab was situated in the foothills of the mountains inside of Dab and was spoken of as being a part of the village.

Most of the land belonging to Maria was situated on the Lukaluka and Kajenamoa side of the village. When walking to Maria's gardens, we often took the pathway behind the site of Saboakai's house in Kajenamoa. Leaving the open village space, the bush closed around the pathway. In the shadows of the trees, small trails, sometimes almost invisible, led in various directions. To an untrained eye, unfamiliar with the place, the forest looked dense and inhospitable. Maria would tell me that this or that tree belonged to a certain person, show me old garden sites that to me looked like forest and nothing else, and tell me stories connected to places we passed by that I could not distinguish as places at all in the apparent chaos of trees, lianas, leaves and pathways. Often Maria would say that our destination for the day was nearby, but to me, who had no guiding points, it felt as if we were walking for hours. While walking, we would sometimes hear the sound of voices or of axes cutting wood. Maria would at once recognise where the sounds came from and know who made them. To Maria and the other inhabitants of Dab, the bush was as familiar and homely as the village, and even small children could tell apart different plots of land and know whose the various trees were.

The division of Dab into three parts also extends to the beach, and the people use their own part of the beach for laundry, fishing with bamboo rods, bathing, washing sago and other activities that usually take place on the beach. The beach of Dab changes through the year as the tides move the pebbles in different directions. During the monsoon season, the tide creates a long tongue of pebbles out onto the reef, doubling the size of the Kulka and Kinakina parts of the beach. On the end of the tongue one reaches far out on the reef, and fishing is good. This is regarded as good times. During the trade wind season, the pebbles are moved the other way, and the beach becomes narrow and littered with logs and debris from the Sepik.

The various parts of the reef are also named, and like the culture hero stones in the village, some rocks in the sea are associated with myths and stories. Further out in the sea, Wogeos name the different parts of the sea according to their distance from the reef, colour and appearance (see chapter 7). The last named part is called 'the bridge' (*kaiuk*), marking the area connecting the Wogeo seascape with that of the mainland or Koil.[12]

Main Kinship Categories

The typical household units in Wogeo were families consisting of parents and their children and often also widowed grandparents and unmarried siblings. Marriage should ideally only take place between members of opposite matrimoieties, but this norm of exogamy is often broken without particular sanctions. Residence after marriage is most frequently virilocal, but this is not a rule. In Dab several

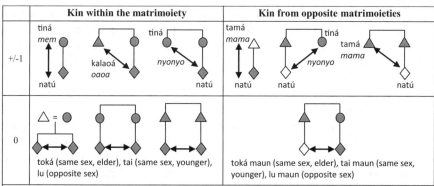

Kin within the matrimoiety	Kin from opposite matrimoieties
toká (same sex, elder), tai (same sex, younger), lu (opposite sex)	toká maun (same sex, elder), tai maun (same sex, younger), lu maun (opposite sex)

◇ = male or female. Colours indicate moiety membership, arrows the relations in question. Terms written in *italics* are terms of address, otherwise the terms are terms of reference.

The charts show only close kin, but the terminology classifies also more distant relatives according to the same pattern, known as 'dravidian-iroqouis' (although in modified form since *maun* is usually used only for cross-cousins of first degree and father's sisters are referred to as *tiná* like mother's sisters).

For classificatory grandparents/grandchildren the term *tubú* is used as a reciprocal term of reference and *bum* as term of address. Spouses are spoken of with the reciprocal term *iaoá*, parents- and children-in-law with the reciprocal term *ianá*, and in-laws of the same generation as *dual*. The term *natú* also means male child and to specify that the child is female, *natú kigrig* is used.

Wogeo kinship terms are not used without a possessive suffix (e.g. *tina-g*: 'my mother', *tina-m*: 'your mother' and so forth) and the terms here are written in third person possessive form ('his' or 'her mother' and so forth).

Figure 1.2: Kinship terminology

couples were living uxorilocally – like Maria and Tarere residing in Maria's place (*maleka*). Some couples might live in the other spouse's village for periods of time, even years, and some move to other villages where they may have rights to make gardens.

The kinship terminology may be classified as a form of the system known in anthropology as Dravidian-Iroquois, classifying cousins together with siblings and aunts and paternal uncles with mothers and fathers, but singling out classificatory mother's brothers/sister's children (*kalaoá*) and cross-cousins of first degree (*maun*) with reciprocal terms as shown in figure 1.2 (see e.g. Hogbin 1964; 1970b: 23). Siblings and cousins (apart from close cross-cousins) are spoken of with reciprocal same-sex and cross-sex terms.

'We Wogeos are all family', people in Wogeo often said. In Tok Pisin they would use the term *famili* (family). In the Wogeo tongue the term *oarooaro* (from liana, *oaro*) can be used synonymous to family. Hogbin wrote that:

> According to Bernard [Gagin] the word *warowaro* [*oarooaro*] is the equivalent of 'kindred' .... 'The term means all a person's relatives, his kinsmen as a whole,' he wrote me in a letter dated 17 July 1973. Obviously it would be presumptuous of me to argue on questions of language, and I can only agree on this having always been the commonest usage. But I have an impression of formerly hearing *warowaro* applied on occasion more loosely, as, for instance, to those of a man's kin and affines who were by chance gathered together when some job had to be done – some of his kindred would be there, some absent (Hogbin 1978: 31).

If Wogeos assume that all other Wogeos are family, there is no real discrepancy between Hogbin and Gagin's interpretations – the people gathered for doing a job for a man would, no matter who were there, be his *famili* or *oarooaro*. When speaking to me, people usually used the Tok Pisin word *famili*, and I cannot argue with the two Wogeo experts about the term *oarooaro*. However, in 2000 when I asked Exter to get a proper linguistic record of the term (in my absence), his informants gave a third and quite unexpected interpretation and claimed that *oarooaro* should only be used for *matrilineal* kin. Gagin once said that 'Wogeo society is getting more and more matrilineal' and the new translation may be seen accordingly, but I do believe that if Exter's informants had been asked the same question in times when an emphasis on their matrilineal identity had been unfavourable, it is not unlikely that they as well would have referred to the more widely defined kindred as *oarooaro*. In the same way as we will see (Part IV) Kulbobo changed his mind in the opposite direction when defining which categories of people are covered by the term *dara ta* (one blood) in his account of conception, the disparate definitions of *oarooaro* show us that the language used to describe kinship relations is not merely a matter of describing given cultural 'facts' but is also a means of argumentation.

Matrilineally related people are usually spoken of as 'true family' in Tok Pisin (*famili tru*). The term *dara ta* would usually be used when referring to the two matrimoieties Taregá (eagle) and Kilbong (flying fox) to which all Wogeos belong. These are known as *tiná* ('mother'), and, when asking people to which moiety they belong, one would use the term *tiná*. Marriage should only take place between the moieties, and people of opposite moieties should treat one another with respect. The criteria of biological matrifiliation is, however, not absolute in the case of moiety-membership, since people from other places who live in Wogeo normally are ascribed to one of the moieties. 'How else can we know who our children should marry,' a woman said to me.

Matrilineages are also referred to as *tiná* or, specifically, *tiná sike* (lit. 'small mother'). A person can only belong to the matrilineage of his or her mother. I was said to be a Taregá, the moiety of Maria, but it was unthinkable to say that I was of her matrilineage. In spite of their indisputable constitution, Wogeo matrilineages are not unproblematic categories, which will be made clear in later chapters.

Daily Rhythms

During my many months in Dab village, the daily routines of the people of Dab were both the background and focus of my research. The day-to-day village life was generally monotonous and repetitive, but sometimes the monotony was broken by visits from people living in other places, prayer meetings, the too frequent occurrence of funeral rituals or other, less frequent, ritual events.

A normal day in Dab as I knew it started with the women getting up at sunrise. They kindled the fire in the hearth and reheated the leftovers from the previous day's dinner before waking up their children. If there was a lot of work to do in the gardens, the women left for the bush before breakfast. Just before eight, the schoolchildren from the villages east of Dab came through the village, and the children from Dab joined them, carrying fresh coconuts for lunch. Most of the women and their older daughters then disappeared into the bush, carrying their baskets and bush-knives, to start their gardening work. Sometimes their husbands and young children joined them, but often the men would lie on their verandas relaxing before they went fishing or began whatever other activities they had planned for the day.

Men participated in gardening mainly when new gardens were made. It was their task to cut down the big trees and to make fences that prevent pigs from eating the garden produce. Men also collected nuts and breadfruits from trees, and they usually planted bananas, but apart from these tasks, women did most of the gardening (cf. e.g. Hogbin 1978: 84). It did happen, though, particularly in the case of young couples, that men joined their wives in their gardens just because they enjoyed each other's company. A friend of mine even used to join her husband when fishing from his canoe, but this was seen as an oddity, since fishing from canoes is regarded as an exclusive male activity. The youngest children were often left in the village in the care of their grandparents or other people who had time to spare, but just as often they accompanied their mothers to the bush.

In the afternoon the women returned, their backs weighed down by the heavily loaded baskets hanging from their foreheads and with bundled firewood on their heads. Also their young daughters usually carried small loads in their baskets, looking quite self-important with their grown-up responsibility. The women threw the firewood down on the ground in front of the houses for it to dry in the sun. As soon as they had washed off the dirt and sweat from their hard work, they started to cook supper. By now the schoolchildren had returned from school, and the older girls helped their mothers. Soon the sound of ripe coconuts being grated could be heard from all corners of the village. Oil was squeezed from the grated coconut meat and mixed with water, and all the vegetables were boiled in this mixture.

People usually ate together with the other members of the household. The mother of the house served the food on plates that each belong to the individual members of the household. Almost every afternoon she also sent plates of food to other people in the village. After supper the young girls washed the plates, while the pots with leftovers were put aside for breakfast the next morning.

As daylight disappeared, people either sat on their verandas or around fires in front of their houses. Often visitors came from other villages – just for the sake of company, to deliver a message, or to discuss plans for collective work, a prayer meeting or a pig hunt. Some nights, larger parties of people gathered around a fire; other nights, families kept to themselves. On moonlit nights socializing was more frequent, and the children played in the silver light that lit up the village space. The villagers sometimes gathered to play games on such nights – 'games of the moon' (*kaleva gongon*). 'Before,' people said, 'we always played these games at full moon. Not only the young people, but all the big men as well. Sometimes people from the whole district met in Dab and played.' Such games should be followed by a food exchange among the parties who had played – usually between the sides of the village. When in season, the nut *ib* (Tahitian Chestnut)[13] was often exchanged for the full moon games.[14] In 1994 the villagers planned an exchange of *kangar* following games we played, but for some reason they did not go through with it.

When I came to the island for my second visit in 1999, the charismatic movement within the Catholic Church had obtained a strong foothold in Wogeo and prayer meetings occupied many evenings. At least once a week there was a prayer meeting in another village, and Dab would be deserted apart from the elderly people and the people belonging to the Seventh-Day Adventist Church. When there were prayer meetings in Dab, the village space would be crowded, leaving no room for other activities than the loud charismatic praying. It seemed as if the meetings filled people's need for socializing, and, on the nights there were no prayer meetings, the families mostly kept to themselves on their verandas. Kulbobo many times complained about this and complimented me on keeping up the custom of lighting a fire in front of my house every night. During the six months I was on the island in 1999 mine was sometimes the only fire to be seen in Dab at nights.

When the moon was up, people usually did not go to bed until after midnight. At other times the village could be quiet already at ten. Sometimes the sound of people passing through the village at night could be heard – it was impossible to walk quietly on the pebbles, and nobody, except sorcerers, could pass through the village unnoticed.

Food, Sharing and Exchange

Women spent most of the daylight hours attending their gardens, and they were joined by men for heavy tasks such as cutting down trees, making fences and gathering nuts or breadfruits from trees. In general it can be said that men worked with trees and women with anything that grows in the ground (see also Hogbin 1938/39: 148). A good woman in Wogeo is one who works hard and always has an excess of food to offer visitors or to give away to neighbours. Hogbin noted that

> More often than not each housewife cooks a surplus in order to give to people who already have in abundance, while simultaneously these folk also cook more than they need with the aim of bestowing in their turn donations which in the literal sense will be just as out of place (Hogbin 1978: 35).

Unless you were invited to sit down and share a meal, a gift of food always needed to be reciprocated. Nearly every afternoon, children were sent between the houses, carrying plates of food: plates that right away or later would be sent back with an equal amount of food (see Lutkehaus 1995b: 153 and Smith 1994:39 for similar practices on Manam and Kairiru). If you were invited to share a meal, the same hospitality would be expected when your host came to visit your house. Having my own household during my last months on the island, I often had difficulties remembering who had one of my plates and who owned all those plates piling up on my veranda; I often experienced the truth of the point that what bears the most potential for power in an exchange is not necessarily what is exchanged, but the time that passes from when the gift is given until its return (Bourdieu 1977: 6-7).

During my first weeks on the island, I was – like Hogbin (1978: 35) – astounded that people bothered to put all the extra work into cooking surplus food nobody really needed. The explanation is quite obvious: these exchanges seldom had anything to do with feeding hungry people. Moarigum said to Hogbin that, 'we have food both for display and to eat. To you it is one thing only; to us it is two things' (Hogbin 1938/39: 324). When people give someone a gift of food, it is as if to say 'I am thinking about you'; it can be a sign of respect, or a boast of how much food one is able to produce without any extra effort. A good woman is a skilled, knowledgeable and hard-working woman who always has a surplus of food to give away. A gift of food was always given when people had helped you in your garden or with any tasks needing a collective effort. The immediate return was meant to compensate the food that is given; it was not the actual return-gift. The 'spirit of the gift', in the Maussian sense, is returned on a later occasion: this is when 'the rope is cut' (*oaro faraik*) as Wogeos say (*faraik* is used for cutting something in halves rather than cutting something off).[15]

That gifts and exchanges are primarily about creating and maintaining relations, Ganem from Moaroka made clear when he explained to me the custom of *moain*. Wogeos always carried a plaited basket (*goate*) with them, traded from the Murik Lakes on the mainland (cf. Lipset 1985). 'Your basket is like a rudder (*singara*),' Marifa had told me. 'Without it you would walk without any direction.' *Singara* is also the word for 'custom'. Most importantly the basket contained betel nuts, lime and betel-pepper: the ingredients for chewing betel, something most Wogeos (except the Seventh-Day Adventists) did whenever they had the chance. Whenever people met along the path in the bush, when working in a garden, or sitting in a village, the first thing they would do was to offer the other person a betel nut or some tobacco from one's basket. 'This custom is one of the most important in Wogeo,' Ganem said. '*Moain* is to let people know who you are. When you give someone a gift from your basket, they will know you and remember your name. If people don't know your name, they don't know you. This is why *moain* is so important.'

As in most of Melanesia, exchange is also an important part of any ritual celebration in Wogeo. Food is exchanged on scales ranging from small direct exchanges of cooked food on plates to enormous displays of baskets of food, pig, coconuts, betel nuts and tobacco. The type of exchange is determined by the occasion: the construction of a new house, funerals or other life cycle rituals, a farewell party, or other events worth celebrating. The exchanges are spoken of as 'work' (*manif*), which refers to the whole event (cf. Lutkehaus 1995b: 358). The actual exchanges taking place during such a 'work' should be an exchange of identities – that is, you receive the same as was given in your name – whereas in the reciprocal 'work', increment may be attempted.

Strathern has pointed out that exchange not only creates ties between people; exchange also 'quite crucially sever[s] and detach[es] people from people. Exchange is essential to the process of personification through which persons are separated by the social relations between them' (Strathern 1988: 191). To which place a person belongs is one of the most significant identities in this concern – like Goleiangaianga distributed food 'to one side and the other side'. During inter-village exchanges (*olage*) after funerals, each village is represented by one or two large baskets that are displayed on platforms or on the ground in front of the house of the deceased, visualizing and embodying the relevant identities and relations of the people present (cf. Carrier and Carrier 1991: 138–45). Other exchanges, for instance exchanges of plates of food (*kalogaloga*) involving only one village, usually place people and their plates according to which side of the village they belong. At a girl's first menstruation, an exchange of plates with food takes place between women at the beach, and at this occasion it is the matrimoieties that determine who should exchange with whom as the women with their plates find their places in two rows facing each other.

'In Wogeo you do not need money', Wogeos often said with pride. You will always be given a roof over your head and food to fill your stomach when visiting Wogeo – to pay for it is seen as immoral (cf. Smith 1994: 165). Still money is getting increasingly more necessary on the island. Wogeos have always been in frequent contact with the world beyond the island, and traditionally, networks of exchange with the nearby islands and the mainland provided items or food Wogeos did not produce themselves – such as tobacco from Kairiru, cooking pots from Turubu, sago and baskets from Murik Lakes, and wooden bowls and ceremonial flutes from the other Schouten Islands (see e.g. Lipset 1985; Barlow 1985). But with the increasing demand of *kana maian* – 'things of iron' as Wogeos called goods that came with colonization and modernization, compulsory schooling, motorized transport (the last Wogeo sailing canoe was made in the 1970s) and western medicine through the twentieth century – money became a necessity also in Wogeo. In the 1990s most families produced copra for cash now and then, and some families had cocoa groves. Men who owned boats caught fish for sale in Wewak when they could afford to buy ice and petrol, and others sometimes took garden produce to sell at the market in Wewak. More rarely people sold a pig to people in Wewak, and some people reared chickens for sale in Wogeo. At the market held outside the church on Sundays, people sold betel nuts, puddings, garden produce and tobacco for small amounts of money. From a visit to Wogeo in 2000, Exter reported that Wogeos had engaged in vanilla production as had many others in PNG following a significant increase in vanilla prices on the world market (cf. McGregor 2005).

In most villages there were a couple of people employed on the mainland. Most of them contributed economically when relatives on the island needed means for arranging funerals or other important celebrations, and they often provided lodging for nieces and nephews going to high school on the mainland. Money was also necessary for the construction of new houses. Nails were used extensively, and more and more people wanted corrugated iron roofs. According to tradition all people in the village as well as other allies should contribute with roof thatch to a new house,[16] and they now had to contribute with money for buying the corrugated iron sheets in Wewak.

The money was, however, never sufficient. This was most dramatically evident when people died because they could not afford the petrol for a boat to take them to Wewak or to the nearest health centre on Koil, only an hour's boat ride away. Some children, girls in particular, did not go to school because their parents could not provide the school fee, especially if they had several older siblings. Also people in paid work sometimes needed help to get all of their children to school. One man who was employed on the mainland in a relatively well-paid job, received money from both his brothers-in-law as well his sister in Wogeo for school fees for his seven children. It was expected that they in turn would receive his help when their own children were going to school, and the children should later in life support and help their benefactors. Like Michael French Smith (1994) describes it for neighbouring Kairiru, life on Wogeo was regarded as 'hard' – even though everyone took pride in the fact that food was never short and that you do not need money on Wogeo.

Mission, Colonial Powers and Change

Hogbin wrote that the first contact Wogeos had with Europeans was at the end of the nineteenth century when a sailor was 'washed up on the island', before anyone alive in 1934 had been born (Hogbin 1935a: 311). The earliest account of mission contact is from 1901 (Swadling 1980; Tiesler 1969–70: 119). The German missionary Francis Vorman, who made a brief visit to the island that year, described the Wogeos as showing 'no signs of friendship' (Vorman [1901]1980: 97). The councillor in Bajor told me that he had learnt from the mission that a missionary had been on Wogeo already in the 1890s and that he had fled the island when the islanders surrounded his hut armed with spears, but I have not been able to verify it. At the time of Hogbin's first visit, he noted that since 1905 'practically every native [meaning males] has spent a period of three or four years on a plantation' (Hogbin 1935a: 311) on the mainland near Wewak or other places like New Ireland. A New Guinean catechist from the Catholic Society of the Divine Word came to Wogeo in 1934 to set up a mission station, although he did not have any success converting people while Hogbin was there (Hogbin 1978: 5). By Hogbin's second visit in 1948, most young people were Christians, and when he returned for his last visit in 1974, 'almost no pagans were left' (ibid.: 9). A mission station with a church and a primary school had been established at Taro, and several German missionaries had lived there for periods of time. Most famous of them was Father Hugo Schultz who was the parish priest for thirty years until 1987. In the 1990s he lived at the mission's retirement home in Wewak. In the 1990s all Wogeos were Christians. Most of them were Catholics but, as already mentioned, there were also quite a few Seventh-Day Adventists (SDAs), most of who lived in Gonamie and Newcamp.[17] Since the late 1980s there had been no resident missionaries or priests in Wogeo. In 1999, the Catholics complained that the Kairiru-based priest, whose parish consists of the six western Schouten Islands and the smaller Wewak islands (eight islands in all[18]), hardly ever came to Wogeo any more.

Political leadership has traditionally been in the hands of men known as *koakoale*. Their eldest daughters and usually their wives, since they should marry daughters of other *koakoale*, are known as *moede*. There were several *koakoale* offices in each village, and according to tradition theywere in charge of different sections of communal tasks and the accompanying knowledge. The 'number one' *koakoale* (*koakoale malala*) was the one responsible for the distribution of food at an *oaraboa* – the most important office established by Goleiangaianga. These positions were inherited, usually from father to son. Mostly the eldest son was chosen, but this was not a requirement if a younger son seems to have better qualifications (Hogbin 1940; see also Allen 1984: 25) or, if a man had more wives, was the son of a higher ranked *moede* or belonged to a different, more suitable matrilineage. Other sons usually got lower ranked positions (see chapter 7). The Wogeo *koakoale* appeared, in the sense that there were several people in the village that were distinguished as being *koakoale* and *moede* and had the capacity to give birth to *koakoale* and *moede*, as an elite opposed to commoners (cf. Lutkehaus 1990; 1995b; see e.g. Liep 1991: 35 on such distinctions in the Massim). In several of the myths Exter and I collected, people who are not *koakoale* and can be labelled 'commoners' are spoken of as *ke boe boro* – 'dogs and pigs' (e.g. Anderson and Exter 2005: 71), but I have not heard this being used at other times.

Towards the end of the millennium the *koakoale* had lost their unquestioned political power. New offices of leadership, called 'luluai', had been introduced by the Germans in the 1920s and continued being used by the Australian colonial government after the Second World War (cf. Bulbeck 2002: 40–41). They were appointed by government representatives, but were usually men already in positions of power – like Gagin's father, Dale. Later locally elected councillors took the place of the luluai, and magistrates were appointed to assist in resolving local conflicts. There were two councillors on the island in the 1990s: one for Bukdi and Takur and one for Onevaro and Bagiava. The councillors headed the 'councillors' committees', and they were the intermediate links between the island and the provincial government. The councillors met in the Local Government in Wewak on a regular basis. The island also had one overall elected leader – Lala from Badiata who is also a *koakoale* – although it was not agreed upon whether this position had any justification, neither traditionally nor within the officially established leadership structure.

In spite of the absence of a resident priest, the Church in the 1990s was active and vital. The Sunday mass gathered most of the Catholics in the two churches on the island, but perhaps even more important were the numerous prayer groups. During my first fieldwork in 1993–94 there was a prayer meeting in Dab once a week, gathering mainly women who called themselves Catholic Mama. They would sit in front of Singero singing songs and quietly saying their Hail Marys. When I returned in 1998, the charismatic group had meetings twice a week in the district to which Dab belongs. The Catholic Mama still had their meetings, but they did not attract the large crowds that the charismatic meetings did. The charismatic prayer meetings were led by 'core groups', consisting of ten to fifteen people, most of them young men and women. Some of these had attended seminars about the 'gift of the Holy Spirit' in Wewak (see Smith 2002: 126–27). In Dab, my adoptive parents Maria and Tarere were leading members of the core group. The core groups would have their own meetings once a week, usually gathering some other people as well. For a small amount of money the core groups also mobilized groups of people to do work like building a house or producing copra, tasks that traditionally involved neighbours and relatives who were obliged to help each other on a reciprocal basis. The money was saved for buying musical instruments for the group, going to meetings in other places, or whatever the money was needed for.

Also the Catholic Mama would do such work, and in addition all the villages had days set aside for 'community work' – usually tasks such as cleaning the path from the village or the open village space. The villages in turn also had the responsibility for the Sunday mass, involving song rehearsals, cleaning the church, and so forth. The programme for communal activities could be quite busy, and during a normal week in Onevaro district in 1998–99 it would be as follows:

Monday – community work during daytime (e.g. communal work in the village, school, etc.).

Tuesday – charismatic prayer meeting for the 'core group' in Dab at night.

Wednesday – charismatic prayer meeting for everyone at night (each of the five villages taking turns to host the meetings).

Thursday – charismatic 'core group' work during daytime.

Friday – Catholic Mama work during daytime, prayer meeting at night.

Saturday – prayer meeting for the children in each village at night, preparing the church for Sunday mass and singing practice for those responsible for the mass.

Sunday – Mass; market afterwards.

(The SDAs have their service on Saturdays and otherwise had their own activities.)

If this program were to be strictly followed, there would not be much time left for work in the gardens or other activities for the parties involved. Usually, however, the prayer groups did not have any work for the days set aside, and the Catholic Mama prayer meetings would easily be skipped if other activities came about. The charismatic prayer meetings were, however, seldom omitted.

In addition to the weekly schedule, both the Catholic prayer groups and the SDAs sometimes had what they called 'community outreach'. The groups went for a day or two (the SDAs for a whole week) to a different village or district in order to spread their message and to work for their hosts. The SDAs also offered classes in readings of the Bible and more practical knowledge such as the use of medical herbs. In connection with such 'outreaches', 'drama nights' were arranged where both SDAs and Catholics would perform small dramas, often with moral messages. The dramas could be quite hilarious, presenting comical parodies of events where people had made fools of themselves, and people of both congregations participated enthusiastically. Afterwards, when back in the villages, people would often spend a lot of time disparaging and gossiping about the other prayer groups or the other Church and their programme, elevating themselves as the morally righteous and true believers.

The Catholic charismatic movement had caused some conflict. The pressure of conformity was great, and several women told me that they were afraid of the prayer group leaders, most of whom did not have any traditional political positions. It was said that people sometimes revealed the names of people practising sorcery while speaking in tongues, but it was hard for me to obtain any reliable information about this since people were not too eager to discuss this with me and it was difficult to interpret what was said during the meetings. The movement had also caused a division in the district where I worked. The leaders in one of the villages were sceptical about the charismatics, and nobody from that village joined the meetings. 'We did not do this before. Why should we all of a sudden have to stand up and scream and shout?' one of them complained (cf. Smith 2002). As a result of these tensions, some people left the Catholic Church and joined the SDAs. Some of them told me that they were afraid of the loud shouting at the meetings and the millenarian visions in the movement, and the SDAs with their disciplined manners seemed to them a more sober alternative (cf. Jebens 2005).

In spite of the enthusiasm for church activities, many people were worried about the fact that often there was not much time left for other kinds of socializing. Some people were eager to discuss this problem with me, and we spent many hours talking about the value of *kastom* in relation to the Church and other changes in the Wogeo way of living. Robbins (2004; 2007) has written extensively about the changes that have taken place as communities have converted to Christianity in Melanesia. The individualistic emphasis of Christianity introduces a radically different notion to societies where the relatedness is at the core of social life. He argues that anthropologists are trained to find continuity when studying change and that they often do this to such a degree that many seem unable to account for radical change. In the case of Wogeo, an emphasis on continuity is not merely the hang-up on the side of the anthropologist. Wogeos were also eager to search for continuity. They would tell me how the practice of confession had its equivalent in the way men had to confess their wrong doings prior to the male penile cleansings in the past, or how the moral code of conduct was the same for Christians as the traditional Wogeo values. With their worries about disappearing customs, Wogeos searched for and found continuity, but it also seemed that the charismatic movement had created a new 'crisis' in this concern. In his efforts to explain the movement in terms of continuity, Kulbobo claimed that the Holy Spirit's presence was the powers of Wogeo that had risen to the surface: 'ol powa bilong ples i kamap long ples klia'. In the next chapter we will see how Wogeo myths are associated with the Bible and the local culture heroes are likened to God and Jesus.

Language

Hogbin wrote that in the 1930s Wogeos took great pride in the Wogeo language and felt that it was the only proper and original way to speak. According to Hogbin they refused to speak any other language when for instance visiting the mainland:

> We have preserved the language of our *nanarangs* [culture heroes] correctly, but these
> people have forgotten the way the *nanarangs* spoke – unless the *nanarangs* themselves

made them talk like barking dogs. It is not fitting that we also should imitate the dogs; these others should rather learn to speak properly' (Hogbin 1939: 154).

In the 1990s Wogeos still valued their language highly and often pointed out how they managed to preserve their language in spite of the extensive use of Tok Pisin. In daily life in Wogeo people spoke approximately as much Wogeo as they spoke Tok Pisin, although some people tended to use Tok Pisin more than others. It also varied how fluently the youngest children spoke the Wogeo tongue (*meme oageva*), but the older children were mostly quite fluent. During my first fieldwork some parents in Dab seemed to speak mostly Tok Pisin to their children 'so that they will be able to communicate properly with non-Wogeos,' as one of them said. In 1999 it appeared as though they had changed their attitude and compared to 1993–94 spoke as much Wogeo as Tok Pisin to their children. It was my general impression that there seemed to be an increased interest in the value of knowing the Wogeo language in 1999, although this was probably also influenced by Exter's work with documenting the language, which prompted many discussions of the value of language.

People did claim, however, that the 'deep' knowledge of the language was disappearing. For instance, only a few people knew how to count beyond twenty in the Wogeo tongue. The Wogeo language as I heard it was always mixed up with Tok Pisin words. Older people complained that the younger ones did not know the language well enough, and when Exter started work documenting the language, the Dab men were quite specific as to who were the best informants and discarded several potential ones as having inadequate knowledge of the language. On this background, Exter's endeavours in writing down the language were most welcomed. As Kulbobo once said: 'I think that if we stopped speaking the Wogeo language, the ground would turn and the mountains fall down'. This statement leads us on to the topic for the next chapter: namely that of the value of *kastom* and the keeping of knowledge.

Notes

1. Additional crops are yam, cassava, breadfruit, pumpkin and numerous kinds of fruit.
2. In Tok Pisin this nut is called *galip*. Another nut is the *oasik* (Okari, lat. *Terminalia kaernabachii*), also highly valued by their trade partners.
3. During my last trip to Wogeo I got the full and tragic story of Oaoa (see chapter 8). Hogbin (1939: 117) described this place as always having been uninhabited.
4. See Parmentier (1987: 58) for similar processes in Belau.
5. *Kalet* also means 'the bush people', Seo (1991: 27) writes, and the term is commonly used to speak about people on the mainland who are regarded as less sophisticated or 'developed' than Wogeos – not dissimilar to the Tok Pisin condescending term *kanaka*.
6. See e.g. Barlow et al. 1986; Hogbin 1935; Lipset 1985; Lutkehaus 1995; Smith 1994.
7. The story is about a young boy who, after having caught octopus (*kurita*) together with his friends, wandered along the beach and came across the house of two old female *nanaranga* (mythical beings). They wanted to eat him and cooked the boy in a pot but only managed to eat his genitals before the boy's parents rescued him and managed to revive the boy. Powerful healing magic is associated with the story. The marks are from the boy's bow and arrow and from the two *nanaranga*.

8. Of the *Exocoetidae* (lat.) family (cf. Hogbin 1938/39: 135).
9. Hogbin wrote that the four major districts were on friendly terms with the district on the opposite side of the island and had a strained relationship with the neighbouring districts (e.g. 1970b: 10). Wogeos agreed with this also in the 1990s but meant that this was merely coincidental and did not refer to any structural order.
10. Dab had, according to the 2000 census, fifty-two inhabitants – the exact same number as Hogbin (1935a: 31) recorded in 1934. Moaroka had sixty-one and Joboe fifty-six.
11. The name of this place is the name Hogbin gave to his house in 1934. It was the name of the place (Ambuala) where he did fieldwork in Malaita in 1933 (Hogbin 1978: 9). Wogeos still refer to the site of his house with that name, pronounced Ambola. In 1993–94 Niabula lived there with his family and the old man Ulbaia and his wife Ima. By 1998 Niabula's children had moved up to the village (*malala*) and the camp was empty.
12. The same term that is used for the rafter connecting the two sides of a house or the night between the old and the new year.
13. *Inocarpus fagifer*, in Tok Pisin, *aila*.
14. We used to play a game that people said was an old game from Wogeo. The songs we sang while playing, however, were from New Ireland.
15. During my last visit to Wogeo, some of the islanders questioned this custom. They said that they should be able to give people food without bestowing upon the recipient the obligation to compensate the gift. I understood their concern better when I found myself in an awkward situation after proudly having given a big plate of self-cooked Wogeo-style food to Nunu, the single woman with seven children, just to realize that the next day she was obliged to reserve a portion for me of a much needed meal intended for her children.
16. See chapter 9.
17. Newcamp had thirty-seven inhabitants and Gonamie, fifty-three.
18. Kadovar, Biem, Rubrub, Wei, Koil, Wogeo of the Schouten group, and Tarawai and Walis sometimes referred to as belonging to Wewak Islands.

⤐ Chapter 2 ⤏

The Legacy of Ian Hogbin and
the Wogeo Culture Heroes

'You know that Gagin knows a lot about Wogeo *kastom*', one of my friends said
as we were sitting on the veranda of my Dab house one evening in 1999. 'And
do you know why?' she continued. 'It is because he knew Hogbin. Hogbin taught
him, and Hogbin knew everything there is to know about our *kastom*.'

Her statement was in a sense the ultimate glorification of the old Wogeo
anthropologist. Throughout the time I had spent in Wogeo, the reminiscence of
Hogbin had been continuously present in most conversations that I had with
people. From the first day that I set foot on the island, people were eager to tell
me about Hogbin's doings and his knowledge of Wogeo. People claimed that he
spoke the language fluently after only a few weeks, that he knew all the songs and
dances, all the myths and magic, and some people even claimed that he, being
Moarigum's apprentice, had killed a person using *iaboua* – death sorcery. I had
heard stories about his return to the island in 1974 and about the enormous food
distribution he had held, how he had planted sweet potato gardens using powerful
magic that no one else knew any longer[1] and how he had scolded people for
disregarding the customary ways.

Often people would refer me to his books in order to find answers to my
questions, and if I pointed out discrepancies between what people told me and
what was written in Hogbin's books, they would either not comment upon it or
claim that his version had to be the right one. What was not found in Hogbin's
book and articles, some claimed, was written down in a secret black book that he
had kept. Only a few held that perhaps Hogbin did not know everything, or they
explained discrepancies as misunderstandings due to the poor knowledge people
had of Tok Pisin in the 1930s (forgetting that Hogbin allegedly spoke fluent Wogeo
after only a few weeks).

Gagin, the leading *koakoale* of Dab, was acknowledged by my friend as a man
with great knowledge of Wogeo *kastom*, and Wogeos unanimously agreed to this
accreditation. But she claimed that this was not due to his position as a *koakoale*;
not because his predecessors, as was customary, had given him the knowledge
associated with his position. She believed Gagin's skills and knowledge were due to
his affiliation with Hogbin. To her, Hogbin had taken the place of the Wogeo elders;
as we will see one could even claim that he had become a sort of culture hero.

In his introduction to the book *The Leaders and the Led* (1978), Hogbin
describes his revisit to Wogeo in 1974. 'Everyone knew me by reputation and

took it for granted that I would fit in as one of themselves. They related many of my doings learnt in childhood, some true, some apocryphal' (ibid.: 11) – not an uncommon experience for returning anthropologists in PNG (see e.g. Tuzin 1997). Hogbin continues to tell how life had changed on the island, and how the islanders complained about their lack of knowledge of the traditional ways. They urged him to teach them what he knew – among other things the way to identify sorcerers:

> 'With each year that passes we still have proof that sorcerers still exist – Christianity hasn't made them give up,' one man remarked. 'Nowadays we're helpless against them because we no longer know how to carry out the inquest that could identify them. If you could teach us what to do surely Marigum [Moarigum] must have given you the training' ... I could assure him, truthfully ... that this was the one series of spells that Marigum had withheld (ibid.:12).

Hogbin (1935/36b: 13) notes after his 1934 fieldwork that he had not witnessed such an inquest at all. In 1993 I did witness an inquest, but some complained that it was carried out according to the Kairiru tradition. They could, however, tell me how it should be (and usually was) done in the Wogeo way – which was not much different from what I had seen and similar to how Hogbin (e.g. 1978: 52) described it. Thus, contrary to what people said to Hogbin in 1974, this knowledge was not regarded as lost in the 1990s. Rather, it was probably the idea that something *more* powerful or authentic had been lost that made people plead with Hogbin to teach them. Ironically Hogbin notes that 'the natives are in any case sceptical about its [the inquest's] authenticity' (1935/36b:13), indicating that the people felt they had lost power from the past also in 1934.

Exclusiveness and secrecy were important for such knowledge to retain its power, and sharing and dispersing the knowledge would most likely evoke a feeling of loss. It might not be the actual spells or prescribed actions that were lost, but the power they possessed by being inaccessible, other than to the select few. Errington and Gewertz (2001) have discussed similar worries about incrementally disappearing knowledge among the Chambri. In making traditional knowledge accessible and understandable to others, the traditional holders of knowledge lose control over this knowledge. Power is transferred to those who can use this knowledge in new ways – for instance in preserving and representing culture as a package of inherited traditions in dialogue with outsiders such as tourists or the government, what the Chambri themselves called 'the living "book" of Chambri wisdom and experiences' (ibid.: 520), a process that Errington and Gewertz call generification of culture (see also Harrison 2000).

The work of an anthropologist inevitably becomes part of such a generification, but Wogeos also accredited Hogbin with the ability to maintain the original power of the knowledge given to him – in contrast to what they themselves had managed. He had allegedly kept the most powerful knowledge in his black book, keeping (and even strengthening, since he brought them with him all the way to Sydney) the secrecy and, hence, its power. One man once told me that a priest working in Wogeo had visited Hogbin in Sydney. He had asked Hogbin if it was true that he had learnt all the powerful knowledge from Wogeo as he had heard. To show the priest some of his skills, Hogbin had according to the story recited a spell (*boasa*) to call for rain. The priest had seen the rain clouds gather and not long after it was raining. The priest had then asked Hogbin if it was true that he could kill a man with *iaboua*. 'Do you want to try me?' Hogbin had replied. The priest got scared and said 'no'.

Stories like this were often told, and particularly one old man often spoke about Hogbin in this manner. He once related a story that I have heard from several people on different occasions. 'You know the story about Goleiangaianga in Gole', he said. 'Nobody remembers this story properly any longer, but Hogbin knew it well.' But before I continue discussing Hogbin's connection to the story of Goleiangaianga below, a closer examination of Wogeo notions of *kastom* and the culture heroes will be pertinent.

The Origins of *Kastom*

One afternoon in 1993 I was sitting with the old man Marifa on the veranda of Singero. I asked him if there was an equivalent term for the Tok Pisin word *kastom* in the Wogeo language. He thought about it for a while and told me to be patient. 'It is not good if I tell you the wrong words', he said. After some time he replied that '*singara nanasa moa*' – 'the rudder of the stories from the past' – best covered the term *kastom*. *Singara* is the rudder of a sailing canoe, but also refers to manners or customary ways (*pasin* in Tok Pisin) (see also e.g. Hogbin 1938: 226). *Nanasa* is used for stories in general and is also a verb for telling stories. *Moa* is the distant past.

According to these stories, people of great skills and knowledge brought *kastom* to the island in the distant past. Hogbin wrote that the Wogeos called them *nanaranga* (e.g. Hogbin 1970b; see also Lutkehaus 1995b). In the 1990s Wogeos usually described *nanaranga* as non-human beings, some of them similar to trolls and giants in European fairytales. In Tok Pisin they translated *nanaranga* with *masalai*. The words *nanaranga* and *nanasa* have the same root. The stories about the *nanaranga* are also often referred to as *nanaranga* instead of *nanasa* (cf. Leach 2000: 165). To teach, *nanarani*, is also from the same word. Most of my informants emphasized, however, that the most important culture heroes were real human beings (*ramata*), and not *nanaranga*. Smith (1994: 74) also notes such differences in opinion from nearby Kairiru Island. In the account of Goleiangaianga, the hero is said to be a *nanaranga* that was transformed into a human (*ramata*). Also in Kulbobo's account of Onka and Mafofo, which I will present below, Kulbobo emphasizes that the heroes were *ramata* but, as we will see, he still uses the term *nanaranga* for Onka and even for Mafofo, who is usually said to be a true man (*ramata*) of Wogeo. Most likely the term *nanaranga* in its strict meaning refers to the figures appearing in the mythical stories in general, without limiting its reference to the more non-human and supernatural qualities in particular. It could be that the present-day emphasis on the human nature of some of these *nanaranga* is a result of the introduction of Christianity with Jesus as the human manifestation of God. As we will see later in the chapter, Kulbobo explicitly compares Onka and Mafofo to God and Jesus. It could also be that the use of the Tok Pisin *masalai*, connoting more of the non-human qualities of the mythical beings, have influenced the way the term *nanaranga* presently is used in Wogeo. However, no matter whether they are regarded as humans or not, it was the heroes (or heroic *nanaranga*) who brought *kastom* and defeated the wicked and malevolent *nanaranga* that made the life of the islanders difficult. As we saw in the description of a tour around the island, various rocks and formations in the landscape are said to be the marks of these heroes and their accomplishments, including the *nanaranga* they killed, adding to the sociohistorical dimension of the experienced landscape.

The first hero who arrived was Goleiangaianga. In the shape of a caterpillar he descended from the sky to the village of Gole, named after the hero. There he initiated *oaraboa* and *kolova* — spectacular displays and distribution of food, the latter to celebrate the initiation of *koakoale*.[2] Later Goleiangaianga was said to have changed his name and travelled around the island, introducing all kinds of customs and useful knowledge. The best-known story about him was from Dab where he called himself Onka. In Dab he established a friendship with the local hero Mafofo, a friendship that turned sour after Onka slept with Mafofo's wife, Moede. Later Onka and, in some versions of the story, Mafofo left Wogeo for new deeds in near and distant places, but first they initiated trade relations with the mainlanders and sailed the paths of trade for the first time. Such travelling heroes are common in the region with its systems of interaction like the Murik trade (Lipset 1997) or similar systems for instance on PNG's south coast (Busse 2005), pointing to a long history of regional engagement and how 'cultural practices come into being over time and through interaction with others'(ibid.: 445; see also Harrison 2000).

Onka, or Wonka as Hogbin wrote, did not have such a prominent place in the version of the myth written down by Hogbin as Wogeos ascribed him in the 1990s. In Hogbin's version the role of Mafofo was emphasized. In *Island of Menstruating Men*, Hogbin introduces Onka merely as 'Mafofo's blood-brother, from a village in the interior' (1970b: 45), and also relates some short tales about the doings of Onka's foolish younger brothers. He did mention Goleiangaianga, but only briefly when referring to rituals associated with *oaraboa* (1970b: 78) and as the 'hero founder' of Gole (1978: 41). In 1971 Hogbin published some myths together with the grandsons of two of Hogbin's main informants: Gagin and Tom Fandim (Dalle et al 1972). Tom Fandim contributed with the story of Goleiangaianga and his journey to Dab. Hogbin wrote in the introduction to the article that

> He [Tom Fandim] belongs to Gol [Gole], and, as is to be expected, the tale magnifies the glory of that village at the expense of the rest. Once the main characters migrated from Gol to the Wonevaro [Onevaro] district on the other side of the island the incidents are identical to those told in Dap [Dab], where I mainly lived (ibid.: 25).

His note concerning Fandim's story is pertinent. Fandim writes that a man who lived in Gole when Goleiangaianga first came, named Tanefoagule [Tanefwagule], was upset that Goleiangaianga had taken his position in Gole, and that he moved to

Dab with his mother. There he took the name Mafofo and gave the name Moede to his mother. I have not heard this part of the Goleiangaianga story while in Wogeo. By Dab people, Mafofo is said to be a true big man of Dab (an autochthon). Wogeos have exclusive rights to the stories belonging to their villages, and thus people in Dab should, ideally, not tell the story about Goleiangaianga (cf. e.g. Hogbin 1939: 157). Likewise the people of Gole should not tell the stories from Dab. As Leach writes about rights to knowledge on the Rai Coast, '[E]xpressing knowledge amounts to claiming inclusion in the relationships (including those to land and spirits) which generate that knowledge' (2000: 165). Any account of Mafofo from a person of Gole would, thus, not be given much importance, including the idea that Mafofo really is from Gole.

In 1999 I went to Gole together with Mats to record the story of Goleiangaianga. An old man was supposed to tell it to us, but when we arrived we learnt that he was very ill. Instead his son would tell us the story, but as he was not sure of all the details the old men of the village came to help him get it straight. They discussed the story for a long time. I understood that they were somewhat reluctant to tell the story to us. They said that there were parts of the story that were very powerful. Parts of it should not be told in public, and particularly not to a woman. I had heard most of the story told on other occasions and had also read it in the above-mentioned publication by Dalle, Fandim and Hogbin (1972). I related parts of the story to let them know what I already knew. They agreed that they could tell the story but omit the powerful parts of it. That I already knew of the content of the story's powerful part from Hogbin's writings was met with some discomfort but could not be helped. We were preparing to start the recording, but then we heard crying from the old man's house. He was dead.

We returned to Dab without the story, but went back to Gole on a later occasion. The discussions about the story were still not finished, but eventually the old man Libaliba told it beautifully. Unfortunately our recordings were stolen during Mats' return journey to Germany in 1999,[3] but in 2000 he recorded it again from Joe Kosman as related in the prelude to this part (which in some respects differs from Fandim's version).

Goleiangaianga's great work was the initiation of *oaraboa*: the ceremonial display and distribution of food. *Oaraboa* is the term for such food distribution in general, but most commonly it refers to enormous inter-district exchanges (see e.g. Hogbin 1970a, 1970b, 1978). A *koakoale* in a village would conspire with his allies to challenge a *koakoale* from another district by inviting him to the feast. The display of food was placed on the platform (*bag*) that was made to look like a canoe, and the pigs were hung on the *boaboaur* on each side of the *bag*. The feast was initiated with a ritual fight between members of opposite matrimoieties. Hogbin (ibid.) described the fight as having the function of relieving tensions and ending old conflicts in order to let peace and fellowship reign during the *oaraboa*. The hosts would perform spectacular dances, and the party would last until early morning. The guests would be loaded down with gifts of food to carry with them back home – like Gule and his companions in the myth. Then it was the guests' turn to reciprocate the gifts, and, later, to return the challenge, attempting to make an even larger feast. Marifa said that *oaraboa* was the most important aspect of

Wogeo *kastom*: conflicts would rest and people would be together in peace. As the story of Goleiangaianga clearly illustrates, abundance of food is Wogeos' greatest pride and concern and, as will be discussed in chapter 8, the *oaraboa* also provides a model for leadership.

Kulbobo and other old men told me that when Hogbin had learnt nearly all the stories of Wogeo, Moarigum had taken him to Gole. In Gole the old man Natoie was supposed to tell him the full story about Goleiangaianga, including a magical spell that is the most powerful and important magic in Wogeo. The spell itself is particularly secret, and the only way to learn it is to listen carefully when it is recited in its proper context. The spell is associated with the initiation rituals of a new *koakoale malala* – 'chief of the village'. For such an occasion the large platform (*hag*) that Goleiangaianga placed in Gole would be built for the *oaraboa*. On each side of the platform, Goleiangaianga's two poles – *boaboaur* – were erected (see Hogbin 1970b: 78).[4] On these slim, high poles, the pigs presented for the *oaraboa* were to be fastened, like sails on the masts of a sailing canoe; but first, the heir should climb the poles, all the way to the top. The story tells that Goleiangaianga had difficulty erecting the poles because of the stony ground. Two women volunteered to hold the base steady while Goleiangaianga summoned the birds and the sun to help hold the poles erect. He then urged the sun to pull the name of Gole 'to the sky till all the heroes of Wogeo and the rest of the islands come to look upon this place as foremost, before all others, famous for its supplies and for its gifts' (ibid.). Since then the men have managed to erect the poles without the help of women (see also Anderson 1996: 133), and it was the spell evoking this power that Hogbin was said to have learnt.

According to what Wogeos told me, Natoie first told Hogbin that he could not teach him the spell since no ritual where the magic should be recited was planned in the near future. But then he changed his mind and sent for Hogbin who, meanwhile, had returned to Dab. Hogbin went back to Gole. There the old man told Hogbin to sit down with his back towards his own back. Two other men also sat down with them – so they were four men with their backs towards each other. Natoie said that they should not be surprised if something happened to him afterwards, since he took a great risk upon himself by reciting the spell. Hogbin would have to take great care of his body after having learnt the spell. He should never marry, since his body would be in a vulnerable state, and contact with women would be dangerous. Also, if he married, the power of the spell would be lost. The man then recited the spell. Afterwards Hogbin and his companion returned to Dab. The next morning a death signal sounded from the slit gongs around the island: the old man was dead.

Hogbin does not write about such an event involving Natoie and the story of Goleiangaianga. He did mention the story of Goleiangaianga and described the way the poles were erected (1970b: 78), but he said nothing about how he learnt it. He did, however, describe how Natoie recited another powerful magical spell, *kinab*, at an *oaraboa* in Gole and that Kaoang, a *koakoale* of Gole, later taught him this spell (see e.g. 1978: 168). I asked Kulbobo and others whether they thought it possible that it was the *kinab* spell that Hogbin had learnt in their Hogbin story, but Kulbobo denied it. He said that the *kinab* spell also was powerful and dangerous but that it was a very different type of spell. The spell to make the *boaboaur* stand erect was indeed something powerful, and it was this magic Hogbin had learnt.

When Hogbin returned to Wogeo in 1974, he found that everyone still 'accepted the efficacy of magic (their word), though not a single spell had survived' (1978: 12). This was certainly an exaggeration since I have recorded several different spells (*boasa*) during my fieldworks, and in the 1990s people still used magic for curing and preventing diseases, securing good crops or catches of fish, stopping rain and so forth. But in the light of the manner in which people spoke about lost knowledge, I can easily imagine why Hogbin got the impression that 'not a single spell' had survived. To Hogbin, Gagin had said that his uncles 'absolutely refused to answer any questions concerning what went on before the missionaries came' (ibid.: 11). They were Christians now and this was something of the past. It could also be that they were afraid of reprisals from missionaries or authorities. While I was in Wogeo, however, the older people on the island were eager to pass on knowledge of *kastom*, although they felt that significant parts of it had been lost.

Most importantly, people claimed that what was regarded as the single most important piece of knowledge was lost. I often heard the story of how the Polish priest who worked in Wogeo in the 1980s had gone to see Hogbin in Sydney. He had asked Hogbin for this important knowledge, and Hogbin had written something down on a piece of paper and told him to bring it back to Wogeo. The priest had done so, and according to the story he had hidden the note in the centre post of the priest's house in Taro. Everyone knew that the note was there, but nobody knew what was written on it. Hogbin had instructed the priest that no one should see it since what was written there was dangerous knowledge and nobody knew how to handle it any more, but still it was important that it was brought back to Wogeo. I asked whether it was possible that it was the spell to keep the *boaboaur* erect that was written on the note, but people meant that it had to be something even more secret and dangerous. Besides, there was still one man who knew the spell of the *boaboaur* alive in Wogeo. Only four villages had the right to erect the *boaboaur*: Gole, Ga, Falala and Dab. When I was on the island in 1994, the old man Sega from Ga came to Dab. He was the last man who knew the *boaboaur* spell. He wanted to erect the poles for a last time before he died so that Sega's heir could learn the magic. But the people of Ga were afraid of this magic, and the ritual was not carried out. Sega died in 1997. The hidden piece of knowledge, written on the note in the priest's house, was even more dangerous. The note in the post was alledgedly still there, and nobody dared take it out. I do not know if the note was actually in the post or not, but considering the power given to knowledge that is not shared or explained, the idea that this spell was preserved as a secret is important. Since so much of the previously hidden knowledge had been shared and unveiled, it is easy to understand why the post of wood was seen as a better keeper of secret than men.

Before I continue with the accounts of Hogbin and knowledge lost, Kulbobo's voice will relate Goleiangaianga's endeavours under the name of Onka. The story about Onka and his companion Mafofo is built around a theme that is found in mythology across Melanesia, known as 'the myth of the two brothers' or 'the hostile brothers' (Counts et al. 1991: 7). Most famous are the two brothers from

Lawrence's book *Road bilong Cargo* (1971[1964]), from the Rai Coast near Madang, where they are known as Kilibob and Manup (see also Englund and Leach 2000). Kulbobo has left out and mixed up some parts in this account that was recorded and transcribed in Wogeo in 2000. In order for the story to be coherent, I have included these parts in the text in non-italics.[5]

Onka and Mafofo

The story I want to talk about is the story of Onka. The name of the man was Onka. The name that the man who appeared first eventually called himself was Onka. He was the man who first came down at Gole. He came down at Gole, he descended upon a high mountain. They call it Vanasoro. He descended from the sky; he descended in a cocoon. The name he called the cocoon was Goleiangaianga. He came down and stood on top of Vanasoro and the ground became dry, sea and ground appeared; the sea dropped, the ground appeared; the island of Wogeo, the island appeared; he said his name was Goleiangaianga. After he had stayed in Gole, he rounded the island. He reached the mountains of Bagiava; he reached Noba and said that his name was Kuliling. Kuliling appeared in Noba; the name he called himself was Kuliling.[6] He stayed there, he stayed and two, three weeks passed; he walked on, he came and reached the mountains of Dab and he said his name was Daro. He came down a ladder.[7] The name he called himself was Daro. His name Onka had not yet appeared. Of his names, three had already appeared: Goleiangaianga, Kuliling, Daro. Three had appeared.

Also Mafofo, a man from Dab, came to stay there. Once Mafofo had sailed to the mainland, Onka slept with Mafofo's wife in the village of the man [Dab].

Onka tattooed his special design on the thighs of Moede, Mafofo's wife. When Mafofo returned to Wogeo, he had dreamt about what had happened and tricked her into walking waist-deep into the sea in order to help him to pull up his canoe. As the salt water reached her thighs, the freshly made tattoo cause her pain. Mafofo saw the grimaces on her face and his suspicions were confirmed. During the night he secretly had a look at the tattoo. Mafofo was building a new men's house (*nyaboá*), and he asked the leading men to come and decorate the house with carvings. He recognized Onka's design from Moede's thighs. Mafofo then asked Onka to climb down into the hole that had been dug for the main post of the house to hold the post steady. Mafofo and his allies then wanted to crush and kill him with the post. Onka understood what they were up to and spat red betel nut juice into half a coconut shell, and as the post was thrust down, Onka made himself disappear but left the coconut shell. When Mafofo saw the red juice, he thought it to be Onka's blood and hurried to close up the hole, satisfied that he had successfully ended the life of the man who had slept with his wife.

Mafofo came back and went ashore and built a nyaboá *[men's house] … and they dropped a post on top of Onka. But Onka went up to Kinabanua and danced. When he danced, this is the song that he made:*

Mafofo, Mafofo, Mafofo o a,	*Mafofo, Mafofo, Mafofo,*
bolova iko dandandi,	*your plans are watery,*
Ngaianga-re mama[o]sadí.	*Ngaianga's[8] are dry.*

The song that he sang was this one. Mafofo sent his mother, Buruka. He said to her: 'Go up and try and see who is dancing at Kinabanua! Is it a village of boys? No, that is the village of my tavag [a term used for men being initiated together]!' He called that man his 'tavag'. The nanaranga call each other 'tavag'. Buruka went up and had a look. The man called Onka was there with his younger brothers, and they danced. 'Mother, what is the matter?' Onka asked her. She said, 'I have come up because Mafofo has sent me to see if you have died or are alive.' He said, 'Go and tell him that I have died. I am here again but this is my spirit that is dancing.' Then the mother returned. Mafofo had told her, 'If it is him, decorate your head with a hibiscus flower when you come down.' So when she came down, she stuck a hibiscus flower into the hair. She came to Dab and he asked her: 'Who dances to the slit gong?' She said 'Onka'. His name became Onka in just that moment. His names were finally four; one name was Onka. She said, 'It is Onka who is dancing, the one on top of whom you dropped the post.' That was it, his name Onka came into being there.

His name Onka came into being, and it remained and remained and remained for good, his name Onka; we keep calling him Onka. He and Mafofo used to fight …. He stayed for good. Then Mafofo told people to decorate the nyaboá *with carvings. The men of the village came and decorated it. He said, 'Not those!' [when seeing Onka's carvings]. Thus Mafofo wanted to see the pattern that was tattooed on Moede's thighs.*

Onka and his people were invited back down from Kinabanua for the initiation of the *nyaboá*. Mafofo tricked Onka and his allies into entering the *nyaboá* together with Moede – at this time women were allowed to enter this particular men's house (Bagura) before it was properly initiated. Mafofo then set fire to the house. When Onka understood what Mafofo was up to, he told Moede and his men to take hold of his loincloth, and he made all of them fly to Kinabanua, hidden in the smoke.

After that, his mother went up into the nyaboá *and looked. She saw that Moede was there, and Mafofo wanted to burn it with fire … burn her with fire. He burned the* nyaboá *with fire, the* nyaboá *Bagura. He set it alight with fire, and Moede went up to Kinabanua and she stayed there for good. Onka married Moede, and she stayed with him for good.*

Mafofo remained in Dab, and they [he and Onka] challenged each other with all kinds of things. They built canoes; they went up to Koil and built canoes; then they came back down again. The canoes were two. One they called Jalaoageva ['Wogeo path']; that was Mafofo's canoe. Onka's canoe was called Oarboit. They called themselves Moanuboa and Liboaboa. This is the song they made:

Liboaboa e, kamá e dekura[9] o,	*Liboaboa, may he rise [with his canoe] like the* kamá[10],
Liboa[o]boa e, kamá e dekura o,	*Liboaboa, may he rise like the* kamá
Liboa[o]boa e.[11]	*Liboaboa.*

The two nanaranga *Mafofo and Onka created this: they built canoes on Koil, the canoes Jalaoageva and Oarboit. Oarboit was Onka's canoe; it came down [to Wogeo] and stood for good in Oakiblolo. Mafofo fastened his canoe. He had not made Jalaoageva for sailing to the mainland. He said, 'I am going to bring my canoe down to Wogeo.' Its name was Jalaoageva. He only brought it down to Wogeo and landed it at Kulka [the canoe landing place in Dab Lukaluka]. He decorated it with carvings, burned it and erected the rails – he worked on it. It became beautiful and he asked his mother, Buruka: 'Mother, what is the name of my canoe?' She told him: 'The name that I will give it for you is Udemtaregá.' The name of Mafofo's canoe was Udemtaregá. When it would rush over the ground, it was like a bandicoot [udem]; when it would rush over the sea, then it would fly like an eagle [taregá]. So its name was Udemtaregá. When Onka saw it, he said: 'Oh,* tavag, *you have done excellently, you have clearly beaten me; your canoe sails best!' Mafofo named it bandicoot and eagle.*

They kept challenging each other in this way, Mafofo and Onka. Onka was like this: Onka is the big man of us, the people of Wogeo. The houses and the nyaboá *they placed in Dab. Everything Onka and Mafofo poured out in Dab.* Koakoale *and* moede[12] *they poured out in Dab. Big houses they poured out in Dab. Nyaboá they poured out in Dab. The* ro *[the rafters in the houses associated with land rights] and all that they poured out in Dab. The bird of paradise [metaphor for the prestige and finery associated with the* koakoale*], too, they poured out in Dab. Koakoale, moede, everything. The big houses they poured out in Dab. They call Dab the village of the birds of paradise [vanua oasá]. That is the village where Onka and Mafofo challenged each other. One side is dry, one side is watery. The dry one, that you have heard about in the song that Mafofo and Onka made. I will sing it once again, the song:*

Mafofo, Mafofo, Mafofo o a,	*Mafofo, Mafofo, Mafofo,*
bolova iko dandandi,	*your plans are watery,*
Ngaianga-re mama[o]sadí;	*Ngaianga's are dry;*

Mafofo, Mafofo, Mafofo o a,	*Mafofo, Mafofo, Mafofo,*
bolova iko dandandi,	*your plans are watery,*
Ngaianga-re mama[o]sadi.	*Ngaianga's are dry.*

The song they sang is this one. That is the song they used to challenge each other with in all kinds of respects. Then they say that one side of the village of Dab is wet: Mafofo's side [Lukaluka/Kajenamoa]. The part that Onka used to sit in is the dry one [Moarmoar]. The house Mafofo used to sit in front of they call Omdara. Like I have told: the canoe Omdara, the spear Omdara, the house Omdara, the Omdara part of the village – where blood floats. The blood is the betel nut spit that Onka spat out.[13] The half of the coconut shell is laying there, the half that he brought down [in the hole made for Bagura's post], that he spat into; it is lying inside the ground. This was the story of Onka and Mafofo.

Like this, it stays important, everything that they made in Dab. Everything they poured out in Dab. The paths they poured out, the canoes they poured out, everything. Their planning, their speeches – everything they disclosed in the village of Dab. Thus the people from all places say that Dab is the village of the bird of paradise. In the village there are many birds of paradise, many houses of the bird of paradise. On whose head do the birds of paradise stand? On Onka's and Mafofo's heads. They are two koakoale. *They made them carry baskets.*[14] *Like that, they poured out goods, all of you from all the villages will hear it like that. The posts, namely the posts they mean when they talk about the posts, those are the posts of the people of Dab. They have names. The names of the posts, of the big* nyaboá *here, Bagura, the names of the posts are Busolaga and Omdara.*

Kulbobo ascribes Goleiangaianga/Onka more of a creator role than Kosman did in his account. Kulbobo says that dry land and ocean appeared when Goleiangaianga landed on Vanasoro. In the joint publication with Hogbin (Dalle et al. 1972) mentioned previously, Gagin contributed with a 'creation song' that ascribes Onka a similar role. However, in most accounts of myths I have heard on Wogeo, people were already present on the island when the heroes appeared – including when Goleiangaianga came.

According to Kulbobo's account, the most important work Onka did was in Dab where he placed named houses and the first *nyaboá* and where he introduced the positions of *koakoale* and *moede*, the latter named after Mafofo's, and later Onka's, wife. Onka and Mafofo were both companions and enemies. Onka and Moede appear as the winning part of the competing relationship – even though Moede cheated on her husband and Onka deceived his *tavag* – a term that marks the close companionship that used to be established between pairs of boys initiated together, usually of opposite moieties.[15] Hogbin wrote that 'while adultery is the theme of many folk-tales I do not know of one where the adulterer is the hero, and the husband is never ridiculed' (Hogbin 1938).[16] If he was right, Onka's heroic status certainly must have increased through the years, being an adulterer. But Mafofo was not ridiculed, and he made the best canoe.

The creation of the trading canoes is also what is usually elicited as the important part of the story – for the people of the district of Bagiava, Onka's canoe Oarboit and for the people of Onevaro, Udemtaregá.[17] Udemtaregá is the property of Dab.[18] Only men from Lukaluka in Dab had the right to build and launch this canoe, and it was built for the last time in the 1970s. At that time it had an outboard engine, and Gagin and Maria with their families were shipwrecked with it on their way from Wogeo. Luckily they drifted ashore on the island of Tarawai and were taken care of by the villagers there. Later the Dab people included their rescuers in their network of trade relations as a token of their gratitude.

The theme of adultery is common to versions of this myth found along the north coast of PNG. Common to these versions is also that the heroes made canoes and left their homes for other places. Also Kulbobo's account continues by telling how Onka and Mafofo initiated trade relations with mainlanders and people from the nearby islands, and how Onka eventually continued on to unknown places. The route they travelled is the route the trading expeditions from Wogeo are thought to have followed ever since. It goes to Kairiru and Muschu to trade tobacco, to Wom near Wewak for tobacco and sago, to Turubu to trade clay pots, to Murik Lakes to get baskets and to the smaller Schouten Islands to trade plates and wood for

making flutes. The paths of trade are known as *jala baga* – 'mainland path'– and
jala kat boe vam – 'canoe and outrigger path', to the other Schouten Islands (cf.
also e.g. Lipset 1997; Smith 1994). The trading partners are inherited together with
land and are known as *lo* (or *bag*, according to Hogbin (1935b: 398), although my
informants reserved the term *bag* for partners within the island). Dab people speak
about these places as where Udemtaregá's *lung* (rollers for launching canoes) lies.
The story of Onka and Mafofo continues like this:

> *I will continue the story of Onka and Mafofo. I will continue and, at the very end of it,*
> *Onka will disappear for good. ... Mafofo went away with Udemtaregá; he sang spells*
> *for it and went away with it, went away with it all the way to a place near Oakiblolo.*
> *He went away with it to a place they call Moanuboaoaoailodi, at Oakiblolo, the place*
> *where Ialoma sits, the place where* oagare[19] *and ginger grow, to Moanuboaoaoailodi.*
> *Mafofo went there and sang spells for Udemtaregá, went there and brought it ashore.*
> *With Oarboit [the canoe] they [Onka and Mafofo] stood together on a small place in*
> *Moanuboaoaoailod, at Oakiblolo. They performed magic on the canoes [by beating*
> *them with* oagare*], bespelled the ropes holding the sails, bespelled the rollers with*
> oagare. *They performed magic on the canoes, beating them with ginger,* jaga[20] *leaves*
> *and all that they prepared there; they bent the mainland [reducing the travelling*
> *distance by magic] there, everything they prepared there. Then they launched the*
> *canoes, and Oarboit and Udemtaregá sailed away.*
>
> *They sailed to the mainland. They sailed until they finally went ashore in Oma*
> *[Wom, near Wewak]; for in Oma, the name of their men's house is Bagura; that is the*
> *men's house in Dab. Its name is Bagura.[21] The rollers lie in Oma, the Lung Lalaba*
> *['big rollers']. Furthermore, they lie in Kandara; they lie in Jagura; they lie in Keba*
> *[Kep]. They sailed along the mainland; [the rollers] lie in Tudubu; they lie in the area*
> *of the* oloolo, *in Sire and Samaf [Samap]; they lie in Kauba [Kaup]; in Kauba, the*
> *name of the men's house is Bagura. The name of the men's house in Dab is also Bagura.*
> *They went on, the rollers lie in Oakun, Magaeta. The rollers lie at Oakun. They lie in*
> *Oagemot: those that lie in Oakiblolo, the rollers of Oarboit. The rollers of Udemtaregá*
> *lie at Kulka beach [in Dab, Lukaluka]. Furthermore, they stayed in Magaeta, stayed*
> *there in Magaeta and Kauba; but we have heard that they came back again.*
>
> *They came down from Boemoa [Biem Island]. They came down. They came*
> *down, came ashore at Badiata; then they separated. One went to this side; one went*
> *to the other side and around Wogeo. Onka came to this side; they unloaded everything*
> *[from his canoe], grasshoppers and all that; sago and all that they unloaded at the*
> *shore; grasshoppers and all that they unloaded around the cape Udir. One turned to*
> *the side of Takur, one went here. They came down, Onka came down, and they say that*
> *he stayed for good, that he stayed in Dab for good. Onka, his name was Onka. He said,*
> *'I am Onka', he came down, thus he stayed for good, saying, 'this is me'.*
>
> *His spirit sailed away, then he returned to the lower side of the island; his*
> *mother had died and was lying there [in the canoe]. Where was he going to go ashore?*
> *Where was he going to bring her ashore, in order for them to bury her? But on these*
> *places they sneered at her and rejected her. He went on and on, asked the people of*
> *Bajor, brought her to that side. Onka asked them, 'my mother is lying on the canoe.*
> *Where am I going to bury her?' But the people of Bajor rejected her. After they had*

rejected her, he sailed with her to the mainland. ... They did not stay on Wogeo, they
returned to the mainland again. They returned, that is they went and went and went
and went and he buried his mother there near Turubu, in Sire. He brought her ashore in
Sire, ... the moanuboa *is there. His mother lies in the village of Sire, Onka's mother lies*
there. His mother was called moanuboa. *His mother lies there. Those clay pots [that*
are traded from Turubu], those are made from Onka's mother whom they buried there.
We trade pots from the people of Tarbu [Turubu]. That is Onka's mother. She called
herself moanuboa. *Pots, they call 'our stomachs'. Our mothers are our stomachs. They*
are those pots.

After that day they did not return any more. They went and went, and Onka and
Mafofo disappeared for good. They disappeared and were no longer there. Today, only
their names remain: Mafofo and Onka.

Among us, the people of Wogeo, if you are a man who wants to perform magic
or whatever you want to do, the people of today say 'God and Jesus'. The writings of
the white ['yellow'] people that have returned to us are about them: they say 'God and
Jesus'. Mary is our mother. Mary's name is like Moede's name. We have Moede – they
have Mary. And our mother, that is her. What is called God is called Onka by us. Only
Onka's name you will call upon. If you want your food to grow well, you will call upon
Onka's name. If a man is ill, if he is dying from it, you will call upon Onka and the man
will rise again. If you prepare kadaga,[22] *you will call upon Onka. You call upon Onka's*
name only. You will not call upon the name of any other man from former times, there
is not any other nanaranga. *Thus we call upon Onka only. Onka's name is big. If you*
call upon Onka only, everything will change. Onka and Mafofo, they challenged each
other. So the people of today say, we say, 'Is Mafofo the worse man of the two? Is the
better one Onka?' We adopt both of them, and both remain with us. And so Onka and
Mafofo sailed away that day; they went and went and were no longer there. Everything
they had already poured out in Dab, like the way we are living. The way we are living
is Onka's tradition [singara]. *Still it remains. Onka is the Big Man, his name only ...*
only he carries everything, Onka. The name of none of our men could stand like his.

Finished, this was the story of Onka and Mafofo; its end is like this. All
kinds of things they poured out in Dab. Thus the end of their story is like this, they
disappeared.

There are other nanaranga; *Kuakua, we in Dab are telling stories about Daro;*
the people of Takur talk about the Ramata Bitanga .... These appeared after Onka and
Mafofo, when they had already disappeared. The story of Onka and Mafofo is already
finished. They had already made the places and islands rise. They had already stepped
over [from island to island] and sailed away and set up the rollers and all things; after
they had made everything, they disappeared. There are many nanaranga *that are still*
here. The end of their story is like this.
Finished!

In Hogbin's writings, Mafofo is said to have made Udemtaregá prior to Onka's
affair with Moede (1970b: 43–45), and the part of the story about how Mafofo
dropped the post on Onka and the doings of the heroes as named Moanuboa and
Liboaboa – most of the latter half of the story – is presented as a separate myth
from Falala (and Oakiblolo) (ibid.: 50–51). The people from Falala complained

to Hogbin that the Dab people claimed that the trading voyages had their origin in Dab. It was in Falala that the two men Liboaboa and Moanuboa had made their canoes and initiated the trade, and it was the people of Falala who should take the initiative to the trading expeditions. The Dab people could join them, but Falala should go first. The Dab people, for their part, saw this claim as preposterous: Dab should go first (cf. Hogbin 1935b: 377; 1978: 41). Kulbobo acknowledges the importance of Oakiblolo (which is commonly grouped together with Falala) in his account, and in the last part of the story he sends not only Onka but also Mafofo to Oakiblolo, creating another argument for seeing Goleiangaianga/Onka as the one and only powerful and adding importance to Mafofo's position (and, thus, Dab).

The initiation of the paths of trade connects Wogeo to the surrounding world – at the same time as these paths opened for loss and the disappearance of knowledge. 'We were too stupid to listen,' Wogeos say, 'and Onka took his skills and knowledge and gave it to other people.' They tell stories of how Onka tried to teach his younger brothers, for instance, how to get sago starch by merely drilling a whole in the sago palm (see chapter 4) or how to get a well of fresh water near their village. The brothers did not follow Onka's instructions, and the chance to have an easier life was lost. Instead they had to work hard. This was also the reason why Wogeo does not have much of a wood carving tradition, people say. Onka gave this gift to the people of Sepik River.

The name Moanuboa is of great importance in Wogeo – not only as one of Onka's names, but as a term designating something of importance – as Onka's mother was said to be *moanuboa*. *Moanuboa* is the name of plants of the *Cordyline* family that are planted on graves and other sites of importance. For instance, the people of Dab planted a *moanuboa* on Tarawai when they initiated *lo*-relations with the islanders. The *moanuboa* plant is also the emblem of corpi of knowledge, such as a specific magic for planting taro,[23] and for *kastom* knowledge in general. When I returned to Wogeo in 1999, old Moita said, pleased with my Wogeo manners, that I had quickly reached the top of the *moanuboa* (*moanuboa ulú*). She picked a *moanuboa* plant and showed me how I had reached the leaf next to the newest and upper leaf. When I had been given all the important knowledge about Wogeo *kastom*, I would have reached the top. *Moanuboa* is also an emblem of peace and harmony, metaphorically held by a certain matrilineage on the island. And, as will be dealt with in Part III of the book, it is used to speak about the offices of leadership Onka/Goleiangaianga instated on the island. Onka as well as his mother were *moanuboa* – Onka even taking Moanuboa as his name.

During my visits to the island, people around the island agreed upon the role of Goleiangaianga as the first hero. I was given different stories about his doings as he travelled around the island, changing his name, but in 1993/94 people seemed not quite sure whether these differently named heroes were one man or not. Some of the older men often wanted to discuss the possibility of this with me, and asked me whether I thought that it was possible that these heroes were all different personifications of Goleiangaianga or Onka. Hogbin referred to those of these heroes that he wrote about as different men, but in Aufenanger's (1972) account of the story from Koil from the early 1960s Onka (Woneka) is ascribed the doings of Goleiangaianga. In 1999, this was not questioned at all: these heroes were one man with different names.

Kulbobo and others maintained that Onka always had been referred to as *Bikpela* (lit. 'The big one' in Tok Pisin), a term also used for the Christian God. Kulbobo once said, 'Onka has given us the breath we breathe'.[24] According to him, this saying came from the ancestors. In his account above, he explicitly likened Onka and Mafofo to God and Jesus and Onka's wife Moede to Mary – similar to what Smith notes from Kairiru (1994: 89) and Lutkehaus from Manam (1995b: 31). Onka gives power to magic like God helps people through prayers. Several men compared ritual cleansings to the Holy Communion, and I often heard myths related with reference to stories from the Bible – like the Garden of Eden or the tower of Babel.

The stories of Goleiangaianga and Onka being the same hero who changes his name can be interpreted as attempts to lessen the gap between Christianity and *kastom* by creating a monotheistic godlike figure. But it could also be that Goleiangaianga/Onka was regarded as such also in 1934 even though Hogbin did not describe him in this manner. It is, however, difficult to establish how these stories have changed and how, whether and in what ways the different myths have merged, but no matter what was the 'true' or more original stories, the discussions of the nature and doings of Onka/Goleiangaianga undoubtedly represent an effort to create a coherent narrative from stories (*nanasa* and Bible) representing different values and traditions. In doing this, Wogeos also expand their networks beyond the regional connections. Onka seems to have been emphasized at the cost of several local heroes and embodies a connection (or relational flow) between Wogeo and a wider world (cf. Strathern 1996).[25]

Some Wogeos thought that Hogbin came to Wogeo in 1934 in order to find the origin of the stories of Onka whose journeys perhaps had led him all the way to England. Moanuboa and Liboaboa were the names Onka and Mafofo were said to have taken before they left Wogeo. Mafofo (Liboaboa) is usually said to have returned to Wogeo, whereas Onka (Moanuboa) left for good. In the Manam Island version of the myth, the two brothers making canoes are called Momboa and Liboaboa and are said to be sons of Moaede (Lutkehaus 1995b: 31–32), whereas the part about the adultery is told as a separate story about Sangania, his wife Moaede and her brother's son Ongka (ibid.: 157–58). On the Rai coast the hostile brothers are called Manup and Kilibob (Lawrence 1971[1964]; see also Counts et al. 1991). In Manam it is said that Momboa is the ancestor of all black people whereas the younger brother, Liboaboa, became the ancestor of white people, and Lawrence (1971[1964]: 65) describes how one of the first European visitors in Madang district were thought to be Kilibob or Manup that had returned (cf. also Tuzin 1997: 71 for a similar mythical theme among the Ilahita Arapesh). In Wogeo I have heard no such explicit statement about what happened to Onka (Moanuboa) when he disappeared. He might have gone all the way to England, one man speculated, whereas another man meant that it was the *stories* about Onka that had wandered all the way to England and that this was why Hogbin came to Wogeo.

To Wogeos, the most important message of these stories is that important powers have their origin in Wogeo, but that Onka took most of it with him. Still Onka left strong powers also to the Wogeos, and people believe that much of this power must have been lost through time – and most of this in recent times. Hogbin was thought to be able to bring back some of this knowledge to the island when he returned as an old man, but allegedly he refused to do so and instead scolded them for not living according to *kastom*. Hogbin had become a mythical keeper of knowledge and, like Onka, he had carried important knowledge (or power) from Wogeo to other places. 'When Hogbin left Wogeo, England prospered and in Wogeo everything deteriorated', Kulbobo claimed. 'He never got married, and the power of his knowledge was preserved.'

The story of Hogbin, knowledge lost and the hidden note show how Wogeos feel that they have lost something significant from their past. The older men feel that their fathers have let them down, but they also feel that they themselves have some of the blame, not taking more interest in what their fathers had to tell them, a disinterest now also found in their children. There is in many ways a discrepancy between the Wogeo pessimism on behalf of their *kastom* and the present day situation. People have always been travelling to and from the island, bringing all kinds of new customs and traditions (cf. Harrison 2000), and Wogeos seem to be very capable of coping with changes and integrating new customs into their lives as well as adjusting their traditions to new situations. However, as Harrison notes (ibid.: 674), it seems that the way traditions and stories are objectified has changed in post-colonial times. Whereas cultural knowledge such as songs, dances, myths and magic in pre-colonial times were objectified and exchanged as prestige goods that would increase their value by being exchanged between groups, their objectification now seems to have taken the form of property as inheritance or legacies, influenced by nation-building processes. Accordingly the failure of properly transferring this knowledge as inherited property from generation to generation within the group would inevitably lead to a sense of loss, adding to the loss of power that follows cultural generification (cf. Errington and Gewertz 2001).

In the next part of the book I will describe customs that point to continuity rather than loss and that Wogeos regard as being of the utmost significance to life and well-being on Wogeo and that were central to Hogbin's work, particularly in *The Island of Menstruating Men* (1970b): those that pertain to what Wogeos speak about as 'looking after the body', namely taboos and rituals focused on people's bodies.

Notes

1. According to Hogbin, the sweet potato was a relatively newly introduced crop in the 1930s and such gardens were rare during his stays (1938/39: 129).
2. Hogbin translated the term *oaraboa* as food festivals (1970a; 1978). See Smith (1994: 39–40) for similar feasts (*warap*) in Kairiru.
3. Exter's luggage with all his notes and recordings were stolen at the airport in Copenhagen. Fortunately we got funding for him to do more fieldwork in 2000, and he managed to collect again nearly all the material that had been lost.

4. See Aufenanger (1972: 1–2) for a reference to the erection of similar poles in Bem (Biem), another of the Schouten Islands and Swadling (1980: 99) for a description from Koil in 1901.

5. I was not present when Exter recorded the myth in 2000 and am not sure why Kulbobo left out these parts. He was quite ill (he died a couple of months later) and might have had trouble remembering the myth properly, but he also knew that I had heard it many times before and knew the story – and that this probably was his last chance to emphasize the issues he though the most important.

6. In Noba, Kuliling was said to have introduced *iaboua*.

7. A ladder made from a bamboo stick, using the bases of the alternating horizontal branches as rungs.

8. According to Kulbobo, this is another of Onka's names.

9. In standard Wogeo, the form of this word would be *dikura*.

10. A fish recognized by Kulbobo in my fish guide as a type of fusilier of the *caesionidae* family (*renbo* in Tok Pisin).

11. Exter notes that 'The interpretation of this song by the speaker differed significantly from occasion to occasion; it seems as if its meaning is no longer transparent to present-day Wogeo speakers (another suggested explanation was, e.g., that kama was a non-Wogeo equivalent of the Wogeo word vama 'outrigger', presumably from the neighbouring Biem language)' (personal communication).

12. The name of Mafofo's (and Onka's) wife that became the title of the wife/daughter of a *koakoale*.

13. *Dara* means 'blood'.

14. Symbols of power, see chapter 7.

15. Another term is *oasaboai* – *wasabwai* in Hogbin's (e.g. 1938: 225; 1970b: 113) writings.

16. Hogbin (1970b: 193) notes how Onka's affair with Moede was used by men to legitimate adulterous affairs.

17. Also in Kragur in Kairiru there is a trading canoe by this name (Smith 1994: 175) (although with a different spelling - Urim Terakau (in Wogeo *d* is pronounced as a trill (*r*) after vowels and the *k* is equivalent to g).

18. Differently named fishing canoes, each with their particular magic and rituals, are also the property of the different villages (Seo 1991).

19. A kind of nettle (Tok Pisin *jalat*).

20. A kind of tree.

21. Also in Kragur village in Kairiru there is a cult house called Bagura (Bakur) (Smith 1994: 83).

22. A drink prepared mainly from coconut milk and herbs for ceremonial and medicinal purposes.

23. Similar to what is known as *tiptip* in Kairiru (Smith 1994: 31–32).

24. *Malmalim ebala ilomte, Onka ilugu ilom* – lit. 'Your breath that is there inside of you, Onka has put it inside of you'. In the article mentioned above, Gagin wrote what he called a 'creation song', translated into English by himself (Dalle et al. 1972: 203). Here Onka is presented as the Creator of the world.

25. Still Hogbin writes in connection with rights to land and residence as sanctioned by *nanaranga* stories, that *nanaranga* and the Christian God could be seen as similar, 'equally real to the particular peoples with which they are concerned' (1939: 154). Although not exactly as he intended, it seems that he had a point – even though Peter G. Sack (1975: 42) meant that he pushed 'the analogy too far'. Hogbin's statement may, however, be truer for the situation in the 1990s than the 1930s.

⊰ Part II ⊱
Bodies, Taboos and Sociality

Prelude

Moita was walking out of the village in front of me with her basket hanging down her back with its straps around her forehead, holding a bush-knife in her hand. We stopped where the path towards Saboakai's house split from the main path. Along the smaller pathway, tall plants of *oaila* were growing. *Oaila* are aromatic herbs used in every cleansing ritual and many medical mixtures on the island. It was early afternoon, and I was *baras* – the Wogeo term for a menstruating woman. My adoptive grandmother, Moita, was going to prepare the cleansing ointment that I was going to rub into my skin the next morning to mark the end of the *baras* period and to cleanse any remainders of polluted blood and smell from my body: we were going to 'wash the *baras* with *oaila*' (*oaila matalosoiak baras*).

We picked bundles of *oaila* leaves and flowers and wrapped them in a banana leaf before we continued towards Saboakai's house. Moita asked someone inside the house if it would be all right if we picked some herbs from the garden surrounding the house. We were told to go ahead. Smaller bushes of what Moita called *oaila maian*[1] grew just outside the house, and we picked some leaves from one of them. Next to it was a Bixa Orrelana tree (*ie*), and we gathered some of its fruits, which contain red seeds used as body paint. In the garden we picked another type of *oaila* (*sibula*), some red flowers (*kamasia*), and a couple of leaves from a *moanuboa*. Moita also dug up a small ginger root (*nges*) and added it to our collection. Ginger is the Wogeo all-purpose medicine and is, due to its heating capacity, used for many kinds of magic – as is common in the region (Paijmans 1976: 149). As we returned to the village, we found a spathe from a betel palm (*kenken bua*) that we took with us, together with some leaves from a plant (*kaboaram*) next to Kumi's house.

We went down to Moita's house in the camp towards the beach. Moita grated some coconut meat. We opened the Bixa Orrelana fruits and mixed the seeds with the grated coconut in the betel spathe. We added the herbs, rubbing them with the oily red mixture. Moita took some of the leaves and flowers and tied them together in small bouquets. Together with the ginger, she wrapped all these up in the sheath and closed it with a piece of vine. In the evening we put the packet on the embers of the fire outside the house for a few hours, then put it aside until the next morning.

At sunrise I went down to the beach together with Moita and Maria and some young girls from the village. We washed ourselves in the sea before we opened the packet we had made the day before. A pleasant smell rose from the mixture and we rubbed the red ointment, called *burenga*, on our skin. The little bouquets of herbs and flowers we tied around our upper arms with the help of the *moanuboa* leaves, and we put some of the flowers and herbs in our hair. The red oil on the women's skin glowed in the golden light from the rising sun over the quiet, pale blue sea.

The palm spathe and the leftovers from the mixture we threw in the sea before we went up to the village. Now I had washed the *baras* away and could freely go ahead with my daily tasks. Later in the day I fastened the herbs and flowers in the ceiling of my house so that everyone could see that it was safe to receive food from my hands. When they had dried, I threw them on the sea.

*   *   *

The event described above points to a salient feature of Wogeo life. One of the subjects I heard about most frequently in Wogeo was the importance of looking after one's body – *lukautim bodi* in Tok Pisin. To 'look after one's body' refers to an ideal that underlies a wide array of taboos, rituals and codes of conduct that are essential to successful being in the world in Wogeo. People told me that in Oageva language they did not use a direct equivalent of the Tok Pisin phrase *lukautim bodi* to speak about this. Rather, the term *ival* covered what they meant when using the Tok Pisin phrase.

Ival can be translated 'avoid' or 'refuse'. The proper way in Oageva to say that I am looking after my body would be to say, 'I am making my body avoid' (*Va baikog uivalki*). 'It is just like when you are using mosquito repellent,' Kulbobo said. The term is also used if someone rejects food when sick, or if someone avoids places or things reminiscent of a person who has died or left the island because it causes too much grief to be reminded of him or her (cf. e.g. Bamford 1998: 160; Gell 1979: 137; Iteanu 1995: 141).[2]

Many aspects of life in Wogeo are guided by taboos and avoidance and accompanying cleansing rituals: to look after one's body is a never-ending work. The most conspicuous taboos are those associated with death, menstruation and childbirth, but also contact with places, certain types of work, and people in certain conditions are avoided in order to look after one's body. Some people used the Tok Pisin words *hygenim bodi* (derived from 'hygiene') to talk about these customs and explicitly drew the connection between the traditional taboos and what they had learnt about hygienic measures in school and from health personnel. In order to have a good life, what is often spoken of in Tok Pisin as *gutpela sindaun long ples* ('sit down good in one's place'),[3] it is necessary to take care of one's body. It should be strong; its skin should be shiny, and there should be enough fat (but not too much) on its bones. In order to maintain a strong and fit body people have to observe the taboos, conduct the necessary cleansing rituals and eat good and health-giving food. 'Your body is holy,' Kulbobo often said, and he thought that *ival* was the closest to having a concept of holiness in the Wogeo language.

It was emphasized in conversations about this that only people who looked after their bodies in this manner could successfully sit (or stand up) in their place in Wogeo, have healthy children and a good future to offer them. Many times I heard people spoken of in connection with the state of their bodies: 'If you look at her you would not believe that she was that old: her skin is tight and fat and her body is strong. It is because she has followed *kastom*; she sits good in her place.' Another statement could be 'His skin is loose [*baikó eitakaoa*, lit. 'his body has fallen down']. He has not followed *kastom*, and, you see, his children do not come to see him; he does not have good food to eat.' A woman spoke about men marrying at a young age (before twenty-five), and said that 'if they marry too young, their skin will be loose and they will grow old before their time. Look at that boy [a man that had just married, at the age of about twenty]; his skin is so loose, he looks like an old man.'

People's bodies – particularly how other people's bodies are objectified – appear in this context as signs, as representing the success people have had in leading a life according to *kastom*; not merely in observing the proper taboos and avoidance but also the manner in which they have 'looked after' their social relations. But bodies are also sites for subjective experience. Gell has described taboos among the Umeda as constitutive of 'the ego as immanent in a network of relations' (1979: 133). He is concerned with grasping 'the oscillatory movement whereby the ego both recoils from the world in constituting itself and is simultaneously drawn back into the world in accomplishing its projects' (ibid.). To follow taboos establishes the self in relation to an external reality as 'intentional acts'.[4] Through life Wogeos enter into different kinds of relationships with others and with their surroundings; accordingly, various types of avoidance (and cleansings) are made relevant. These channel the relations that the social person is made up of into proper paths and, thereby, are important in the constitution of the person vis-à-vis other persons and entities in the phenomenal world.

In the light of this perspective, the dialogical relation between bodies as representation and bodies as 'a ground of being-in-the-world' (Csordas 1999: 184) becomes evident. The subjective bodily experience of being-in-the-world is moulded by avoidance and cleansing practices that are made relevant through life; at the same time, people's bodies become signs of these practices or, rather, of the success people have had in following them.

I will argue that avoidance practices in Wogeo not only elicit ideas about health and hygiene, but also create and make manifest connections and disconnections between the beings and entities in the world. On the one hand, it will be useful to see these connections and disconnections as a relational flow between persons who are categorized, among other things, by the states of their bodies. On the other hand, these connections and disconnections can be seen as a result of the susceptibility of human bodies as they move in a phenomenal world that, reciprocally, is affected by human presence in it. In other words, I will elicit the material or embodied emphasis of Wogeo sociality as it is made evident through avoidance practices.

Notes

1. *Maian* means 'iron' and refers to something that has come from overseas – in this case from the mainland.
2. In order to say that something is tabooed or forbidden, Wogeos use another word – *dol* (which means 'finish') – e.g. *limá dareka, limá kankan dol*, 'her/his hands are bad, do not eat from her/his hands'; *vaine mos gongonki dol*, 'do not sleep (play) with a pregnant woman'.
3. Cf. Eves 1997: 183 for a similar emphasis on 'seating'.

4. More specifically, he writes about food taboos and elicits how eating (and the equivalent acts of intercourse and killing) both positively (by eating) and negatively (by not eating) is constitutive of the ego.

❧ Chapter 3 ❧
Differentiation and Connectedness: Blood, Flutes and Gender

When I started to take part in Wogeo daily life, I soon learnt to move my body according to what can be called Wogeo etiquette. Women in particular have to move in specific manners when in the vicinity of men. If a man or, more importantly, a group of men are sitting down, a woman should walk around them, at least a metre or so away; if she has to walk close to them, she should walk behind their backs, gather her skirt, bend slightly down and excuse herself. This is also a general rule for anyone walking close to people sitting down: one should avoid letting the lower parts of one's body come close to anyone's face. This could at times be quite tricky, for instance when I spoke with groups of men on the veranda of Singero. Then the women of the house, including myself, would have to crawl or slide away from them before standing up on the narrow veranda. Usually the men would be helpful and turn their backs towards us so that our passage would be easier. Little girls were often shouted at when ignoring these rules – 'Don't you know how to excuse yourself?!' They were told to sit down properly (*moado moang*, lit. 'sit good'), gathering their legs and pulling their skirts down over their knees. This was particularly important when eating, and should anyone step over food lying on the floor, this would be almost as bad as actually stepping in it. Such etiquette clearly channels the bodily experience of being in relation to others, and the gendered difference in these rules of avoidance and the emphasis on the lower part of the body are related to ideas of pollution and cleanliness (cf. e.g. Eves 1998).

Polluted Blood

In Wogeo it is said that pollution from contact with that which should be kept separate is accumulated and contained in the blood (*dara*) and will result in disease. Such blood needs to be removed from the body and is recognized by its dark colour. Women get cleansed regularly through menstruation. A menstruating woman should not cook or give anything to a man since 'blood is hanging from her hands' (*limá dara daboeka*) or 'her hands are bad' (*limá dareka*). Her body is regarded as being in a vulnerable state and she should not walk around too much or work in the gardens. These precautions are mainly to protect the woman and not because she is in a polluting state. On the contrary, if she works in the garden while menstruating it is regarded as promoting growth – 'like magic', Kulbobo said – but since it would also increase her bleeding, she should abstain from such work. She should relax and take care to keep warm – coldness is a dreaded state of being, associated with fevers, weakness and death (and 'bad times' caused by too much rain and wind) (see also e.g. Hogbin 1970b: 84; 1978: 45).[1] A *baras* woman should not bathe in fresh water since such water would increase the flow of blood. She should bathe in salt water at a particular spot on the beach – in Dab between Kulka and Oare (see Fig. 1.1). There she should immerse her body and take care to resurface in a different place to where her blood was floating. 'If I was to wash in water mixed with my sick blood, I would get old before my time,' Tangina told me. She hung her wet clothes for drying at a place on the beach where no man, by accident, would walk underneath them. In the past she would also have worn special clothing or a grass skirt so that everyone knew which state she was in. She would also have had to enter and leave the house through a hole in the floor so that she would not cross a doorstep where a man could walk afterwards (Hogbin 1970b: 136–37).

There are also certain places a woman should not go while *baras*. Some Wogeo *nanaranga* love the smell of a menstruating woman – in Onevaro district there was one living by a small stream near Taro where the school is. Gamuia told me that her grandfather, Marifa, had forbidden her to go to school while *baras* because of this *nanaranga*. But Gamuia had seen the girls who lived in Taro bathe in this place all the time, and nothing happened to them. Because the power of the church is getting stronger, he has become less dangerous and is hardly ever seen any more, she said, and she had eventually disregarded her grandfather's advice and went to school even when *baras*. Tangina, who was some years older, replied that when she was in school they had often heard the *nanaranga* blowing in his conch shell (*taur*). This *nanaranga* was also attracted to the smell of sex (*luma*) and fish, and a girl from Kinaba had been taken ill some years ago after bathing in the stream with the smell of fish on her hands. A man in Moaroka had known the magic (*boasa*) for this *nanaranga* and had made her well again. 'But I think the *nanaranga* must have married the girl,'[2] a friend of mine said. 'She kept getting ill over and over again, and eventually she died.'

During my stays in Wogeo I repeatedly heard people, both men and women, complain that women did not properly observe the *baras* taboos anymore. The increase in cases of tuberculosis over the last twenty to thirty years was often blamed on the disregard menstruating women showed for the *baras* taboos. I found, however, that this was not an accurate description of the situation – at least not in Dab or Onevaro district. All the women I knew abstained from cooking, working and touching men while *baras*, and it was generally agreed upon among my female friends that they would not let go of these taboos. Besides, these days of the month were their only real free time: while they were lying in front of the fire or playing with their children, their older daughters, other women of the household, or their husbands had to cook.

Also the younger girls I knew usually kept the taboos. One girl of about twenty admitted that she did not observe the taboos that strictly when she was in Wewak (where she was quite often), but while in Wogeo it was unthinkable not to. She and others pointed out that town life was easier. They had tap water and soap, cooked on stoves on tables, and additional hygienic precautions were not all that important. My young friend also said that in Wewak she also tried to go far away from people to bathe in salt water while *baras*. There was one particular spot at the edge of the beach in Wewak, among some cliffs, where she used to go. But then the stories said that a spirit (*masalai* in Tok Pisin) used to 'turn the head' of menstruating women in this place, even white women she said, and she became afraid to go there – even though the power of the church was getting stronger.

When the flow of blood stops, women should undergo the ritual cleansing at the beach. In the 1990s, most women were satisfied to use soap, but some still did this in the traditional manner, like Moita taught me, when they felt like it. Any women who want to can join in this event, whether they are menstruating or not. The women who are not *baras* do it to 'feel fresh' and because they enjoy the companionship, they say. The ointment, *burenga*, was used for most kinds of cleansing rituals and also sometimes used when a particularly important garden was to be planted. No matter what the occasion, it would take away the smell of anything impure and prepare the body for most tasks. Tangina said that she often planned to cleanse herself in the traditional manner when *baras*, but that usually she was too tired to be bothered with the work of making the ointment when she had soap and did not really have to. Besides, the red paint was known to give people a headache (which, in my experience, it did).

Nobody explicitly said that they expected me to follow the taboos or conduct the cleansing ritual. During my first fieldwork I did not cook on my own, and that I was *baras* was not really an issue at all. But when I established my own household and started to give away food, the only appropriate thing to do was to follow the taboos. That I carried out the traditional cleansing was met with approval, even though everyone knew that I had a sufficient supply of soap. Particularly the older people were extremely satisfied with this. Kulbobo said that, due to his tuberculosis, he was reluctant to receive food from anyone but the older women who did not menstruate and knew how to look after their bodies. But with me it was different, he said. I did not live with a man; I was following *kastom*; I cleansed myself properly, and therefore he felt it safe to eat food that I had cooked.

The blood from girls who are menstruating for the first time is not regarded as polluting. The first *baras* is for 'opening the road', people said. They have also not yet had sexual intercourse with men. Sexual contact between men and women is regarded as a dangerous undertaking, and people often pointed this out to me in the same manner as Hogbin had written about it:

> The established doctrine is that the members of each sex would be safe and invulnerable, healthy and prosperous, if only they were to keep to themselves and refrain from mixing with members from the other sex group (Hogbin 1970b: 87).

'If men were to themselves and women to themselves, there would be no disease and everyone would be happy,' people told me. They also said that the sexes are conceived as polluting each other mutually. A woman past menopause, however, is regarded as less threatening to the opposite sex since 'her road is blocked' and she has also learnt well how to look after her body.

First Menstruation

A girl menstruating for the first time is regarded as particularly vulnerable since she is in a transitional state. She has to undergo a series of rituals, and during these her body is 'emptied' (*ia kusí eoalisi*). The most elaborate rituals are held for girls known as *moede* – daughters of *koakoale* (as is the case for the Manam moaede, Lutkehaus 1995a:202; 1995b: 179–201). For other girls people organize shorter versions of the rituals to be described below, and in the 1990s a few girls did not go through any celebration at all. The main features and the taboos followed are, however, mostly the same (see also Hogbin 1970b: 125–36).

As soon as she starts menstruating the girl is taken into the bush, to the land where her parents have their gardens. There she climbs through a liana (either *suve* or *oaro iamuna*) that is split in the middle and, afterwards, closed again. Afterwards she climbs over a young tree – for instance a *kangar* – and her body will grow strong and tall together with the tree.[3] After climbing through the liana, her body becomes like an empty container (*jiraboa*) and has to be filled with good food and medicine (*kadaga*) that will make her body grow strong and tall.[4] She should keep warm and be accompanied by other young girls who have not yet menstruated – also referred to as *baras* – who sleep close to her at night. She is also given food with ginger and chilli (a dish known as *sur*) to make her hot. Her mother does not participate in the rituals at all; rather it is the women belonging to the same place as her who organize the rituals – often her father's sisters (cf. Lutkehaus 1995b: 195).

During this period, the girl observes a series of taboos meant to protect her body. She covers her head with a scarf, and, when walking in the sun, she hides

Photo 3.1: A young girl climbing through a liana at her *baras* celebration

her body under a blanket or towel. She does not touch her skin or the food she is eating with her hands but uses a fork or a cassowary or flying fox bone. To eat fish is prohibited since it could cause various skin diseases. She does not decorate her body in any manner apart from the mixture of coconut oil and red soil (or, if such soil is not available, Bixa Orrelana seeds) that is rubbed into her skin every morning. Like other menstruating women she does not bathe in fresh water since it would increase the flow of blood.

When she is in this transitional phase she visits all the villages in the district and other places to which she might have a particular connection. There she climbs through lianas on the ground of the people with whom she, as an adult, will stand in particular relations of exchange and alliance. People also like to get the *baras* girls to come and work in their gardens because it is, among other reasons, regarded as promoting fertility or merely because it is a chance of getting work done. Then she and the other *baras* girls are ritually cleansed on the beach of the village, before they and their companions are invited to a meal in the house of the woman who has invited the girl. In the house the older women dance and makes hilarious jokes and stunts hinting at the future sexual life of the girl[5] – referred to as *nibek* of the women. *Nibek* is anything associated with the male cult in general and the flute spirits in particular (equivalent to what is known in the region as *tambaran*[6]).

Lastly she is, in company with the young girls and many of the women from the district, taken to a particular spot on top of a mountain where her childhood is symbolically buried – in the shape of things she has touched while *baras*. Now she has changed her body from that of a child to a gendered, adult woman who has entered into important social relations of exchange and alliance (cf. Lutkehaus 1995b: 200): she has walked the paths between the places to which she has particular relations, paths that she later will follow in work and ritual.

The completion of the girl as a woman is celebrated with an *olage*, an inter-village exchange of cooked food – the higher the status of the girl, the more people are involved. In 1993 I participated in the *baras* celebration of Marajina, Gagin's eldest daughter. Since she is a *moede*, a female *koakoale*, the celebrations were particularly extensive. They lasted for a whole month and were completed with an *olage* where baskets representing seven villages and two enormous pigs, particularly bred for the occasion, were exchanged. In every *olage* all exchanges between the villages within the district – five in the case of Onevaro – are obligatory. At Marajina's *olage*, two additional villages (Koablik and Falala) joined in since her father had particular allies in these places.[7] With the pork distributed evenly to the various baskets, the baskets are displayed together on a platform or a canvas, together with green coconuts and betel nuts, and then the baskets are randomly redistributed between the villages.

After the *olage* for a *moede*, all the women dress up in all their traditional finery. The *baras* girl is given the traditional decorations of boar's tusks and dogteeth, shells and feathers that belong to her as a woman of the place and of her matrilineage. Then they all parade through the village from east to west and back again before lining up in front of the girl's house where gifts of traditional decorations and clothing are exchanged in her name. Some gifts are given directly

to the girl whereas others are exchanged between the guests. The next day she
and her companions are taken to a particular spring, in Onevaro at a place in
the bush beyond Badiata, where they drink and wash in fresh water. Afterwards
she is given a meal of fish and breadfruit. All the taboos are now lifted, and the
ceremonies are finished.

When she had gone through the rituals, the girl was in earlier times seen as being
ready to marry, but not to have children – her breasts should grow properly first:
they should hang. In the 1990s both men and women seldom married before they
were well into their twenties, but it was not uncommon that girls have children
out of marriage while in their teens. When speaking about this, people would sigh
and say that these young ones did not follow *kastom* and did not know how to look
after their bodies.

Strathern (1993: 44) has argued that '[M]elanesians regard bodies as images of
a kind, and, in the process of growing up, one kind of body has to be replaced by
another', and in the process 'half of a whole becomes one of a pair' (ibid: 48).
The non-gendered, childish body (the product of a gendered pair) is substituted by
a gendered, adult body, ready to engage in sexual relations. In Wogeo the taboos
followed and cleansings conducted during the first *baras* are not about protecting
other people from contact with the *baras* blood. Rather, they are focused on
protecting the girl as her childish, non-gendered (or asexual) body is changed into
a gendered adult woman, placed in a network of social relations that is embedded
in the landscape through which she has walked during the rituals. Her vulnerable
body should, during the rituals, not be exposed to potential harmful influences from
the external world but be guarded through taboos and the physical barriers of cloth
and the red oil. She should not speak too loudly, not participate in play or dancing,
eat heating food and be heated by the company of other girls. When the transitional
phase is completed, she re-enters daily life with a body ready for sexual relations
and, accordingly, she will be polluting to the opposite sex when *baras*.

Childbirth

When a woman gives birth, large amounts of bodily fluids are released from her
body. These are dangerous to others to such a degree that nobody should touch her
body or the baby after the head of the baby is visible: the woman is now *boaruka*.
Women give birth at particular places at the beach. When the baby is born, the
mother should herself cut the umbilical cord and throw the afterbirth into the sea
or bury it under the pebbles in the sea. Then she should bathe herself and the baby
in the sea before retreating to a house built for the occasion, a *boaruka* house (cf.
Lutkehaus 1990: 148). In the past the house was usually built at the outskirts of
the village, or even in the bush if the woman had older children who were likely
to disturb her (see Hogbin 1970b: 137), but in the 1990s pregnant women were
afraid to stay in the bush because of sorcerers and so their husbands usually built
the *boaruka* houses next to or even under their house in the village.

There she should stay for a whole moon, without contact with any men. When
going to wash in the sea, she should take care that no men see her, and only
women would give food to her. As is the case for menstruating women, washing in

fresh water would increase the flow of blood, and she should therefore bathe only in salt water until she leaves the *boaruka* house. She should also take care not to touch her body or her food with her hands.

If complications occur during birth and other women have to assist, they should also 'sit in *boaruka*', or at least observe taboos similar to a *baras* woman for a period of time afterwards. They should later be duly compensated for their hardships through gifts of food and clothing – 'to wash their hands'. If the child is going to be given away in adoption and the adoptive mother is eager to have a child as if it was her own, she could decide to assist in the birth and sit in *boaruka* together with the birthmother and also breast-feed the baby if possible. Physical contact with the baby does not pose a danger to other women, but the father will usually wait until the mother leaves the *boaruka* before he touches it.

Many young women are afraid to give birth in Wogeo, I was told. 'It is hard for us women here in Wogeo. In town it is easy.' Tangina said otherwise: 'I am afraid to go to the hospital in Wewak. Who should take care of me there?' Other women said that they found the hospital too dirty. Others again could go to Wewak to give birth in order to be near a doctor, but not go to the hospital. However, if other women should have to assist them, it was seen as a more troublesome affair to go through the work of 'washing their hands' in Wewak than if it had happened in Wogeo. Of the women in Onevaro that I knew of who gave birth while I was there, three gave birth in Wogeo and one in Wewak.

Male Cleansing and the Male Cult

Women get purified from the illness that has accumulated in their blood through their monthly menstruation. Men do not have this innate capacity, and they have to get rid of their sick blood in a different manner. The title of Hogbin's book *The Island of Menstruating Men* (1970b) refers to the way men used to cleanse themselves from polluted blood, although in the 1990s they objected to calling this 'menstruation' due to the term's reference to the female uncontrollable bodily function. A couple of times a year, men would induce bleeding from their penis by cutting it, traditionally with a crab claw – a variation of customs commonly found in PNG (see e.g. Keesing 1982: 7; Paulsen 1992; Tuzin 1982). This operation is called *sara*, and afterwards the man would follow taboos that were stricter than those a *baras* woman observed. While I was in Wogeo, I was told that only a few older men still went through this ritual regularly, but in 1994, one young man said that there were several young men who had wanted to learn how to do it. 'Look at us, we are not tall and strong anymore like they were in the past,' he said. He himself had been too afraid of the pain to go through with it, he said, but said that some of the others had done it.

In the past the cleansing ritual was taught to the young men after they had gone through a series of initiation rituals associated with the male cult. The most important series of rituals in this cult occurred when the young boys were ritually purified of contamination accumulated in their bodies as a result of the intimate physical contact with their mothers during birth and upbringing. Girls did not have to go through any such rituals since they were of the same sex as their mothers.

For the boys it was necessary to go through these rituals not only to get rid of the polluted blood but also in order to initiate their physical growth as men (cf. e.g. Keesing 1982: 5). A certain myth provided the outline for these rituals:

Once there was a little boy called Nat Kadamoanga. He was not like any other boy. When he was still in his mother's womb, she died and was buried under the house of her parents. But the little child was not dead, and he nurtured himself on the sticky white sap from the roots of a breadfruit tree. One day his grandparents heard him cry; they opened the grave and found Nat Kadamoanga. They took care of him as if he was their own son. He was a very curious boy, and one day, as he was walking in the bush, he heard the most beautiful sound. Enchanted by the sound, he tried to follow it. He walked further into the bush, and after a while he came upon a nicely decorated house. The sound came from the house. He climbed up the ladder and went inside. There were no people there, but he found the source of the sound – a couple of flutes playing all by themselves. He took one of the flutes and tried to figure out how the sound was made. He put it to his mouth and tried to blow into it. The sound changed, and amused by this he tried to make melodies. The two women – Malouna and Sinamoa – who owned the house, were working in their garden not far away, and when they heard the change in the sound from the flutes, they quickly returned to the house. When they saw Nat Kadamoanga, they got very angry. They said 'Oh you naughty boy; you have done wrong to us now. You went into our nyaboá [cult house] and you took our flutes; what will we do with you?' But they calmed down and let the boy play with the flutes for a while. One of the women started to tease the boy, and after a while they had sexual intercourse. Afterwards he wanted to keep on playing the flutes, but no. Not a sound came from the flutes. 'Oh no,' said the women, 'you really have done wrong to us now as you have slept with us. But don't worry. We will teach you to play the flutes. But it will be hard work and a lot of pain; you have to be strong.' They went into the bush and returned with oaila and coconuts. They rubbed his tongue with sandpaper-like leaves until it bled, ordering him not to swallow the blood. They gave him the fluid from the coconuts mixed with oaila [kadaga] to wash his mouth, and asked him to try to play again. A little weak sound came. The boy practised and practised, and again the women sharpened his tongue. This went on and on until the boy was able to play properly. The women then got serious with him, and told him: 'You were very wrong to come into our nyaboá and play with our flutes. The house and the flutes now belong to you and all men; no woman will ever again come inside the nyaboá or see a flute, and the flutes will never again play by themselves. Because of your stupidity, every boy has to learn to play the flute like you have done. If not, they will not grow and become men.' So they spoke, and so it became (Anderson 1996: 1–2; see also Hogbin 1970b: 100–1).[8]

The myth is about a little boy who had not been contaminated by the dangerous passage through the birth channel of his mother or by drinking milk from his mother's breasts. He kept himself alive by drinking the white sap from a breadfruit tree, and he was removed from his mother's dead body by his grandparents and brought up by them. (Old women past menopause do not, as mentioned earlier, present any danger to men.) He found the *nyaboá* and the flutes that were the property of women. Women possess the powerful capacity of innate fertility and growth, and the flutes, thus, played by themselves. 'Flutes are empowered by female beings of supernatural dimensions' Herdt (1982: 87) notes as characteristic of ritual flutes in many places in PNG. Nat Kadamoanga, who was not like other boys,[9] found the house and the flutes. Alas, he made a grave mistake. He tried to take control over the flutes, to force their sound. Gris from Dab once said: 'I think that if Nat Kadamoanga had not stolen the flutes, it would still be the women who owned the *nyaboá* and us men would have the hard work of cooking.' Because of Nat Kadamoanga's actions, men lost the innate ability of growth. From now on they had to learn to play the flutes in order to become men. In the 1990s Wogeo men often complained that they were not as tall or strong as they used to be in the days of the cult.

There is an apparent analogy between playing the flutes and sexual intercourse. In other places in PNG where similar myths and rituals are found, this analogy is made quite explicit. Among the Gimi the flutes are said to originate from women's vaginas, and the monthly menstruation is blood from the wound that was made when the penis/flute was retracted from the female body (Gillison 1980; see also Lutkehaus 1995b: 216–17).[10] When the young Gimi boy stole the flute, he forgot to remove the pubic hair the woman had put in its opening to stop the sound. That is why the Gimi men started to have beards (Gillison 1980: 156). Also some Wogeo men said that men's facial hair is a mark from Nat Kadamoanga's attempt to play the flutes, indicating that analogies between vagina and flutes are part of Wogeo men's deliberations about the myth as well. After Nat Kadamoanga had played the flutes and they had stopped playing by themselves, he had sexual intercourse with the women. As a result he could neither play the flutes nor grow into a man by himself. He had to be cleansed from the influence of the women through bleeding from his tongue, and only then would he be able to play the flutes properly and successfully initiate his growth. The women taught the boy this work, but from then on this was the task of initiated men as a part of the male cult.

The flutes were played at most significant ritual occasions – like large food exchanges, the initiation of a new *nyaboá*, the initiation of young boys, and so forth (see Hogbin 1970b). The flutes were taboo to all women and children, and they were told that the sound of the flutes came from spirits, or spirit monsters as Hogbin (ibid.: 58) called them, known as *nibek*. *Nibek* is also used for the flutes themselves and things associated with the male cult in general. Hogbin wrote that Wogeo men said that the monsters were to be regarded as 'figments of the culture heroes' imagination', but that 'when the occasion calls for the presence of the monsters, the behaviour of both sexes seems to indicate unquestionable belief' (ibid.).[11] When the flutes were played, women and children stayed indoors until they again were inside the *nyaboá*. Old Moita told me that she had been very afraid when she heard the sound. 'We hid inside the houses and closed all openings as well as we could. Oh, Iamoe, we were so afraid. *Nibek* is something bad [no good]!' There was one exception, Kulbobo told me. Moarigum's wife, Iamoe, was a big woman, a true *moede*, he said. At Moarigum's funeral, when *nibek* came, she did not hide. The old woman remained at Moarigum's grave, covering her head with a piece of clothing. She must have known, he said.[12]

Wogeo men said that it was all right that I heard and wrote about *nibek*. After all, I had already read about it in Hogbin's book, and as long as I did not talk to the other women about the flutes, it did not matter. The women also seemed quite disinterested in the whole thing. The flutes have been gone for a long time, ever since the missionaries had convinced Wogeos that the cult did not have a place in a Christian world, people said. Since then the church had changed its policies in this regard and Gagin once told me that he would like to start making the flutes again. He had been to Manam and heard the flutes being played there. But the older men said no. The power of the flutes (and the spirits) was too strong, and nobody had the appropriate knowledge to control them any longer.[13]

The male cult was often spoken about as 'the school of the beach' (*skul bilong nambis* in Tok Pisin). The young boys would go through a series of initiations with the other boys of the same age. As they entered this world of men, more and more of the secrets of male growth and power would be revealed to them. In addition they would also be educated by experts on different areas of life, referred to as *tilab* (teacher): they would learn the necessary magic and skills for making gardens, arranging food distributions, fishing and so forth, as well as myths, songs and dances. The first stage of the men's cult was when Nibek was said to eat the little boys. The 'eating' was when the boys, dressed as men, entered the *nyaboá* for the first time. Inside the *nyaboá*, the secret was revealed to the terrified boys: there was no monster, just a couple of flutes. In the next stage they were taught to play the flutes.

The male cult disappeared as the Catholic Mission got a foothold on the island in the 1940s and 50s, and there were only a few older men who had participated in the initiation rituals left on the island when I was there in 1993–94. Marifa told me about the time he was initiated as part of the last group of boys who learnt to play the flutes. He took great pride in telling me the story of the last initiation, and I will let his voice tell the story as I have transcribed it from a taped interview (in Tok Pisin) in 1994 (Anderson 1996: 12–15; see also Hogbin 1970b):

Number one is when the boys are putting malo *[bark loin-cloth] on and* nibek *is eating them – all the young boys, just as I told you before. Then they all dress up and go to the village. Then they stay there for a while, waiting. When the breadfruits are ripe, it is time for school number two. Now they all go to the beach. Just like in the story of Nat Kadamoanga and Malouna and Sinamoa, before they all followed this story, they did this again. We – me, Sanganie, Buljaua, Talbul, Sanakoa, some are dead – we went down. The men did this work with us. We were the last. They made a house for us on the top of the mountain where Tarere now is making a garden. We went to that house to learn to play* nibek. *We stayed there and tried to play. After some time the men said: 'Alright, now you must go to the beach.' They made a house for us on the beach just down here. Tafalti was teaching us, he was the* koakoale *of the beach. We slept on the beach. No woman was to see us. We stayed on the beach, and we went and got breadfruit and roasted it on the fire. We had to clean it well and ate it using a bamboo knife. All the men got* oaila, purpur, *coconuts, and made* kadaga. *They made holes in a row in the pebbles on the beach. They put banana leaves inside and made the* kadaga *inside the holes. When we drank we went in a row from one hole to another, drinking from all the holes. Okay, later this day we went and sat down in a line on the beach. Tafalti got this leaf; you have seen women using it for washing dishes, a sharp leaf. We held out our tongues and he sharpened [rubbed] our tongues with the leaf. One by one we stood up, he sharpened our tongues, and we sat down again. He got ginger, chewed it and spat in our mouths. We could not spit around, we had to sit close to a fire and spit in the fire, all the blood. When it had stopped bleeding, all right, we washed our mouths in the sea. We went and sat down again. They made* kadaga *again and we drank. In one day we did all this. We stayed on the beach and ate breadfruit only. The next day many men came. 'Alright,' they said, 'you go ahead and play now.' Two got up, played, not very good, they sat down again. Two others got up, played, and so it went on. The men sat and listened. We did not play too well, the flutes did not sing well. We had* kadaga *to drink all the time, it did not finish. It cleans the stomach and the thoughts, you will think only of playing the flutes. The men sang for us, just like Malouna and Sinamoa, sang for teaching us to play:*

Egelo gelo gelo gelo gela gelo	*Play, play, play*
Egela gelo, o o a	*Play,*
Natare Kadamoananga	*Nat Kadamoanga*[14]

They did it like in the story. We played and played, and after a while some of us played well. Me, Sanakoa, Buljaua, Talbul, we played. We played and played; a whole moon went by. Three moons we stayed on the beach. When we had learnt it well, all right; we went to the bush and cut bananas and greens. We wrapped it all in leaves and roasted it on the fire. We could not eat fish. Then we went to the mountain above Kinaba and danced and played the flutes. We slept in the bush. Then we went to Falala and played there. Then we came back. We went to the mountain of Joboe where the big stones that looks like a house are, played there, and then we went to sleep at the beach of Joboe. We played there too, slept, and went back to Dab. When the Japanese had finished fighting with America, they did this work with us. Now we slept in the house where the Japanese had stayed on the beach of Dab, you know where it was. We could not go back to the first house. Then they dressed us up with malo and all kinds of nice bilas *[Tok Pisin for bodily decorations]; shells, paint, and so on. They called us* iamuna, *like Marajina [Gagin's daughter] was* baras. *Now we went to the village and all the women could see us. They had cooked for us, and we entered the village and lined up. The women came with the food and carried it around us. We went to a house and ate on the veranda. Then we went down to the beach again and stayed there. Lastly we went to Badiata. Now it was time to drink water. We had only had coconuts to drink, like the* baras. *We went to the water near Badiata. You have been there at Marajina's* baras *celebration. We drank and washed, and then we went to Badiata where they all had cooked food for us. We ate in the* nyaboá. *We went back to Dab. We could walk around now, seeing all the women. But they had marked one year for us; in one year we could not go with women 'making wrong'. It was a strong taboo. We marked out a* pangal *[Tok Pisin, stem of a coconut leaf], and when it got dry and fell down, it was our time. If we broke the law, we would get sick. When the time to do wrong to women had come, each of us had a man to teach us. We could not go without him bossing us. He gave us medicine to keep in the mouth, medicine from a tree. Now we could go to a woman. They chose an old, old woman for each of us, a woman with name. She would train us. Afterwards we had to go to the beach and wash our bodies in the sea. Then the men who were bossing each of us had another medicine, a banana we call* titi. *If you eat this, your urine becomes yellow. He made* kadaga *with this banana, and we drank it.*

Then all the germs from the woman got out.[15] *We were the lasts. Now all the young men go and sleep with women to their own liking. Everyone becomes sick; young girls have children without a man.* Nibek *has not seen the young men; now they are all wrong.*

Strathern (1993: 50) has written about Melanesian initiation rituals that through these rituals, boys grow in the company of men in the same way as a foetus grows in the mother who contains it. In Wogeo this analogy was made quite explicitly: the man carrying out the cleansing of the tongue had the title *koakoale* of the beach (*koakoale one*), and afterwards he was, like a woman who has given birth, referred to as *boaruka* (Hogbin 1970b: 93).[16] He was subject to all the taboos of a *boaruka* woman, having 'given birth' to young men. Also men who tore down an old *nyaboá* (and, thereby, made place for a new one) and men who erected the poles for a new *koakoale* to climb were *boaruka* (ibid.: 93–94).

In 2000, Mats recorded a song from the genre called *ririk* from Kenai, a *koakoale* of Falala. Kenai had for many years been worried that none of the younger men in his village wanted to learn about the customs of the past. In 1994 he told me that he had planned to buy a tape recorder to record the stories, songs and spells that he knew. As far as I know, he had not done so by my last fieldwork, and in 2000 he was happy to get the chance to sing for Mats while visiting Dab. He wanted to sing a song that he had learnt while being initiated (Anderson and Exter 2005: 85):

When we went down to the beach, what did we perform there? We performed boarboar *[chants]; their mother, the* nibek, *danced them on the beach. I will perform them since Dale [Mats] has come; ... he will bring them to his place – in our place they will not exist any more. When we will die, these things will have gone. The men will be here; this will not. The women cannot understand. Only we. ... The two of us [Kenai and Kulbobo] are sons of* koakoale. *In fact, only the two of us remain. ... Well, I will sing the chant; you will hear it:*

O ma[o]ma[o], o ma[o]ma[o], [17]	*Father, father,*
o a o a o ma[o]ma[o],	*father,*
o dan o Sibik e a deka[o]lila[o]ng[18]	*may the water of the Sepik be good*
o ma[o]ma[o], o ma[o]ma[o],	*Father, father,*
o a o a o ma[o]ma[o],	*father,*
a o Sibik e o dan[o]ú o a dekolilaong.	*may the water of the Sepik be good.*
O nyonyo, o nyonyo, o a o a o nyonyo,	*Mother, mother, mother,*
a o Sibik e o dan[o]ú o a deka[o]lila[o]ng	*may the water of the Sepik be good*
o nyonyo, o nyonyo, o a o a o nyonyo,	*mother, mother, mother,*
a o Sibik e o dan[o]ú o a deka[o]lila[o]ng.	*may the water of the Sepik be good.*
Kabain nga. Kadok!	*That was all. Finished!*

That the water flowing past the island from Sepik River should be good (i.e. clean) is meant to promote fertility and prosperity. When the sea is clear, the reef is easily visible and fishing is good. When the tide is strong and unfavourable for fishing, it is impossible to see even half a metre ahead and good swimming skills are necessary to avoid being pulled out into the sea by the tide. In addition, the sea can be full of all kinds of organisms causing one's skin to itch and burn. The image of the clean, flowing water can be seen as an analogy to the cleansing from the tongue (and, later, the penis), necessary for the growth of the boys. As we will see in chapter 6, the flowing water from the Sepik is also used as an image in other cleansing rituals.

The intercourse with the old women was meant to reciprocate the milk the boys had received from their mothers, Marifa said. Milk is seen to be the same type of substance as semen, and frequent intercourse in the beginning of a pregnancy will secure sufficient milk in the mothers' breasts. Lala said that the young boys also got the 'wind' (breath, *win* in Tok Pisin) to play the flutes from the old women, the free flow of which Nat Kadamoanga had broken when he tried to control the flutes and slept with Malouna and Sinamoa. The Wogeo equivalent to soul or essence of life is 'breath' (*malmalim*, 'your breath', cf. Hogbin 1970b: 180) and the 'wind' used to play the flutes may be seen as a manifestation of this flow of life or innate fertility. Old women do not give birth any more, and they are therefore free to give this power to the young boys so that they can play the flutes and grow properly.

One old man added another event to the final stages of the initiation: we had to follow an old *moede* to the beach in the morning. We would hide as she relieved herself, and then we would take some of her faeces and eat it. It was a punishment for what Nat Kadamoanga had done, he said.

Gendered Differentiation

In accordance with the emphasis on the relational and contextual focus of Melanesian ethnography, the male initiation as described above should not be understood merely as representing a 'culturalized' world of men, providing an explanation of male dominance, opposed to a 'natural' world of women (see also Hugh-Jones 2001: 248–49). Rather, the gender symbolism at play provides images of shifting, complementary female and male qualities or capacities.

Marilyn Strathern (1988) has claimed that as products of the social relationships that created them, Melanesian persons are as dividually constituted as they are individually. As a realization of those relationships children can be seen as non-gendered or androgynous (male/female) entities with an innate potential for differentiation. In order to be able to enter into productive relationships, they need to be transformed from 'half of a whole' into 'one of a pair': they need to be made 'incomplete' (Strathern 1993).

In a similar fashion Roy Wagner has written about Papuan conceptualizations of the innate. He claims that, rather than abstracting a social order from that which within a Western natural science paradigm is seen as a 'natural' and self-evident order of differentiated beings (such as men and women, human beings and animals, living and dead – similar to the taxonomies of biologists), Papuans conceive this order to flow 'more or less spontaneously in the world' (Wagner 1977b: 397).

> It is immanent in man, other creatures and in the cosmos itself, and may not be 'created' by human agency, but only tempered, constrained and invoked. It constitutes the thread, or strain of similarity and contiguity among all the diverse classes of beings that inhabit the world. What we are disposed to call 'humanity' or 'social relationship' is for Papuans the very ground of being; it is not a distinct property of man, but rather man's greatest resource (ibid.).

The differentiated beings in this world are analogous – both similar and different. The similarities are seen as the 'innate property of being', and differentiation is the responsibility of man. Social and ritual life is about maintaining and renewing the differences between people, spirits and animals, and between men and women. In that sense gendered incompleteness is not a given and absolute property of the human body, but rather a potential that is invoked and maintained. This continuous work of differentiation maintains a necessary 'beneficent relational flow' (ibid.). Or, as Sandra Bamford has phrased it, 'Unity and disjunction become twin moments in the ongoing flow or elicitation of social life' (Bamford 1998: 159). Wagner further states that

> The flow in the first instance is the thing that we recognize as human sociality, and in the second it is fertility, spiritual power and the 'knowledge' of the diviner or shaman. ... [T]he anthropomorphic innate is perceived as a flow of human potential across the physical diversity of the landscape (Wagner 1977b: 398).

The flow 'in the first instance' is human sociality – we use the analogies or figurative symbols to think about or create social relations (such as those between men and women). Differentiation – and the creation of beneficial social relations – stops the flow and attaches the analogies to bodies or other entities. Or, to phrase it according to Strathern's perspective, 'decomposes' the composite, androgynous person – makes it 'incomplete' (Strathern 1992: 83).

We can see the theft of the flutes as an image of a primordial act of gender differentiation (or 'decomposition'). 'Because you've stolen for yourself something we intended for everybody, no female will from now on look at a flute or have anything to do with one. You males can keep them,' Hogbin (1970b: 101) wrote in his version of the myth. The flutes were intended for everyone, and their capacity to play by themselves can be interpreted as representing an unrestrained flow of fertility. But then Nat Kadamoanga tried to take control over the flutes. The spontaneous flow of fertility stopped and, since then, had to be facilitated through a gendered complementarity. Men and women are gendered and made incomplete in different manners according to their relationship to this flow of fertility – Wagner's flow 'in the second instance': 'For women it is easy; for us men it is truly hard work,' Wogeo men complain. Men had to work hard to learn to play the flutes in order to grow, whereas female fertility is an inherent capacity of their bodies. Female fertility, as an enduring and unchangeable fact, does not need to be created but merely couched into being, nor does it need to be accounted for to a similar degree as male growth and power. 'Men play flutes, women bear infants,' as Hogbin's (1970b: 101) informants said.

The need to keep the flute myth and the associated rituals hidden from the women could be discussed at length, but I will only dwell briefly on this question here. Donald F. Tuzin (1997) has written about how the Ilahita Arapesh in 1984 publicly 'killed' the *tambaran* by revealing the secret of the original female power to the women. The women did not seem particularly surprised (ibid.: 161), but Tuzin noted that they did become more assertive. According to Smith (1994: 81), in Kairiru, one of Wogeo's neighbouring islands, the cult was abandoned already in the 1930s at the behest of the Catholic Mission's first emissary. Women and children were shown the secret ceremonial objects of the cult and told that it was the men who made the sound of the *tambaran*. In Wogeo, no such revelation had, to my knowledge, taken place. Only a few of the people alive in the 1990s had experienced the *nibek* and the male cult, but men were still eager to discuss it. Even though they said that women still should not be told the secrets, the men did not seem to mind women overhearing our discussions on the matter. The cult and its secrets are also described extensively in Hogbin's book (1970b), but Wogeo men did not regard this as a problem. When discussing Hogbin's writings, men said that written words detached from real life could not give a full understanding or evoke the same powers as *hearing* the words could.

Even though people know that the flutes were no monsters but merely a pair of flutes, the flutes themselves are still regarded as powerful objects (cf. Smith 1994: 82). As already mentioned, Gagin had, after hearing the flutes played in Manam, suggested to Wogeo elders that they should start making the flutes again. Marifa and others had refused to do this. 'These things have strong powers,' Marifa said, 'and we do not know how to control them anymore.'

Kulbobo often emphasized that experience was central to understanding. Considering that the men were more interested in discussing the rituals than the myth and that only a few of the oldest ones could actually tell the myth, it is likely that the part of the cult that was most salient to men in general was the actual performance of the rituals – including the physical exclusion of women and their fear of the *nibek* – rather than the secret of the theft itself. The separation from the boys' mothers, the cleansings and the mastering of the flutes was, quite physically, what made men of boys. The lack of growth and the frequency of diseases were due to the lack of practice of the rituals. When discussing secrets and experience among the Baktaman, Fredrik Barth has argued that

> instead of developing a 'theory' of growth and health and fertility ... develop a 'mystery' of these themes. Secrecy is an essential precondition of this mystery. It dramatizes and inculcates a deep emotional experience of the *partial* nature of our understanding compared to the uncharted fullness of reality (Barth 1975: 221).

Similarly most of my male informants did not engage in discussion of the meaning of the myth of Nat Kadamoanga as a 'theory of growth and fertility'. The myth and other similar stories were *tok piksa* ('picture talk' in Tok Pisin), both Marifa and Kulbobo emphasized. They were representations of the mystery of fertility and growth that was 'something for the big men only'. At least from the 1990s retrospective perspective, it was the myth itself, and not its interpretation, that seemed to have the character of a philosophical elaboration over gender differentiation, and it was the business of the *koakoale* rather than something all men had present in their minds.

*   *   *

The rejoining of the fertile unity (or flow) – when 'two bodies become one' as people say – is a dangerous undertaking. It evokes the strongest power there is – the power of life – and proper avoidance and cleansings should be observed. But still such connections are seen as being an enduring source of disease – 'If men and women were to themselves, nobody would be sick.' With this in mind, I will continue by looking further at taboos and accompanying ideas associated with the work of looking after one's body.

Notes

1. Coldness is also associated with spiritual beings (Hogbin 1970b: 81).
2. Cf. Eves for a similar example from Lelet, New Ireland: 'It is said that the larada [equivalent to *nanaranga*], seeing that a person does not exhibit shame, decides to marry that person, a euphemistic way of saying that the larada has sexual intercourse and colonizes the internal spaces of the body' (1997: 182).
3. Young boys went through similar rituals at their initiation (cf. Hogbin 1970b). See also Tuzin (1982: 338) for a description of how similar physical connections are made between young initiands and the growth of certain trees among the Ilahita.
4. I have described such rituals in connection with Gagin's daughter Marajina's first baras at length in other places (Anderson 1996; 1998).
5. Both the ritual cleansings, the application of oil and the horseplay of the women are found in the first menstruation rituals in Manam as well (Lutkehaus 1995a).
6. See e.g. Tuzin (1997).
7. At this *olage*, five baskets and two pigs were also exchanged in Kijua's (Maria's daughter) name since she was expected to menstruate soon and it was convenient to join the two exchanges. Fourteen baskets were displayed at this occasion, a relatively large *olage*.
8. I have heard this myth in slightly different versions, but they all agree upon the main theme as presented in this version from a taped interview with Marifa (see e.g. Gillison 1980; Lutkehaus 1995b; Gregor and Tuzin 2001; Tuzin 1997 for references to similar myths from other places in Melanesia as well as in Amazonia). Lala had a version I have heard only from him: he called the women Dabdab and Tatamona and said that the little boy had come from Sepik.
9. His name means something like 'a good boy' or 'a boy in a good state' (by Marifa his name was translated as 'he who is on his own'). Hogbin (1970b: 100) translated it with 'man locust', but I have not heard this translation (words for locust are e.g. *fit* and *vajike*).
10. Among the Sambia, where semen from older men is ingested by young boys in order to promote their own growth, playing the flutes explicitly appear as a metaphor for homosexual fellatio (Herdt 1982: 61).
11. In the Sepik such spirits associated with male cults are commonly referred to as *tambaran*.

12. Hogbin (1935a: 332) wrote that he suspected the older women to know that 'deception is being practiced'. Leach (2000: 169) notes that on the Rai coast near Madang women past menopause could freely enter the male cult house and see the tambaran. Among the Hua women past menopause are even initiated into the cult (Meigs 1984).

13. Lutkehaus writes that the Manam no longer fear the flutes and that women know that they are not spirits. 'They do, however, remain symbols of the authority of the tanepoa labalaba [chiefs], and of male power in general' (1995b: 318).

14. Wogeos often 'pull' the words as they say when they sing. Natare Kadamoananga is Nat Kadamoanga.

15. One young man claimed that eating this banana would cure gonorrhoea.

16. When Marifa went through this procedure, his older brother Tafalti had this title.

17. The vowels in square brackets are added to the words for the purpose of rhythm.

18. This word is not from Wogeo but probably from the neighbouring Biem language; a Wogeo equivalent would be *dekalingó* (Exter, personal communication).

⊰ Chapter 4 ⊱
Desired and Undesired Connections

As far as avoidance and creation of beneficial fertile flows are concerned, it is not only contact between human bodies which is precarious; also bodies and their physical environment are connected in this sense. When planting a new garden it is important that the bodies of all the workers are in good condition and that they observe the proper taboos prior to and after the work. You need to trust people when asking them to help you in your garden, Maria said. It is therefore more important to bathe and smell nice before you start working than to wash off the dirt afterwards. Smell is important in this regard. Strong smells, like the smell of fish, sex and menstrual blood, are regarded as polluting and should be avoided. One has to wash at once after having sex in order to get rid of the smell. When I was ill once, I was told that I should take care when I was given betel nuts from younger people – they could not be trusted to have washed off the smell of sex. There are also certain *nanaranga* in the bush that are attracted to such smells – like the one who lives near Taro that was mentioned in the last chapter. When particularly important gardens are planted, people would make *kadaga* and *burenga* and place the drink and the ointment at the entrance to the garden. The workers would drink the *kadaga* and rub *burenga* on their skin before entering the garden. 'Then your body is clean and smells nice, and you feel fresh when you start to work,' Maria said.

A human body transfers pollution not only to other bodies, but also to other entities and places it encounters. This connection is not only a matter of bodies carrying pollution and, thereby, contaminating what they come in contact with. A different sort of connection is made evident by another type of avoidance. When a woman has planted sweet potatoes, a task usually carried out by women, she should not wash in saltwater *afterwards*. This would make the sweet potatoes she has planted dry. The same is the case with men who have planted bananas. The connectedness (or 'thread of similarity' (Wagner 1977b: 397)) between the human body and what it encounters is, thus, salient beyond the direct contact. What the woman does with her body continues to affect the sweet potato she planted after she has left the garden – as it does before she enters it.

A similar connection between a person's body and its encounters is made when a man has caught a big fish. If he enters a garden the same day, the fish will climb over the garden fence in the shape of a pig and eat the taros or sweet potatoes. Similarly, if someone has *eaten* a big fish or pig the day before planting a garden, the ghost of the animal will eat the garden produce. Or, when the Palolo worms (*manuan*[1]) came ashore to breed in November 1993, Gamuia told me that she could not participate in the yearly catch of the worm because they would make holes in the taro she was going to plant the following day.

As Mary Douglas (e.g. 1966) has done, anthropologists often point out that taboos and avoidance keep categories that should be kept apart separate. 'To follow a taboo ... is to shore up a system of cultural distinctions and to prevent connections from forming between cultural domains that must not be mixed' (Bamford 1998: 158). In the case of the taboos referred to above, it seems that they also do the opposite: they demarcate a unity between categories that seem separate. Sandra Bamford makes a similar point when she describes food taboos among the Kamea in the New Guinea highlands. 'Taboos frequently do mark off categories of persons and things. But they are also the means by which such distinctions are constituted in the first place' (ibid.: 159) she states, and continues by describing how certain food taboos constitute a unity between a mother and her son. Boys are subject to a number of food taboos. If they breach these, it would hardly affect their own bodies, but their mothers would suffer hardships: 'she would sit in the house all day long where she would eventually die' (ibid.: 162). Later on, when the boys are initiated, these taboos are transferred to their mothers and the young men are free to eat anything they like. The taboos establish the 'essential similarity' between the two at the same time as they anticipate the differentiation that will come when the boy is initiated (ibid.). Kamea male initiation is as much about decontainment from the mother as it marks the entrance into the male cult, Bamford claims. Also in Wogeo a unity between a mother and her young son can be seen through the fact that her *baras* blood is not polluting to him before he starts puberty – the time when he earlier had to initiate his own growth through playing the flutes and rid his body from female influence.

If we return to the example of the Wogeo woman and the sweet potato she is planting, we can say that a unity is made between her body and the potato – to the extent that she can secure the growth of the potato by following taboos focused on her body beyond the direct contact. In the same manner a connection is made between a man and the fish he catches or the pig he feeds. A man should not eat a pig he has fed himself – if he did so his body would be covered with boils. At a later stage the sweet potato or the pig will perhaps be given away in exchange, and we can certainly see how exchange objects can be labelled 'inalienable' and how giving away such an object can be to give away a part of oneself. The woman can be seen to give away a part of herself not merely due to the work she has invested in the produce but also due to the unity that is made between her and the potato (or a man and his pig).

Gell (1979) made a similar point in his analysis of Umeda taboos. Among the Umeda, a man who eats a pig he himself had killed would engage in auto-cannibalism – the ultimate anti-social act. In Wogeo, food is the main vehicle for creating and maintaining social relationships. Food should not only be eaten when hungry but as importantly it should be given away, expanding the person into the network of relations that constitute it rather than closing it off into a self-contained entity (see also Sørum 2003). At the same time, giving away food establishes the person vis-à-vis and separate from others (cf. Gell 1979; Strathern 1988). Food as a mediator for, or objectification of, connections or relations is an important part of Strathern's analyses. Or, to use the notion of 'flow', we can see such gifts as embodiments of a relational flow. Taboos and avoidance facilitate flows (or connections) as well as cutting them as a person's life trails through the landscape of time and space.

Pollution and Diseases of the Place

In conversations about taboos and cleansings, what is described by the term *ival* (avoidance), Wogeos often provided a much more concrete and pragmatic explanation: 'In your country everyone has soap and hot water in the tap. The doctors have gloves and disinfectants. We do not. That is why it is so important to follow this *kastom*,' one man said. In addition to securing good harvests and proper relationships, the taboos protect people against illness (*somoa*) as a result of dangerous contact – like gloves protect the doctor from contagion and mosquito repellent protects the skin from mosquito bites.

Some illnesses in Wogeo are said to be outside the domain of medical diagnosis and healing – in Tok Pisin these are referred to as *sik bilong ples* ('disease of the place'). If you have such diseases, people told me, a doctor would not necessarily find any physical causes. The doctor will make all kinds of tests and then tell you to go back home, saying: 'You have an illness from your place that I cannot cure.' Disease of the place can, however, also cause illness with symptoms similar to tuberculosis (*somoa ngaia*) and asthma (*somoa ngasa*) as well as hepatitis, and a medical doctor can also diagnose them as such.

Such illnesses are often said to be caused by contact with people and substances associated with *baras*, *boaruka*, *sara* and *manvara* (people who have touched a dead body). Such contact is referred to as *langana* (also tuberculosis is often said to be *langana*, particularly from contact with *baras* blood). If it can be established that the sick person has received food, betel nuts, tobacco or similar from people with 'bad hands' (*limá dareka*), his or her disease will probably be said to be *langana*. And if a cause cannot be proven, diseases like tuberculosis will often be said to be *langana* anyway since such contact is not easy to confirm. Hogbin wrote that contact with *baras* blood resulted in a 'fatal disease characterized by swelling of the tissues' (1970b: 83). He also wrote that contact with men who had conducted the *sara* operation was more serious and resulted in certain death. Contact with *manvara* can result in malaria or malaria-like symptoms (*maoak*).[2]

Langana is usually blamed on people being careless in their dealings with dangerous bodily substances. But people can also use these substances intentionally to make people sick. A woman may deliberately touch her husband's food if angry with him (cf. Hogbin 1938: 230) but these substances can also be used to harm people through what Wogeos call *muj* (cf. e.g. Hogbin 1935/36b). *Muj* is equivalent to what Wogeos label *poisin* (poison) in Tok Pisin.[3] Kulbobo divided *muj* into two subgroups. The first group makes use of harmful substances in order to make people ill. The best-known method is to take some contaminated *baras*, *boaruka* or *sara* blood, put it on a piece of tobacco and let it dry in the sun. When the victim smokes this tobacco, he or she will get ill in the same manner as from other contact with these substances. A more difficult, but certainly more fatal, way of poisoning someone is to take a piece of a corpse, burn it on the fire and mix the ashes in food or water or cooking oil that the victim would consume. Snake poison or the liver from a puff-fish can also be used. In the last case the victim's stomach would swell up like the fish. There is also the more recently introduced use of battery acid. One young boy who died during my first fieldwork was poisoned in this manner, people claimed. His guts had been eaten away as though they were corroded, people said. He died while in Wewak, and battery acid was at that time said to be something only mainlanders used but, in 1999, Kulbobo included this with the other local means of poisoning.

The other group of *muj* that Kulbobo listed was what in anthropological terms could be classified as contagious magic (e.g. Keesing 1981: 509). The perpetrator would take something that the victim had touched, like hair or a cigarette-butt. Then she would say a magical formula (*boab*) over it and afterwards burn it on the fire. The culprit should take care not to touch the object herself, lest she would bring harm to herself instead of the victim. Another way is to put a spell on a *moanuboa* leaf or a piece of vine and then tie it into a loose knot. In the dark of the night the offender would go to the victim's house and gently call out her name. When she answers, the perpetrator would pull the knot tight and then burn the leaf or the vine on the fire. The victim would choke to death. A similar method is to put a *moanuboa* leaf invested with magic on a path where the victim would step over it.

Muj and *langana* are always immanent dangers when receiving gifts of food, betel nuts or tobacco from someone, and people should take care from whom they accept such gifts. This is a difficult task since it is a very strong statement of rejection to refuse such gifts. A way to avoid this is not to eat the food right away, but to carry it with you and secretly throw it away. Accordingly, it is a statement of trust and friendship to eat such food in the presence of the giver. Kulbobo, who had been sick with tuberculosis for many years, said that one of the reasons he was still alive was that he was very careful about whose food he was eating.

Boab is the term for malevolent magical spells in general, like the ones used in the latter group of *muj*, but in this case it refers to certain types of spells. These are not primarily meant to harm anyone in particular, but are made to protect crops from gardens or trees in the bush (cf. Hogbin 1935/36b: 4–6; 1978: 47–49). If a big food distribution or other type of exchange is planned, a person might want to taboo a garden or, more commonly, betel nut palms or other trees.[4] He would say a magical spell and spray his saliva on the palm and then mark it with leaves around the stem of the palm. If people still climbed the tree and ate the betel nuts or whatever was tabooed, they would get strong pains in their bodies, fall ill and eventually die. Only the person who had cast the spell could heal the sick person, so the thief would have to admit his wrongdoings in order to survive. Wogeos often pointed out that, as good Christians, they had abandoned all such bad customs. But in the next sentence they could tell me about this and that person who was known to still use *boab*, and several times I heard that illness was caused by *boab*. *Boab* was a means to protect one's property, it was relatively uncomplicated to put to use and since most people owned the knowledge of *boab* and it was seen as the least harmful of the malevolent magic, it was allegedly the most frequently used.

All malevolent spells (*meme jon*, lit. 'bad tongue') are dangerous to the person saying them. Spells get their power from the breath from the stomach together with the words spoken (cf. Hogbin 1970b: 180). Confidence in the power of the words is also necessary for the spell to work. The spells are usually said to a piece of ginger or betel nut, and these are then chewed and the saliva is sprayed upon that which will be affected by the spell: for instance a betel palm in the case of *boab* or the sick person in the case of benevolent *boasa*. If the spell is particularly powerful (or the sick person very ill), the saliva excretion will increase. Should the magician swallow the saliva, he would himself be the affected by the power. One old man who died during one of my stays in Wogeo was said by some to have died because he had owned many *boab* and had used them a lot. Involuntarily he had swallowed a little saliva now and then while saying his spells. When he grew old this had accumulated in his body and, as a consequence, some people claimed, he died.

Germs, Smell and Language

So far I have dealt with direct physical contact between bodies, such as sexual contact or contact with people regarded as being in polluting states, and I have written about contact between human bodies and what they physically encounter in the phenomenal world – such as garden produce or pigs or fish. Further I have written about bodily substances as mediators of dangerous contact, most prominently *baras*, *sara* and *boaruka* blood as well as sexual fluids. As described above, saliva can also be a dangerous substance. Saliva can carry magic – both benevolent and malevolent magic. The power of the magic came from the words together with the breath from the stomach. Breath and spoken words are a kind of flow that differs from the flow of substances described above in that they cannot be seen or touched. To this kind of flow I will also include smells and what Wogeos described as 'germs'. As we will see, this adds another dimension to the analytical notions of connectedness and avoidance.

A class of what Kulbobo labelled 'place disease' is *oabel*. *Oabel* does not itself refer to a class of disease or a cause of disease, but to breaches of certain taboos that will make a disease worse. These taboos are connected to work with sago and *ngabir* (giant taro, lat. *Alocasia macrorrhiza*) and with certain *nanaranga*. As already mentioned, *nanaranga* can be the cause of people getting ill, like the girl who the *nanaranga* in Taro 'married'. They are also known to 'eat' the spirit (*vanunu*, lit. 'shadow') of people. Only people who know the proper magic for the particular *nanaranga* can cure such diseases. *Oabel* is different.

If someone has done any kind of work with sago or *ngabir* in the bush and someone is sick in the village, they should not enter the village until after sunset and after having washed in the sea. If they do not observe this rule, the person's illness could worsen and he or she could die, even if the wrongdoer has not come anywhere near the sick person. One man told me that he thought many of the beliefs regarding taboos and disease to be mere superstition, but *oabel* was different, he said. He had seen too many cases of people getting seriously ill because of *oabel* to doubt it. 'I do not know what it is. Maybe it is like smell or germs flying through the air.' Kulbobo referred to this as *oabel dafan va* – literally meaning, '*oabel* are getting me'. He translated this as *oabel* is 'shooting me' or 'biting me' – like a stinging nettle that comes near one's leg in the bush.

Work with sago and *ngabir* are spoken of as *nanaranga* work. Both of the plants have myths connected to them. In Onka's time, people said, Wogeos did not have to go through the hard work of cutting down the sago palm, pounding the marrow or washing out the sago starch. They merely had to drill a hole in the palm and the starch would pour out from the hole. One day Onka told his two younger brothers to go and get some sago. The two were particularly lazy and, as they walked into the bush, they complained about the hard work. They decided that it would be much easier if they cut down the palm and took it to the village. Then they could have the sago supply near their house. But when they entered the village with the sago trunk, Onka got angry and said that because they had cut down the palm, everyone from now on had to work hard to get sago: the starch would not flow by itself any more (see Hogbin 1970b: 48 for a similar myth).

There is an analogy between this story and the myth of the theft of the flutes. Again, foolish men had tried to take control over a fertile flow but, instead, disrupted it and were punished by having to work hard to regain what they had attempted to control. Accordingly, sago-production is mainly the men's task.

In another myth, the origin of *ngabir* is explained. Because they had quarrelled with their parents, a young girl and her brother ran off into the bush. There they came upon the *nanaranga* Ngabirkara. Terrified, they climbed up into a tree. Ngabirkara had seen them and tried to shake them down. The girl was afraid of falling down, and said, 'Brother, let the tree get small!' Nothing happened. Then she said, 'Papa, let the tree get small!' Still nothing happened. She said, '*Kandere* [mother's brother], please let the tree get small,' but not until she said 'Husband, let the tree get small!' did the tree shrink so they could easily climb down. They went with him to his house, and the girl became Ngabirkara's wife. He was not happy that the little brother was moving in with them and the boy had to stay under the house. He was only given leftovers to eat and his sister had to pass the scraps down to him through a hole in the floor. But when Ngabirkara went into the bush during the daytime, she let him in and gave him good food to eat. Finally both of them were fed up with the situation, and one day when Ngabirkara had gone fishing, they set fire to the house and ran back to their village where their parents were happy to see them again. In the meantime, Ngabirkara had spotted the smoke from his burning house and returned in a hurry. He understood that the two had run off and he set out following their tracks. In the village people had prepared themselves, and when he arrived they threw hot *mumu* (stone oven) stones and water on him so that he cooked to death. They buried him on the beach, and some time later an *ngabir* grew on the spot where they had buried him.[5]

Ngabirkara's relationship to the girl is that of a husband who had sex with her. He disrupted the unity between the girl and her brother and attempted to control the flow of unconditional care between them. The situation was unbearable and Ngabirkara was killed. Representing this primordial husband and disruption of relations based on birth, *ngabir* still grows on Wogeo. In Hogbin's version of the myth, the *ngabir* grew on the spot they had buried his penis (1970b: 31–32). Again, as for the sago, an analogy can be made to the flute myth in the sense that it represents a broken beneficial flow. Thus, the work with *ngabir* is a hazardous activity.

The placing together of invisible 'germs' as in the case of *oabel,* words and smells as constituting a particular type of flow, illustrates an aspect of the relation between bodily states and the phenomenal world that will be salient also later in the book. Smells in particular elicit this relation.

Smells are central to ideas of well-being and health in Wogeo.[6] Wogeos are always acutely aware of smells, bad smells (*boabou*) in particular. Many times a day I would hear people blow wind from their noses (instead of sniffing it in as a Norwegian would do), loudly exclaiming *samting smell hia!* (Tok Pisin, 'something smells'). Some smells are not merely unpleasant but also dangerous to people's health. Most of all the smell of sex – *luma* – is bad. As described above, all the cleansing rituals in Wogeo involve the use of the pleasant smelling herbs *oaila.* If used after washing, this smell on people's bodies prepares them for all kinds of important activities and rids them of pollution. Rather than the presence of dirt on the skin, smells tells people whether one is properly cleansed or not.

If we see smells in a semiotic perspective, they are particularly potent signs since they always refer to something different from themselves. 'Smells should be symbols *par excellence*' (Sperber 1975: 118). Gell has written about smells that they

> ... are characteristically incomplete. They are completed, in the first place, by their source, which is where they become so highly concentrated that they cease to be smells and become substances. Apart from this, a smell is completed, not only by its source, but also by the context. Because smells are so intimately bound up with the world, the context of the smell is not other smells (in the sense that the context of a linguistic sign is the rest of language, only in relation to which it outlines its distinctive meaning) – but simply the world (Gell 1977: 27).

He further states that '[t]o manifest itself as a smell is the nearest an objective reality can go towards becoming a concept without leaving the realm of the sensible altogether' (1977: 29). Here Gell takes a saussurian semiological view of language as a system of signs that are only given meaning in relation to other signs, but his description of smells as signs appears more similar to the semiotics of Wagner (1986b) with its focus on the relation between the sign and the signified. Signs are given meaning in a dialectical process of concretization and abstraction between the perceived macrocosm (the phenomenal world) and the microcosm of abstractions. Smell would, according to this view, belong to the larger microcosmic realm of signs that includes both verbalized and non-verbalized signs at the same time as it is concretized in the macrocosm through experience. As such, smell as a sign is not all that different from for instance a linguistic sign.

In Wogeo smell can signify bodies in polluting states (e.g. the smell of sex or menstruation), and it can signify bodies that are properly cleansed (the smell of *oaila*). Seeing connections between bodies and between bodies and the phenomenal world as flow, smells can be seen as a type of flow. And this is potentially a quite dangerous one, since it can be disembodied from its origin and move far away from it – carried on people's bodies or through the air. For some important activities that are associated with Wogeo *kastom*, the smell of foreign things, particularly soap, is potentially harmful. When the Palolo worms (*manuan*) come ashore to breed once a year and Wogeos gather to collect this delicacy, the smell of soap would keep the worms from coming ashore. The smell of *oaila*, on the contrary, attracts them, and all participants in the catch should have rubbed red oil with *oaila* (*burenga*) on their bodies. In this case the smell of soap and *oaila* stands not primarily for states of cleanliness; rather, soap stands for the world beyond Wogeo and *oaila* for purified states according to Wogeo *kastom*. As Gell has noted, 'the response to smells is typical rather than specific, general rather than particular' (1977: 28). Likewise, in the welcoming ritual of washing people with *oaila* that was described in the introduction, the *oaila* rids people's bodies of the smell from foreign places.

Another kind of disembodied sign or flow that can have a similar effect is words or, perhaps more accurately, language. In Wogeo there are two activities in particular where this analogy is evident. The first concerns a certain fruit, called *veka*. It is round, orange-sized and green with four large boat-shaped seeds in the middle of the white, sweet meat. The fruit is highly valued, and the Wogeos claim that it only grows on Wogeo.[7] People have tried to plant its seeds in other places, but they do not grow. According to a myth, a *veka* fruit drifted ashore on the beach of the village of Moaroka. It then changed into a woman and when the woman died, a *veka* tree grew where she had been buried. The fruits should be collected before they fall to the ground and at exactly at the proper time, lest they go sour. When collecting this fruit it is of the utmost importance that one does not speak Tok Pisin or English or any foreign language. Also, one should not look towards the mainland. If these taboos are broken, all the fruits from the tree will be sour and inedible.

The other activity concerns a certain type of red soil that is found in the mountain beyond Badiata. The soil is the preferred ingredient for the cleansing ointment *burenga*, rather than the red seeds from the Bixa Orrelana, but the seeds are often used instead since they are easier to obtain. When going to the spot where the soil is found, nobody should speak at all, and if one has to, one should whisper and definitely not in Tok Pisin or English. If people should breach these taboos they would get lost and not be able to find the path down from the mountain. Once some men brought a tape recorder and played Western pop music on this mountain, and, if someone by coincidence had not passed by and helped them, the men would for sure have been lost – they spent two days on the mountain before they found their way down, and their dogs died there, people told me.

'Your body is holy' Kulbobo said and referred to *ival* as describing what he meant by holiness. He continued by drawing the parallel to place: 'You have to look after your body like you look after your place (*kaba*). You have to sweep your area and keep it tidy and plant flowers on it.' Things 'of the place' – like the red soil and the *veka* fruit – should be kept well in the place. English and Tok Pisin words, the view of the mainland and the smell of soap all signify the world beyond Wogeo and bring unwanted contact between what is 'truly' Wogeo and what is not. I will return to such analogies of body and place in the next part of the dissertation.

It appears that Wogeos regard the boundaries of bodies as fragile or easily penetrable. Essences from other bodies or entities can, like smell or 'germs', enter bodies or other entities or places and affect them in positive or negative manners according to the relations between them. A series of avoidances is therefore necessary to secure not only the well-being of individual bodies but also of the relations in which they exist. The expansion of the social person into a network of relations and bodily movement in a phenomenal world needs to be channelled in the proper directions by cutting certain connections and creating others (cf. Strathern 1996). Similarly, bodies are gendered through processes of disconnections and connections – both in mythology and ritual. Bodies or persons are not composed or constituted independently of the relations of which they are a part or the landscape in which they move: it may well be said that it is relations rather than things or persons that are the ultimate constituents of the world (Gell 1999: 35).

Notes

1. Lat. *eunice viridis*.
2. Another type of place disease is somoa nibek – the result of breaches of any of the taboos associated with the male cult. It was important that the young men restrained their sexual drives until they had been properly educated on the matter and they had passed through the different initiation classes. If they should sleep with a woman before their time, they would eventually get ill – perhaps not before they grew old. The only way to avoid this was to acknowledge their wrongdoings so that the 'big men' who knew the proper *boasa* could help them. Also women who entered a *nyaboá* would get this illness – unless when it was new and *nibek* had not yet visited the cult house. I never heard any specific details of the symptoms of *somoa nibek*, but one old man who had problems urinating and another who died from an intestinal disorder were said by some to suffer from *somoa nibek*.
3. *Poisin* is also used for sorcery in Tok Pisin (cf. Mihalic 1971: 159), but Wogeos usually use the term *sanguma* for *iaboua* when speaking Tok Pisin.
4. Kulbobo explained it in this manner: *Va neg vanua obariki* – translated by Exter as, 'I am making my place prosper (by putting taboos on it)'. In 1998 a district on the island had tabooed nearly all their breadfruit trees, betel nut palms, coconut palms and *galip* trees because they wanted to sell their produce in the town market in order to raise money for various purposes. They had not used *boab*, though, people said. It was often emphasized when we spoke about this that hardly anyone used *boab* any more; they were satisfied with just 'marking' the trees or gardens.
5. I was told a much longer version of the myth but have extracted only parts of it here. For a full version, see Anderson (1996, ch. 5) and a slightly different version in Hogbin (1970b: 31–32).
6. See also e.g. Gell (1977) and van Oosterhout (2001).
7. I have not been able to verify this claim. The fruit looks similar to *Casimiroa Edulis* (white sapote). Hogbin also notes that the veka is particularly valued (1938/39: 309).

⊣ Chapter 5 ⊢
Death and Disconnections

The relations that make up a Wogeo social person are most clearly made evident at death. In the rituals following a death these relations are made manifest, concretized and embedded in the sociogeographical landscape where the deceased has lived his life as paths to follow for generations to come. In this chapter I will present the rituals following a death in Dab as an illustrative example of the embodied and relational emphasis of Wogeo sociality. I will describe the taboos and cleansings the people involved need to follow in order to protect themselves from the coldness of death and to dispose of the spirit of the dead, and I will show how the rituals manifest and dissolve the network of relations that the dead person has been immersed in through his life: the network that constituted the deceased as a composite social person (or dividual) and that now has to be unmade or disentangled until only the memory and name of the person is left so that someone else may fill his or her place.

Summing up the argument of the last chapter, taboos and cleansing rituals in Wogeo can be interpreted as disconnecting or stopping flows of similarity at the same time as they create or make explicit other connections or similarities. Yet another example points to a different sort of connectedness that affects a person's ability to secure a good harvest from the garden he or she is planting. When a woman is going to plant a garden and she has visitors sleeping over at her house, it is important that neither they nor any members of the household leave the house before she wakes up. If they did she would wake up and feel that she has been left alone. She would worry and be sad, and this would spoil the new garden. Similarly, if someone close to you is leaving for another place, you should not plant a garden the day after. 'We call this *boasava*,' Maria said (cf. Hogbin 1970b: 187). Wogeos do not like to be alone, and unwanted and unexpected disruptions of social relationships are threatening and leave people unable to succeed in their efforts. As the final rupture of social relationships, a lot of work is involved in coping with death.

Manvara

Relations between the living and the dead are perhaps the most obvious disconnection or differentiation necessary to secure productive relationships, and following a death, a series of taboos are followed and cleansing rituals conducted in order to properly disconnect the dead person from the world of the living. A dead body, no matter how the person died, is extremely dangerous to handle.

The coldness from the body can easily enter the body of anyone who touches it, and the result can be deadly. Also those who have touched a corpse carry with them this coldness, and, unless they observe the proper taboos and conduct the necessary cleansing rituals, they present a danger both to themselves and others. Therefore only a few people take upon themselves the task of handling a corpse. These people, referred to as *manvara*,[1] should all be healthy and fit. Mothers with young children seldom do this work, nor does a woman who has many people she should cook for. Most *manvara* are men who are not too old and do not have too many household responsibilities and young women. They are usually also close relatives of the dead, since people who are emotionally involved have the strongest motivation to undertake this dangerous work, but also people who have certain rights in the deceased's estate are sometimes *manvara* to secure the continuation of their rights.

Immediately after a person has died, the *manvara* are designated. They wash and dress the corpse, while others transform an old canoe into a coffin. At one death I witnessed, nobody immediately volunteered to be *manvara*, and the body was manoeuvred – without anyone touching it – onto a bed-sheet so that they could handle the body without direct contact. The people present clearly felt uncomfortable with the incident. But, as they said afterwards, they could really not be blamed, since the deceased did not have any close relatives, and his adoptive son, who seldom came to see him, was in Wewak. The man had not succeeded in establishing close and lasting relations through his life; he had been sick for a long time and did not have a proper house to live in: he did not 'sit good' in his place. Later on a few people willing to be *manvara* were still found (cf. Hogbin 1935/36a: 19 for an account of a similar incident in 1934).

Usually, however, it is not difficult to designate *manvara* – except at times when there have been several deaths in the village and people are tired of this kind of work and need to continue with their daily routines. The *manvara* immediately start to follow certain taboos that disconnect them from their ordinary social and physical surroundings. Like male and female initiands, they should not touch their own or other people's bodies with their hands. They should eat with forks or, traditionally, a piece of bone, and they should drink through a straw. They should also not mingle with other people but stay at certain places on the beach during the day, and at night in a corner of their own in the village. Before, people also used to protect their heads from the sun with palm spathes. Their bodies are in a precarious state and are seen as particularly receptive to damage. The sun on their heads would make the hair grey, and also their joints and teeth are susceptible for premature symptoms of aging. If they were to carry on their daily tasks without precautions, the flow of life that each of them embodies could be disrupted, and their bodies would reach the threshold of death ahead of time. When the funeral is finished, the *manvara* go through a series of cleansings in order to rid themselves from the coldness of the dead and to cut off the connection to the spirit of the dead person: to make the dead 'sit down'.

The Death of Ulbaia

On 2 February 1994, one of the oldest men in Wogeo died. His name was Ulbaia. As a young man he figured in a photo in one of Hogbin's books (1970b: 179),[2] and when I came to Wogeo he must have been in his late seventies. He lived with Niabula on the beach where Hogbin had his house built in 1934.

In the morning we heard crying from the beach. Maria and I ran down and heard that the crying came from the small hut that had been built for Ulbaia and his wife Ima. From the village we heard the death signal being beaten on the wooden slit gong so that the news of Ulbaia's death should be spread around the island. Several women gathered outside the little hut and cried since there was no room for them inside where Ima and Niabula's son Oadakai were sitting. Soufa, Ulbaia's adoptive daughter, cried the most – her grief seemed unbearable.

Ima and Oadakai started to pass Ulbaia's belongings out of the hut. The women broke his plate and threw the half-eaten food into the sea so that no one would risk taking in something that his spirit was attached to. His clothes and his basket were put aside since they should be buried together with him. His knifes were distributed amongst the women. Soufa came with a bed sheet, and she and Oadakai wrapped the dead body in it. Soufa hung rosary beads around Ulbaia's neck and put on his hat and sunglasses. Kumi, Soufa's brother and her husband got Ulbaia's old canoe and started to make it into a coffin. The dead body was going to be placed inside Kumi's house, since Ulbaia and Saboakai's (his adoptive son) house in Kajenamoa had collapsed during a rainy night some weeks earlier. First they had to move an old sick man living in a little shack next to Kumi's house. If he got close to the dead body, his illness would worsen and he could die.[3] Pregnant women should also stay away from a dead body. When the coffin was ready, the dead body was carried to Kajenamoa by the two who had made the coffin together with Soufa and Oadakai.

These four young people, together with Ulbaia's adoptive granddaughter and two other men were going to be the *manvara*, the chief mourners, for Ulbaia (cf. Hogbin 1970b: 94–95, 158–67).[4] They were the only ones who should touch the dead body and take upon themselves the dangers involved in physical contact with the coldness of death and the spirit of the dead. During the following weeks they would have to keep to themselves, since the coldness from the dead body was on their bodies. They had to go through a series of cleansing rituals and rituals meant to chase away the spirit of the dead man, and they had to take several precautions to protect themselves while being *manvara*.

Tarere said that it often was matrilineal relatives who ended up doing this work, since they were the ones who really cared, but that this was not a rule or 'law'. Hogbin (1970b: 161), on the other hand, writes that the men digging the grave should be of the *opposite* matrimoiety from the dead. In the case of Ulbaia's *manvara* (some of whom also dug the grave), all of them except one were of the opposite moiety of Ulbaia. I had, however, difficulty determining the relations between Ulbaia and all the people involved. Nobody seemed willing to give me the 'true story' of Ulbaia's kinship relations or they claimed that they did not know – probably due to adoptions in the past that were not publicly spoken of.[5] However, apart from Oadakai (who was of the same moiety as Ulbaia and belonged to Moarmoar), all the *manvara* had in common their affiliation to Kajenamoa, the place where Ulbaia had belonged: they were all *dan Kajenamoa*. In addition, two of the *manvara* had rights in *kangar* and sago growing on Ulbaia's land, and if they did not take upon them the work of *manvara*, they could lose these rights: Ulbaia's heir Saboakai could 'cut the rope'.[6]

As the body was carried to Kumi's house, Ima followed, still crying and with her head covered by a towel. When the coffin had been placed inside the house, people started to arrive from other villages to cry for Ulbaia. Nyem, his adoptive daughter who was married in Bajor, was one of the first. She sat down inside the house together with Soufa and Ima, whereas the other visitors sat down outside after having shown their respect and grief inside the house.

The young boys in Dab had gathered green coconuts as refreshments for the mourners, and people seemed to appreciate the sociality of the event. More and more people came. We could hear them already before they entered the village space, crying and singing Ulbaia's name. Only some of the men cried, but they all carried *moanuboa* that they threw upon the roof of the house, as was customary. Niabula took one of them and threw it away, explaining to me that it had roots and that if someone took it and planted it in the garden, Ulbaia's ghost would hunt the place. 'Before', he said, 'we used to throw taro-plants on the roof, but in this *kastom* was wrong' (see Hogbin 1970b: 159). It was a waste of food, Niabula said, which made good sense since the taro crops, due to various diseases, had diminished severely in recent decades.

Many of the mourners came from Bajor. Bajor was Ulbaia's mother's place, and the mourners were of his matrilineage. Ulbaia's adoptive daughter had married in Bajor to follow this path. Some of the men from Bajor burned down a big, old mango tree that belonged to Ulbaia to show their grief. Saboakai cut down one of Ulbaia's coconut palms. At the death of a young mother some months later, people from her matrilineage even attempted to destroy the house of the woman's parents – an extreme expression of grief. Battaglia (1992: 9) describes similar practices from Sabarl as a part of the work of 'forgetting' the deceased – 'remembering in order to forget' she argues is a central function of Sabarl mortuary rituals.[7] Houses are representations of the reproductive life of the deceased and destroying them can be seen as an 'intensification of forgetting, as if to confront it' (ibid.). In the case of the death of the young Wogeo mother above, her mother later gave me jewellery that had been given to the woman at her first *baras*. She did not want to keep them and be reminded of her loss, she told me. Similarly people often take upon themselves to follow personal taboos when someone dies – for instance by not eating certain foods or visiting certain places that remind them of the deceased. But forgetting is not an appropriate term to describe what Wogeos want to achieve with these practices: to be forgotten is an appalling prospect to Wogeos. The attempt to destroy the house of the parents of the young mother was explained as an expression of anger: the woman was taken away too early, and the house as a symbol of security and containment was attacked. Cutting down trees of the deceased is better understood as symbolically marking the end of a person's life rather than as an attempt to remove traces of it: at a girl's first menstruation, young trees as symbols of expected growth were used in the rituals; at deaths trees are cut down, finishing the flow of life. To avoid certain foods or places is a way of displaying one's grief and keeps the memory of a person alive as much as it makes one forget. Similarly the mother's gift to me was as much about not having to be reminded too often as an attempt to forget at the same time as she made sure that I would remember her.

In the past, people were buried under their houses. In the 1990s graves were usually dug next to people's houses and were marked out with fences and flowers and sometimes stones to keep memories of the dead alive. The dead remained as part of their *maleka*. I was told that there was a bit of an argument between the Dab people and Ulbaia's relatives from Bajor as to where Ulbaia should be buried. The people from Bajor meant that he should be buried where his mother came from, but the people in Dab did not even consider the possibility. It was in Dab that Ulbaia had lived his life and left his work, and it was here that he should be buried. This was a subject that often came up when people died, particularly at the death of young people and children. The mother's relatives as 'one body' with the deceased are more attached to the dead than anyone else, something that also is made apparent in the ritual releasing a widow from her obligations to her husband. Widows are supposed to mourn for about a year, and during this period they do not cut their hair. Then the man's matrilineal relatives throw a party for her and cut her hair, the final separation between the spouses, and she is free to find a new husband. Close matrilineal relatives in this sense resemble Annette Weiner's (1988) description of matrilineal relatives as 'owners' of a deceased in the Trobriands, similar also to the roles of a Wogeo girl's mother and maternal aunts at her first *baras*, and the *manvara* are similar to the Trobriand 'workers'.

The mourners were given food to eat, and some men started to dig a grave at the place where Ulbaia and Saboakai's house had its place: in Ulbaia's *maleka*. There was a short ceremony around the coffin inside the house, led by the Catholic catechist. The children laid flowers in the coffin and the lid was nailed on. The coffin was then carried to the grave. Some people thought that they should have waited until the next day with the burial. According to custom, Ulbaia should be allowed to sleep in the house for one more night, they argued. The reason for the hurried funeral was that Saboakai wanted to go to Wewak that night. In the end the boat he was supposed to go on did not turn up, but the burial was still carried out that afternoon.

Ima was sitting next to the grave, still covered with a towel. Soufa was crying next to her. The grave was filled with earth and then with a layer of gravel. A lamp was lit and hung over the grave since it was getting dark and Ulbaia should not sleep alone in the dark. This was important, since sorcerers get the power to make themselves invisible from newly dead bodies. When the grave was lit up, no one would dare get close to it.

After the burial, the *manvara* went down to the beach. They washed themselves in the sea with wild ginger leaves and *oaila*. In particular they should rub their joints. Upon returning from the beach, they went through a procedure meant to strengthen and protect their bodies. The *manvara* went to the grave and stood in line in front of it. A man acted as ceremonial leader and gave them a mixture of lime and ginger (over which he had recited a spell) and they rubbed their hands with the mixture behind their backs. The mixture was also rubbed under their feet. If his or her hands did not turn red, it was a sure indication that someone else was going to die. The ginger was said to heat the *manvara's* bodies. Then the man in charge presented a piece from a Sea Fan coral (lat. *Gorgonacea*) that had been heated on a fire; the *manvara* should chew on this – once on each side of their mouths. The coral looked like a miniature tree and was almost unbreakable. Biting on this coral strengthened the teeth of the *manvara* so that they would not lose their teeth. Premature aging is an immanent danger to be prevented in all the life cycle rituals on Wogeo, and in the case of death, it was particularly the teeth and the joints that should be looked after: problems with these body parts are particularly associated with old age. Lastly the *manvara* were presented with betel nuts fastened on pieces of the root of a tough weed (*brumstik*). Taking care not to touch the nut, they dipped it in some lime from a shell that was provided; then they chewed the betel nut. This was also supposed to strengthen their teeth. All of the ingredients of the ritual were then placed on the grave.

Most of the visitors had now returned home – only a few of them stayed behind. They were going to sleep outside Kumi's house, guarding the grave and keeping each other company. This gathering was called *kiamiam* and usually lasted for about a week. *Kiamiam* is a reduplication of *kiam*, which means 'cold' or 'to be cold'. Maria explained *kiamiam* as: 'We are cold and are warming ourselves around the fire.' The *manvara* kept to themselves, at a distance from the rest, lighting their own fire closer to the grave. The exception was Soufa: she slept with Ima inside the house. If the corpse had been left in the house in the canoe-coffin, the mourners would have sung for the dead, people told me, at least according to tradition. One song in particular was important: a song that is also sung for a new canoe. This would help the dead person to properly 'steer his canoe'. It is said that if you go down to the beach just before the sun rises on such a night, you can see a canoe with the dead leaving the island.

The next morning the *manvara* again went to the beach to wash themselves. Then they smeared ashes (*jim*) on their faces. There are two places on the beaches of Dab where the *manvara* can sit without presenting any dangers to others: beyond Oare, the beach in the direction of Joboe, and at Kinakina, the beach on the side of the village towards Kinaba. Since Ulbaia belonged to Kajenamoa, the *manvara* now went to Kinakina.

They returned to the village just before noon, and sat on the veranda of Kumi's house. We talked for a while, and the *manvara* pointed out that people did not follow the taboos properly these days. They were supposed to drink only with a straw and should not touch their skin or the food they ate. But people did not worry about this anymore. 'Are you not afraid to get sick?' I asked. Some of them laughed, but it turned out that two of the *manvara* carried a cassowary bone to scratch themselves with, and claimed that, at least on the first day, they drank only through a straw.

I sat down next to Soufa, and she started to tell me about how the previous day had been. In the morning she had brought some sago for old Ulbaia. He had eaten some and gave the rest to his dog like he used to. He drank a coconut, ate half of the coconut meat and gave the rest to Ima. Soufa took his wet bed sheets with her to wash them. When she returned, Ulbaia had fallen unconscious outside the hut – as he had done several times lately. Soufa and Ima carried him inside. 'You know, Iamoe, he was so heavy, and I am only a woman.'[8] He regained consciousness but was in no pain and did not complain. Soufa called his name and he looked at her and recognized her. She comforted him and told him that now he could rest his body. Soufa ran up to the village to get Kumi, her brother by birth, but on her way she heard Ima starting to cry and realized that her father had died. 'I was so sad, Iamoe. I saw his puppy licking the tears off Ima's face.' Later Soufa had taken Ulbaia's basket and his walking stick to her house. 'The others wanted to bury it with the body, but I kept it. I am not afraid. I want papa's spirit to come back to me.' In the night Soufa had slept with the basket in her bed. She had woken up in the middle of the night and felt that she could not move. Her body was heavy. She wanted to shout but could not and realized that it was Ulbaia's spirit that made her feel that way. 'But if papa wants to come back like that, it is all right. I was not afraid, only happy to be close to him,' Soufa said.

Later the *manvara* again went to the beach. They washed in the sea and rested in the shadow until late in the afternoon. Saea came with some food for them and they ate before they again smeared ashes on their faces and on the rest of their bodies. They went up to the village. In front of Kumi's house, some of the villagers had formed two rows, outlining a pathway. They had each prepared a stick from the stem of a sago leaf onto the tip of which they had fastened a leaf from a stinging nettle (lat. *Laportea*). If, by accident, you got near this nettle in the bush, your leg or arm would burn and itch for days – a most unpleasant experience. Wogeos use such leaves for pain relief, maintaining that the sting from the nettle would chase the real pain away.[9] As the *manvara* walked towards the house, they raised their arms over their heads, and people beat them with the sticks tipped with the nettle: those on one side on their chests and those on the other side on their backs. The people holding the sticks had also been given a piece of bespelled ginger. The ginger was chewed and the saliva sprayed over the *manvara* as they walked by. Both the ginger and the nettle heated the *manvara's* bodies, and the beating was supposed to chase away Ulbaia's spirit. During the celebration of a girl's first *baras*, an imitation of this custom is carried out when the girl returns to the village after having 'buried' her childhood on the mountain (Anderson 1996). Then the *manvara* entered Kumi's house where the corpse had been placed. Inside the house some women held branches crawling with ants and burning palm leaves over the doorway as the *manvara* ran through the door. Screaming and shouting, the women shook the branches and the burning leaves so that the ants and the glowing embers from the fire fell down upon the *manvara*. Then the women ran out and threw the branches and the leaves into the bush. The people who had beaten the *manvara* followed and threw away their sticks. Now they had chased the spirit of the dead away from the house.

Inside the house, the *manvara* were given betel nuts and ginger that they chewed and sprayed on their skin. Plates of the special dish *sur* had been prepared. *Sur* is, as already mentioned for the *baras* celebration, a mix of boiled vegetables, grated coconut meat, ginger, chilli and *oaila* and has the effect of heating people in dangerous, transitional states (see also Hogbin 1970b: 56). Some of the *oaila*

Photo 5.1: Mourners beating the spirit away from the *manvara*

leaves were removed, and the women pressed these on the *manvara's* bodies: on their jaws, on the front and back of their upper bodies, and on their legs and arms. This was again to strengthen the joints. Afterwards the leaves were placed under the floorboards. There they would dry and then be thrown on the sea. The *manvara* now carried with them the plates of *sur* and went to a place beyond Oare, the beach towards Joboe.

There the *manvara* went into the bush and found some mud that they dissolved in the sea. They dived into the sea and surfaced where the mud was mixed with the saltwater to hide from the spirit. If there had been any muddy freshwater nearby, they would have washed there, but since there was no such water in the vicinity, the *manvara* instead mixed mud in the sea. They rubbed their skins with the rest of the *oaila* from the food and immersed their bodies in the sea again. When resurfacing, they 'dried' their bodies with a white coral stone that afterwards was thrown into the sea. Pieces of ginger infused with magic were chewed and the saliva sprayed on a stone that they then moved around their bodies in circles. Afterwards the stones were placed among the roots of a large tree on the beach, 'making the spirit of the dead and all his worries sit down'.

Afterwards the *manvara* rubbed their bodies with roots from a certain tree that they had grated and mixed with white soil from the mountain. This mixture was described as cold. After all the procedures which were intended to heat the bodies of the *manvara*, these cool substances would bind the power from all the magic. They dressed in new clothes since the clothes they had worn the last day and night were contaminated with death and so needed to be washed or burned. A small fire was lit into which the *manvara* threw some fresh leaves that made a crackling noise. They jumped over the fire several times in order for the smoke to take away the smell and the coldness of death and again chase away the spirit. This ritual was also imitated at the *baras* celebration. Then they sat down and ate the *sur*: 'Now we can touch our bodies and eat with our fingers again.'

At sundown the *manvara* returned to the village, and the *kiamiam* continued. In the night Oaiari, *koakoale* of Kinaba, told me a story:

> *A long time ago there lived a woman called Gamuia in Moaroka. Her husband died, and Gamuia's grief was immense. Just before daylight, when people had fallen asleep, Gamuia went down to the beach. As she sat there, she saw a canoe filled with spirits of the dead. She saw her husband get into the canoe and they paddled quietly away, towards Kinaba. Gamuia could not bear to see her husband disappear, and she followed along the beach. She went to the beach of Kinaba and saw the canoe pass by. She continued to Tabele on the beach of Dab and saw the canoe on its way towards Joboe. She carried on and saw the canoe passing by the beaches of Joboe and Badiata. At last she reached the point beyond the place where Newcamp is now situated, near some stones in the sea. This place is known as Taoaoa and is a place of spirits. She sat down and saw the canoe come ashore. Her husband climbed out of the canoe and walked up on the beach to see the place for the last time. When he returned to the canoe, Gamuia grabbed hold of his loincloth. He turned around and said: 'Why have you come here? You have to go back to Moaroka.' 'Now, I cannot go back. I want to follow you,' Gamuia answered. She climbed into the canoe together with her husband. The canoe sailed towards Koil, and, since then, no one saw Gamuia again* (see also Hogbin 1978: 92).

Oaiari continued by telling me how Wogeo people believed that the spirits leave for a different place for a while – nobody knows exactly where – and then they return to their village; near their house. There they help their relatives and look after their house and their land. 'My father is buried near my house,' Oaiari said, 'and every time I have to do something important, like planting a big garden, I go to my father's grave and ask for help.'[10] The spirit of the dead is called *mariaboa* or *vanunu*, the latter literally meaning 'shadow'. Hogbin (1970b: 55) wrote that *mariaboa* was reserved for the spirits of the dead whereas *vanunu* was the 'spiritual essence' of living people. My informants did not make such a clear distinction – it was the same, they said. Kulbobo said that the equivalent to 'soul' in the Wogeo tongue is *malmalim* – literally 'your breath' – interpreting 'soul' (breath) as the essence of life and 'spirit' (shadow – *vanunu* or *mariaboa*) as what is left when the breath of life is gone.

I told Oaiari that in Hogbin's book I had read that the dead lived in a place in the centre of the island (Hogbin 1970b: 51; see also Smith 1994: 76), and Oaiari said that this was not the case. He had never heard of such a place. Before I had asked Tarere and Marifa the same question, and they also denied any knowledge of the whereabouts of the after world. Hogbin wrote that the dead found their way to Taoaoa and then ascended up to the place in the mountains. A possible explanation of this discrepancy is that the direction the canoe of the dead is said to take is described as upwards. A 'place on top' (*vanua iata*) could, thus, be interpreted both as 'a place on the top of the island' or 'a place in the upward direction'.

The following two days the *manvara* stayed on the beach during the day and returned to the village at sunset. They slept in Kumi's house and kept to themselves. Visitors from the other villages, together with the Dab people, kept on sleeping outside on the verandas or near Kumi's house at night.

On the fourth day the *manvara* went to the stream between Moaroka and Taro and went through the same ritual cleansing as they had done in Dab. In the afternoon all the people who had participated in the *kiamiam* gathered in front of Kumi's house. The women had cooked and carried plates of food with them. Some of the plates were presented to the *manvara* on Kumi's veranda, and the rest were placed on the ground in two groups. The women gathered around one group of plates and the men around the other, and we all ate. This was a communal meal and no exchange was involved.[11] It marked the break up of the *kiamiam* and was called as *jim masaoa* – literally meaning, 'empty ashes'. *Jim* in this context referred both to the ashes of the fires around which we had been warming our bodies and the ashes the *manvara* had smeared on their bodies. 'It is as if we all have had ashes on our bodies – like the *manvara* – and now it is finished,' Kulbobo later explained me. Saboakai, who had not yet left for Wewak after all, made a short speech and declared that when he returned from Wewak they should have an *olage*, an inter-village exchange of food in baskets. This was going to be the last work for Ulbaia, and pigs should be slaughtered. By arranging this *olage*, Saboakai would 'stand up' in his father's place (*malekati*). If he did not do this, he could not rightfully claim the place of Ulbaia and the rights that were marked for him. After the meal the visitors retuned to their villages – apart from the *manvara* and Nyem, Ulbaia's adoptive daughter. The *manvara* still had to go through ritual cleansings in Joboe and Jelalab.

In the same manner as both male and female initiands had to visit all the villages in the district in order to initiate and manifest their social relations within the district, the *manvara* had to do the same in order to finish off the dead person's relationships and make his spirit 'sit down' in the places with which he had relations. When going to another village, the villagers had to present the *manvara* with food. When they had gone to Taro in the morning, the people of Falala had sent for the *manvara*. They had gone there in the early afternoon. In Falala, Kalabaia had slaughtered a pig and cooked it for the *manvara*. This pig was the reciprocal gift for a pig Ulbaia had killed in connection with the death of Makanga. Kalabaia's wife, Keke, had called Makanga 'younger sister', and since none of Makanga's descendants were able to present a pig, Kalabaia took upon himself the obligation to reciprocate the gift from Ulbaia. The *manvara* had eaten on the beach in Falala.

I was told that we should expect two more pigs as reciprocal gifts in connection with Ulbaia's death. Mango, a *moede* from Badiata, should give one pig, since Maria's adoptive father had given a pig when Mango's father had died. Because all of Maria's elders were dead, Maria had told Mango that she wanted the pig to be reciprocated at Ulbaia's death, since Maria and Ulbaia came from the same side of Dab. The second pig should come from Talbul and Munjal, a *koakoale* and his wife in Joboe. Ulbaia had killed a pig when the man Kalabaia of Joboe had died. Kalabaia did not have any descendants apart from his daughter who was a Seventh Day Adventist and, thus, did not have any pigs. Talbul was obliged to look after Kalabaia's affairs in Joboe, and it was therefore his duty to reciprocate Ulbaia's pig. Such reciprocal gifts are spoken of as 'cutting the rope' (*oaro faraik*), meaning that the tie of exchange is cut. The gifts should either be presented to the *manvara* and the people of Dab while the *manvara* are still in mourning, or they should be presented at the planned *olage*. As it turned out, neither of these two pigs was presented at the *olage*. Probably they would be reciprocated on another occasion in someone else's name but then for someone closely related to Ulbaia or his place in Kajenamoa.

Decomposing the Composite Person

Strathern has written that 'a Melanesian death required the active severance of persons and relations' (1992: 99). As Ulbaia's *manvara* wandered through the landscape in which he had lived his life, his spirit was attached to the bodies of the *manvara*, and they had to 'seat him' in different places in this landscape. For the period of mourning the *manvara* can thus be seen as functioning as vehicles for his spirit and also for his social personhood – that is, his social relationships. Temporarily released from their own social networks (cf. Iteanu 1995: 143), the *manvara* acted out Ulbaia's set of relationships, following his pathways for a last time as well as physically washing off his spirit, and he would remain as a 'shadow' (*vanunu*) detached from the world of the living, although still connected to the places where he had led his life.

The wanderings of the *manvara* mainly followed pathways to the other villages within the district. All proper *manvara* rituals within the district should, as for the *baras* rituals of a young girl, follow these pathways. In people's daily lives it is relations to the villages within the district that are made most relevant, and in all funeral rituals within the district the connections to these places are manifested as obligatory pathways for *manvara* to follow. But when visiting the various villages, the relationships unique for the particular person are also made relevant: it is people with particular relationships to the deceased who give food to the *manvara* and cut ropes of exchange involving the dead person. Some of these relationships are determined by which side or *maleka* the deceased belonged to and others are based on kinship, marriage or other alliances – like the pathway to Falala in the case of Ulbaia. Pathways beyond the district are always about such particular alliances.

For the survivors, deaths disrupt social relations, evoke grief and loss and remind them of the precarious nature of life. The mourners gathered for the *kiamiam* comforted each other and worked through their grief together. Hogbin noted that the mourners (including the *manvara*) were referred to by the term for a dead spirit (*mariaboa*): 'People deny that such folk are actually ghosts but maintain that association with the deceased leads to a resemblance' (1970b: 159). The mourners gathered for the *kiamiam* can also be said to embody the social personhood of the deceased, although in a different manner from the *manvara* who took it upon themselves to carry Ulbaia's spirit on their bodies. As the cast of his significant others, the people participating in the *kiamiam* manifested and visualized the network of social relationships in which Ulbaia had been immersed through his life – that is, those that remained; Ulbaia was an old man and had already cut many of his significant relationships (those which had not been transferred to the next generation) through participating in other people's funerals. Whereas the *manvara* walked his pathways in the landscape, the participants in the *kiamiam* instead came to his *maleka* and manifested his composite social personhood (or network). They came to his *maleka* to honour and remember his life, and when the *kiamiam* was dissolved, when the 'ashes were empty', they disentangled and decomposed this social network that was uniquely Ulbaia's. Saboakai, as standing up in his father's place, would not be immersed in the same network, since his kindred and alliances were different from his father's: it was in the quite physical *place* of his father he stood up.

The Last Work for Ulbaia

A final work (*manif*) in the name of the dead was yet to be carried out – the *olage*. Battaglia has written about mortuary exchanges in Massim that 'these exchange events function as temporary memorials, culturally inscribing social relationship as an ephemeral coherence "located" in the particular person being honoured in his or her physical absence' (1992: 4). As a similar kind of temporary memorial, the display of food at Ulbaia's *olage* was the final manifestation of the relationships for which he had been the locus. It was held about a month after the *jim masaoa* and was one of the largest distributions of food for many years. Ulbaia had been a respected man in Wogeo.

Twenty-two baskets (*kamina*) of food, seven plates of food, seven pots of rice and five pigs were exchanged.[12] All the food was displayed in front of Kumi's house before it was distributed to the parties involved. Both Nyem and Saboakai had killed one pig each, and Maria contributed with the third pig. The fourth pig was a wild pig caught in the bush, and Badeoa from Joboe contributed the last one because his mother had called Ulbaia's mother 'sister'. Badeoa was also married to Gouso, Ima's daughter, and the food was given in her name as well, but his own relation to Ulbaia was in this context given pre-eminence. The pork was distributed to all the baskets.

Nyem contributed the largest part: four baskets and five plates. Badeoa presented three baskets of food. The families of those who had been *manvara* gave together nine baskets. Then all the five villages of Onevaro presented one basket each that were exchanged amongst them, as was customary at any *olage*. On this occasion it was said that these baskets were intended for the women who had taken part in the *kiamiam*.

Nyem gave her baskets to Niabula, his daughter Tangina and Ima's son Kalasika, since they had helped look after her father, and she gave one to the *manvara*. Badeoa gave his baskets to Saboakai and Niabula for taking care of Ulbaia, and the last one was given to the *manvara*. Apart from the baskets for the *manvara*, the baskets were reciprocated with an equal amount of food, but these were not included in the display. The gifts to the *manvara* should not be reciprocated. The same was the case for the basket that each of the villages in

Onevaro had contributed to give to the young boys who had done various sorts of work during the mourning – like gathering coconuts and betel nuts. The baskets from the *manvara* were exchanged among the *manvara* themselves.

The plates of food were presented to the men who had participated in the *kiamiam*. Maria explained to me that they got separate plates because the women were numerous, and it would be a disgrace if there was not enough food for the men in the baskets. In my experience, however, as a rule important men were given food separate from the women at any ceremonial occasion. The men were individually marked out rather than grouped together as the women were. The wives of the men on the receiving end of these plates contributed with reciprocal gifts of food.

Ulbaia's *olage* honoured his name and completed the work of putting his spirit to rest. At the same time the people who were not closely affiliated to him were compensated for the effort they had made in doing this work. The *olage* finally cut the relations that had been elicited as the central constituents of Ulbaia's social life during the funeral: relations to his immediate family and allies, to his fellow villagers and to the other villages in the district. The food representing these people was brought together in the display as a temporary memorial, and the large amount of food manifested the success he had had in establishing and maintaining relationships through his life. Then the food is distributed to the participants who carried it with them, dissolving the display and, thereby, cutting the ties. The work for Ulbaia was finished, and Saboakai could take his place.

Cutting the Skin

After this 'last work', the *manvara* and the villagers need to go through a final cleansing ritual. After all deaths, all the people in the village of the deceased – and others who have participated in the mourning – are prone to sickness. They have been close to the coldness of death, and contamination might have accumulated in their blood. In order to regain their strength and health, therefore, *manvara* and the whole village go through a ritual cleansing of their blood. The description is based on the rituals following a different death since I was not present at the last work for Ulbaia.

At sunrise one morning not long after the *olage* had been carried out, everyone went down to the beach. They formed a line with their backs towards the sea. A ritual expert took a *moanuboa* and walked from east to west along the line of people, sprinkling saltwater on their backs with the *moanuboa* while spraying ginger invested with magic from his mouth on them. Then they turned around and the procedure was repeated on the front of their bodies.

Then some of the women took a piece of broken glass or a razor and cut the skin of the mourners. They made small cuts on the joints and on the hands and feet as well as on the chest, stomach and upper and lower parts of the back. It should bleed properly, and if people had pains anywhere, they cut there as well. Before cutting, they washed the spots with a leaf and the water from a red coconut (*ni tongatonga*). After cutting they put on red soil from the mountain beyond Badiata mixed with the coconut water and two types of grated vine (*oar* that 'enters the cut' and *samite* that 'cleans out the sick'). Then they put on white soil from Wewak, again mixed with coconut water and the same vines. The red soil is powerful and hot, whereas the white soil is cold and binds the power. Finally they washed the cuts with coconut water mixed with the vines but without the soil.

Later all the young men in the village came to the beach with loads of green coconuts. Everyone gathered under lean-tos or shady trees, and the men start to scrape the coconuts in order to make *maoir* – a variation of *kadaga*. The elder men who knew the different spells and ingredients for the various types of *maoir* supervised them.

One *maoir* was particularly for the *manvara*: coconut meat and water were mixed, bespelled ginger was added and then hot stones were put in it. This type of *maoir* would cure *kol sik* (Tok Pisin for 'cold sick' – malaria and similar fevers). If people eating this were already sick, they would vomit and get diarrhoea, letting out the disease. Other types of *maoir* were for 'cleaning the stomach' and for other favourable purposes. The basic ingredients were water and meat from coconuts, with different herbs and bark from various trees added. When all the bowls of *maoir* were ready, the ritual experts chanted magic over them while moving wild ginger leaves over the bowls. Then the *manvara* ate from the one bowl that was heated, and then the rest of the crowd was served from the other bowls – men first and women afterwards.

Afterwards everyone ate *sur* that the women had prepared. The whole day was spent on the beach, eating, fishing and talking. Everyone was relieved that the taboo period was over and that the work for the dead was done. Some had gathered the ingredients for making *burenga* – the red ointment used by *baras* women – and the next morning the *manvara* and the villagers who wanted to would go to the beach, wash and rub their skin with the red oil, and their bodies would again be fit and prepared for carrying on with their ordinary lives.

* * *

Since dead people are not seen to easily accept their new state of being, people have to help placing the dead in their proper place. The spirit of the dead is attached to the people who handle the dead body and will stay with them unless they make him or her 'sit down' – not only as he or she is buried in his or her place (*maleka*) but also in the other places he is related to. Dead people – that is, their 'shadow' – can also remain near places they were attached to if they are not properly put to rest. It is particularly difficult for people who have died as a result of the intentional acts of others to get to accept their new status. A young man who was said to have been killed by *poisin* in 1993 was seen many times standing at the path between Dab and Joboe under a betel palm that had belonged to him. He had too many worries over his death, people said. For weeks people were terrified of walking along this path at night. Eventually one man got a piece of ginger, bespelled by an old man who had the proper knowledge, and took it with him to the place. As he approached he saw the dead boy standing there. The man told the dead boy with a friendly voice that he should go and sleep now. He chewed the ginger, spat some of it on a stone, and threw it at the ghost. And after that, no one saw the dead boy again.

In Wogeo, most deaths are explained by human agency or as effects of human action, and people are always in fear of death. Many precautions are therefore taken to protect oneself – both the state of one's body and the state of one's social relations. In the course of life people need to observe proper avoidance and conduct the necessary cleansings, and they have to maintain social relations in the appropriate manner (particularly through sharing and exchanging food), in order to 'sit good' in their places. When deaths occur, the success people have had in life in these matters are made manifest, and the efforts of the dead are commented upon and visualized through the cast of people participating in the mourning. They do a last 'work' (*manif*) in the name of the dead, and they eat a last meal for him or her. As the significant others of the deceased gather to do a last work for him or her, they act out their relations to the deceased for one last time, and their social relations are disentangled and cut. As the *manvara* walk through the landscape the deceased has invested with his or her life, his or her social (and platial) identity is decomposed and embedded in the landscape as histories to be remembered and paths to be followed for future generations. This landscape of places, paths and history is what I will turn to next.

Notes

1. Hogbin (1970b: 95) writes that also men who had summoned the *nibek* spirit were *manvara*. This was not relevant in the 1990s since the spirits were no longer summoned.
2. He is not mentioned elsewhere in Hogbin's writings.
3. Sanganie died some months later.
4. Hogbin (1970b: 159) wrote that the mourners were referred to by the term for spirits of the dead: *mariaboa* (*mariap*). I never heard this term used for mourners: only *manvara*.
5. For instance was Badeoa's role in Ulbaia's funeral not only important due to his marriage to Gouso, Ima's daughter, but also because of relations through his mother. Ulbaia belonged to the same moiety as himself.
6. For a further elaboration of Ulbaia's kin-relations, see chapter 9.
7. To forget the debts of the deceased are an important part of forgetting the social person in Sabarl funerary rituals. In Wogeo debts are not necessarily forgotten at a person's death but may be transferred to the heir of the deceased, other relatives or people belonging to the same side of the village.
8. Usually both men and women pointed out that women generally were physically stronger than men, and I guess Soufa here wanted to emphasize her efforts in helping her father.
9. Species of *Laportea* are commonly used as a counter-irritant throughout PNG (Paijmans 1976: 139).
10. See Smith (1994: 78) for similar notions in Kairiru.
11. What they called in Tok Pisin *bung kaikai* (lit. 'meeting food').
12. I was not in Wogeo at this *olage*, but on my request, Tarere made a detailed account of the exchanges that took place.

❧ Part III ☙
Landscape, Knowledge and Leadership

Prelude

'Mother carries the place' (*tiná vanua ebaj*) goes a saying in Wogeo. Roger M. Keesing (1993: 103) has pointed out that 'The symbolic construction of the earth as female, linking the fecundity of the soil to the fecundity of motherhood, seems deeply grounded ... in human primary experience.' So also in Wogeo: 'The ground is like a mother,' Wogeos say. Lutkehaus has noted from nearby Manam that 'the female body and the processes of human reproduction is a symbol of, and metaphor for, the social body ... and for social reproduction' (1995a: 199). Likewise, analogies of maternity are prominent in many aspects of Wogeo life – or, to be more accurate, innate female fertility and its lack in males; or unrestrained fertility (or flow) in opposition to controlled and instigated growth.

In the gardens women work with everything in the ground. Men usually plant bananas, they cut down trees, they climb the trees and shake down nuts, and they make the fences around the garden. Women plant taros, sweet potatoes and yams, and they remove the stones from the ground (cf. Hogbin 1938/39: 148). In a game sometimes played at full moon, Wogeos sing songs portraying women as taros and men as bananas.[1] Once Moita wanted me to plant a banana sprout in her garden so that when I had left, she could say that those bananas belong to Iamoe. She showed me all the stones in the hole she had dug, good for drainage to the roots of the plant. 'When we see these stones that are good for the plant, we say that "mother is sitting",' she said: *Tiná emoado*. In a song for a new canoe, quoted by Hogbin, the tree that has been cut down, carved and burnt is likened to a dead child, bereaved from its mother (its roots): 'O mother, mother, your child is dead; it lies stretched out and still ...' (Hogbin 1935b: 383).

Femaleness and motherhood are associated with soil, roots and seatedness, and maleness is associated with trees growing from the roots or the ground. In the powerful spell based on the myth of Goleiangaianga, a mother was holding the poles in a hole in the ground so that the men could climb the poles, like a tree rooted in the ground. The *veka* tree grew where the *veka* woman had been buried. Nat Kadamoanga kept himself alive by drinking sap from the roots of a breadfruit tree before he was found in the grave of his mother. Boys' umbilical cords are hidden in newly planted banana plants, and a girl menstruating for the first time should step over a young tree so that she will grow tall and strong with the tree (Anderson 1996). The souls of dead people are made to 'sit down' on the bases of old trees.

Kumi once said that 'Young people are like the stem of a tree; old people are like the leaves – all as necessary for the well-being of the tree'. The roots of trees are deeply planted in the place, and the branches reach out, intertwined with vines and lianas holding them steady. This image is given of the ideal state of the village in a magical spell supposed to secure the well-being and security of the village after the major food festivals of the past, the vines and lianas being metaphors

for kinship and exchange relations (Hogbin 1936: 271; 1970b: 182; 1978: 168).
Hogbin wrote about the spell:

> The headman who taught me the spell showed me how the *waluo* and *dabara* creepers
> grow up and cover a tree completely. So thick is the tangle of vines that in a gale the
> branches cannot rub against each other. Also, since the whole tree resists the force of
> the wind, it cannot be blown down. Further, as the creepers have thorns it is impossible
> to climb up and take away the fruit. The magic makes the village just like one of these
> trees. The inhabitants do not rub against each other, which means that they do not
> quarrel, other places are not able to overthrow it by force, and outsiders cannot come
> in and kill the villagers with sorcery. ... While reciting the spell the headman has to
> stand with his feet planted firmly wide apart. This 'makes the place steady' (Hogbin
> 1936: 272).

As suggested in the introduction, the relationship between a body and its physical
surroundings is, however, not merely a matter of analogies and symbolic
representations. In a phenomenological perspective, the bodily, sensual experience
of moving in a landscape is the basis for how we establish meaningful worlds.
Or, to use the words of Richard Eves (1997: 175), 'The body in its movement
through space is integral to the process by which the world is known, valued
and inhabited.' The image of rootedness is powerful because it is based on the
experience of the body seated in place and the body standing up and walking
through the landscape.

In this part of the book the focus is moved from the body to the landscape in
which it is placed. James Fox has elicited three different aspects that are central
to the understanding of the 'power of place': the organization and valorization
of space; the landscape of specific places and social memory; and the social
knowledge in an ordering of places (Fox 1997b: 8). In Wogeo, directions and
sides are ascribed positive and negative values and organize movements and
activities in the landscape accordingly. Landscapes are construed in terms of sides
and directions and accompanying values[2] – not merely as a matter of subjective
spatial orientation, but also conventionalized so that the island as a whole appears
as ordered in sides and directions. Further, the landscape consists of places
and pathways channelling movement (or flow)[3] between places. To Wogeos,
the geographical landscape of places and pathways and the social landscape of
people in relation to each other must be seen as mutually constituted. Belonging
to places is the most significant constituent of a person's identity, and they strive
to 'sit good in their place'.[4] Being in these places 'gathers' experiences, thoughts,
memories and histories around places and the pathways between them (Heidegger
1993[1954]; see also Casey 1996: 24). Or, said in a different manner, people's
movement along pathways between places gathers the people and places they are
related to into meaningful landscapes that are as social as they are geographical.

In the previous chapters it was described how taboos and avoidance focused
on individual bodies through experience, and representations can be seen as a part
of the constitution of persons vis-à-vis other persons and the phenomenal world.
The next chapter will take a different point of departure and first describe how

landscapes are constituted by people's experience of, and movement in, them and how landscapes as 'social landscapes' can be both images of, and loci for, the ordering of people's identity, belonging, relations, power and history. Secondly it will discuss the status of knowledge in Wogeo and how the offices of leadership and the distribution of knowledge are embedded in the landscape. This leads up to the topic for last part of the book: kinship and the politics of belonging.

Notes

1. The Manam similarly see taro as female and banana as male (Lutkehaus 1995b: 321).
2. Cf. e.g. Tilley (1994: 16), Tuan (1977: 34).
3. Cf. Roalkvam (1997).
4. This is also the case for the Lelet of New Ireland where, according to Eves (1997: 184), to be properly 'seated' is 'a highly desirable state'.

⊰ Chapter 6 ⊱
Sides, Pathways and Directions

Chasing the Stars

The Pleiades, the little cluster of stars in the zodiacal constellation Taurus,[1] is known as *baras* in Wogeo. If one looks at the night sky at the same time every evening throughout one year, these stars (*itú*) appear to move across the sky, from east to west. They mark the passage of a year, and *baras* is also what the Wogeos call a year.[2] When the *baras* stars are seen at a particular spot above Koil at a certain time of night, the New Year celebrations start (see also Hogbin 1938/39: 138–39).

In the rituals described in the previous chapters, the directions east to west and opposite were important – as in the first *baras* celebrations when the 'new woman' paraded through the village from east to west. East, the direction of the rising sun, is 'up' (*iata*), and west, where the sun sets, is 'down' (*bija*). The directions of up and down are associated with positive and negative values (cf. Fox 1997b: 5), and when walking around the island, one should start out in the upward and good direction to show one's good intention. In the cleansing on the beach following a death, the ritual expert moved downwards, from east to west. The spirit of the dead travelled upwards, towards east, in the good direction. The *baras* stars, like the sun, move downwards. As the stars move downwards, the Wogeos 'chase the stars' (*itú dafuraiak*) until they reach the lower end of the island where they are 'cut off'. When they chase the stars, they also chase all the diseases and pollution that have accumulated on the island through the year. As people's bodies are fragile and in need of constant care, so is the ground, and like a menstruating woman, Wogeos also regularly cleanse their island of pollution. Below will be described the various stages of the rituals as they start on the top of the island and move downwards.[3]

The first stage of the rituals is called *Itú die Lalaua boe Badiata* – 'The stars of Lalaua and Badiata'. The people of Badiata, at the upper end of Wogeo, are the first to 'beat the slit gong' (*giramoa datuk*) for the New Year (together with people of Lalaua in Koil). They do this some time in January.[4] As the stars rise over the horizon, they 'count the stars' with beats on the slit gong. When the stars are up, they start to sing and dance until daylight. On this night Wogeos say that 'the fence (*oar*) of Sepik River is opened' so that the water will flow freely past Koil and Wogeo, carrying with it many kinds of good things – such as the trading partners from Murik or logs that gather fish underneath them and that are good firewood when drifting ashore. A particular song was always pointed out to me when talking to people about the celebration in Badiata. It is about two men who carry a pig on a stick between them – a song associated with a particular star constellation.[5] The scene is dramatized with two men carrying a man impersonating the pig, and the villagers then chase the dancers downwards (westwards), out of the village, with a lot of noise and mock fights.

Then everyone goes down to the beach and washes with a type of *burenga* known as *ngadur*. Every matrilineage has its own type of *ngadur*, and the recipes are the secret property of the lineages. Afterwards the villagers return to the village and drink *kadaga* with the same ingredients. 'You have seen that some families have really tall and fat children. They have a powerful *kadaga*', Kulbobo said.[6] The *ngadur* and the *kadaga* will secure health for the people, particularly the growth of children. 'We drink *kadaga* to change the body', Kulbobo said, 'your good body will come' (*baikom detafas kalingó*). The ritual secures good crops and catches of fish for the next year as well – it maintains the well-being of the island. 'We change the ground[7] and good times will come' (lit. 'good island will arrive' – *vanua kalingó medetafas*).

The next stage of the rituals takes place some time in March when the stars are seen directly above the island and is called *Niu ba lalaba* – 'The big one'. Then it is the people of the middle part of the island – from the districts of Takur, Bukdi and Onevaro except Badiata – who chase the stars. At this celebration, people do not dance but beat slit gongs and drums and sing songs. In Dab they sing about all kinds of things that drift past the island with the tide from Sepik. The songs should not be sung on other occasions, but can be sung by anyone in the village during the celebrations. Some have been composed recently, other have been passed down through the generations. One song that has been passed down goes like this:

Fake kata kefat lona	A tree comes floating near the reef
Uldi dalele dalako bija	Its crown leans over and comes ashore
Uldi dalele dalako bija	Its crown leans over and comes ashore

'We sing this song so that good things will come from the sea', Kumi said. 'Like when the trees from Sepik drift by. Sometimes you can see that an insect like a grasshopper sits in such a tree. It comes ashore, and the grasshoppers climb off – just like people come by boats and Iamoe [my name] comes with cargo for the store in Dab and *lo* [trading partners] come with baskets from Murik.' In his account of Onka and Mafofo, Kulbobo also used the image of grasshoppers to describe the goods brought home from the trading partners. The image of the flow from Sepik was also used in the male cleansing from the tongue (see chapter 3). Another song is about *lo*, and, like the song about trees from the Sepik, this song is also about good things that come in this direction – even though these *lo* (from Sire and Samaf villages) are going to Wei Island and not Wogeo:

O kam oloolo, kam oloolo,	You *oloolo*, you *oloolo*,
kasabren[a]ren-te,	you are carrying so heavily,
ka-lako m ba[o]ia?	where are you going?

| *O kita-ne talako, talako Oeia,* | We are going, going to Oeia! |
| *o a o a o, o a o a o!* | o a o a o, o a o a o! |

The two songs cited above demonstrate the importance ascribed to connections to other places and relations beyond the island and the goods and wealth these relations bring to the island. Another short song is about securing another form of wealth: good catches of fish. The song simply asks a certain fish called *kura*[8] to open its mouth wide and to eat the bait on the fishhooks. In Tok Pisin Wogeos call this fish *bikmaus*, meaning 'big mouth'.

| *O ika ma kura-te, oaoam faoatí o,* | Fish *kura*, open your mouth wide! |
| *o a o a o, o a o a o!* | o a o a o, o a o a o! |

These songs should not be sung at any other times of the year, lest their power will be broken and good times will not come and the trading partners will not arrive.[9]

At daylight the people of the upper villages on each side of the island (Joboe and Gonamie) start chasing the stars from their village downwards to the next one, with mock-fights and a lot of noise, throwing sticks and hammering on pots and plates. When they reach the next village, the people from that village join in and continue in the same manner until they end up in Moaroka in Onevaro and Ga in Bukdi. Afterwards they wash with *ngadur* and drink *kadaga* as they did in Badiata.

In April the people of Bagiava on the lower part of the island beat the slit gong for the New Year. They 'cut the ropes' of the stars in order for them to 'go down into the sea'. Otherwise the procedure is the same as in Onevaro, although the beat of the slit gong is slightly different. One song that is sung in Falala goes like this:

Nat ta egongon Kada ilode	A boy is playing in Kada
Egongon kura mage	Playing by gathering sea in his arms
Egongon kura mage	Playing by gathering sea in his arms

Kada is a stream near Falala, and the boy is pictured playing where the stream comes out into the sea, trying to gather saltwater with his arms. 'They sing this to gather plenty of everything, like fish and so forth', Kumi said. The people of Bagiava then chase the stars to the beach beyond Juga before they wash with *ngadur* and drink *kadaga*.

The last celebration is in the village of Oanaba in Koil. There they look in a hole in the reef and see the reflection of the stars in it. Then they 'pull the *baras* up' – and a new year begins.[10]

Wogeos do have a traditional calendar that is the same all over the island, marking seasonal crops and the seasons of the south-east trade wind and the monsoon (see Hogbin 1938/39: 137). But even though the month for the catch of the *manuan* (Palolo worm) is said to be the last month of the year all over the island, the year does not end at the same time at the different places on the island. Rather, the end of the year moves downwards with the stars. The night of the celebration in the villages is spoken of as *vanua kaiukdi* – 'the bridge between the islands'. Probably it is the Wogeo translation of the rituals with the term 'New Year' which creates this discrepancy: after all Wogeos say that it is the island that changes, not the year. The 'changing of the island' can better be comprehended using the image of the island provided by Kulbobo: as a canoe in movement forwards or upwards (to the east) with the sea streaming downwards (to the west) along its sides. Like the tide from the Sepik that leads good things to Wogeo and the stars that travel downwards in the night sky, the passage of time flows past the island.

The Island as a Canoe

One afternoon during my second visit to Wogeo, Kulbobo asked me to come and sit with him. He had drawn an image on a flat stone: the contours of a canoe with an outrigger. 'Wogeo and Koil (the neighbouring island) are like a canoe and its outrigger (*kat boe vam*)', he said. His intention was to explain to me the

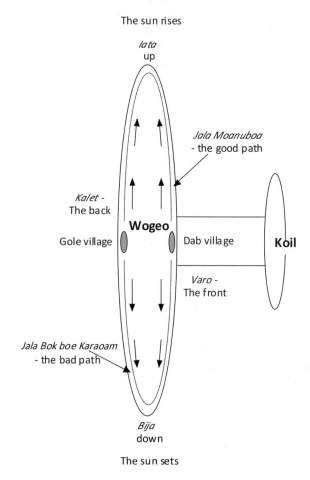

Figure 6.1 Koil and Wogeo as *kat boe vam* (canoe and outrigger)

distribution of power on the island, and I will return to this later in the chapter. First he told me about the different parts of the canoe: where the sun rises, in the upward direction, is the bow of the canoe. The aft is where the sun goes down. The image of the island as a canoe bears few similarities to the two islands as they appear on official maps (see Fig. 6.1), but corresponds well with how I had experienced the landscape during the time I spent on Wogeo.

The image was first drawn without any specific reference to directions and sides, but with the image of the canoe in mind, these aspects of the Wogeo conceptualization of space became clearer. The idea of the front and the back was first explained to me by referring to the front and the back of a body. 'The front [*varo*] is like the side you turn towards people. The back [*kalet*] is like that which is behind your back, like what you hide behind your house', Marifa said. Accordingly, the front of the island is, as already described, the side facing the mainland and the other visible islands, where the trading partners live and where boats usually come from. The back of the island is the side facing the 'empty ocean' (*boka masaoa*). In the villages, 'back' is the side towards the bush or the beach, and 'front' the side facing the village space (cf. Hoëm 1995 for similar spatial conceptualizations in Tokelau).

As you walk around the island, the mainland and the nearest islands disappear from sight when leaving Newcamp, at the upper end of the island (*iata*).[11] Walking along the beach towards Gonamie in Takur and in Bukdi, there is nothing to see but the vast ocean. Kairiru and, later the mainland, appear again after the mountain between Ga and Juga, the lower end (*bija*). As for Koil being placed in front of Dab, this also seems appropriate when walking along the coast on the front side. The canoe-like shape given to both of the islands is not peculiar since islands often appear to be long and oval-shaped when approached by sea. With this image of Wogeo in mind, it is easier to comprehend the movement of the stars from the top of the island until they are cut off at the canoe's stern.

This 'map' of Wogeo is imbued with values. It has already been mentioned how the front was regarded as more developed and sophisticated than the back. The directions up and down are valued as good and bad and are based on the movement of the sun and the stars. Upwards (forwards) is the good direction. A canoe steering forward also provides an image for *kastom* (*singara* – 'rudder') and leadership (*singare* – 'to steer'), like Kulbobo had told his eldest son: 'The canoe Dap is your canoe; you must look after it, you must steer it.'[12] During the chasing of the stars, pollution is chased from the upper to the lower end of the island. This leaves a clean and fresh path for the New Year, marked by the *baras* stars that through one year will move downwards across the night sky until they 'go down' in the sea off the lowest part of the island – or for the canoe to continue its travel upwards.

From Maria, Mats and I recorded a spell meant to stop long-lasting rainfalls (Anderson and Exter 2005: 90–91). Also here the movement from east to west was significant. The spell listed the names of rocks found along the coast of Onevaro, moving downwards from Jelalab. Maria chanted in a quiet, monotonous manner, but the mentioning of place names evoked movement (cf. e.g. Feld 1990; Fox 1997a; J. Weiner 1991); a journey downwards along the coast of Onevaro, asking the rain and the wind to stop in each place until the wind and the rain eventually were asked to go ashore near Taro and the hold-up in the bad weather would then be 'met with shouts of joy' (Anderson and Exter 2005: 91).

People moving in the downward direction are said to follow the path called *Jala Bok Karaoam*[13] – the 'bad path'. Bad things should move downwards. Hence, people entering a village from the bad path, that is, moving in a downward direction from where they started could be suspected of having ill intentions. Likewise, if someone in a village is sick and help is needed from a different village, the messenger should ideally go upwards, on what is referred to as the good path (*Jala Moanuboa*). This is, however, an ideal representation. People say that the good and the bad paths are not relevant if the villages in question are close. Nobody would suspect a Dab person entering Kliaba – ten minutes walk to the west of Dab – of having bad intentions merely because they were moving downwards. But if people come from the opposite side of the island, which path you move along can be significant. When I walked around the island together with my Dab friends, we started walking upwards, along *Jala Moanuboa*. If visitors come for an important occasion, like an *oaraboa* or a meeting regarding sorcery or something similar, the path they follow could signal their state of mind. This would have been particularly pertinent in the case of warfare in the past. Sorcerers have their secret paths crossing the interior of the island.

As well as referring to directions (upwards and downwards), this also defines the two sides (*valú*) of the island, with the villages of Dab and Gole in the middle. When in any village on the island, people would refer to the side on which the pathway came into the village as up and down or as the good or bad path. But

Photo 6.1: Women following a pathway to give away food

when speaking about the island as a whole, the paths Jala Moanuboa and Jala Bok Karaoam were conceived as starting in Dab and Gole, hence dividing the island into two sides: up and down. The organization of space and social relations into sides is common in Oceania[14] and I will return to this later in relation to the spatial organization of the villages.

Landscape of Paths and Places

The relationship between space and place is central in many studies about landscape. Space has commonly been regarded as prior to place in the way human geographer Yi-Fu Tuan describes it: 'What begins as undifferentiated space becomes place when we get to know it and endow it with value' (Tuan 1977: 6).[15] Tuan himself gives priority to the moving body through space and sees places as pauses in movement (ibid.). Another point of view is presented by Eric Hirsch who sees place as 'foreground actuality' and space as 'background potentiality' (1995: 4). Place has a 'here and now'-character whereas space becomes more indefinite: as a horizon (see also Leach 2003: 197–201). Casey (1996) takes a quite different position. He argues that it is place that is prior and general whereas space is created from movement in and between places, and this phenomenological stand leads us back to the concept with which this book started: that of dwelling.

Much of the anthropological literature on place draws on an essay by Heidegger entitled *Building dwelling thinking* (1993[1954]).[16] As described in the introduction, 'dwelling' (*wohnen*) signifies the nature of our being-in-the-world (*dasein*): as 'dwellers' the world is revealed to us through our dealings in and with our environment (1962: 95) – we do not see and interpret it as if we are set apart from it. Heidegger (1993[1954]: 350) denoted *wohnen* as meaning, among other things, 'to stay in a place' or 'to dwell at peace' (ibid.). To Heidegger, this implied that in the nature of man's being there was a capacity to safeguard and protect the place in which he dwells (cf. Krell 1993). In German, the terms *bauen* and *wohnen* are derived from the same term, and Heidegger points out that the original meaning of 'building' (*bauen*) is 'dwelling' (*wohnen*). People build *because* they dwell, they do not build *in order to* dwell (see also Ingold 2000: 153, 185–86). He also undertakes a trickier step and states that in the same manner as building is related to dwelling, *thinking* is related to dwelling. Our experience of dwelling (or being-in-the-world) is the basis for our thinking in the same manner as dwelling is the foundation for building.

Heidegger uses the example of a bridge to clarify his reasoning. The bridge across a river brings together the riverbanks on each side of the bridge. It makes the water pause as it meets the pillars of the bridge and it provides shade for the people who travel under it by boat. It constitutes a channel for movement in the landscape since people who want to cross the river will do so over the bridge. The bridge as a place lays bearings on how people experience the landscape. But the bridge also created the place in the first instance – not only its own existence as place, but also the riverbanks and the pathways leading to the bridge. Prior to the bridge, the riverbanks were not seen as related to each other. There was the river, there were the riversides, and people's movement in the landscape followed other channels than when the bridge was built. The bridge *gathers* the landscape around it.

Landscape becomes, in this sense, a set of relational places, linked 'by paths, movements and narratives' (Tilley 1994: 34; see also Bender 2006: 306). Barbara Bender has written that the term 'landscape' can apply to 'the creative and imaginative ways in which people place themselves in their environment' (2006: 303).[17] The image of Wogeo as a canoe is a very imaginative and totalizing one, with a great potential for conventionalization, belonging to a microcosmic realm of representations in the Wagnerian sense. In the macrocosmic realm, meaningful landscapes of places and pathways are brought into being through our experience and movements in them. It is as an abstraction of such experiences that the image of the island landscape as a canoe has been made. In everyday living, however, this generalized and conventionalized imaged landscape is concretized (and detotalized (cf. J. Weiner 1991)) in people's movement and actions. When walking along a pathway, people will relate to the directions and sides elicited by the image, although probably only seldom with the image of the canoe in mind. But when the need arises, the image can be evoked and referred to and will find resonance among Wogeos.

As mentioned above, the image of Wogeo as a canoe was first drawn for me in order to explain the distribution of power on the island. Dab is regarded as the capital of the island, and it was here Onka and Mafofo initiated the trading routes to the mainland (*Jala Baga*, lit. 'Mainland path') and the other Schouten Islands (*Jala Kat boe Vam*, lit. 'Canoe and outrigger path'). Dab is situated on the front and in the middle, at the bases of the important outrigger that holds the canoe steady. The image of the canoe can, in this way, be a politically powerful tool, but I have also been shown other maps with different emphases. Most islanders do, however, agree that there are *two* villages, Gole and Dab, which are more important than the others. They are said to be the original villages on the island, Gole being the oldest one as the site where Goleiangaianga descended from the sky. Dab and Gole together are the 'middle places'. Another image that was often used to explain the distribution of power was that the island is like an eagle (*taregá*): Dab and Gole are its body, and its wings stretch outwards, encompassing all the villages on the island (Fig. 6.2). The eagle is a common figure in Wogeo mythology, representing heroic capacities. The eagle is also the name of one of the matrimoieties. People belonging to Dab and Gole are sometimes referred to as *taregá ramata* – 'eagle people'. Gole, as the first place, is the head, and Dab the tail.

Hogbin also wrote about the particular importance of these two villages but ascribed it to the impressive personages of the two headmen Moarigum and Kaoang (in Gole) at the time of his research. People from other villages would deny the claim that these two villages were above the others, and 'the mythology furnishes little guidance, for interested parties make a habit of distorting or suppressing different versions to validate present conditions' (1978: 42). Also in the 1990s most Wogeos would elevate their own village compared to others – for instance, friends from Moaroka could say things like: 'We know that everyone elevates Dab and Gole, but you should know that Moaroka is also an important village. It is not a small place! Many customs originated in Moaroka. Many people first come ashore

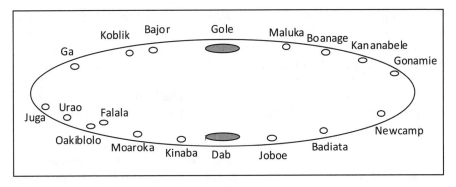

Figure 6.2: Idealized map of the island in the image of an eagle with its wings spread out

in Moaroka. The coconut came first to Moaroka. The *veka* came first to Moaroka.' But even so, people I spoke to all around the island agreed to the importance of Dab and Gole and pointed out that the Dab and Gole people were *taregá ramata*. In the 1990s the myths of Goleiangaianga and Onka certainly provided 'guidance' in this concern – as did the way the landscape was conceptualized. It is still pertinent to remember, however, that the Dab people were my primary informants and that my knowledge therefore inevitably has a Dab bias.

Village Landscapes

All the villages are divided into different parts. People in general claim that all the villages around the island are organized in the same manner, similar to the 'eagle-map' of the island with two sides and the middle (as in Fig. 6.3) and with the pathway leading through the village. The middle is the place where the male cult house (*nyaboá*) used to be built. A village is referred to as *malala*, which, according to my informants, literally means 'cleared, flat place', but the Austronesian term *vanua* (proto-Austronesian *banua*, see e.g. Keesing 1993: 94) for place, island and

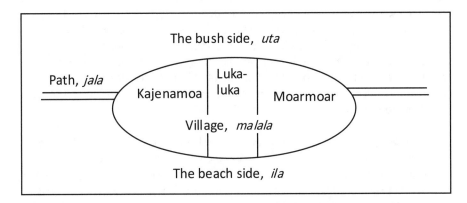

Figure 6.3: Idealized division if the village is in three parts, as in Dab

country is also used for the village. In Wogeo, *vanua* means 'island' but is also used for 'place' when some sense of belonging is connoted. *Malala* is reserved for the physical village, i.e. the settlement, whereas *vanua* refers to the whole area of the village, including the land in the bush and on the beach that belongs to the village.[18] If asking a Wogeo person which village he or she belongs to, one normally uses the term *vanua* (*vanua iko kaba?*). It is illustrative that the original site of Dab on the mountain is called Dabvanua – literally Dab's place of belonging or origin.

The parts of the villages are important: they are the most significant loci of belonging and identity in Wogeo. In Hogbin's writing through the years he made several attempts to describe the basic organizing feature of the localized groupings (*dan*) in Wogeo.

> The inhabitants of a village form a local unit, but each unit is split into two, and usually the half is more important than the whole. … Recruitment to this type of grouping is not defined by unilineal descent, and for an understanding of the principles it is necessary to know something about leadership, rights to land, and kinship (Hogbin 1970b: 18).

Hogbin described these groupings as the people living in clusters of houses grouped around the house of a *koakoale*: one cluster on each side of the male cult house. In his first reports from Wogeo he labelled these groups patrilineal clans (e.g. 1935a; 1935/36a) and stated that 'both succession and inheritance follow the male line, and the society is in every way predominantly patrilineal in sentiment' (1935/36a: 209). The term *dan* that is used for the groups literally means 'water' and is also a euphemism for semen. Hogbin interpreted this as referring to the patrilineal foundation of the groups, although his informants did not necessarily agree (e.g. 1935a: 316). In a later article he wrote that the local groups did not have a distinct term at all and said that the Wogeos 'deny them status as separate units' (1939: 120) but later he again changed his opinion about how to write about the groups. Following the lead of other kinship studies in the region he wrote that cumulative patrifiliation[19] resulted in what might seem as patrilineages, but that this had nothing to do with the local ideology (e.g. 1970a: 308). However, already in 1935 he noted that, 'the kinship system is clearly not a rigid framework to which everything must be adapted. … it is much more like a net which may be pulled and pushed about, and even cut and joined together again' (1935a: 317). Eventually he ended up using the concept of 'kindred' for describing the main organizing feature in terms of kinship, and referred to the work of Derek Freeman from Borneo (Freeman 1961; Hogbin 1978: 30–35).

> The [Wogeo] social structure … may be said to be based on kindred, the people whom a person recognizes as his cognates. A kindred is always centred on single individual or a set of full siblings, and the links are traced through males and females. … each person or series of siblings is the focal point of a unique kindred, which exists only for as long as he or they remain (Hogbin 1978: 30).

Freeman's argument was that kinship alone was not sufficient to explain belonging in the case of the Iban of Borneo; also residence had to be taken into consideration. Hogbin led a similar argument when discussing corporation and said that it was not only 'genealogical propinquity' that should be in focus: 'it ignores geographical propinquity' (ibid.: 32). 'The questions to be settled are, who live together and why?' (ibid.: 33). But, as Paula Brown noted when reviewing Hogbin's work, his analysis 'leaves some questions still' (Brown 1980: 136). Among the Iban, residence was based on what Freeman called 'utrolateral filiation' – that is, married couples settled in either the husband's or the wife's place (Freeman 1962: 26). Continuity was focused on the *bilek*, the residence unit within a longhouse, and its property, rather than on a line of descent. A focus on continuity embedded in place rather than lines of descent may prove to answer the questions Brown saw as unanswered in the case of Wogeo as well (cf. Leach 2003).

When Hogbin returned to Wogeo in 1974 for a last visit, almost thirty years after his 1948 fieldwork, he found that the organization of the houses into two clusters had dissolved due to the disappearance of the male cult house that divided the village in two (Hogbin 1978: 10–11). He noted, however, that the villages were still spoken of as having two sides and a middle (ibid.). In the 1990s I found that these parts of the village were still of great importance. If there can be said to be clearly defined local groups at all in Wogeo, they are the people who count themselves as belonging to the same part of a village as each other. All named houses had their particular place within the part, whether they were built or not, and when people spoke of belonging, they would say that they belonged to a specific part of a village. *Dan* is a general term for groups of people, but in the 1990s it was mostly used for people belonging to the same place – e.g. *Dan Kajenamoa* in Dab. The reasons given for a person's belonging to a place were not necessarily based on principles of descent or filiation. The different ways such belonging is created will be returned to in the next part of the book.

The parts of the village are important in many different respects. In daily life it is the parts that are the main foci of belonging and cooperation. They define where people spend most of the day and who works together with whom. Each part is further related to a certain part of all the other villages in the district with ties of reciprocal obligations and belonging, and on some occasions these parts participate on the same side of an exchange. Whenever people from different villages are visiting each other, they always go to the certain part of the village they are visiting that is related in this manner to their own place to sit down, receive and give *moin*, rest and eat. They maintain relations in the social landscape embedded in the geographical landscape by walking along the paths, acting out both the connectedness and the difference between the places. These paths between the different parts of the villages are often followed in the case of adoptions and marriages. When people spoke about the ideal form of adoption, they would tell how the newborn baby was also carried in a *kamina* basket along the path from its place of birth to the place of its new parents.

As already mentioned, people generally claimed that all the villages on the island were organized in the same manner, with all the parts having different names, like Moarmoar, Lukaluka and Kajenamoa in Dab (see Fig. 6.3). When I

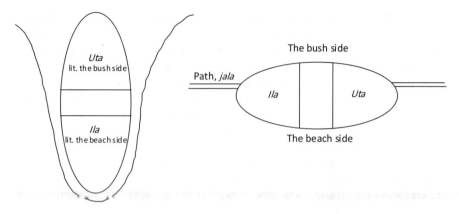

Figure 6.4: The village of Gole on the mountain and on the beach

went around all the villages on the island during my last visit and asked people about the organization of the particular villages, I found that this was not accurate. Not all the villages were organized in the same direction – this was especially true on the back of the island – nor were all the villages spoken of as having three parts. After having discussed this with various people it ended up solving a problem that had puzzled me for a long time.

Earlier (Anderson 1996) I had written extensively about the different parts of the villages since these were the prime loci of belonging. What seemed problematic, though, was that I did not manage to find a generic term for these parts: people always referred to them by their names. As explained in an earlier chapter, the villages on the back were the last ones to move down to the beach, a matter people from the front sometimes referred to in order to emphasize their superiority compared to the people from the back. In Gole the posts from the old houses could still be seen at the old village site. The old village site was on a narrow mountain ridge, and the village was divided into three parts: one towards the sea, the middle one, and one towards the bush (Fig. 6.4). The male cult house was placed on the outer end of the ridge towards the sea. The part facing the sea was called *ila* and the part towards the bush, *uta*. These are the generic terms for the side towards the bush and the side towards the sea wherever you are – they are directional terms like up and down. When Gole moved down to the beach, they organized the village in the manner that Dab and most other villages were organized, thus turning the village 90°. But the parts of the village kept the names *ila* and *uta* even though they no longer complied with the directions that the terms designated (see Fig. 6.4). When talking to older people in Dab, they said that the original site of Dab on the mountain, Dabvanua, also had the parts *ila* and *uta* and not Kajenamoa and Moarmoar.

When my linguist colleague started his work of documenting the Wogeo language, he found that in Dab the parts of the village were referred to as *malala* (e.g. *malala Kajenamoa*), a term I had understood was reserved for a village as a whole. The use of *malala* in connection with the sides I had interpreted as, for instance, 'the Kajenamoa side of *malala*'. In some of the villages on the back, however, they referred to the parts as *valú*, the term for sides or halves.[20] When I then asked people in Dab, they said that *valú* could be used (e.g. *valú Kajenamoa*, meaning 'the Kajenamoa side'), but that *malala* was preferred. After having checked this in most of the villages on the island, there seemed to be different variations on a continuum from the conceptualization of the parts as sides (*valú*) found in Gole to a conceptualization of the parts as more independent and named places (*malala*) as Kajenamoa and Moarmoar in Dab. It is, thus, likely that a change has taken place in the conceptualization of the division of the village as sides to a conceptualization of the village as consisting of named places following the move from the mountain sides to the beach, as seems to be the case for Dab and the other villages in the district of Onevaro.

Parmentier (1987) has written about place, myth and history from Belau in Micronesia. The Belauans organize their villages in sides, and Parmentier's interpretation suits well to describe the Wogeo conceptualization of sides as well:[21] 'A Belauan side is not like our notion of a side of a house or a side of a mountain, but rather is one-half of an oppositional pair in which both halves are identical, yet inverse' (ibid.: 111). In Dab, the emphasis on Kajenamoa, Lukaluka and Moarmoar as more independent places probably also has to do with Dab's political importance as 'the capital' of Wogeo: the middle place. This again is related to the division of the island into up and down and the good and the bad path. The *koakoale* of each of the two sides of Dab were said to have an overruling responsibility for the upper (the *koakoale* in Moarmoar) and the lower (the *koakoale* in Kajenamoa/Lukaluka) parts of the island. In accordance with how the upper part and the path *Jala Moanuboa* are spoken of, Moarmoar is regarded as a good place. In Moarmoar one should not fight, and when peace talks were held during times of war in the past, the meetings were always held in Moarmoar. Kulbobo described Moarmoar as 'dry' when he told the story of Mafofo and Onka. Moarmoar was dry – Kajenamoa, watery. Discussions about *iaboua* and planning of war were always held in Kajenamoa. Lukaluka, which is usually linked together with Kajenamoa, is also watery, but it is also 'a place with two faces,' people would say. 'You can never be sure if you are told the truth in Lukaluka.' I do not know enough about the other villages to say if the sides of the villages elsewhere were given the same qualities, but all around the island such qualities were connected to the named houses, which will be discussed later.

It was also said that only Gole and Dab had a middle part that was not merely the site of the male cult house but also contained named houses, but this is positively not true. Four of the five villages in Onevaro had a middle part with named houses, and this was also the case in several other villages on the island. Again, this could be due to the historical development in the organization of the villages, but more importantly the idealized image of the structure of the villages points to the privilege given to Gole and Dab as middle places, dividing not only the village into sides, but the whole island. Lukaluka in Dab is regarded by all Wogeos as an important and powerful place.

The Belauan and Wogeo relations to the landscape as far as social organization, history and politics are concerned share many similarities, one of which is that there is a 'contradiction between the village as a source of ideas of temporal permanence, structural stability, and spatial order, and the village as the locus of constant political, ecological, and demographic change' (Parmentier 1987: 59). From a distance Wogeos conceptualize the socio-geographical landscape in an ordered and uniform manner, emphasizing sides and directions. That the actual organization of the villages was different from this ideal topography was seldom commented upon and people were usually not interested in discussing it any further when the topic was raised. This idealized conceptualization of the landscape will be significant in my argument in the next chapters and points towards the relative fluidity and mobility of people in opposition to the anchoring and structuring capacity of places – places where people 'sit down' or 'stand up' (cf. Eves 1997). The next chapter will focus on leadership and on how traditional offices of leadership are embedded in the landscape.

Notes

1. 'Open cluster of stars, in the zodiacal constellation Taurus, about 400 light-years from the solar system' (Encyclopædia Britannica Online 2002).
2. Similar conceptions are found among the Usen Barok of New Ireland (Wagner 1986a: 40).
3. Unfortunately I have only had the chance to get spoken accounts of this event. I have, however, discussed these rituals thoroughly with people and, together with Exter, also recorded songs that are sung during the celebration.
4. Hogbin (1938/39: 139) wrote February.
5. Boro-suk and Boro-baj, lit. 'taking pig' and 'carrying pig'.
6. Hogbin (1938/39: 138) wrote that only male children were washed, but people made no such distinction when telling me about the rituals.
7. *Jer detabul*, lit. 'turn the ground'.
8. Species of rock cod and grouper of the *Serranidae* family.
9. People agreed, though, that it was all right for Kumi to sing them for Exter and me so that we could record the songs – as long as no one else heard them and we recorded them outside of the village.
10. I am not aware of when they do this in Oanaba, nor do I know exactly how they celebrate in Koil. In Manam, the New Year celebration is called *barasi* and is also associated with the Pleiades and is analogous to the cleansing of a menstruating woman or, more specifically, to a first-time menstruating woman (Lutkehaus 1995b: 146; 1995a). The Manam secure fertile crops for the coming year by washing palm-sized *barasi* stones representing the various crops and applying a coat of red oil to them before all the villagers wash and drink *ngaduri*. The New Year is celebrated at the end of the rainy season (in May and June) when the Pleiades can be seen at the top of the volcano crater in Manam. Lutkehaus does not note any difference in time in the celebration around the island.
11. The mainland is only visible from Wogeo on clear days.
12. *Kat Dab, kat iko. Iko mogodome, iko mosingare*. Similarly one of Hogbin's informants said: 'a village without a headman is like a ship without a captain' (Hogbin 1940: 32).
13. I do not have a proper translation for this term, but Kulbobo said that it meant 'something that bites'.
14. See e.g. Hoëm (1995, 2003); Hviding (1993, 1996); Parmentier (1987); Roalkvam (1997, 2003).

15. Casey (1996: 14) and Ingold (2000: 54–55) criticize anthropologists for axiomatically regarding space as prior to place, and they both mention Weiner's *The Empty Place* (1991) and Myers' *Pintupi Country, Pintupi Self* (1986) as examples of this point of view.
16. First published with the German title *Bauen Wohnen Denken* in 1954.
17. See e.g. Hirsch and O'Hanlon (1995); Hoëm and Roalkvam (2003); Parmentier (1987); Weiner (1991) for other recent studies of the salience of place and landscape in the region.
18. In Manam *malala* similarly refers to public space, whereas village, homestead and a place in general is *anua* (Lutkehaus 1995b: 262).
19. See e.g. Allen (1984), Barnes (1962) and Scheffler (1985).
20. *Valú* is also used, for example, for half of a song with two parts.
21. He refers to 'side' as one out of four fundamental spatial diagrammatic icons: side, path, corners and larger/smaller (Parmentier 1987: 59, 108).

⊰ Chapter 7 ⊱
Knowledge and Leadership

About once a week in Dab I would wake up to the sound of the 'bell' (an empty bombshell from the Second World War) being beaten. This was the call for a village meeting. I would drag my tired body out onto the veranda and sit and watch as people slowly began to line up in front of Singero. Often there was a lot of waiting involved, since people seemed to find these meetings a nuisance and only reluctantly found their way to the line. I use 'seemed' since such slowness and apparent disinterest in communal events is as much a matter of 'style' as indicating a real disinterest. After some months in Wogeo I found that I also was moving my body in the same lethargic and disinterested manner as I climbed down the ladder to join the others. While standing in line, only a few people would look at the speaker with attention. The rest seemed to have their minds elsewhere, and some could even turn their back to the speaker without any apparent reason.

The meetings were normally called on Monday mornings, the day marked for 'community work'. During my first year in Wogeo the councillor on the front of the island usually lead the meetings in Dab. If he was not present, a member of the councillor's committee usually replaced him. The speaker would slowly walk up and down in front of the line of people, speaking with the loud and self-confident voice that men used when speaking in public, pulling the words and pausing a lot between passages. Mostly he would speak in Tok Pisin, mixed with a lot of English words – one of the more popular being 'community development' and, in 1999, also 'human integration development' (cf. Smith 1994: 6). Usually the subject was the distribution of the chores of the day: such as cutting the grass along the path between the villages, clearing the village space of weeds, cleaning the church or sweeping the gathering place in Taro. At some point during nearly every meeting the speaker's voice would turn angry, and he would reprimand the villagers for not carrying out their duties or scold people for lack of moral conduct. Usually this concerned too much gossip in the village, arguments about pigs getting into people's gardens, or long-standing quarrels within a family. Sometimes separate meetings were called in order to resolve such quarrels.

One such meeting took place during my first visit to Wogeo in order to solve a conflict between a widowed father and his daughter. The daughter had been angry with her younger sister because she did not carry out her household chores when returning from school in the afternoons. The older sister had beaten her with a stick, and the younger sister had run away to her half-sister in another village. Later in the evening, the father came over and shouted that she had no business beating his youngest daughter. He claimed that he was so upset that he was going to burn down his house (a common way to express one's anger in Wogeo, but usually only as a threat[1]). The man was well known for his temper, and no one seemed to take much notice of the incident. He did not burn down his house, but over the following days his daughter refused to cook for him since he had reprimanded her in public. After some days her husband became tired of the conflict and asked Ioun from the councillor's committee to call the meeting.[2]

Ioun talked for a long while about how the conflict could disrupt the family. Anger between parents and children should not last more than a day and the involved parties should say what was on their minds and make peace. The father then talked for a long time. It did not matter whether his daughter fed him or not but she was not allowed to beat his other daughter. The older sister mumbled a few words. Ioun then concluded that the younger sister also shared some of the blame, being lazy, but the older sister should leave punishment to her father. In the afternoon all the inhabitants of Dab should meet and share a meal and that should be the end of the affair.

In the evening the sound of the bell could again be heard and all the villagers gathered in front of Singero. The women carried plates of food, and we all sat down. Ioun stood up and started to speak again: now the parties involved should promise with their hand on the Bible not to argue anymore. All the three 'sections' of leaders were present, he continued: himself from the councillor's committee, Tarere and Tagaoera from the church and Kumi as a *koakoale*. Now everyone had to stand up. Ioun talked about how important it was that both parents and children weighed their words and their anger. Tagaoera said some words about how families are falling apart these days and that it is a Christian duty to look after the family. Tarere said that now they should make a promise while putting their hands on the Bible. If they broke the promise, they would be punished with sickness and misfortune. Tagaoera then made the youngest sister swear with her hand on the Bible always to listen to what her sister told her to do. The older sister had to promise not to beat her sister or be angry with her father. The father was standing at some distance with his arms folded. He was reluctant to come over when they insisted that he also should put his hand on the Bible. Eventually he came over but did not touch the Bible or promise anything. Instead he shook the hands of everyone present, including his two daughters. Nobody made any further comments and everybody sat down. The men present then ate, as did the father and his daughters.

The events around this conflict well illustrate the distribution of the recognized positions of authority at the village level in Wogeo. The councillor's representative led the meeting and did most of the talking. The representatives of the church advocated family values and brought the Bible to settle the dispute together with the communal meal. Such meals are the traditional way of manifesting reconciliations: to restore peace and harmony in the village (Hogbin 1938).

A *koakoale*, a traditional leader in the village, was also present. Older men often complained about the weakened power of *koakoale*.[3] As in this case, *koakoale* did not play any important part in village meetings or conflict resolutions during most of the time I spent in Dab. When Gagin was home for Christmas in 1993, however, the situation was quite different: then there was no doubt as to who was the leader in Dab. Gagin as a *koakoale* stood out as a highly respected man with great authority. Everyone listened to what he had to say, and men who were otherwise speaking with authority would become humble in Gagin's presence. The village was always filled with people while he and his family were there. We celebrated the first *baras* of his eldest daughter; a traditional *tangboal* dance was arranged; there was always plenty of food, and people were light-spirited and enthusiastic. In Gagin's absence there were no *koakoale* to take his place. The ones who were eligible did not want the responsibility or did not have sufficient authority or support. Gagin, with his education and experience combined with his strong interest in Wogeo *kastom*, seemed to have a perfect combination of knowledge and competence to fill this position.

Forms of Leadership

Leadership in Oceania can hardly be discussed without reference to Marshall Sahlins' (1963) distinction between Polynesian chiefs in inherited offices and Melanesian self-made big men. Sahlins' typology has, however, received a great deal of critique – in particular his description of the Melanesian big man (e.g. Allen 1984; Godelier and Strathern 1991). Leaders that base their power solely on the accumulation and distribution of wealth are found only in some cases in the region, and hereditary offices of power – such as the Trobriand chiefs (e.g. A. Weiner 1976; see also Liep 1991) or the Wogeo *koakoale* – are not uncommon in island Melanesia.

Maurice Godelier introduced a third type of leader, based on his Baruya ethnography: the great man (Godelier 1986; Godelier and Strathern 1991). Great men are found in societies where male initiation rather than ceremonial exchange is central to public life, and where symmetrical rather than asymmetrical exchange is common. Accumulation of wealth is not necessary for social reproduction and a great man's status is ascribed and constituted by ritual. 'Domination is achieved through the ritual and other powers that great men have at their disposal, and through a male ideology promulgated in initiation rites that sets men's general powers against women's' (M. Strathern 1991: 1).

Wogeo leaders appear to possess characteristics from all these types of leadership: their offices are inherited (although they have to show their abilities of leadership to be true leaders), they engage in competitive exchanges and they are associated with male initiation. Perhaps they are better described as what Mark Mosko (1991: 97) half-seriously labels Melanesian 'odd men'. Such typologies are seldom suitable to describe the varieties of real life, but as Tuzin writes in his chapter in the collection: 'It does not matter that typologies – perhaps all of them – are fated to be overturned … a typology's undoing is also its moment of methodological fulfilment' (1991: 115).

However, in order to describe the offices of *koakoale* in Wogeo, I will take an alternative point of departure, based on a slightly different typology and accompanying conceptual tools. Based on similar themes as Godelier, Lamont Lindstrom (1984) argues that we can make a distinction between knowledge-based and wealth-based societies in Melanesia (see also Harrison 1989). 'In knowledge-based societies, men achieve power through successful manipulation and control of information and ideology' (Lindstrom 1984: 304). Lindstrom maintains that distribution of knowledge as the basis for inequality is found in societies where material production and exchange is based on principles of equality rather than increment (similar to what is the case in Godelier's great man societies). Unlike the typical big man systems where leaders achieve renown and power by accumulating and distributing wealth, leaders in knowledge-based societies attain and keep their position by demonstrating and, to a certain extent, sharing or exchanging their knowledge.

Chapter 3 introduced Wagner's notion of how the continuous work of differentiation maintains a beneficial relational flow. The flow in the first instance was that of human sociality, and in the second instance, fertility, spiritual power and knowledge (Wagner 1977b: 398). Knowledge is also part of the beneficial relational flow – a 'flow of messages' as Fredrik Barth (1975: e.g. 105) has described the system of communication of the Baktaman. Secrecy channels the flow of knowledge: it 'places limits on the relationships' (J. Weiner 2001) where knowledge is transferred; or 'cuts the network' (Strathern 1996) in which knowledge flows. Further, the flow of knowledge is channelled, cut or limited by placement and matrilineal belonging. Some bodies of knowledge are transferred (or flow) within the matrilineages whereas other knowledge is channelled through offices embedded in the landscape. It is to these flows of knowledge I will turn next.

Knowledge and Leadership

Traditionally Wogeo political power is associated with the distribution of certain types of knowledge (cf. Hogbin 1978: 44; see also Smith 1994: 31–33): knowledge people say that Onka left before he continued on to other places. This knowledge is spoken of as having been passed down through generations, as part of what Wogeos call *kastom* or *singara* – that which 'steers the Wogeo canoe' through time. Some 'sections', to use Kulbobo's word, of this knowledge are conceived as being more important than others and, in particular, this is knowledge associated with *oaraboa*. Only specifically chosen leaders would learn what is seen as the full corpus of knowledge. After the rituals that initiated the highest ranked leaders (*koakoale malala*, 'Chief of the village'), these new *koakoale* would spend some weeks in a little hut called *boaruka* – the term applied to the house a mother has to stay in after she has given birth (the term also designates a mother after birth). Kulbobo said that they could also sit in the *nyaboá*, the men's house (cf. Lutkehaus 1995b), but they would still be spoken of as 'sitting in *boaruka*'. While in *boaruka*, all men of knowledge on the island would come to see them in order to give them important knowledge. Only then would the new *koakoale* become good leaders, and, as the keepers of this comprehensive corpus of knowledge, they were truly powerful men.[4]

Lindstrom (1984: 293) distinguishes two types of knowledge as important in this concern: 'operational' and 'interpretative' knowledge. Operational knowledge can be instructions or scripts for 'ritual and other behaviour' and includes knowledge about land, history, names and genealogy as well as knowledge about national politics, language and the 'modern' world (ibid.). Such knowledge can be exchanged and even become a commodity. Interpretative knowledge concerns explanation and interpretation – the creation of meaning. Its potential for power and hierarchy is about 'semantic creativity', about communication of meaning and truth, and cannot be commoditized in the same manner as operational knowledge.

In relation to religious traditions, interpretations or explanations are commonly referred to as 'exegesis' – particularly regarding the explanation of religious texts. In his ethnography on ritual and knowledge among the Baktaman, Barth (1975) argues that anthropologists too easily describe their informant's elicitations of customs as representing a local exegetic tradition without taking into account the influence of the anthropologists' enquires that might launch "informants' in intellectual careers as analysts of their own society' (ibid.: 225). In carefully taking this into account while in the field, he discovered that the Baktaman do not have much of an exegetic tradition. The rituals of the male cult become meaningful primarily through experience. Barth maintains that the symbolism of the initiation rituals of the Baktaman is best explained as cast in analogical codes – similar to how Wagner (e.g. 1977b; 1986b) discusses symbols and meaning formation. Barth opposes the complex analogical symbolism in Baktaman ritual to verbalized communication in digital codes. Analogical codes are built on metaphors, 'which each separately derive their meaning from an analogy between symbol and that which it symbolizes' (Barth 1975: 227) whereas verbal communication would reduce the complexity of these ritual symbols. In Wogeo I usually got no explicit interpretations or explanations for ritual practices and taboos – this, for instance, was the case for the elaborate *baras* rituals – indicating that experience rather than verbalized explanation is primary in how rituals become meaningful to Wogeos also. Like the Baktaman, Wogeos can be said to have developed a 'mystery' rather than a 'theory' of fertility and growth. The Baktaman world in the late 1960s and the Wogeo world in the 1990s are, however, quite different. The Austronesian-speaking Wogeos have always had extensive contact with neighbouring groups through networks of trade and also, for a long time, with missionaries, anthropologists and other people with whom they engage in cultural exchange; in contrast the small Papuan Baktaman group lived in relative isolation at the time of Barth's fieldwork. Interpretations and representations of cultural notions thus have quite a different history in Wogeo compared to among the Baktaman. Wogeos also have an extensive oral tradition in terms of 'formal speech acts' (cf. Howell 1986), like myths, songs and spells.

None of my informants, male or female, had problems understanding what I meant when I used the word 'meaning' in connection with myths and customs, but women would seldom engage in discussing 'meaning' with me. They would usually refer me to men whom they saw as being in charge of such interpretative knowledge – not necessarily because they were unable to provide explanations but because this was a male domain. Kulbobo was clearly the type of informant that Barth referred to above in that he saw in me a chance to 'lift up his name' in becoming my teacher. My presence and Kulbobo's ideas of what I wanted to hear clearly influenced what and in what way he taught me. But I do not believe that this disqualifies his lessons as representations of Wogeo views of the world. Besides, the way he and others taught me was based on imagery and analogies that only became meaningful through the *experience* of participating in Wogeo life. Often he, and other men as well, would not elaborate upon the meaning of what we were discussing but rather used metaphorical images or told me a myth, which is a collection of such images. This was particularly true of Marifa, my oldest informant. In this sense, myths can be seen as explanations for practices. Sometimes, when I asked about a certain myth, Kulbobo said that it had no meaning in itself and used a metaphor that surely was not based on conventional Wogeo imagery but that he considered as being more intelligible to me: it is like a 'photocopy', he said, and meant a carbon copy. 'You see this paper and you know it is a copy of the real paper.' For instance he commented on the myth of Nat Kadamoanga in this way without giving further elaboration upon its meaning. In this sense, myths appear both as scripts for and representations of practices as well as explanations for these. As such, they comply with Lindstrom's definitions of both operational and interpretational knowledge.

I cannot be sure to what extent and in what way the knowledge given to male initiands in general, and to the *koakoale* sitting in *boaruka* in particular, was explicitly exegetic or explanatory in nature. An indication is, however, provided by Kulbobo who distinguished the different ways of saying how knowledge was passed on in the cult – 'the university of the beach' as it often was called: 'I show you the work' (*va manif uvatak iko*); 'I give you instructions' (*nanauva va ovandi iko*); 'I give you the story' (*nanasa va ovan iko*), and 'I tell you the 'talk' (*filava va obale iko*). To 'show work' to the initiands refers to ritual procedures and other types of work according to *kastom. Nanauva* refers to rules for proper conduct – like taboos and cleansings. Kulbobo translated *nanauva* with 'law'. *Nanasa* means stories in general, like stories about people, land and houses, and to myths in particular (*nanasa moa* – 'stories from the past').[5] The word for teaching, *nanarani*, is derived from this word. These three forms of knowledge – *manif*, *nanouva* and *nanasa* – can be labelled operational and the use of the term 'give' underlines Lindstrom's point that operational *knowledge* is something that can be given away or exchanged. But, as discussed above, *nanasa* can also be seen as explanatory and would then appear to belong to a category of interpretative knowledge.

Filava is different in that it is 'spoken' or 'told' and not 'given' or 'shown'. It refers to statements, speech or words about specific things or events.[6] The verb *filefile* can mean 'to give a speech' – like the leading men stood up and talked in the conflict resolution described in the beginning of this chapter. In Kulbobo's account of Onka and Mafofo he said that, 'Their *bolova* [planning], their *filava* they 'broke' in the village of Dab,'[7] presenting *filava* (and *bolova*) as an important genre of how Onka's knowledge is presented. *Filava sangarar* is the Wogeo term for 'metaphor' or 'parable'. *Sangarar* means 'close to' or 'similar', for instance that a village is 'like a tree' or that a house is 'like a mother'. In Wogeo such images or analogies are common means of explanation, of which I have already presented several examples – such as Kulbobo who said that Wogeo is 'like a canoe' or Moita who showed me the stones in the ground to tell me that 'mother is sitting'. Wagner writes about such imagery that 'An image can and must be witnessed or experienced, rather than merely described or summed up verbally. ... Image, of course, can be verbal – a trope or metaphor – but then it will retain metaphor's peculiar intransigence to glossing' (Wagner 1986a: xiv). Such images are used by all Wogeos, even though only a few may be able to elaborate upon their meaning, and, when they do, their elaborations may be quite different.

> *None* of these glosses are universally accepted – but, then, none of them has to be. The image presented in the metaphor *contains* or *elicits* them all, and all that is necessary is to retain the image itself. ... cultural convention exists at the level of the image, not that of its verbalized gloss. The key operations here are those of elicitation – a use of the image to provoke an appropriate response or understanding – and containment, the facility to encompass a number of possible interpretations (ibid.: xv).

Filava sangarar can thus be said to belong to a category of interpretative knowledge, as do myths that often are loaded with such images. Most of Kulbobo's lessons to me were phrased, at least at the outset, in such ways.

Even though it is possible to make a distinction between operational and interpretative knowledge in the case of the above-mentioned bodies of knowledge, it is not necessarily uncomplicated to distribute the various bits of knowledge to one category or the other. If myths and other 'talk' can be seen as scripts for, representations of, and explanations for customs, on the one hand, and if experience is as important in meaning formation as verbalized knowledge on the other hand, it is better to conclude that such knowledge has both operational and interpretational qualities, based both on experience and verbalized imagery or explanations.

Here it is pertinent to note, however, that what Lindstrom labels interpretational knowledge is not identical to an 'exegetic tradition'. Interpretational knowledge is the ability to 'convert personal interpretation into socially common knowledge' (Lindstrom 1984: 294). A local exegetic tradition will be a basis for a person's personal interpretation – whether this personal interpretation is in accordance with or in contrast to this tradition. In so-called knowledge-based societies men gain power by successfully communicating their interpretations. It might be useful to draw on a traditional exegetic tradition veiled in secrecy and obscure metaphors, only sparingly giving their insights. But in other contexts it might be convenient to redefine the situation altogether and even reveal secrets, creating a new and different platform for their power (cf. Errington and Gewertz 2001).

In Wogeo, the young *koakoale* who were sitting in *boaruka* were, among other things, given the knowledge to control the wellbeing and fertility of the island. Amongst the most powerful knowledge given to them were spells that would cause droughts, long-lasting rainfall or strong winds; the power to erect the *boaboaur* that pigs were fastened to during an *oaraboa*; the *kinab* spell that would secure the prosperity and peaceful relations of the village after an *oaraboa*, and the control of *iaboua* – death sorcery. The last leaders to 'sit in *boaruka*' probably did so in the 1940s. Such *koakoale* were the men who most aptly could demonstrate their interpretative knowledge in a convincing manner. They already had people's attention and respect, and if, in addition, they had rhetorical skills and charisma, they could increase their standing as leaders by being able to convince their followers of the truth of their definitions and explanations of events. Like his grandson Gagin, Moarigum had been such a man. More than fifty years after his death he was still spoken of with awe and respect. It was due to his affiliation to Moarigum that Hogbin had received 'all the power of Wogeo', people said.

I have heard Moarigum's wife, Iamoe, described as being 'above' Moarigum: she was a true *moede*, being both the daughter and wife of a *koakoale*, and gave Moarigum the right to live in the powerful house Singero. This was, however, an extraordinary case: everyone spoke of Iamoe with respect, and she must have been an exceptional woman – Hogbin describes her as 'as much of a personage amongst the women as he [Moarigum] is amongst the men' (1938: 226; see Hogbin 1978 between pages 84 and 85 for a photo of Iamoe [Yam]). Hogbin writes that the position of *moede* had to be earned by demonstrating authority in women's affairs and being a good wife to her husband, always having an abundance of food to offer guests. In 1934, he wrote, there was only one *moede* in Wogeo, namely Iamoe (1978: 43). I learnt about the *moede* position differently: the eldest daughter of a *koakoale* was a *moede*, and if she married a *koakoale*, she would continue being a *moede* all her life. But, in the same way as a *koakoale*, a *moede* only became truly powerful by successfully demonstrating her authority and knowledge. *Moede* could have quite a great amount of power: they could stop fights, control the flow of food at exchanges and influence political processes backstage. 'Women think good thoughts located in the stomach and men bad thoughts located in the head,' people said.

'Everything goes in fours'

Kulbobo had been sitting together with his cousin, an important *koakoale*, when the cousin had been given knowledge from his mentors (*tilab*). This *koakoale* did not sit in *boaruka* since the custom at that time had been abandoned, but he was still given large parts of the important knowledge.[8] Kulbobo was a young man at the time and had been instructed to sit quietly and listen but not to tell anyone what he learnt. In spite of his promise of secrecy, he felt it important to teach me what he called the 'full knowledge' of Wogeo. Knowing that his disease would soon end his life, he seemed to regard this as the last chance to demonstrate his knowledge. As much as a means of preserving Wogeo *kastom*, Kulbobo's endeavour to pass on his knowledge to me was a way of manifesting his position as a true *koakoale*. Kulbobo wanted my 'book' to show people that he had been a man of knowledge, similar to how the power and knowledge of Moarigum and the other great *koakoale* of the 1930s and 40s had been made manifest and kept in Hogbin's books. Kulbobo was also one of few who openly questioned whether Hogbin knew it all or not, opening the possibility that my 'book' could reveal new truths and, thus, lift his name up.

Among the knowledge Kulbobo gave me that Hogbin did not write about concerned the distribution of the most powerful offices of authority in Wogeo. Onka laid the foundations for Wogeo's overall leadership, and he placed this overall power in Dab, at least according to the Onevaro people. 'Everything in Wogeo goes in fours', Kulbobo said:

You know we count everything in fours, like we count coconuts.[9] There are four districts on the island, four original villages and four pathways. The districts were Onevaro, Takur, Bukdi and Bagiava. The villages were Gole, Dab, Ga and Oaoa.[10] The pathways were Kureo, Damsalaga [crossing the island], Jala Moanuboa and Jala Bok Karaoam [rounding the island]. In Dab Onka left four houses, four ro, four baskets, four men, and four women. The houses were Singero, Ruma Bua, Omdara and Bagura. The ro were Saoang Ngaud, Giririmba, Tokodub and Tarajimba. The men were Saoang, Ngaud, Kintabi and Boaiak. The women were Moede, Buruka, Makena and Segilma. These were the first.

When Kulbobo first drew the map of Wogeo as a canoe, he wanted to tell me about the four baskets (*goate*). As already mentioned all Wogeos carry a basket with them everywhere they go. The baskets referred to here are different: they are embodiments of a specific kind of power. There were four baskets on the island: two big ones and two smaller ones (the size refers to the power of the baskets, not the actual size). From the outset all of them were in Dab. Two of the baskets belonged to Moarmoar and the other two to Kajenamoa and Lukaluka. Then Moarmoar sent one to Koil and Kajenamoa/Lukaluka sent one to Bajor. Kulbobo drew the map of the canoe in order to explain this to me and he drew the baskets as shown in Figure 7.1.

These baskets were indeed powerful, both for good and bad. The *koakoale* who held the right to such a basket could in some cases decide over life and death and he was feared and respected. First of all this has to do with sorcery. Some Wogeos

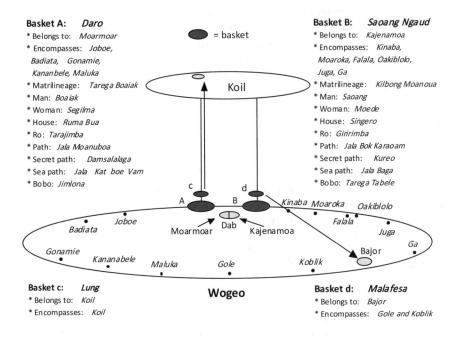

Figure 7.1: The baskets of power (*jonga*)

have the knowledge of how to kill people with magic called *iaboua*.[11] According to most people, Goleiangaianga initiated *iaboua* while he was in the village of Noba (presently Falala) after he had left Gole. Others would maintain that *iaboua* came from outside of Wogeo. Summing up the accounts I heard of *iaboua*'s origin, it was generally agreed that Goleiangaianga initiated the practice as a means of sanction but that some people started to misuse it, and the practice got out of control. It was usually claimed that these people belonged to matrilineages that had come to Wogeo from overseas.

Common to the accounts saying that *iaboua* originated in Wogeo was that *iaboua* originally was a good thing, used as a means of control and sanction. If a person had killed someone without a good reason or committed adultery or other crimes without paying compensation, the leading men on the island could agree that it would be a proper punishment to kill the man with *iaboua*. The complainants would approach one of the *koakoale* holding a basket and present their grievance. He would contact the other *koakoale* holding baskets, and, if they all agreed that *iaboua* was called for, they would put a *jonga* (circular boar's tusk) in the basket and an assassin would be contacted.[12] If someone used *iaboua* without having a *jonga* in one of the baskets, he or she could expect that they themselves would be murdered. The relatives of the victim could later go and ask the *koakoale* whether he had a *jonga* in the deceased's name in his basket. If he did, and the *koakoale* agreed, they could themselves put a *jonga* in the basket and revenge the murder. In the 1990s, people claimed that *iaboua* was out of control, and many deaths were suspected to be the result of sorcery.

The baskets were said to encompass the different areas of the island. The *koakoale* holding the basket in Moarmoar would control the upper part of the island, and the *koakoale* holding the one in Kajenamoa/Lukaluka, the lower part of the island – except for the district of Bukdi, which was controlled by the *koakoale* holding the basket in Bajor. When given the right to a basket, they also got the rights to names, houses and *ro* associated with the basket. In addition they were in charge of the specific paths on land and sea and the secret path crossing the island that people on *iaboua* missions used. They also had assistants called *bobo*, meaning 'butterfly'. They were informants about people's doings – 'like a butterfly that flies around and comes and sits on your basket'. The identity of the *bobo* was not publicly known. Kulbobo could only tell me the details of what the baskets in Dab contained in terms of names of houses, paths and *bobo*.

The *koakoale* were given the baskets to carry when they were dressed up in their inherited finery at the completion of the male initiation. Wogeos inherit rights to wear certain jewellery and body decorations with particular names and designs, resembling what Lipset (1997) has called the 'heraldry' of descent groups in Murik. In Wogeo such heraldry is often the property of matrilineages but people also inherit jewellery and rights to wear certain designs from their father. As is the case for the Manam chiefs (*tanepoa*), the *koakoale* are the only ones who are allowed to carry circular boar's tusks (*jonga*) and other sorts of 'chiefly regalia' (Lutkehaus 1995b: 289) – like the baskets of power that also are called *jonga*.

The baskets also contained other sorts of power and knowledge, but Kulbobo did not tell me much about this. He was the last one who really knew anything about them, he claimed, but this was something from the past that was not good. The most important thing to understand in relation to the baskets was the ability and necessity of controlling *iaboua*. All the four baskets were gone, people claimed. The men holding the baskets had decided that it was time to abandon the customs that were not beneficial for the people of Wogeo, and, since *iaboua* had been out of control for a long time, the 'good work' of the baskets was lost anyway. The last basket – the one belonging to Moarmoar – was said to have been buried together with a man who died in Badiata the day I set foot on Wogeo for the first time in 1993. He had the right to live in Ruma Bua in Badiata and was what is called 'one house' with the basket-holder in Moarmoar. The other baskets had also been buried, although people would make a point of saying that 'we are not sure, but they *say* that they have buried the baskets'.

Koakoale and Matrilineages

According to Kulbobo's elaborations, the two *koakoale* in Dab holding the baskets were the most powerful men in Wogeo. These offices are associated with two matrilineages – *tiná* Boaiak and *tiná* Moanoua. *Tiná* Boaiak is the lineage holding the basket in Moarmoar and the house Ruma Bua, whereas *tiná* Moanoua has the basket of Kajenamoa/Lukaluka and the house Singero. Marriage is nominally exogamic on moiety-level, that is, a Taregá should marry a Kilbong, and a son is therefore usually of the opposite moiety from his father. In spite of the rule of exogamy, marriages within the matrimoiety are not uncommon. Marriage within a matrilineage is, however, regarded as particularly bad. I know of only one such marriage in the Onevaro district, and the couple had gone through a lot of trouble before people accepted their marriage.

As a rule a *koakoale* inherits his position from his father of a different matrilineage, and this causes a situation reminiscent of what has been labelled the 'matrilineal puzzle' (see e.g. Holy 1996: 102). How can the continuity of these offices belonging to the matrilineages be secured when patrifiliation is the norm of inheritance? Since adoption is common in Wogeo, a solution for securing the continuity of the matrilineage in the associated *koakoale* position could be for the *koakoale* to adopt his sister's son. This is, however, the only form of adoption that is strictly tabooed: you should not call your mother's brother (or any man in your matrilineage) 'father'. Viriavunculocal residence, which is the solution for men holding matrilineally inherited chieftainships in the Trobriand Islands (e.g. A. Weiner 1988; see also Allen 1984: 30), is also not an option for Wogeo *koakoale*: they should inherit their father's position.

'We exchange', Kulbobo said. If a *koakoale* in Moarmoar is of the Moanoua family, he should marry a woman from the Boaiak family. A *koakoale* of the Boaiak family in Kajenamoa should marry a woman from the Moanoua family. The sons of these marriages would then have the proper identity for the offices: only a Moanoua man will stand up as a true *koakoale* in Kajenamoa, and only a Boaiak man as a true *koakoale* in Moarmoar. According to this notion, it is only in every second generation the sides have a *koakoale* of the proper matrilineal identity.

These matrilineages are also associated with the values ascribed to the sides of the island. As the upper part of the island, the path Jala Moanuboa and the house Ruma Bua are regarded as 'good', so is the Boaiak family. On the other hand, the Moanoua family associated with Kajenamoa, Singero, and the path Jala Bok Karaoam, is regarded as possessing dangerous knowledge and is often said to be 'no good'. This is not primarily attributed to 'naturally' inherited tempers but due to what Gagin has described as the 'tasks' or specializations of the lineages – similar to what Lutkehaus (1990: 187) describes as the 'special capabilities' of certain chiefs (*tanepoa labalaba*) and their descendants in Manam. Simon Harrison (1990: 66) points out that such ritual specialization of descent groups in Melanesia is typically associated with ideologies of rank. Allen (1984: 25) notes that such ranking is uncommon in societies with patrilineal descent systems, and uses Wogeo (based on Hogbin 1978) as an example of a society with patrilineally inherited leaders without ranking of lineages. It is quite to the contrary, then, but still in adherence with Allen's thesis that specialized and ranked *matrilineages* can be added to the Wogeo ethnography.

Gagin describes the Moanoua family in the following manner: 'A warlike family. Talks about wars, initiates wars and trouble, kills, murders, leads others to war, leaves no time for peace and harmony. They are warriors all their lives.' The emblem of this family is a spear adorned with cassowary feathers (named Salagalaga). They also possess a magical stone with the capacity to make people strong warriors. One man of this lineage told me that he had this stone in his possession. It was a very small stone that one could keep in one's pocket. He had several times tried to throw it away, since he thought its powers to be of no benefit to the people, but somehow it always turned up again. He just let it lie there and never wanted to use it, he said.

The Boaiak family has two branches, and, according to my informants, it is the branch called Boaiak Saumgum that is in charge of Moarmoar and Ruma Bua. The Boaiak Saumgum lineage is described by Gagin as 'A planner of peace: Plans discussions about peace, plans and initiates feasts, big ceremonies and *tangboal* dances, organizes inter-district celebrations. Restores peace throughout the island.' According to Gagin, this lineage is 'symbolized by the *dabara* vine' that is used to make garden fences. '*Dabara* holds fast so that there will be no trouble, no wars, and peace and harmony will prevail on the island.' Their emblem is a *moanuboa* – the *moanuboa* of peace.

Kulbobo meant that the *dabara* vine was the property of the Moanoua family and that the Boaiak family had a vine that was called *boaboag*. With these they could 'tie together' the place where it was 'broken' – at times of conflict and unrest. Parts of the *kinab* spell that was recited after an *oaraboa* uses the image of a tree with vines: 'The tree standing tall, fastened securely, covered entirely, with *oaluo* and *dabara* vines. My beloved village, fastened securely, covered entirely, with *oaluo* and *dabara* vines' (Hogbin 1936: 271; 1970b: 182; 1978: 168). Kulbobo had not heard of the *oaluo* vine but it could be that this was another name for the *boaboag* vine of the Boaiak family.

The Boaiak Saumgum matrilineage has a history that is significant here. Boaiak Saumgum lived in the village of Oaoa, one of the four villages reckoned to be the original and most important ones on the island. Oaoa was located in Jelalab Bay on the far eastern side of the island, on the upper end of the canoe as described in chapter 1. On this spot there is not only a beautiful beach, there are also large flat areas of land that are ideal for gardening; but in spite of this, the area has not been inhabited or cultivated for at least a hundred years, people said, and probably more. Hogbin (1939: 117) describes the area as never having been inhabited. According to how people counted the generations that had passed, it must have been sometime in the middle of the nineteenth century that a conflict arose between the Oaoa villagers and the people of Badiata. The leading men on the island had a meeting and decided that they wanted to eradicate the village and its inhabitants from the face of the earth because of their wrongdoings. Boaiak Bolova did the planning – *bolova* is the word for 'planning'. During the dark of night, a crowd of men attacked the village and killed all the villagers – men, women and children. Only a few people had been told about the plans and had been promised refuge by their allies; among them were Boaiak Saumgum, one of the leading men of Oaoa. He escaped with his family to Boaiak Bolova, who was *koakoale* in Dab. In order to avoid further conflict, Boaiak Saumgum was said to belong to the same matrilineage as his host, who actually belonged to a different branch of a more encompassing family and, through time, this became the generally accepted truth, and only a few people knew the true story. Below follows the story as Gagin wrote it in a letter in 1998:[13]

Forefather Boaiak (Saumgum) lived in Oaoa, a village on the eastern tip of the island, with his people. The village was heavily populated. A woman from Badiata was murdered at Saoalo Ilod. As that area of land was not within the boundary of Badiata, and Oaoa land boundary was up to Koarug River, the blame for the death was given to Oaoa village and its chief. Badiata landmark is up to Vaf creek, and not to Koarug River. Badiata then planned a revenge against Oaoa village. A boy had been adopted from Tiná Moanoua from the village of Taro (present site of the Catholic Mission) by Badiata folk in the part of the village called Kurita. The boy grew up to be a young man and he was the one to make war on Oaoa village. All planning of the war was done in Dab by Boaiak (Bolova), the chief of Moarmoar. All six villages of Onevaro district combined (Taro to Badiata) surrounded the village of Oaoa and killed men, women and children early one morning. Some people escaped in canoes to Koil and Oei islands and a few to Takur District. The warrior arrested Boaiak (Saumgum). The chief came with his own house and rebuilt it in Dab. So the house Masa-masa Matam Nara came into being in Dab from Oaoa, through the chief Boaiak (Saumgum).

Boaiak Saumgum held 'the *moanuboa* of peace' and this was the reason he was not killed: he was a man of peace. Boaiak Saumgum was said to 'hide' within the Boaiak of Dab's matrilineage, meaning that they were spoken of as being of the same family. The house Masamasa Matam Nara was a mark of the peaceful relationship established between them and the boy of the Moanoua family who started the war. Kulbobo's (of *tiná* Moanoua) marriage to Sanum, from the Boaiak Saumgum family, that gave him the right to live in Masamasa Matam Nara was said to follow this 'path' or 'story'.

In 1993/94 people would usually not disclose who was of *tiná* Boaiak Saumgum unless it was obvious that the people present knew the story. People would often describe this lineage as 'no good'. In 1998/99 the situation seemed to have been altered, and I eventually got an explanation for this change. A different matrilineage of the Taregá moiety was regarded as having come from the mainland. They were said to stir up problems, behave immorally and use *iaboua* frequently. In order to give them a chance to change their manners, the Boaiak Saumgum lineage had, several generations ago, given them the *moanuboa* of peace, and Boaiak Saumgum took it upon themselves to be the scapegoat for *iaboua* suspicions (how they actually managed to do this I am not sure). Through the years, the lineage allegedly from the mainland changed for the better. Eventually it was decided that Boaiak Saumgum again should hold the *moanuboa* of peace. But this should happen when a *koakoale* of Moarmoar again was of the Boaiak Saumgum lineage. The last one had been Boaiak, the older brother of Bagasal whom Hogbin described as *koakoale* in 1934.[14] Boaiak and Bagasal's sister, Segilma, had married in Falala and her daughter, Sola, was sent back to Dab to marry Moarigum's son, Tafalti. Her son was then supposed to stand up as a *koakoale* of the Boaiak Saumgum lineage in Moarmoar with the *moanuboa* of peace. But Sola did not get any children of her own, and it was decided that Moita from Gole of the Saumgum lineage should marry Gabis, another of Moarigum's sons, for the same purpose. She fell in love and married Dalle, the *koakoale* of Kajenamoa, instead, and her son (Gagin) should thus 'stand up' as *koakoale* in Kajenamoa. In another attempt to get a man from the Boaiak Saumgum lineage in the Moarmoar *koakoale* position, Moita's daughter, Sanum, married Kulbobo. In their son, Kintabi, there was finally a *koakoale* who could be given the *moanuboa* of peace. He also had the support of his mother's brother Gagin, and at the feast for the establishment of Kintabi as a *koakoale*, Kintabi was given the *moanuboa* of peace by a man from the matrilineage that had carried it for the last generation (his full name was Tom Hogbin Kintabi, named after Hogbin since he was born just after Hogbin's last visit to Wogeo).

Gagin, *koakoale malala* of Kajenamoa/Lukaluka, is of the Saumgum linage. His wife, Iakena, is of the Moanoua lineage, and his eldest son thus has the proper matrilineal identity to stand up as true *koakoale* in the Kajenamoa side of Dab. He has been given the name Jaran after a great *koakoale* in Kajenamoa/Lukaluka prior to Moarigum, and Gagin has already held a feast initiating him into the position. Kintabi and Jaran will, thus, stand up as proper *koakoale* with the right matrilineal identity on each their side of the village – like famous ancestors with the same names had done before them.

But there are more *koakoale* in Wogeo than the ones holding baskets, and other aspects of the offices of *koakoale* need to be investigated in order to understand the political landscape in Wogeo.

Koakoale and Place

The offices of *koakoale* and the different bodies of knowledge at the village level are further connected to the spatial organization of the villages. Kulbobo once decided to teach me about the villages in accordance to this. 'You want to learn about places? Today I will teach you about the areas of the village. First there is *malala*, the village. Then there is the beach. We have three *moanuboa* in Wogeo,' Kulbobo said. '*Moanuboa* of the beach, *moanuboa* of the bush, and *moanuboa* of the village.' He continued telling me the words for the areas all the way out to the deep blue sea, and then from the village all the way up to the mountain:

Moanuboa Raoa: from the village to the sea
Malala – Village (the settlement)
Raoa – Beach
Mavat – Reef
Lona – Where the reef descends to the deep (where the fish are plentiful)
Gig (gig ilodi) – The deep blue ('inside the deep blue')
Loa – White, shining 'paths' on the surface of the sea
Masaoa – Empty ocean
Maraoa – Where you are first able to glimpse boats or hear the noise from the outboard motors
Kaiuk – The area ('bridge') between the island's *maraoa* and the mainland's or other island's *maraoa*

Moanuboa Koab: from the village to the mountain
Malala – Village
Oen – The area close to the village with mango trees and coconut palms
Koab – Bush, where most of the gardens are
Duguva – The bush at the beginning of the riverbeds
Bulum – Mountain
Duguva damare – The inner most part of the bush belonging to the village.

As already described, *moanuboa* is the name of plants of the *Cordyline* family and Kulbobo called it a 'holy plant', using the English words. *Moanuboa* are planted as marks of significance, for instance on graves (cf. Lutkehaus 1995b: 313), but *moanuboa* are also symbols of bodies of knowledge and the right to use it.[15] There are *moanuboa* of powerful magic for planting taro, others for planting coconuts, for fishing and so on (see Seo 1991 for 'magic of the reef' – *lona*). In the following it is the *moanuboa* as marks of *koakoale* offices and the associated corpuses of knowledge that is discussed. Mats recorded the following account of the *moanuboa* and the *koakoale* from Kulbobo as part of the documentation project:

> *Our grandfathers and fathers in the past used to call it* moanuboa. *Not the* moanuboa *that you plant in your gardens. ... They say that one* moanuboa *stands on the beach, one stands in the village, one stands in the bush. ... They say that there are three* moanuboa; *in the past they were Moanuboa and Liboaboa. Who was Moanuboa? It*

was Onka, his name was Moanuboa. He said his name was Moanuboa.[16] *One was Liboaboa. Then they left their names. … He [Onka] said: there are three* moanuboa; *one stands on the slope of the beach, one stands in the village, one stands in the bush. These* moanuboa, *they are men of* binga *[power of bringing wealth, abundance]; their names are* moanuboa.

Kulbobo here refers to Moanuboa as one of the names Onka called himself and that he 'left' this name (together with Mafofo who 'left' the name Liboaboa). Names in Wogeo are much more than identification marks: names are like positions or offices that are filled. When you are given a name, you are also given a certain place in the village. When speaking about *iaboua*, for instance, people would say that this or that person 'had name' in *iaboua* – meaning that they had knowledge of *iaboua*. The name Moanuboa in the above account represents the corpus of knowledge necessary to lead the people, knowledge left by the great leader Onka.

According to the stories told, Onka divided the corpus of important knowledge he left into three sections – in three *moanuboa*: one on the beach, one in the bush and one in the village. Among the three *moanuboa*, the *moanuboa* of the village is ranked the highest. The knowledge and obligations associated with this *moanuboa* concern first of all the display of food and the following exchange during the great *oaraboa* of the past. The *koakoale* who 'stands on the beach' (*koakoale one*) – the *moanuboa raoa* – has the overall responsibility for trade relations, fishing and gathering from the ocean as well as the coconut palms, and they are responsible for the presentation of food from their area during an *oaraboa*. He is also in charge of the rituals associated with male initiation. The corpus of knowledge and obligations following the *moanuboa koab* concerns work in the gardens, gathering in the bush and pig hunting and, hence, the presentation of food from this area.

Each *koakoale* had second-in-commands, called *ngaro*. The *ngaro* should use their authority to support the work of the *koakoale* and ensure that the *koakoale*'s instructions to the commoners were followed. *Ngaro* means 'teeth' and is reminiscent of what the Manam refer to as the '*tanepoa*'s jaw' (Lutkehaus 1995b: 303), inherited positions with the responsibility of delivering the *tanepoa*'s messages. In Wogeo, these positions seem more flexible. When the areas of the various *koakoale* were in focus, it was the *koakoale* of that section who was the sole leader, and the other *koakoale* had to obey him and even function as his *ngaro*. When the *koakoale* of the bush organized the harvest of a garden, even the *koakoale malala* should obey his instructions.[17] Kulbobo continues:

The moanuboa *that stands on the beach, he sails out for* ngada[18] *and all that; he brings wooden plates and tobacco and baskets.*[19] *He brings fish to the shore; that is the task of that* moanuboa. *They say that he who sails out in a canoe, he who stands on the slope of the beach, is a* koakoale. *His name is* Moanuboa. *One* moanuboa *stands on the beach.*

One stands in the village, the big koakoale *stands in the village. The things that are with him are the* nyaboá, *the houses, the* boaboaur, *the bag [ceremonial platform]; all this is in the village. When there are feasts for the big houses, then it is the task of that* moanuboa. *The* moanuboa *that stands in the village, he is the biggest. When he speaks, all kinds of things come.*

One stands in the bush. One moanuboa *stands in the bush. He stands in the bush; what does it mean? He stands in the valleys and herb gardens. What you throw in front of the platform in the bush, he takes care of it ['carries it']:* kangar, taro, banana, *ngabir, ula [Singapore taro], sweet potatoes; everything in the bush, whatever you plant for food.*

He gathers coconuts – the bird of paradise of the beach they call him who stands on the beach where the coconuts sprout – and throws them into the village, throws them into the herb gardens, into the valleys and herb gardens. The big koakoale *in the village, the* moanuboa *that stands in the village, he speaks; the things from the beach come, he places them down for the people. The women and men rejoice for them. The one in the village tells he who stands in the bush, 'The women and men are crying for that thing,' and he gives it to them. He gives it to the one in the village, and the one in the village places it down for the commoners ['dogs and pigs']. ... This is the* moanuboa. *The exact making of the story of the* moanuboa *is like this.*

When we discussed the three *moanuboa*, Kulbobo again used the image of the eagle: 'It is like an eagle: the body is the area of the *koakoale malala*, and its wings reach out towards the mountain and the sea.' The basis for this leadership structure is both the spatial organization of the villages and the *oaraboa* and the associated knowledge. In Dab both the sides, Moarmoar and Kajenamoa/ Lukaluka, have the three *moanuboa*, but most people meant this to be special to Dab and Gole as the middle villages – the rest of the villages had three *moanuboa* for the whole village. On the back of the island the *moanuboa* of the beach was the *moanuboa* of catching flying fish. The canoes in the cave of the mountain Iamoe (see chapter 1) were made for this purpose. The people of the back did not arrange trade expeditions, and the task of catching flying fish was the important duty of the *moanuboa* of the beach.

Kulbobo's account continues:

I will speak about kolova[20] *and* oaraboa. *It is the big* moanuboa *in the village who orders* oaraboa. *He will talk to the one on the beach who will give him fish; he will put the fish down as* oaraboa *for the women and men; he will call them to the* oaraboa. *Those are the* moanuboa. *Those three men of* binga *[power of bringing abundance/wealth] order* oaraboa. *The one on the beach will give something; he [in the village] will make* oaraboa *for the women and men; they will eat fish. He will order goods – baskets and pots and tobacco, necklaces from dogs' teeth will come from the mainland. The one in the village will place it down for the people in the village; he will order an* oaraboa. *The one on the beach does not speak; he only brings things and gives them to the one in the village who orders an* oaraboa. *He gives it to the commoners. Then he turns around, tells the one in the bush, 'give me* kangar; *the commoners are crying for* kangar!' *He will give an* oaraboa *for them; taro and banana will appear; he will place them down for them: that is an* oaraboa; *he places down coconuts for them: that is an* oaraboa; *ib [Tahitian chestnuts]: that is an* oaraboa; *oatala [type of nuts]. So this is what is called* oaraboa.

Oaraboa *and* kolova *are something of the* moanuboa. *Who are the* moanuboa? *That is Onka, he changed his name; he said his name was Moanuboa. They say that those men have* binga. *They are* koakoale *of* binga, *those three* koakoale. *When they give everything, that we call* binga. *Binga, that is the power of the* koakoale. *Iaboua is* binga; muj *is* binga; *all that, that is* binga. *That was all; this is* binga, *this they call their* binga. *Finished, the end of [the account of] the* moanuboa *is like this.*

Binga is the power of the *koakoale* – the power of bringing in abundance, of bringing wealth. A *koakoale* is said to 'carry' *binga* (*binga ebaj*); Kulbobo said that in the past, when you saw a man adorned with boars tusks, necklaces of dogs' teeth, feathers of cassowary and bird of paradise, carrying a decorated basket, you would say, 'Oh, that man has *binga*.' He was a man that could make great *oaraboa*, who could distribute an abundance of food to his fellow villagers. He had the skills and knowledge of Goleiangaianga, the hero who gave Wogeos the skills and knowledge of how to produce and exchange an abundance of food.

Koakoale and Exchange

As already described, the largest exchanges (*oaraboa*) in the past were competitive displays of food between *koakoale* involving people from two or more districts on the island (see e.g. Hogbin 1970a; 1978). One *koakoale* would invite a *koakoale* from another district to participate in a feast. Often the inviting *koakoale* had to trick the other one into accepting the invitation. To participate in a large *oaraboa* involved hard work for both parties, and other work would have to be set aside. The inviting *koakoale* could, for instance, pretend to be very ill and ask the other one to come and see him one last time before dying. In the allegedly dying man's house, the not-so-sick-after-all *koakoale* would then throw a certain kind of coconut onto his visitor's lap, and the challenge of *oaraboa* was given (see Hogbin 1978: 156). The inviting *koakoale* would put on an enormous display of food. Large amounts of food had to be gathered, and the preparations for such feasts could take years. Hogbin writes that at an *oaraboa* in 1934, 15 pigs, 5 tons of taro, 3 tons of *kangar*, 200 ropes of banana, 'at least 5,000 green drinking coconuts, and hundreds of bunches of areca nuts' (1935a: 320) were displayed. The *koakoale malala* would tell the *koakoale koab* to make gardens, and they would summon their *leoa* spirits – men impersonating spiritual beings (*leoa* means 'mask') – to protect the crops, patrolling the forest with their frightening appearance (Hogbin 1938/39: 319; 1970b: 59–71).[21] As long as they were present, people had to be careful not to harvest foodstuff tabooed for the *oaraboa*. The *koakoale one* would also summon a *leoa* to taboo coconut palms awaiting the *oaraboa* and organize expeditions to get tobacco from trading partners. The *koakoale malala* would make sure he had a sufficient number of pigs to slaughter. For this, he needed help from all his allies. First of all this would be his fellow villagers and those belonging to his side of the village in particular. The other villages in his district would also join in and sometimes also allies from other districts. I was told that sometimes the whole island would participate in such feasts with the villages of the upper side of the island allying against the villages of the lower part. On such an occasion, the two sides of Dab would be on opposite sides of the exchanges. When everything was ready, the *nibek* spirit was called to the village, and the feast started. The food was displayed on the platform, and on some occasions the *boaboaur* would be erected, making the whole display appear as a sailing canoe with masts (see e.g. Hogbin 1935a: 320). After the initial mock fight, peace would reign in the village. The *koakoale malala* then distributed the food. Then people would eat lots of food, dance and socialize all night long. Some of the food would be carried back to the villages. Later, the invited *koakoale* would have to reciprocate the gifts – a considerable work that often would take a year or more – and, later, he would try to return the challenge by putting on an even greater feast (see Hogbin 1978: 169).[22]

Binga – the power to produce in abundance – was an important part of the power of the *koakoale* and they would compete in throwing the largest food distributions. There seems to be an element here of what Lindstrom distinguished as characteristic of 'wealth-based' societies, again pointing to the fact that even though the distinction between wealth and knowledge-based societies can be a useful heuristic device, complex realities seldom adhere to such categorizations. In the case of Wogeo, the ability to make a great *oaraboa* is closely connected to the status and distribution of knowledge. Even though the ability to stage the greatest food distributions was the means to 'lift up one's name' and become a powerful leader, this was not merely the result of actual accumulated wealth: it was the result of the knowledge the leader possessed, the *moanuboa* he carried. The ability to distribute the food properly, that is, knowing who should receive which portions of the display and call them by name, was often pointed out to me as one of the most important skills of the *koakoale malala*. The magic the *koakoale* and their collaborators possessed was what made the crops abundant, and a *koakoale* who aptly demonstrated the quality of his knowledge was the *koakoale* who could maintain the support of his allies. They knew that as long as he was in power, there would always be food and prosperity in the village. If people did not support their leaders, they did so at the peril of evoking the anger of the *koakoale* who also possessed powerful means of sanction – like magic to bring about long-lasting rainfalls or droughts, to make earthquakes or strong winds, to kill with *iaboua* or *muj* or to stop using the magic securing the prosperity of the village. Also this is *binga*.

In the 1990s the largest ceremonial food distributions that took place were of a more modest form, known as *olage*. The largest *olage* that took place during my visits was the one described in chapter 4, following Ulbaia's death. Such ceremonial exchanges are spoken of as 'work' (*manif*) in someone's name: at funerals, a girl's first menstruation, the construction of a new house, or similar occasions. The exchanges were the 'work' that made a new house into a proper house, a girl into woman, or made the dead sleep properly in the ground and their heirs to 'stand up' in their place. The people who arrange such work kill pigs for the *olage*, and others who feel they are obliged to might also slaughter a pig. The pigs provided by people who are not necessarily obliged to contribute have to be reciprocated at later, similar work (cf. Jeudy-Ballini 2002). All the people involved carry with them baskets of cooked food to the *olage* – some representing whole villages and others intended for particular people, like the *manvara* at Ulbaia's death. The cooked pork is then distributed equally to all the baskets, and people would receive a basket with the same amount of food as they gave. The exceptions are those who are given gifts as a return for some particular work they may have done – like being *manvara*, building a house, or following a first time *baras* girl through her rituals. They will receive food on plates or in baskets that are not exchanged. The people who participate in an *olage* can later expect the reciprocal participation of the people who arranged the *olage* in their own *olage*: this is what is spoken of as the real exchange: this is how the 'rope is cut'.

Also in *olage* there is a competitive aspect. The largest *olage* will be remembered for a long time, and at a person's death his or her descendants will increase their own standing by 'lifting up' the name of their parents. Also, at *baras* celebrations of *moede* and exchanges marking the coming of age of new *koakoale* the size of the *olage* can add support to the standing of the person the *olage* is for. In fact there is a competitive element involved in all exchanges – even those taking place in the villages every afternoon. The direct exchange, that is the gift of food and its compensation, should be approximately identical but it is the gift of food that is given in return on a later occasion (that also should be compensated by an equal amount) that is spoken of as the real exchange. At this occasion the woman may try to give a larger portion of food than she received; as a mere show off, as a token of respect or gratitude, or merely because one had more food that day. To conclude we can say that principles of increment are present in Wogeo exchanges, but the ability to compete in exchanges is closely connected to the possession of knowledge.

Changing Expressions of Knowledge

In the 1990s the division of the different responsibilities and knowledge of the *koakoale* was no longer of the same importance as in the days of the great *oaraboa* and the male cult. The large inter-district *oaraboa* of the past were no longer arranged, and, although quite extensive food exchanges were still arranged, they were rare events. The knowledge following the offices of the *koakoale malala, one* and *koab* were, thus, not relevant to the same degree as in the past. But I did meet a *leoa* spirit in the district of Bukdi in 1999; *koakoale* there had summoned it to taboo large amounts of crops in their forest in order to sell them at the market in Wewak. The money was intended to meet various needs in the district as a whole. People pointed out, though, that the *leoa* was not as dangerous or powerful as in the past, but my companions seemed genuinely frightened when we unexpectedly met the *leoa* on the path between Gole and Koablik. There was also made a small platform close to the path where the spears of the leading *koakoale* in the district were placed together with marks of the crops that were tabooed. In Onevaro they have not called for the *leoa* for a long time, and nowhere on the island were the *nibek* spirits summoned any more.

There were still men who were labelled *koakoale* in all villages. One or two would always be elicited as the most important ones, but several others would be mentioned as well. Discussions about present day *koakoale* would usually evoke disagreements as to who was making empty claims of being *koakoale* and who was truly *koakoale* or *ngaro*. If they could point to some *koakoale* ancestor they might find it desirable to claim inheritance of the title. Since the events where their power and knowledge would be proven were rare, they could do so without meeting too strong resistance. If I asked people in Dab about each and every man, nearly all of them would be called *koakoale* for some purpose. It should be noted, though, that Dab had few inhabitants while I was there and that they, as the 'middle place', had three offices of *koakoale* on each side of the village. It could therefore be that this multitude of *koakoale* is more conspicuous in Dab and other villages with few residents than in the more crowded villages like Ga and Bajor of which I do not have the same knowledge. Since the sections of responsibility were no longer that important, the *koakoale* appeared more as an elite opposed to the commoners than as leaders responsible for their 'sections'. Only particularly apt *koakoale* would stand out as real leaders – as Gagin did.[23] That Gagin and Kulbobo's respective sons should stand up as *koakoale* in Kajenamoa and Moarmoar seemed, however, still to be important.

The magistrates, councillors and the councillor's committees were usually, but not necessarily, men who were also *koakoale*. Demonstrating their knowledge of the world beyond Wogeo they often used phrases quite foreign to most Wogeos – like 'human integration development'. But Wogeos are not easily impressed by empty oratory and often spoke sarcastically about such speech. For instance when representatives of the PNG health authorities had a meeting in Onevaro district in 1994 about, among other topics, family planning, hygiene and malaria prevention, I was the only person from Dab present. The meeting was a rare event in the often dull daily routine, and many people found it entertaining. But my Dab friends said, 'We have heard it all before; it is only talk. Why bother?' Similarly, when a former Prime Minister of PNG was going to visit the island, people were not eager to participate. 'Why should we do all this work for him, prepare food and put on dances. What has he ever done for us?' What did impress my Wogeo friends, however, were islanders who had made it because of their education – who made money and used parts of it in Wogeo to, among other things, contribute with pigs, rice and tinned fish at exchanges. Knowledge that did not result in prosperity and benefits for the people was not worthy of the same respect.

In 1998, however, the charismatic movement seemed to have made new types of knowledge important. During the frequent praying meetings the children sang hymns in Tok Pisin, accompanied by men playing guitar; many people spoke in tongues – most of them women – and some were more active than others. The leaders translated the obscured words and spoke continuously with strong, persuasive voices, sometimes putting their hands on the heads of people who would fall down. The meetings could last for hours, and it was difficult to distinguish them from each other. People sitting on their verandas were urged to come and sit with the others. And everyone came. In Dab it was only Saboakai, Kulbobo and the few Seventh Day Adventists who did not take part. Sometimes I would sit with Kulbobo at such occasions. First I thought Kulbobo to be critical of the movement, but when we talked about it, I got a different story. He had encouraged the revival, he said. 'And look, now all the power of Wogeo has come up in the clear' (*Ol powa bilong Wogeo i kamap long ples klia* in Tok Pisin) (see also Robbins 2004: 138). To my knowledge this statement did not refer to any revealing of the secrets of the male cult as had been the case in such revivals in other nearby places (see e.g. Leavitt 2001; Tuzin 1997). Rather he referred to the experience of the Holy Spirit and his messages in the shape of tongue-speaking.

The messages were, as far as I could elicit, usually translated as being about moral decay and the need to 'sit good' in the place, but some people were also able to reveal *iaboua* perpetrators when possessed by the Holy Spirit.

Even though the consequence of the arrival of the first missionaries in the 1950s was the collapse of the male cult and the end of the large *oaraboa*, the church in the 1990s was not seen as destructive for Wogeo *kastom*. The collapse of the cult and the disappearance of the *oaraboa* were usually blamed on misreading of the Christian message both on the side of the missionaries and the first converts, but not on Christianity itself. 'We should have thrown away the bad things and kept the good things,' people often said. The codes for moral conduct according to *kastom* and Christianity were conceptualized as essentially the same, and it was people's lack of moral conduct – like promiscuity, gossip, egoism and *iaboua* – that was corrupting good life.

In his book about conversion to Christianity among the Urapmin, Joel Robbins (2004) takes as a point of departure three models of cultural change, and all three of them seem to describe some aspects of the situation in Wogeo.[24] The way Wogeos emphasized the basic similarities between Christianity and Wogeo *kastom*, can be seen to fall into the category of change that Robbins calls a model of assimilation: people fit new circumstances into old categories (ibid.: 10). But this appears to be a retrospective view in the late 1990s rather than describing what actually went on in the 1960s and 70s when Christianity was rapidly adopted by most Wogeos (cf. Hogbin 1978). The model that Robbins (2004: 10) labels the model of adoption, where two cultures exist side by side, may be better suited to describe what actually happened at the time of conversion: Christianity was seen as incompatible with *kastom*, and the first converts did not wish to transfer the traditional knowledge to the next generation. Through time, however, the gap between the two has lessened and categories from both cultures have been stretched to fit, similar to what Robbins aimed to describe with a third model: that of transformation (ibid.), with the emphasis on the basic similarities between *kastom* and Christianity as a result.

In the late 1990s, however, the charismatic movement represented a new change. Most of the prayer group leaders had no traditional positions of power, but they now stood out as leading men in their villages. Some young girls confided that they feared them. Sin and redemption were common topics of conversation, and people did their best to appear as the most committed members of the groups. In Robbins' book, an Urapmin Christian leader describes how the experience of being able to read and understand the Bible had given him new knowledge that could be made relevant in everyday life: 'the Bible and Urapmin life suddenly made sense together, rather than as two mutually exclusive frames of meaning. And his ability to bring them together made him a leader' (Robbins 2004: 133). The prayer group leaders in Wogeo could read the Bible, they had been attending courses in Wewak to receive the gift of the Holy Spirit, and in that way their experiences were similar to that of the Urapmin leader. But the strong position of the prayer groups in Wogeo can also be explained in the light of what traditionally gives power and authority in Wogeo (as among the Urapmin, who are closely related to the Baktaman): namely knowledge, secrecy and the power of experience.

The ability to translate the words of people speaking in tongues is a prime example of interpretative knowledge. As the *koakoale* could recite spells and myths with complex imagery and hidden meaning passed down from Onka and use them as means to interpret events and influence people's lives, the prayer group leaders could interpret messages from God (or even Onka who is often spoken of as the same as God).[25] Moreover, people did not have to rely on their leaders exclusively to guide them: they were themselves functioning as vehicles for the messages, and they were experiencing the 'power of the place'. As in *kastom* spells and myths, the messages were opaque, but whereas 'knowers' traditionally would give their interpretations sparingly and, thus, maintain their exclusiveness vis-à-vis others (Lindstrom 1984: 302), interpretations were now freely given to anyone who wanted to listen. The power of the place had indeed 'come up in the clear'. No wonder people were more enthusiastic about these new demonstrations of knowledge than towards long speeches about 'human integration development' and other phrases that are no less obscure than those used when speaking in tongues or in magical spells.

Secrecy or hiddenness is a crucial aspect of power relations in Wogeo (cf. Lindstrom 1984: 301). The basis of gendered power in the male cult was the secret of the original female powers of unrestrained flow of fertility. People's matrilineal identity should ideally be kept hidden and is a source of extensive political manipulation – as is also the case with adoption. When interpreting customs, myths and rituals for me, Kulbobo and other men often stated that what they told me was the secrets of the *koakoale*, diminishing the importance of alternative interpretations. The secret messages of tongue-speaking can be interpreted similarly but are also different, since the content of the tongue speeches does not represent a known and 'complete' body of knowledge. They are seen to come directly from God, and the interpreters do not empty their fund of power by sharing their knowledge or understanding.

Men were given important bodies of knowledge in the male cult – the 'school of the beach'. The men who initiated them were, like women who have given birth, *boaruka*. The young *koakoale* receiving the knowledge associated with their coming office were sitting in a 'birth hut' (*boaruka*) (cf. Hogbin 1970b: 93). Women have the innate power of life, whereas men had to instigate their growth in the male cult. Whereas women have the innate capacity of being cleansed of disease through menstruation, men had to manually bring about their cleansing. When the *nibek* flutes were in the hands of women, they played by themselves; when men stole them, they had to learn to control them in order to maintain the fertile flow. At an *oaraboa* the *boaboaur* poles were made to stand erect by evoking the power of female rootedness with the help of spells imaging mothers holding the base steady as substitutes for roots. Unmediated fertile flow and power and its successful control are necessary for the well being of the island and its inhabitants. Even *iaboua* was a positive power when in control of competent *koakoale*. Out of control it was a destructive force. Yet another analogy may be drawn in this concern. Most commonly it was women who spoke in tongues at the prayer meetings. If the gift of the Holy Spirit is seen as the 'power of the place' released into the clear, it appears obvious that it is women who are the vehicles for this unmediated, spontaneous manifestation. Men's interpretations may accordingly be seen as 'cutting' this flow: decomposing it into intelligible speech.

Knowledge, Truth and the Vatican Council

One afternoon towards the end of my first fieldwork, an old man from Kinaba was supposed to tell me the story of the origins of *iaboua* in Wogeo. He was from a matrilineage often accused of using *iaboua*, and he had invited leading men from as many of the matrilineages as he could so that they would hear what he said. In that way he hoped to avoid gossip and suspicions of telling untruths. I was not yet fully aware of the implications of the matrilineages' association with *iaboua*, and had no particular expectations for the interview. I soon discovered, however, that the occasion was somewhat extraordinary. The men gathered outside of Moita's house; I served coffee, and the atmosphere seemed tense. The old man related the story about how *iaboua* had spread from its place of origin and had come to be associated with his matrilineage. The story he told was a variation of other stories of the origins of *iaboua* that I had already heard, but before I had the chance to ask any questions, he started to talk about the pope in Rome. He asked me whether it was true that the Catholic leaders sometimes meet to decide changes in the interpretations of the Bible – that they would sit in a closed room until they agreed on new meanings. I said that I had heard they could do something like that, but unfortunately I did not follow his lead. Rather I tried to get back to the question of *iaboua* and matrilineages. The old man often wanted to discuss Christianity and hear stories from Israel, and I interpreted this as yet another sidetrack in that direction. The gathering soon dissolved, and Tarere later complained that the old man had not completed his story. Not until later did I realize that I had been a very bad fieldworker that afternoon. In spite of many attempts, I did not manage to take up the thread with him when I returned five years later. Still I am confident that he had tried to tell me something important – not about the Catholic Church but about knowledge and politics in Wogeo.

His interest in the Vatican Council points to important aspects of Wogeo politics and knowledge management. The image of leaders sitting in a closed room is reminiscent of *koakoale* sitting in the *nyaboá* – the male cult house – where they discussed questions of knowledge: like rituals, magic, *iaboua* or land rights, or like we were sitting outside of Moita's house in the banana garden, talking about the origins and use of *iaboua*. A question that springs to mind is whether the man's suggestion of a potential change in meaning is a radical idea to Wogeos or if his choice of parallel was due to already established notions of flexibility in the knowledge politics of Wogeo. I have already discussed how ideas of 'true' *kastom* and history were crucial to my informants when the issue of what 'my book' should contain came up, indicating that the true meaning of *kastom* was seen as absolute and indisputable. According to this notion, the only possibility to nuance the picture is to reveal additional or deeper layers of truths. Kulbobo often talked about the knowledge he 'gave' me as *dip save* – 'deep knowledge' in Tok Pisin.[26] Barth has described the knowledge revealed in the male cult of the Baktaman as 'Chinese boxes': each stage of the cult presented deeper and truer knowledge that in the previous stages had been obscured (Barth 1975). Similarly I was given knowledge that was said to be the secrets of the *koakoale* that sometimes would contradict the more public versions of the issue in question. A discussion aimed at *changing* meanings instead of *revealing* deeper layers of meaning, thus, seemed to contradict the way meaning was represented according to tradition. But the image of the rudder (*singara*) as tradition allows the people actually steering the canoe to decide the direction, guided, but not necessarily predetermined, by the stories from the past (*nanasa moa*). What we were discussing that afternoon was not religious doctrine or a comprehensive body of knowledge that can be labelled Wogeo *kastom*: it was histories of named people and the implications of these histories in people's lives. Such histories are always the subject of extensive arguments and manipulations in Wogeo, and even though people would always claim to have the true story, they also knew that maintenance of consensus about the truth of such stories is at the core of Wogeo politics.

The old man had lived all his life with the suspicions associated with his lineage. It was his lineage that had temporarily been given the *moanuboa* of peace in order to get the chance to improve their conduct. It could be that his story was intended to comment upon the decision of returning the *moanuboa* to the Boaiak lineage – either as a parallel to the Catholic practice of secret discussions of changes in meaning or as a questioning of the legitimacy of the claim of the ownership of the *moanuboa* of peace. But it could also be that he wanted to initiate a discussion about the fairness of ascribing the doings of individuals to whole categories of people – the matrilineages. On another occasion I discussed this with a relatively young man from Bajor. He was a powerful man, and he said that with the changes that had come with the introduction of Christianity it was clear that Wogeos should get rid of the *iaboua* suspicions that were troubling so many people on the island. I thought the man meant that *iaboua* suspicions were often groundless and exaggerated and this was why he wanted to put an end to them. I asked how he thought it might be possible to change this, and it turned out that I had misinterpreted his intentions. In accordance with the general attitude among Wogeos, he replied that the only way was to throw all the people of the matrilineages that were known to use *iaboua* in prison. If the old man's intention was to start a critical discussion of collective guilt in using *iaboua*, it surely was a radical suggestion.

Any conclusion about the man's intentions would be mere speculation on my side. Still, the event points to notions that will be the topic for the next and last part of the book: the way histories of people, places and kinship can be seen as arguments in an ongoing process of establishing a proper social landscape – what we can call the politics of belonging. In order to 'sit good' in one's place one has to be in the right place, show proper conduct and look after one's body properly. The only way to success in this regard is to create and maintain a consensus that one has followed the right path and that one's moral conduct has been impeccable. The search for 'true' histories is important in this regard. Lindstrom writes about politically significant knowledge of land in Melanesia:

[T]he information which men put forth to make claims to a plot of land concerns the history of its tenure, its name and its boundaries. Thus, in the Trobriand Islands, the recitation of the history of the land is not only a 'mythical charter', in Malinowski's terms, but is also a means of argumentation (Lindstrom 1984: 296).

The sides and pathways of the landscape on the one hand, and the matrilineages as manifestations of female fertility on the other, channel the flow of power and knowledge. But the landscape and matrilineages are also the main sign vehicles for how belonging and relations – the sociality of the living people – are constituted. The histories of people, matrilineages, houses, places, *moanuboa* and events in terms of genealogies and movements in the landscape can all be seen as arguments in ongoing processes of establishing proper belonging and relations as well as achieving and maintaining power and position.

Notes

1. Hogbin (1935/36b: 241; 1978: 103) described how the man's father, also known for his temper, made the same threat in 1934. Moarigum once allegedly did burn down his house in anger (Hogbin 1940: 8; 1978: 103).
2. Ioun was the oldest of Moita's second husband Bon's sons with his first wife. He was from Badiata but had a strong affiliation to Dab, both through his maternal grandparents and his father's mother.
3. Hogbin describes the *koakoale* as 'more than a mere headman, but less than a chief' (Hogbin 1938: 224).
4. 'Knowledge' in Wogeo language can be translated with either *iamaiama*, which also means 'thought', or with *maleva*, which is knowledge more in the sense of competence or skills. For instance, one can say *Nat buti iamaiama maleva tabo*, meaning 'The small child does not know (*maleva*) to think (*iamaiama*).' Or one can say *Ramata iare, iamaiama ia bitanga tuga*, meaning 'That man, his knowledge (*iamaiama*) is indeed great'.
5. *Nanasa* is also the verb for telling stories.
6. *Filava moala* ('talk from the past') is Onka's words (Onka *meme* – lit. 'tongue'), *filava gongon* is jokes ('play talk') and *filava buti* is rumours ('small talk').
7. *Bolovadí, filavadí – kanakana duru domafora Dab malala.*
8. My guess is that this happened sometime in the 1950s.
9. The numeral system in Wogeo is based on four: 1:*Ta*, 2:*rua*, 3:*tol*, 4:*koik*, and then 4+1, 4+2 and so on (e.g. 7 – *koik boe tol*). To exemplify this, the Wogeos always use the way coconuts are carried and counted. They are tied together four and four, and people count these bundles of four rather than the coconuts one by one.
10. Hogbin wrote that there were five districts (e.g. 1970b: 10). Ga, the fifth, is now included in Bukdi, and my informant said that Ga, which is only one village, had been an anomaly. Oaoa was one of the largest villages on the island but was, as already mentioned, destroyed – perhaps in the beginning of the nineteenth century.
11. See Hogbin (1935/36b; 1970b: 149–50) for detailed accounts of the practice of *iaboua* (*yabou*).
12. Hogbin does not write about the baskets but he notes that 'as a rule informants, if their own relatives have been killed in this way, claim that the man who was *kokwal* [*koakoale*] of the clan took vengeance by himself bewitching the sorcerer' (1935/36b: 14; see also 1938: 229).

13. I have changed the orthography of names to the style used elsewhere in this book in order to avoid confusion, and I have also corrected some spelling and grammatical errors.

14. Boaiak was dead at the time, and truly it was he who was *koakoale*, people told me, but his son, Itanefa, was not old enough at the time. Bagasal was described by Hogbin as 'a complete nonentity, who in most matters was overshadowed by his younger brother Wiawia [Oieoie]' (1938: 226).

15. This is similar to what the Kairiru-people call *tiptip* (Smith 1994: 31–33).

16. Cf. Aufenanger (1972: 9).

17. Hogbin (1978: 38) mentions the *koakoale* one but not the *koakoale koab*. In *The Leaders and the Led* he writes that 'each Wogeo headman has a virtual monopoly within his residential cluster on magic relating to group tasks and group wellbeing' (1978: 190). My guess is that this discrepancy between Hogbin's account and Kulbobo's is most likely due to Moarigum's uniquely powerful position in Dab in the 1930s and 40s and the absence of other strong leaders. These were probably mostly spoken of as Moarigum's *ngaro*, and the contextual ascriptions of *koakoale* and *ngaro* dependent on the 'section' in focus, may not have been made relevant or were difficult to notice. In the above quote he also ignores the *koakoale one*, which he mentions elsewhere.

18. Food such as meat, fish or nuts that are added to the staple meal of vegetables.

19. From the *lo*.

20. Food distribution for a new *koakoale*.

21. Hogbin (1970b: 58) writes that these taboos are associated both with the bush *leoa* [*lewa*] and a bush *nibek*. I have not heard about the latter.

22. The Manam arrange similar inter-village exchanges called *buleka* (Lutkehaus 1995b).

23. Another example is Gris in Moarmoar who held the *moanuboa koab* and, at least post mortem, was said to be skilled in his section of responsibility. After he died in 1997 it was claimed that, 'the axe has fallen down': food in Moarmoar was no longer abundant.

24. Inspired by Marshall Sahlins (e.g. 1985).

25. Robbins (2004) writes that the Urapmin strongly emphasizes seeing rather than hearing in achieving knowledge, and for them it was dreams and visions from God that really empowered the Christian leaders.

26. *Nau yu go dip, kisim dip save, go andenit long graun na tanim ol ston long graun bilong Oageva.* 'Now you are going deep, receiving deep knowledge, going under the ground and turning all the stones in the ground of Wogeo.'

⊰ Part IV ⊱
Politics of Belonging

Prelude

One afternoon in 1994 I asked Lala, the elected leader of the island, about traditional conception beliefs. Lala laughed and shouted to the nearby people: 'Listen, Iamoe wants to know how children are made!' and people laughed along. In addition to the comic situation my question created, people seemed to find it somewhat awkward to answer it since we were all aware of the same biomedical explanation of conception. Eventually Lala told me that, traditionally, Wogeos believed that a child was created by blood from both parents and was then nurtured by all the good water from the food the mother ate. Menstruation blood has nothing to do with the conception and growth of a child. Such blood is bad or sick blood (*dara somoasomoa*), and the blood that creates a child is good blood (*dara kalingó*).[1] Hogbin wrote about conception beliefs in Wogeo in the 1930s and 40s that

> they frankly admit that they do not know exactly what takes place. Three suggestions were put forward by intelligent informants – that the conjunction of semen (*jabejabe*) and the female secretion (also called *jabejabe*) results in the formation of the embryo, which is nourished until birth by the menstrual blood; that the blood contains the seed and that the semen and secretion, 'like the white of an egg,' provide food; and that the semen and secretion coagulate the blood and then seal it in the womb. The fact that maternal and paternal kin are sometimes distinguished as 'blood' (*dara*) and 'water' (*dan*), a euphemism, as is admitted, for 'semen', seems to indicate that the first suggestion is to be regarded perhaps as the orthodox point of view (Hogbin 1971: 174).

Hogbin was presented with three different theories of conception, and none of these were similar to the version Lala told me. Later I got additional versions of what was regarded as the traditional conception beliefs. During my last fieldwork, Kulbobo was, like Lala, somewhat reluctant to talk about this, but he eventually told me a version of the process that was similar to the one Lala had told me five years earlier: a child is made when mother's and father's blood meet. The foetus is then nourished on the water in its mother's womb that later turns white and becomes milk in her breasts.

Some days later, however, he said to me that we had to talk about it again: 'It is not good if I tell you lies'. Men and women each have their 'water', he said. When he translated to Oageva he used the word *nigi*, which also is used for coconut oil ('water' is *dan*). According to Kulbobo, *jabejabe* that Hogbin wrote about is the fluid of saliva and vomit and has nothing to do with reproduction. Women's water (or oil) is transparent or light green (*nigi gingina*), and men's water is white (*nigi bungbunga*). The female fluid is like the water you transpire or that which comes in sores and 'oils' the joints. The male fluid (semen) later creates milk in women's breasts. Men therefore have to eat lots of white food – like breadfruit,[2] *kangar* (almonds) and *oatala* (another nut with white meat). Milk that men drank from their mothers' breasts when they were infants also helps to make their semen white. It is only semen from intercourse that results in babies and the following ones that produce milk in women's breasts. At other times the passage is blocked. This semen also makes the coming mother fat and healthy. When men and women have intercourse, the male and female fluids meet and turn yellow, like the yoke of an egg. Then you can see a little stripe of blood in the yellow. This later becomes like a little snake, then like a small lizard with a tail, and eventually it becomes a baby. This version appears more similar to two of the versions presented to Hogbin. Kulbobo meant that the foetus did not become alive until about the eighth month of pregnancy. Intercourse is regarded as beneficial for the foetus until you can see the stomach of its mother growing. From then on intercourse would block the birth channel and is tabooed. The mother should take care not to eat certain kinds of food during pregnancy. Among them are some types of yam that have in common their rough skin and some kinds of fish that look ugly. One should also not eat, touch or walk underneath flying foxes. Breaches of these taboos will affect the looks of the child – for instance contact with flying foxes would give the child pointed ears.

Although emphasizing different types of substances and different ways of nourishing the foetus in the womb, all these versions of conception have in common the equal importance given to male and female contributions. I tried several times to discuss this in relation to the idea that matrilineally related kin are spoken of as sharing blood, but most people did not engage in my attempts to talk about this, and it did not seem as if people made any connection between ideas of descent and the substances involved in conception. Kulbobo was an exception. After telling me his revised story of the traditional conception beliefs, he said that Wogeos share blood with kin on both the mother's and the father's side, and that the idiom that the matrilineages are of 'one blood' was not important. For the matrimoieties it was important, though, since they decided whom one should marry.

Some weeks after this discussion, Kulbobo once more called me over to his veranda. He said that he had given the matter a lot of thought, and *now* he was going to tell me what really went on during conception. Kulbobo told me that there were not two fluids (*nigi*) involved, but four. Women contribute with the transparent or light green water (*nigi gingina*) as told above, but in addition their bodies contain yellow water (*nigi kaoera*) that is a mix between the water above and the white semen from the father. This water accumulates in the womb and constitutes food for the foetus. Men contribute with semen (*nigi bungbunga*), but also with blood (*dara*). The little stripe of blood in the yellow in the mother's womb that later would become the foetus was the blood from the father. I asked why Kulbobo had not told me this in the first place, and he replied that this was the 'hidden talk' of the *koakoale* in the men's house. 'You see, a *koakoale* has to be of *koakoale* blood'. If a *koakoale* does not inherit the title and the blood from his father, he will not have true power. It is correct that matrilineages are of 'one blood' or of 'one skin' (*kus ta*), but as far as the father's contribution to the conception of the child, '*kastom* is a little wrong', Kulbobo declared.

At first I was not sure what to make of these stories. First it had appeared both to Hogbin and me that Wogeos had an ideology that focused on patrilineal descent, but when probing into this, we had both found that this was superficial. It seemed that people emphasized matrilineal succession as the continuation of consanguinity, although not always in public, and in my masters thesis (Anderson 1996) I had written about the balancing of the public and seemingly counterfeit emphasis on patrifiliation on the one hand and matrilineal descent on the other. I hoped to find analogies to the ideas of descent and consanguinity in the traditional representations of conception, but without success. However, after having observed Kulbobo's great effort to find the 'true story' in this concern, it became more clear than ever to me that the 'cognatic dilemma' was not merely a dilemma to anthropologists with a preference for lineage theories (cf. Hviding 1993).

Even though Kulbobo had told me earlier how true *koakoale*-ship alternated in generations since inheritance of the powers associated with the titles had to remain within a matrilineage, he now told me that a *koakoale* had to continue the blood of his *koakoale* father in order to have power. And it seemed as though he had changed his story of conception accordingly in order to facilitate this argument. An apparent question is whether he changed his story in order to convince me of his right to power or if this really was 'hidden talk' of the *koakoale*. I can, of course, not answer that question, but Kulbobo's efforts in explaining conception illustrate how, as Hogbin (1935/36a: 37) also noticed, no one 'kinship system', providing an encompassing explanation for consubstantiality, succession, inheritance, local organization and belonging, can be elicited in Wogeo. Patrifiliation and matrilineality are principles of continuity that continuously have to be negotiated and balanced: they are connections that need to be emphasized or toned down according to the situation. The work of balancing the mother's and father's sides in the creation of continuity and in channelling the flow of rights and property will be the focus of this part of the book.

Notes

1. This is similar to beliefs among the Usen Barok of New Ireland: 'the maternal blood cannot be menstrual blood, which is 'dirty', but must be *clean* blood' (Wagner 1986a: 62).
2. The male initiands also had to eat breadfruit while learning to play the flutes.

⊰ Chapter 8 ⊱
Kinship, Place and Belonging

In the chapters on bodies and avoidance I described how Wogeo social persons partly can be seen as being constituted through channelling and cutting connections between people and what and whom they encounter through the course of life. In my analysis of these processes I made use of, among others, Strathern's and Wagner's perspectives on Melanesian sociality, emphasizing the relational and contextual composition of Melanesian persons (or 'dividuals'). I will continue by describing Wogeo kinship and social organization with the same focus. Wagner (1974) and Strathern (1988) have questioned the applicability of concepts such as *society* and *group* to Melanesian realities, and I believe fruitful insight in Wogeo social organization can be gained by combining these perspectives with a further elicitation of the images made from, and infused in, the landscape.

As has been suggested in the last chapters, placing people in proper places can be said to create the most visible and socially relevant organization of people in day-to-day life in Wogeo: the landscape, conceived of as ordered and enduring, continuously orders the mobile people – it places limits on relationships. To belong to the same place is the most 'group-like' identification in terms of daily interaction and shared belonging in Wogeo. Then there are the categories of people that are seldom explicitly made visible in the geographical landscape but that are fixed and unchangeable in a social universe: people who in anthropological kinship terms should be called matrilineages and are said to be of 'one blood' (*dara ta*) or 'one skin' (*kus ta*). The matrilineages are seldom spoken of or visualized as social units. Still they can be said to constitute corporate units in the sense that they are seen as moral bodies: what a person does is, in some concerns, attributed to the matrilineage as a whole. The matrilineages are embodied in every Wogeo person: a part of the person that is made relevant according to the situation. But matrilineages are also manifested apart from the composite persons, namely in the shape of named houses to which I will return later in the chapter.

'The dead weight of old kinship categories'[1]

The relationship between sharing place and sharing blood is complex and often laden with tension – both as cognitive categories and social units – and it is not strange that Hogbin struggled to find a way to describe Wogeo social organization: 'Kinship in Wogeo can be manipulated indeed so very readily that one almost hesitates to speak of a "system" at all' (Hogbin 1935/36a: 37). Wagner (1988: 39) has noted that 'The greater part of the anthropological literature is founded on a necessity to fix either groups or units (or both) as a beginning point in analysis.' In the 'heydays of structural functionalism' (Holy 1996: 71), descent theory dominated studies of social organization to such a degree that it was taken for granted that in most small-scale societies the relevant groups were localized descent groups, and descent-based systems of inheritance were seen to work as the counterparts to Western legal and political institutions. The aim seemed to be to isolate some sort of overall system that would provide the logic for a wide range of phenomena such as group formation, consubstantiality, patterns of residence, marriage and the transfer of rights. Even today anthropologists imprecisely claim that a society *is* (or people are) matri- or patrilineal, connoting anything from unilineal local descent groups to ideas of consubstantiality.

> [T]he game became one of turning kinship into jurisprudence and corporate economics, the study of 'descent systems' and of the 'institutions' formed in tribal societies by the descent of rights and property. Social anthropology became the science of descent groups, and descent groups and their constitution came to be crucial in accounting for the core function of integrating society and keeping it together. ... Groups were a function of *our understanding* of what people were doing rather than of what they themselves made of things (Wagner 1974: 197, original emphasis).

In the 1950s and 60s anthropologists working in New Guinea were fascinated by the apparent similarities between African unilineal descent systems and kinship systems in the New Guinea Highlands, and analysed these societies accordingly: as composed of unilineal descent groups. Barnes called it 'the African mirage in New Guinea' (Barnes 1962: 5). After closer scrutiny, however, the presence of too many non-agnates in the seemingly patrilineally organized local groups, among other characteristics (ibid.: 6), indicated that these systems were founded on other criteria as well as descent, and the solution to the 'problem of groups' had to be sought elsewhere. But the discussions were still founded on kinship and descent as recruitment principles to groups, with concepts such as cumulative filiation and kindred as modifying alternatives. Kinship was to anthropology what logic was to philosophy, as Robin Fox (1967: 10) stated.

In other places in the region, the search for the obligatory groups focused on cognatic descent and raised what Ward Goodenough (1955) called 'a problem in Malayo-Polynesian social organization'. The problem arose from the question of how groups were formed when cognatic descent determined inheritance and succession. Cognatic descent appeared to form corporate groups similar to unilineal descent groups, but descent alone could not determine *how* these groups were made: why people ended up belonging to a group through the one parent rather than the other. 'Conceptualized as a kind of inverse to lineal holism, the workings of cognatic kinship seemed incapable of yielding a model of a whole' (Strathern 1992: 90).[2] Individual choice and preference appeared to be significant in deciding to which group a person should belong. Structuralist lineage theories came under attack, and process and individual choice became central foci in Oceanic kinship studies (e.g. Firth 1957; Scheffler 1965). Concepts such as 'cumulative filiation' and 'kindred' were put to use in attempts to solve the 'problem' (see e.g. Barnes

1962; Freeman 1961; Goodenough 1955; Scheffler 1985),[3] and residence and locality were emphasized in analyses – pointing towards the significance that place has been given in Oceanic studies since the 1990s. A quote from Hogbin's last book from Wogeo shows how his analyses followed this development:

> In my earliest publications about Wogeo, going back to 1935, I spoke of the persons born into a cluster of houses as forming a patrilineal clan or patrilineage. This was wrong. Later, with second thoughts I described them as a descent group. If no longer grossly inaccurate, this was misleading. Recruitment is not by descent from a distant ancestor, unilineal or cognatic, but by filiation, being someone's offspring, usually the father, occasionally the mother, and hence inheriting that person's right in land. Cumulative filiation down the years has the effect of creating what are putative descent groups, but this is incidental, a by-product, and has nothing to do with the local ideology (Hogbin 1978: 35).

The fact that people spoke about descent and lineages when discussing belonging, did not necessarily imply that these were the actual and most important recruitment principles to groups (see e.g. De Lepervanche 1967/68). The questions that should be posed first in any analyses of kinship, descent and group formation are: what is shared, and what is transferred for what purposes in which contexts?

The 'Problem' of Groups

According to the perspectives of Wagner (e.g. 1974; 1988) and Strathern (e.g. 1988; 1992), Melanesian socialities are not adequately explained by presenting structures of groups in relation to each other – groups in which individuals become members through birth and marriage and, thus, enter into relationships with others through their membership of these groups. Melanesian social persons 'contain a generalized sociality within' (Strathern 1988: 13), and this embodied sociality is constituted and made explicit as the Melanesians act out their relations to others. As the frequently quoted passage in *Gender of the Gift* says: '[S]ocial life consists in a constant movement from one state to another, from one type of sociality to another, from one unity (manifested collectively or singly) to that unity split or paired with respect to another' (ibid.: 14). A shift in focus away from prestructured groups to dividual persons seems partly to solve the 'problem of groups'.

> In a society in which both social units and the relations or alliances among such units are articulated through social relationships, a unit *in its constitution* is never really alienable from its relations with others. It reproduces itself through alliances with others, and allies with others through its own mode of reproductive constitution (Wagner 1988: 40, original emphasis).

If the primary goal in the discussions about groups is to understand how, and together with whom, people act in the world, it is not problematic to say that in Wogeo there are groups. The constitution of the local groups is, however, different from what was assumed in the golden age of descent theory and by those who saw kinship as the 'logic' of societies (see also Hogbin 1970b: 25).

In the case of Wogeo two key principles can be elicited as significant to how people create and conceptualize their relations based on shared belonging: shared belonging to places and shared substance transferred matrilineally ('blood' or 'skin'). Although these seemingly provide criteria for the creation of clear-cut groups, this is not necessarily the case. Rather, place and blood (or 'mother') are parts of every Wogeo person, parts that are contradictory and often in conflict. Which is given salience depends on the context, and they both define the person vis-à-vis other persons, in different situations with different casts of people (see also Leach 2000). But they also concern belonging together with others, and it is in the sense of shared belonging that these parts of the social person are collectivized, and social units are made and unmade depending on the situation. Like a Melanesian child can be seen as 'androgynous' and in need of being made 'incomplete' in order to enter into reproductive, gendered relationships, the cognatic person is 'decomposed' as it enters relations based on shared belonging: 'The "cognatic" or androgynous person becomes depluralized, decomposed, in the creation of the "unilineal" single-sex person' (Strathern 1994: 209). Whereas the blood-side of Wogeo persons is constant and unchangeable but seldom spoken of or manifested in social space (cf. Scott 2007b: 67), the place-side is a subject for continuous negotiation and recreation through discourse and visual manifestations such as house building or food exchanges, and people can belong to more than one place.

The idea of consensus as a significant factor for the placing of people and the transfer of rights will be central in developing this argument further (cf. Scheffler 1965: 292). I argue that consensus in this concern becomes more substantial than merely agreeing upon rules for inheritance and succession: it is at the core of Wogeo politics. Wogeos relate to a multitude of principles for establishing belonging to a place, and the maintenance of power and position is closely connected to the ability to achieve and maintain a consensus about certain histories or 'pathways' which lead people to their proper places and titles. In other words, the ability to make people agree, and keep on agreeing, that the path followed is the right one. The process of establishing such platial identity is about cutting flows or networks (Strathern 1996), about emphasizing particular relationships, histories or pathways in favour of others; or, as James Weiner posed it, about placing limits on relationships (J. Weiner 2001; see also Roalkvam 2003).

Before elaborating on the importance of such consensus in the next chapter, it will be necessary to look into the basic conceptualizations of kinship and belonging that Wogeos refer to when talking about their social life, starting with the ideas about shared place as opposed to shared blood.

Shared Places

During an ordinary day in Dab, people did not encounter only other fellow villagers: every day people passed through Dab on their way to other villages, and some of them would usually take the time to stop, eat some betel nuts and chat for a while. Others came to visit people in Dab, to help someone make a new garden or to work on land they had near Dab. Likewise, people from Dab would often go to another village in the district to work on garden land they had there, to help someone in their work, or, for instance, to visit someone who was sick. There were also prayer meetings a couple of times a week in different villages, and often there were funeral ceremonies to attend or a food exchange of some sort. Still, in daily interaction, it was the relations between people living close to each other that were made most relevant as people carried out their daily tasks. Most days the women worked in their gardens – sometimes accompanied by their husbands, children who were not in school, other women of their household such as a mother or mother-in-law, a sister-in-law, an unmarried sister, or others who happened to stay there for a while. Due to the threat of sorcerers, nobody liked to be alone in the bush, and, if no one was free to accompany a woman, she would take her dogs or not go at all

When a new garden was cleared, a larger work force had to be mobilized. A general norm was that the people belonging to the same side of the village, those who were spoken of as *dan ta* (one *dan*), should help each other in such tasks. When the women from one side of a village were clearing a garden in 1998, one of them stated, 'We from our side always help each other. Look at those from [the other side]; they always work one by one.' Her statement did not necessarily describe the situation accurately, but it did point to a norm of loyalty to the side of the village to which a person belonged. Other women would also sometimes join in – sometimes all the women of the village, as well as other people affiliated to the place in some way: through women who had married out, well established alliances or other relations. The different sides of the different villages were also connected to each other in relations of alliance, also spoken of as *dan ta*, and these relations influenced women's choices of who to help making new gardens.

In many ways Wogeo can be said to be a 'place-based society' (Anderson 1996; 2003a), place having a similar position as the house in so-called house-based societies.[4] In such societies a house is

> a corporate body holding an estate made up of both material and immaterial wealth, which perpetuates itself through the transmission of its name, its goods, its titles, and down a real or imaginary line, considered legitimate *as long as this continuity can express itself in the language of kinship and affinity*, and, most often, of both (Lévi-Strauss 1983: 174, my emphasis).

Houses in Wogeo are also much more than the actual built structure, and their continuity is spoken of in terms of kinship and descent, but it is the place – that is, the side of the village – that is the prime focus for continuity and belonging. The social units that are most relevant and visible in daily life in Wogeo are based on shared belonging to a place, and names, titles, land rights and certain corpuses of knowledge are conceptualized as belonging to, and embedded in, the place. Wogeos emphasize patrifiliation when matters regarding belonging to places, names and land rights are in question but, as will be made evident, this is as much a way of speaking about the transfer of rights as designating the actual paths of inheritance.

The people who live in the same place can in certain situations be labelled corporate bodies, but this depends on the context. The people who join together for instance in clearing a new garden are often the people living in the same part of a village, but other relations could also be made just as relevant in gathering people for such work. At ritual exchanges, the people belonging to the same place often participate in the same side of the exchange, but not necessarily. They can sometimes be seen as 'moral bodies' in the sense that one could say, 'the people of Moarmoar are people of peace', but this would be dependent on what was being discussed. The salience of place is not primarily about corporation but about belonging. People in places constitute social units in a manner comparable to what Schneider has said is the case for Yap: 'If there are no people, land alone does not constitute a *tabinau* [the Yap local groups or estates]. And people without a relationship through land cannot constitute a *tabinau*' (Schneider 1984: 21).[5] Along similar lines James Leach (2000, 2003) comments on Peter Lawrence's problems in describing social organization on the Rai coast:

> instead of looking for corporate and enduring groups based on the shared ownership of land (which he did not find), he might have looked to how people gain identity directly from the land on which they produce themselves as social entities. This is different from looking for the basis of 'society', as a set of structural relationships, made visible in land ownership (Leach 2003: 27)

In Wogeo this platial identity is created in many ways, descent being one of them: there are many pathways leading to a place. That someone follows his or her path (*ia jala*) is a frequently used explanation of how a person has attained his or her place and position in a village. The ideal representation of succession is that of being the biological child of the person who previously held a particular position but this is frequently not the actual path of inheritance. Adoption is common in Wogeo, and many of the adoptions I recorded had taken place in order to follow pathways. Marriages also follow pathways, and the types of pathways that adoptions and marriages follow are manifold.

The notion of 'path' is commonly used in the Austronesian-speaking world to elicit relationships and life trajectories. In Wogeo the notion of path is most of all about repetition: about creating and maintaining relationships and not merely the path made and followed as life unfolds (cf. Parmentier 1987: 109). To follow a path to a place is to follow 'in the steps inscribed by others whose steps have worn a conduit for movement which becomes the correct or 'best way to go" (Tilley 1994: 31; see also Hviding 2003; Roalkvam 1997: 170). To follow a path is to choose one direction and exclude others; to obviate some connections by emphasizing others; to channel one type of flow while stopping others.

In order to find the proper pathway for a person to follow, Wogeos look to the history of the place. These histories are seen as embodied in the rafters of the named houses in the villages, called *ro*. Each *ro* is connected to certain pieces of land and the histories of the *ro* are the histories of the people who have held rights in them and, thus, in the land associated with them.[6] The roof of a named house thus becomes 'a sort of diagram of the utilization of the agricultural land in the neighbourhood' (Hogbin 1939: 161). When people in Wogeo talk about their land, they talk about their *ro*. It is the histories of the *ro* that give people guidance when

Photo 8.1: *Ro* in the house Singero

there are no obvious successors to the *ro* or if there are too many successors. The history of the *ro* also tells people the proper names to give to their children.

The histories embedded in the *ro* often describe movements in the landscape, movements that constitute pathways to be followed. Common origins for such pathways are daughters' marriages in their mothers' native villages. Adoptions also follow such pathways: a child is often sent to its mother's village. Through time, and with repeated marriages and adoptions, these pathways become strong and clear and often people are unable to point to its origin. Other pathways are cleared (*jala osar*[7]) as the result of particular events involving people belonging to different places. Gagin wrote in a letter in 1997:

> *Nowadays an inside core of a Wogeo culture seems to follow a question of a 'right to' something; as followed on from a path, 'jala-di' meaning as descended from a known historical event which would have had occurred earlier as a privilege granted to someone for his unconditional service or a good deed.*

Other pathways again had to do with the movement of houses, and all these kinds of pathways or histories are what Gagin referred to as 'logical' stories or arguments.

The right to the *ro*, or a person's inscription into the history of a particular *ro*, is partly attained by naming. All names belong to the parts of the villages, and most male names as well as some female names within these places belong to the different *ro*. There are only a given number of names on the island, and a person cannot take a name that is occupied. The same name can exist in several villages but then as a different 'version' of it – for instance, there is one Boaiak in Badiata and one in Dab. Lindstrom (1984: 293) describes the local groups in Tanna (Vanuatu) as 'name sets', and this may be an adequate description for local groups in Wogeo as well (see also e.g. McWilliam 1997: 103). Like Onka as Moanuboa 'left his name' and, thereby, positions of power and knowledge that were to be filled by *koakoale*, Wogeo names can be seen in a similar manner: they are like positions in the landscape that are filled by living people and become vacant when people die.

In this, Wogeo local organization appears similar to what Harrison (1989; 1990) refers to as a 'realist' polity: a model of the social world consisting of enduring social groups (e.g. totemic clans) and names that transcend the actual living people – as opposed to a 'nominalist' polity where groups and positions are the outcome of people's actions and last only as long as the people embodying them are alive (see also Scott 2007b: 14–16). Inspired by Lindstrom (1984), Harrison argues that there seems to be a correspondence between these polities and what he calls magical and material politics (Lindstrom's 'knowledge-based' and 'wealth-based' societies referred to in the last chapters). Typical highland societies, with their 'self-made' big men, grand exchanges and flexible local organization, he associates with a nominalist polity, and societies with inherited positions and a hierarchy partly based on knowledge or ritual specialization (e.g. societies in Sepik and on the north coast of PNG) he associates with a realist polity.

Hogbin wrote that when a child is named, 'a senior relative goes through the list of the child's ancestors and living kinsmen until the appellation already selected has been reached ... The idea seems to be that a linkage should be demonstrated between the youngster and his various cognates, first those of the past, then those of the present' (1970b: 61). I have not myself witnessed such a naming ceremony. People said that they usually did not follow this *kastom* anymore, and that the child's paternal and/or maternal grandfather merely tells the parents the name of the child. Even so, Hogbin's description of the naming ceremony clearly elicits the notion of 'following history' through naming. Through naming, a person takes the place of the person who previously had the name belonging to the place. Continuity is created through following the history of the place, the name and the particular *ro*. Biological filiation is only one of many ways to follow such histories. Here it should be noted that, to Wogeos, the distinction between biological filiation and filiation through adoption is important. Belonging is given through naming and by placing people in proper places, and adoption and biological filiation in this concern work in the same manner. The distinction between these two is, however, significant in other ways, and this will be discussed later in the chapter.

Notions of lineal descent and the transfer of rights and belonging are founded on an urge to create continuity through time. Rather than limiting the analytical focus to genealogical relations, we should pose the question of *how* people create such continuity and expect biological filiation to be one among many possible alternatives. Levi-Strauss' analysis of the house demonstrated that continuity could be created independently of lineages, even though kinship and descent were the language used to describe this continuity. Melanesian ethnography provides examples of yet other alternatives. For instance Leach (2009: 188) describes how knowledge associated with places is shared and transferred in, for example, filial relations and becomes an essence that creates similarity and continuity. Bamford (2007: 44) describes how continuity among the Kamea does not rely on filiation at all but on connections to the nonhuman environment. In the case of Wogeo there are various ways of creating continuity, but most of all continuity is based on the history of the places. These histories, and the *ro* and pathways, will be returned to in more detail in the next chapter.

Dan, the term for people belonging to a place, does not designate a given social group but is, as Hogbin noted (e.g. 1978), a polysemic category. *Dan* is used to speak of groups in general, such as 'the people on my side', 'the people supporting me', 'the people from my village' and similar (cf. Anderson 1996; 2003a; Schneider 1984). Not all of the people said to be of such a *dan* live in one place, and the totality of the people said to be of one *dan* are never brought together as a visible group – if they can be determined at all. A person could easily be assigned to a different *dan* within the same discourse about land rights or, for instance, in a food exchange. Gagin once said to me that maybe *dan* was *samting hangamap nating* (Tok Pisin for 'something hanging in the air'), implying that it had no real or concrete reference. *Dan* literally means 'water' and was explained by Hogbin as being a euphemism for semen (e.g. Hogbin 1935a: 316). Semen is sometimes spoken of as *dan*, for instance when Kulbobo was talking about ideas of conception, and since Wogeos often stated that 'the side of the father is the side of the ground; the side of the mother is blood', it could be possible that *dan* in this concern connotes semen. However, the term *dan* connotes other ideas as well – for instance that something or someone is not trustworthy or solid (like 'watery' tricks, lies, someone with 'two faces', a person who talks too much). In relation to groups, *dan* can perhaps also imply something that is not regarded as 'true' or whole: the cognatically related people of the place in opposition to 'true family' – the matrilineages of 'shared blood' or 'skin'.

Shared Blood

In his writings Hogbin did not mention matrilineages but referred to the matrimoieties as the only matrilateral organization. I was in Wogeo eight months before I learnt about the matrilineages, and it was not easily obtained information. They believed that the matrilineages should be kept hidden (they are *kana mustaki*, 'something to hide'), and people would sometimes even deny that such lineages existed (cf. Scott 2007). Since recruitment to the matrilineages is only achieved through birth, it would seem impossible to keep this identity hidden given that there are only about nine hundred people on the island. Probably most grown-ups have an idea of the matrilineal identity of the people in their district, but they do not necessarily agree with each other. Through time, people have done the best they can to obscure these matters, and it was hard to get a reliable picture of who belonged to which matrilineages – as in the case of the Oaoa lineage described in the last chapter. Hogbin noted that '[d]espite moiety membership following the female line, people remember men's names better than those of women, and there is thus more chance of a person's identifying his great-grandfathers than his great-grandmothers' (1978: 26). Seen in the light of the hiddenness of the matrilineages, it is not surprising that Hogbin noted that people appeared to remember fewer of their female ancestors than their male ones.

Matrilineal identity is kept out of common discourse because some matrilineages are regarded as 'no good' and have a reputation for using *iaboua* more often than others, or for stirring up conflicts and fights. Throughout history, attempts have been made to destroy such matrilineages by means of *iaboua*, murders or sterilization of their female members. Most deaths in Wogeo are seen as being the result of human agency, and deaths are frequently blamed on the use of *iaboua*; since *iaboua* knowledge is associated with the matrilineages, it is obvious that people do not wish to draw attention to their matrilineal identity. The secretiveness of the matrilineages is maintained since people do not speak about them in public, although they are sometimes gossiped about with lowered voices at night. 'A little knowledge is always there', Marifa said. As was the case with the matrilineage from Oaoa, some people have also taken refuge under other, better-regarded and more powerful matrilineages so that they would be spoken of as belonging to their protectors' matrilineages.

Gagin writes about the origin of *iaboua* in the following manner:

Sanguma [iaboua] *originated in Noba (old village of Falala) on the hill above Moajeje creek. The knowledge became known to a person (an ancestor) named Kulingling.*

Kulingling (of a Kilbong matrilineal line) was in his garden that morning for a secret mission, about taro magic, having in his hand a tanget *[Tok Pisin for Cordyline] 'Moanuboa', reciting magic for the better growth of his garden. Goleiangaianga (Onka) transformed into human [form] appeared to him. He showed him the skill, the magic; gave him the* kawawar *[Tok Pisin for ginger] for it with a* tanget *and told him to kill a dog and perform the spells and magic to give the dog its life. The person did so. He then said you have now got the skill of* sanguma.

In order to avoid implicating named people, I have omitted here the part of the story that relates how, and through which people, *sanguma* was spread and continued at the time of Jaran, the generation before Moarigum.

...It was [during] Jaran's reign that sanguma *became popular and spread. People may say before Jaran's time there was no* sanguma. *During the time of my grandfather's reign (Moarigum)* sanguma *was properly controlled, so I was repeatedly told.* Goate *(basket)* bilong sanguma *hanged in Singero house in Lukaluka (Dab).* Kebo Nyaboá *(sanguma skill) was then said to protect all chiefs around the island. Matters dealing with their mere survival were referred to* Kebo Nyaboá (sanguma) *to see to it that matters happened rightly in favour of chiefs whoever it may be. But the death of Moarigum using* kebo sanguma *... changed the trend and caused upset to the pattern.*[8]

Usually when I discussed the use of *iaboua* and the matrilineages with people, they would claim that such and such a family that was known to use *iaboua* had come from the outside. Some people told me that originally there were only two families on the island: Taregá and Kilbong. Then there came new families from the outside, and problems arose. One old man told me a different story and said that originally there were only Kilbong on the island and that they did not 'sit down' good until a Taregá woman came from the mainland and brought peace and order. On the other hand others would claim that all Kilbong came from the outside. Some people would agree to the foreign origins of their own family and tell the story of their family's arrival on the island, whereas others would deny that their family had a foreign origin. It is, thus, not possible or of any use to elicit one version of the stories of the origins of the families as being more authentic or authoritative than another.

The matrilineages were said to hold different *moanuboa* in addition to those associated with *koakoale* positions. They had the right to these various corpuses of knowledge that was passed down through generations within the lineage. For instance, the matrilineage of a man who died in the spring of 1999 possessed a *moanuboa* for taro – that is, fertility magic for taro. At the funeral the man's half-brother (with a different mother) threw a decorated *moanuboa* on the grave. As a token of grief he wanted to bury the taro magic with the dead so that nobody could use this magic again. Before the grave was covered with earth I saw another man, from the same matrilineage as the one who threw the *moanuboa*, pick it up from the grave and carry it away. The deceased's brother from the same mother later told me that the man had removed the *moanuboa* because he thought that his matrilineal relative did not have the right to do what he did. He had learnt the magic and had the right to use it, but he did not control it. 'It was not for him to bury this *moanuboa*. He does not belong to our family and has no right to make such a decision. If [the other man] had not removed it, I would have done it myself.' The man who had tried to take control of the *moanuboa* was a leader in his village and a man of great influence. If he had succeeded in his attempt to control knowledge belonging to a different lineage, he would have further increased his standing. For the true brother of the deceased the act was seen as an insult, and his explanation for his anger was that the man had also been given away in adoption and was no longer even the son of their common biological father.

In addition to owning *iaboua*, other types of magic, designs for body decorations and carvings, and so forth, some of the matrilineages were said to have certain tasks or specializations in society – both for good and bad – as already described for two of the lineages in the last chapter: the Moanoua and the Boaiak Saumgum families. Another lineage (Boaiak Bolova) played, according to Gagin, a 'leading role in planning of any form of killing – by spearing, magic or sorcery' but did not take an active part in them. It is important, however, to keep in mind that how these ascribed capacities are described varies according to who is talking – as is the case for all stories about origins and identity in Wogeo.

Houses and Matrilineages

The matrilineages are also associated with the named houses on the island. A named house, or a 'big house', is a house that has a history and exists independently of the built structure. Kulbobo said that there were originally only four named houses on the island. These were Singero, Ruma Bua, Omdara and Bagura. Ruma Bua was the 'dry' house that Onka was said to 'sit in front of', and the 'watery' Omdara was where Mafofo 'sat'. Singero, the middle house in Dab, was also associated with Mafofo. Bagura was the male cult house in Dab and Gole and does not exist in any other places on the island.[9] The other three houses were then sent around the island, most of them as dowry or following adopted children, but also as gifts to allies. When a house is 'sent' to another place, it is the house in the sense of its name, design, magic and properties that is sent. The original house will still remain on its original site. At least one of these four houses exists in most villages. Singero was, for instance, present in Maluka in 1999, and the old man, Taregá, who lived there was happy to tell me that we were 'one house'. In 1993 when Burenga of Badiata died, Marifa in Dab gave a pig for the food exchange in Burenga's name since they were of 'one house' – they were both living in Ruma Bua: in Badiata and in Dab (but were of different matrilineages). Then there are houses that came into being later and that have usually only been built within one of the four districts, although some of these have also been sent to other districts – like the house Masa-masa Matam Nara that came to Dab from Oaoa, and Baiau that came from Oakiblolo. Taregá Tabele had its origin in Dab and has since been sent to Boanag.

The matrilineal families own the named houses, but people of the matrilineage do not necessarily live in their houses. When a person inherits a *ro*, he or she also inherits the right to live in a certain house associated with the *ro*. The houses, thus, contain the people belonging to the place where it is built. The inheritance of the *ro* follows many kinds of pathway, and most of them are not matrilineal. The matrilineal families will often try, however, to send some of their own blood to the house through adoption and marriage, and such adoptions and marriages constitute common pathways into a place.

Some Wogeos would claim in private that their matrilineage owned the land associated with their house. Scott (2007b: 71–72) describes a similar situation among the Arosi. The Arosi were reluctant to disclose the narratives of matrilineages and their ancestral land in public, but in secret Scott was told the histories of the lineages and how they were the true owners of the land. To openly tell the true stories would cause conflict . In Wogeo, however, most people did not agree that the matrilineages had rights to land and that remained the case whether asked in public or in one-to-one conversations. During my first fieldwork Marifa often pointed out that to involve matrilineages in discussion of land rights was indeed wrong: 'Before we did not mention *tiná* when talking about the land; this was a strong taboo!' Still there is no doubt that the most powerful matrilineages have a strong attachment to certain areas of land and a great deal of influence on how the land is utilized. For instance, some people of the Moanoua family living in other places often claimed that land belonging to the *ro* Giririmba in Lukaluka and associated with Singero was theirs – a claim that was met with anger from the people in Dab, even from people belonging to *tiná* Moanoua. The loyalty towards one's matrilineage is not necessarily imperative when one's platial belonging is involved. But Gagin's claim that Wogeo society was getting 'more and more matrilineal' could indicate that matrilineages are becoming more important in this regard.

The main point to be made here is that there often is a strained relationship between the people of the place and the people owning the house on the place, in much the same manner as Parmentier (1987: 67) describes as a 'systematic disharmony' resulting from the combination of patrivirilocal residence and a matrilineal bias associated with houses in Belau; and Battaglia describes a 'fundamental tension between [matri]clan- and place-based allegiance' (1992: 4) among the Sabarl in southern Massim. In discussions of descent systems, similar situations have been described as the matrilineal puzzle (Richards 1950): members of the exogamous landholding matrilineages are born and raised apart from their land because of a norm of patrivirilocal residence after marriage (e.g. Scott 2007b: 22; A. Weiner 1976).

In Wogeo, the people of the place will strive to strengthen their ties to the place by preventing the matrilineage that owns the house on the place from gaining too much power, whereas the matrilineage will try to place their own people in the house. Since daughters usually move away from the house when they marry, this requires a continuous effort on the side of the matrilineages. Parmentier concludes that in Belau this 'disharmony' means that 'village loyalty is disjoined from kinship affiliation' (1987: 67), but for the Wogeos I would say that, although kinship affiliation is important, village loyalty does not depend on it. Central to the understanding of the ways Wogeos create continuity and belonging is the practice of adoption.

Adoption

Adoption is, as already mentioned, common in Wogeo as it is many places in Oceania (Anderson 2001; 2004; see also e.g. Brady 1976; Carroll 1970). For instance Sanum and Kulbobo had given away four of their six children in adoption and but adopted two, and Maria and Sanum's mother, Moita, gave away all of her four children in adoption and then herself adopted a girl together with her second husband in Badiata.[10]

People told me that ideally the adoptive mother should take the child just after birth and go through the same ritual cleansings as the birth mother,[11] although I know of only one such adoption in Dab. As a general rule adoptions should not be spoken of, and a child should not know that it was adopted, but this secrecy was more common in the past than it is today. In the 1990s, people knew about most adoptions, but still it was not normally considered proper to talk about them. My survey from 1994 indicated that nearly 50 per cent of the Dab villagers were adopted. In 1934 Hogbin noted that at least eighteen of Dab's fifty-two inhabitants were adopted (1935a: 318), and, since adoptions were kept secret to a greater extent then, it is not unlikely that the number was even higher.

The term for adoption is *oalaoala*, which literally means to take something out of something and add it to something else,[12] and adoption should be distinguished from fosterage, which is spoken of as 'looking after' a child. Adoption does not necessarily involve transfer of care for the child – an adopted child can live with its biological parents or with both sets of parents – but it is always about naming and the transfer of belonging and rights in land. Fosterage involves only transfer of nurture.

Childlessness is, however, not the only reason for adoptions, perhaps not even the most common one. Adoption is one of the most important means for the people of the place to strengthen ties to the ground independent of the continuity manifested in the matrilineages. As an illustrative scenario we could imagine that a man was married to a woman belonging to the matrilineage that owned the named house he lived in. If the matrilineage of his wife had a strong interest in the house and the place it was built upon, the man could, in order to strengthen his position in the place, adopt a child who would follow a pathway that was connected to the man's own history or to the history of the *ro* independent of his wife's matrilineage. In that way his child would be from a different matrilineage to that of his wife, and he would be the creator of continuity – not his wife's matrilineage. Or, if a house did not contain any people of the matrilineage that owned it, the matrilineage could attempt to send one of their children to the house in order to manifest and strengthen their relationship to the house and the place. A man can also increase his or his matrilineage's influence by spreading his or his sister's children. We could also imagine that the ideal adoption for a man who lives in a house that his matrilineage owns would be the adoption of a child from his own matrilineage. Obviously this would give him (and his matrilineage) a strong foothold in the place where the house is built. He cannot, however, adopt a child from his own matrilineage. Such adoptions are the only form of adoption that is explicitly tabooed in Wogeo: 'You should not call your mother's brother father.'[13] Such adoptions have taken place, though, but these are indeed something to hide.

During my last fieldwork I was told of a few such adoptions in great secrecy, and I cannot disclose them here.

Some adoptions are made exclusively in order to follow pathways, that is, to commemorate certain events or to honour alliances. Adoptions can also take place as a sort of peace offering: 'If you have something from my body, the two of us cannot be cross', Tarere said, and some adoptions have been done to make peace between former enemies. One woman in Dab is adopted from Falala in this manner. Her father in Falala was involved in a bitter conflict with a man in Dab. A *koakoale* of Moaroka took upon himself to be a mediator, and he said that the man from Falala should send his daughter in adoption to Dab. This he did, and the relationship between the two men then stayed peaceful.

Adoption in Wogeo does not, as mentioned, necessarily imply a total transfer of care for the child, but it is always about creating a proper belonging for the child by giving it a name and rights that are spoken of as belonging to a place. It is as much about where a child should belong as about who should raise and nurture it. The relations that produced it are not replaced by a new set of relations as would be the ideal in, for example, Norway (cf. e.g. Howell 2001; 2006); adoption in Wogeo rather *adds* relations that become part of the constitution of the child as a social person. In Strathern's perspective (1988), a child is an objectification of the relation between a man and a woman. When a child is adopted it becomes an objectification also of the relationship between the biological parents and the adoptive parents (or one of the parents). At the same time the child enters a relation to its adoptive parents that is similar to the relation it has to its biological parents and thus becomes an objectification also of their relationship. All these relations are parts of the construction of the child 'as the plural and composite site of the relationships that produced [it]' (ibid.: 13). The relations of which a child is the product show which place is the right one for the child: 'a white stone belongs in a white place, a black stone in a black place,' a Wogeo woman said to me when speaking about adoption (see also Anderson 2001).

* * *

When it comes to inheritance and succession, Wogeos strive to maintain a balance between the two main principles of belonging, and there cannot (or need not) be any single 'system' or regular pattern of pathways followed to establish a person's platial belonging. There is, on one hand, a tendency to emphasize patrifiliation, and even patrilineality, in discourses about succession, and virilocality is the general norm of residence. On the other hand, the matrilineages own the houses and wish to gain influence in the place. The work of maintaining the balance between the two, as is often a function of adoptions and marriages, is continuous and endless and the source of conflicts. Adoption, succession and inheritance, as well as matrilineages and houses, will be the topic of the next chapter, which deals with inheritance and land rights in Dab. From neighbouring Kairiru, Smith quotes a man who, when discussing genealogies, said, 'we fight with stories' (Smith 2002: 114). In a similar fashion, when talking about the stories of the *ro* in Dab, Kulbobo said: 'This is politics, Iamoe.'

Notes

1. McKinnon (1995: 172).
2. See also Carrier and Carrier (1991: 11–25); Hviding (1996: 131–36, 2003).
3. See Scheffler (1985) for a discussion on Meyer Fortes' distinction between the concepts of filiation and descent.
4. Carsten and Hugh-Jones (1995); Lévi-Strauss (1983).
5. See also Hviding (1993, 1996, 2003).
6. Hogbin notes that the various parts of the dress of a leoa spirit, called to protect tabooed crops prior to an *oaraboa* (that is, the obligation to make them), also goes with the *ro* (1970b: 62). The trading partners (*lo*) on the mainland are also inherited with the *ro*.
7. *Jala osar* literally means to clear an old path that is overgrown with vegetation or to clear a new path. Marifa used the phrase when he explained to me how an adoption could follow a path. If the relation between the two parties (adopters and birth parents) had not been kept strong through exchanges, the adopters would send a pig to the birth parents prior to the adoption in order to 'clear the path'.
8. In Kulbobo's version of the story about Onka in Onevaro (see chapter 3), Kuliling (Kulingling in Gagin's account) was one of Onka's names. Gagin refers to this as the name of a man who received the magic (the 'ginger') for *iaboua* from Onka. In Gagin's version *iaboua* was introduced only a few generations before Moarigum, whereas others, including Kulbobo, would say that *iaboua* came in the mythical past. Common to Gagin's account and others I have heard is that they ascribe to women (and, hence, the matrilineages) the role of spreading and starting to misuse *iaboua*.
9. It is, however, found several places in the trade network.
10. Contrary to my findings, Hogbin (1935/36a: 27) wrote that there were few families with both biological and adopted children. Probably this discrepancy is due to the greater extent of secrecy surrounding adoptions in the 1930s.
11. This is contrary to what Hogbin (1935/36a: 23) wrote.
12. I have also heard it interpreted as meaning to peel off the bark of a tree, and Kulbobo used the image of taking a page out of a book.
13. Hogbin (1935/36a: 21) wrote that the only relation that should be avoided was adoption of children from the opposite moiety of the adoptive mother (in which case the child would call his classificatory mother's brother 'father'). He explains this with the rule of moiety exogamy: since the child then would have to learn that it is of a different moiety than that of his or her mother in order to choose a proper spouse, it would be impossible to keep the adoption secret. Since Hogbin was not aware of the matrilineages, and the moieties are, like the matrilineages, spoken of as *tiná*, it was impossible for him to draw any connection to the matrilineages.

⤝ Chapter 9 ⤞

Dab Village – its Land, Houses and People

The last chapter described how the *ro* in a named house are connected to the land and the histories of the people belonging to a village. Here we will take a closer look at the *ro* and the land of Dab. By towards the end of my first fieldwork, I had learnt to orient myself in the bush of Dab and was able to make a rough map of the land belonging to the part of the village that I knew best. I walked with Maria through the bush, and she pointed out the various sections to me, using trees, pathways, stones and other formations in the landscape to demarcate them. Figure 9.1 shows the map that we made of the land belonging to Kajenamoa and Lukaluka in *vanua* Dab – Maria did not know enough about the land in Moarmoar to include that part of the bush. In addition to gardening land, people also hold rights in certain trees – particularly almond and breadfruit trees.[1] Those who have the right to the land in which trees are rooted own most of them, but rights in trees can also be given away to people living in other places. Anyone can pick the occasional nuts that have fallen to the ground anywhere, but larger amounts should only be harvested from one's own trees. Rights in single trees are upheld as long as people gather the fruits from the trees, and if they contribute with roof thatch when someone is building a new house in the village to which the tree belongs. It was also not a big deal if people made a garden on land not belonging to them if the intention was to produce for daily consumption only. As long as people did not cut down fruit or nut trees or destroy large trees, it did not matter, according to Maria. But if the garden was made with a particular event or ritual in mind, it was different. It would mean that the food produced in the garden was to represent someone as belonging to a certain place, and where the food had been produced would, thus, become significant.

The rights to the land of the village are associated with the *ro*, and the *ro* in the ceiling of a house constitute in this manner a map of the village land. As we saw in the last chapter, a house is also associated with the matrilineages and, as discussed in the introduction to this book, great significance is given to house building. Below I will describe the construction of Singero in Dab.

The Construction of Singero

When I returned to Dab for a second visit in October 1998, my Dab family had temporarily moved to the house of Maria's mother Moita on the beach. Singero had been torn down, and a new house was under construction. People said that I was really lucky to come when they were going to complete the house since Singero was regarded as one of the most important houses on the island. Many

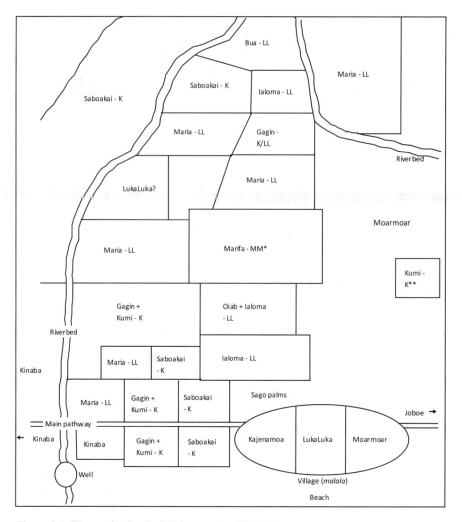

Figure 9.1: The garden land of Kajenamoa and Lukaluka

LL stands for Lukaluka, K for Kajenamoa and MM for Moarmoar.

* Marifa's plot (of Moarmoar) is also marked off since the land is regarded as being inside the land belonging to Kajenamoa/Lukaluka.

**Kumi has inherited this plot within Moarmoar's ground from Saoang (also of Kajenamoa) who was particularly fond of this piece of land. In the 1990s, Matarena of Moarmoar had a garden here.

significant and socially important rituals and events accompanied the construction this important house.

As described in the last chapter, Wogeos distinguish between 'big', named houses and houses that are merely dwellings. A named house has a certain place in the village (*ruma maleka*), a history and a name. It has a particular design and capacities and is associated with a certain matrilineage. Wogeo houses are mostly made from bush material, and a good house lasts for fifteen to twenty years. Then people have to build a new house, but in the case of named houses, it is the same house that is rebuilt – not a new house. Named houses, with their names, designs, capacities and values, exist independently of the actual built structures. In this way they can be given away to other villages – that is, as a replica, since the original house will remain in its place (*maleka*).

The various parts of such a house are imbued with meaning – both as a construction and as a dwelling. The gables are designed and fastened by *koakoale* from the corresponding sides of the village; the end posts have names associated with the matrilineal families and the sides of the village; the rafters in the ceiling are connected to the various sections of land surrounding the village, and the roof-thatch should be made and fastened by the set of people having rights in the land of the village. In this manner a house can be seen as a microcosm of the social and physical composition of the village: an embodiment of its estate, history and social relations.

Singero has its place in Lukaluka, the middle part of Dab: in front of the culture hero stone Mafofo and opposite the site of the Dab *nyaboá*, Bagura (cf. Hogbin 1939: 159). Singero is said to be a 'watery' (*dandan*) house since it is associated with Mafofo. One cannot be sure that one is being told the truth in Singero – just as Mafofo tried to trick Onka in various ways. In the same manner, Lukaluka is said to be a place with 'two faces'. Lukaluka (and Singero) is in the middle of the village, with Kajenamoa in the downward direction and Moarmoar in the upward direction – it 'faces' both the good and bad sides. Ruma Bua in Moarmoar is a good house, a house of peace. If anyone in fear of their life enters Ruma Bua, no one can harm them. Kajenamoa, on the other hand, is the place where meetings regarding sorcery and conflicts are held. Omdara, the house often associated with this side or direction (and with Mafofo) and spoken of in Tok Pisin as a *haus nogut* ('bad house'), was not present in Dab during my research, and Taregá Tabele in Kajenamoa is, to my knowledge, not ascribed any particular qualities.

All named houses should be treated with respect, lest the houses lose their strength or power: they become 'watery' (*dandandi*) – as could have been the case with Singero in the two following examples, one from my own research and one from Hogbin's work. In 1998 a married woman and her lover had sex in a named and important house. It was discovered, and the head of the household got very angry. They had disrespected the house, and it was no longer 'dry'. It was demanded that the couple should pay a fine of several hundred Kina or the equivalent in pigs in order to make the house strong again. To disrespect the house is a grave offence – as it also is to be violated in any manner inside a house. Hogbin (1940: 18) described an incident when some money had been stolen from a basket hanging from a rafter in Singero. The owner of the basket was very upset, and, before the culprit was found, Moarigum's wife Iamoe gave him some of her own money to compensate his loss. Iamoe was of the matrilineage that owned Singero, and Moarigum got the right to live in this house through Iamoe. When Iamoe gave the money, she acted as the owner of the house in which he had been violated – something that was her responsibility as owner rather than Moarigum's, who was just the head of the household.

Bagura, the *nyaboá* in Dab, and Singero are like the king and the queen of Wogeo, Kulbobo said.[2] Bagura had not been built for decades, and Singero was the only house in Lukaluka in the 1990s.[3] When I arrived in October 1998, the framework of the new Singero was ready. Most of the roof beams had been fastened, and people said that it was almost completed. The parts missing were the main supporting roof beam (*kaiuk*) from one side of the house to the other, the main rafters (*ro*) in the ceiling and the roof-thatch (*vato*). A house is seen as completed when the thatch covers the roof – even though the walls and the floor may not yet have been made.

Under the houses nearby, *vato* were piled up, and I heard that several people were busy making more. The *vato* are made from the leaves of the sago palm, and making *vato* is seen as the hardest and most time-consuming part of building a new house. First the leaves have to be gathered. The sago palms have long, sharp spikes on the stem, and great care needs to be taken when collecting the leaves. Bundles of leaves are carried to the village and the marrow of every single leaf has to be partially removed in order to be able to fold it. This is tedious work, particularly since the leaves are edged with tiny thorns that easily penetrate the skin and are almost impossible to remove. After the marrow has been removed, the leaves are stitched together four by four with tiny pieces of wood from the stem of the sago leaves – shorter leaves inside of the longer leaves. Then the leaf bundles are folded over a stick – about thirty on each stick – and stitched onto it with rattan, collected in the mountains. One *vato* thus consists of around 120 single leaves. A big house like Singero demands about 400 *vato* – made from 48,000 single leaves. Many people are usually involved in this work, as will be made clear below.[4]

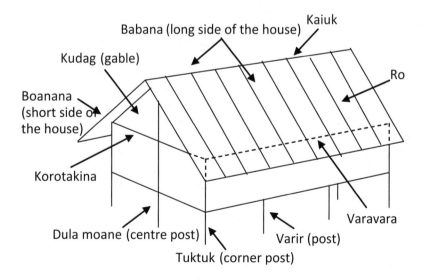

Figure 9.2: The terms for the most important of the parts of a house

When I arrived, most of the *vato* for Singero were ready, but the preparations for the food exchange (*olage*) that should conclude the fastening of the *vato* took another week. Meanwhile, the *kaiuk* and the *ro* were made and tied to the roof. The *kaiuk* is like a bridge, Kulbobo said: 'It brings together the two sides of the house.' *Kaiuk* is also the term used for the vast area of sea between the island and the mainland where no boats can be seen and no engines heard from the shore – like 'a bridge' between Wogeo and the mainland. In the New Year celebrations, the night of the celebration was also referred to as *kaiuk* (*vanua kaiukdi*) – the 'bridge' between the old and the new year or, literally, island. In houses, the *kaiuk* brings together the two sides of the village, and the gables (*kudag*) on each side represent the two sides of the village. The *kaiuk* in the roof of Singero was made from a long, thick liana. It had been hard to find one that was long and straight enough, Tarere explained, but the search had been worthwhile since it was stronger and more enduring than a tree trunk.

Then the *ro* were fastened. It was the people who had rights in the land belonging to Dab who made the *ro*. The parts of the *ro* that would be visible under the edge of the ceiling were carved and painted in different designs, some of them elaborate in the likeness of animal heads (e.g. snakes and lizards), others with simpler 'marks'. People claimed that in the past all the *ro* would have been beautifully carved, but in the 1990s usually only a couple of *ro* in a house were carved. Each man had his favourite design, but he could make whatever design he wished. In the case of the new Singero, many of the men of Dab put effort into making the *ro* beautiful, and most of them were carved and decorated with leaves and paint on the day they were fastened.

All the houses in a village have the same set of named *ro* (see also Hogbin 1939: 160–65). In Dab there are sixteen *ro* – eight on each side (*varo*, the front and *kalet*, the back) of the house – and this is also the rule in most of the villages on the island.[5] A *ro* was often explained to me as being 'the ticket to the land'. Each *ro* is connected to plots of land in the bush: some *ro* have many or big plots; others have few or smaller ones. 'The rafter is the root, and the land grows from it,' said one of Hogbin's informants (ibid.: 163). The *ro* are divided into two or three groups according to the different parts of the village – in Dab, those to the west, to Kajenamoa; those to the east, to Moarmoar; and those in the middle, to Lukaluka. At the time of Hogbin's fieldwork the *ro* were said to truly belong to the *nyaboá*, the male cult house. They were also made in the named houses, but these were copies – 'the *nyaboá* is the model and … the others are imitations' (ibid.), Hogbin wrote. In the 1990s, the *nyaboá* was not built, and the *ro* were made only in the named houses.

Most male, and some female, adult members of the villages own the right to at least one *ro*. The 'largest' ones (with most land) are usually owned by the highest ranked *koakoale* of that part of the village. When people in Wogeo talk about their land, they talk about their *ro*. 'If you like to learn about our land and the history of our land, you have to sit down with the old men in the villages and ask them about the *ro* in their houses,' I was told when I first came to Wogeo.

Some days after the *ro* had been fastened in the roof of Singero, the time for covering them with *vato* had come. Many people had come to the village – and the men gathered around Singero while the women were busy cooking. Some of the men were splitting up rattan that was going to be used to fasten the *vato*. 'Look at them,' Kulbobo said. 'They are all Kilbong; they belong to *tiná* Moanoua.' This family was said to own Singero,[6] and it was their responsibility to help to build the house. I did, however, also see men from the Taregá moiety involved in this work, and I guess Kulbobo spoke as if they were all Kilbong in order to emphasize this family's connection to Singero.

Most of the *vato* were now placed in rows on the ground in front of the *ro*. Iaman from Joboe beat the *giramoa* (slit gong) to call for those who had not yet arrived. Iaman was known as one of the most skilled *giramoa* players on the island, and the message, made up by several beats of different length and strength, could be heard several villages away.[7] Soon the last men arrived, and some of the men then climbed up onto the roof – one on each *ro*. On the tip of long sticks, they were given *vato* and started to tie them to the rafters. When they had reached the *varavara* (see Fig. 9.2), Kulbobo and Jabat from Kinaba stood up and spoke. 'Now is the time to come forward and talk if anyone has something to say', they said. Jabat was the son of Moarigum's adoptive sister, and thus had a strong connection to Lukaluka. Kulbobo spoke as a *koakoale* of Dab and as a member of *tiná* Moanoua – Singero's owners. Nobody else spoke, and the men who should contribute *vato* to the various *ro* carried them forward and placed them in front of the *ro* – first those from Dab, then those from the other villages.

Vato are like money, Wogeos often said. If anyone holds rights in a tree or a piece of land within the area belonging to a *ro*, they have to contribute one or two *vato* to fasten onto the *ro* when a new house is built. If they do not do this, the rights can be taken from them. The *vato* were placed on the ground in rows in front of each *ro*, and the *vato* displayed on the ground constituted a map over the rights to the land belonging to the *ro*. The cast of people gathered were the people affiliated to the ground in Dab, and their rights to the ground and trees of Dab were concretized in these rows of *vato* in front of the *ro*.

The *vato* were then fastened, and the work continued until the one side of the roof was covered with *vato*. Then the procedure started over again on the back of the house. Kulbobo and Tarere supervised the work. People said that there were often a lot of arguments and even fights at this stage of the work. Conflicts regarding land rights would be brought to the fore and had to be negotiated and settled. This did not, however, happen in the case of Singero or at the construction of the other two major houses that I have witnessed. When the work was finished, the men who had participated sat down on the floor inside the house – those affiliated with Kajenamoa and Lukaluka on that side of the house and those affiliated with Moarmoar on the other side. The women then carried in plates of food for them to eat. We all rested for a while before it was time for the main food exchange – *olage* – for the house.

Each village in Onevaro district contributed to the exchange with one large basket (*kamina*) of food that had been cooked in stone ovens.[8] The baskets were meant for the women who had made *vato* for Singero, and they were supposed to be displayed in front of the house. This time, however, they were placed in the garden in front of the house where Maria and her family were living at the time.

Two more baskets were added, intended for the young boys who had helped work on the house. The food in these two baskets was a combined contribution from all the women present. Several large plates of cooked food were also presented. They were for all the men who had helped build the house – the women from Dab gave to the men from the other villages, whereas the women from the other villages gave to the men in Dab. These plates were carried to the men, who once more had gathered inside Singero, and were exchanged between the two sides. The baskets, apart from the two for the young boys, were then exchanged so that no one received a basket to which they had contributed. Afterwards everybody sat down to eat, and some of the food that was left was carried back to people's respective villages. Now Singero was a house proper.

Singero's Traditional Design

Some days later the *kudag* were made and attached to the gables. With the help of some young boys, Kulbobo made the *kudag* on the Moarmoar side, and Saboakai made the one on the Kajenamoa side. They were made from plaited strips of bamboo, and the two men painted them with different designs according to their own liking. Both Kulbobo and Saboakai were from the Moanoua matrilineage, and they were *koakoale* in their parts of the village – Saboakai had his *maleka* in Kajenamoa and Kulbobo in Moarmoar. Kulbobo asked me to photograph him under his *kudag* and told me explicitly that among all the photos I had taken of him, this was the one I should send him. He was also happy that my room was made on the Moarmoar side so that I would sleep under the *ro* belonging to his side of the village. Hogbin (1970b: 77) wrote that the house of *koakoale* often had a statue of a man with 'an enormous penis fully erect' attached to the *kudag*

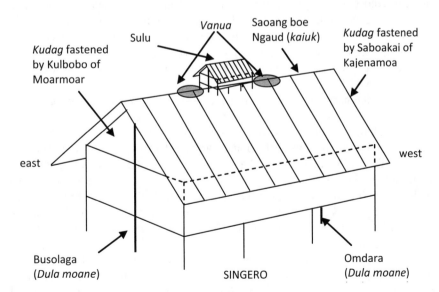

Figure 9.3: The names of the parts of the traditional Singero

on each side – something that would have made the representations of the two *koakoale* and their power quite evident.

In Hogbin's time, Singero had had a distinct design. But in the 1990s, houses in Wogeo were built in a plainer, common PNG style, and according to the preferences of the individual house owners. Earlier the style had been different: the roofs on most houses in Wogeo reached down over the veranda so that people could more easily hide and defend their house, and all the named houses were built according to their own particular design and decoration. Singero had extended gables on each end of the roof, giving it a look that resembled the typical style of the *nyaboá* on the island.

Singero also had a small house, called Sulu, made on the top of the roof (see Fig. 9.3 and photos in Hogbin 1970b: 71; 1978: pl. 1). On each side of the house Sulu, small patches of ground were planted with tiny plants, called *vanua*. I never heard any explanation of these peculiarities on the roof of Singero. Old Marifa used to laugh when he spoke about it – he found it quite amusing – and said that it was only for fun (*bilas tasol*, 'only a decoration' in Tok Pisin). Considering Singero's importance and position in the 'middle place' of the island, however, I believe that it is not too presumptuous to interpret the little house with the two *vanua* on each side as an image of Singero and Lukaluka dividing the island into two sides as described previously.

The posts on each side of the doorway into Singero were named and should traditionally be carved and fastened by the two leading *koakoale* in Dab, representing the two leading matrilineages. The two main bearing posts on each side of the house (*dula moane*) were also named and powerful. In Singero the one on the western (downwards) side was called Omdara, as was the name of one of the four most important houses in Dab belonging to Kajenamoa. In Omdara a woman can be tricked into marrying a man if she sits under a particular *ro*. The name referred to the fake blood (*dara*) that Onka made from betel nuts when Mafofo tried to kill him by pushing the post into the hole where Onka was standing. It was also the name of the spear that should be placed in the front of Udemtaregá – Lukaluka's big trading canoe. The right to build and sail Udemtaregá belonged to Lukaluka where Mafofo's *maleka* was.

Busolaga, the name of the post on the opposite side, was also a name for the ceremonial spear (*lilibur*) with cassowary feathers carried as an emblem by the *koakoale* belonging to the Moanoua family.[9] Busolaga was the post of Singero, and Omdara was the post from the house Omdara, Kulbobo said. These were the two main houses in Kajenamoa/Lukaluka, even though Omdara had not been in Dab for a long time. The two posts were said to be in both of these houses. Ruma Bua in Moarmoar had the two posts Oaring and Bulbag. The *kaiuk* of Singero was called Saoang boe Ngaud, which is also the name of the main *ro* in Kajenamoa. Saoang and Ngaud were also two of the four male names that Onka was said to have instated in Dab.

The two most important *ro* in Dab are called Tarajimba and Giririmba. The rights to these two *ro* are associated with the leading positions in the two sides of the village. These two *ro* are in all the villages, people often told me. When I checked this out around the island, people did not cite these two names for the main *ro* in all the villages. The man who followed me around on the back of the island got annoyed when I asked people about this. 'Listen Iamoe', he would say. 'What I have told you is the truth. These two *ro* are in all the villages, but in some places they are only in the *nyaboá*.' People in the villages in question did not necessarily agree with this, but Tarajimba and Giririmba are found in many (although not all) villages around the island, and these two, together with the *ro* Tokodub (the *ro* where the *iaboua* basket used to hang) were the only three of the sixteen *ro* in Dab that had their own names and not the names of men. I will continue by presenting the inheritance and the history of the various *ro* in Dab.

Inheritance of Rights

The inheritance of rights in a *ro* is usually spoken of as following a principle of patrifiliation. On closer scrutiny this is, as already discussed in the last chapter, often not the case for the actual transfer of rights. Both men and women can inherit cultivation rights, and they can also inherit from people other than their parents. Hogbin wrote that women could inherit land or get rights to land as dowry, but they would entrust these to their husbands and not speak about them as 'their' land or make decisions about the cultivation (1939: 138; see also 1970a: 307). He noted, however, that a man cannot use his wife's dowry land as dowry for his own daughters, and if his wife dies without children, her land returns to her kin (1978: 84). The women I spoke to all referred to the gardens they cultivated as 'theirs' – whether they themselves or their husbands had inherited them – and I wonder if perhaps a female anthropologist speaking to women about ownership of the gardens would have received different answers to those Hogbin did in the 1930s. In his description of the *ro* in Dab in 1933 (1939: 162–63), he wrote that as many as eight of the fifteen *ro* he accounted for had been inherited from women (by men). However, only one of the women described as having passed on *ro* in Hogbin's account is included in the histories of the *ro* that I collected. Some of the others appear as having passed on partial rights – in trees or pieces of land belonging to certain *ro* – and the obligation to make *vato* for the *ro*, but most of the histories of the *ro* that I collected emphasized lists of Dab men stretching back in time as principal right holders. Only two women, some three or four generations ago, are mentioned as having passed on principal rights to *ro* (as was the case in Moaroka). In 1999, Maria was the only woman in Dab who was regarded as a proper *ro* holder. Two other women were each looking after their *ro* but were not spoken of as *ro* holders (but both of them still talked about the gardens as 'theirs'). It therefore appears as though female links in the histories of the *ro* are more easily forgotten than male ones. Considering the 'hiddenness' of the matrilineal ties and that matrilineal transfer of land over generations is seen as something that should be avoided, this makes sense. On the other hand, several of the men whom Hogbin described as *ro* holders have also been left out in the accounts given to me. The histories of the *ro* are recounted to fit the present situation, and, as I will demonstrate below, there are always various alternative links or stories to emphasize when deciding who is to hold which *ro*.

When comparing my own data to Hogbin's account of the construction of the *nyaboá* Bagura in 1933, continuous lines of patrifiliation cannot be found for many of the *ro*. In the 1990s only two or three of the *ro* holders actually living in Dab had inherited their rights from their biological fathers. When discussing the paths of inheritance with people, they would not regard inheritance following non-filial links as abnormalities, but would tell me how inheritance always follows histories or pathways – patrifiliation being only one such pathway. To underline the legitimacy of their claims, people would, however, still use lines of patrifiliation if possible. In 1995, Gagin wrote in a letter to me:

> *[I]t is important to follow stories or pathways in Wogeo kastom as far as the individual and family rights of ownership are concerned. When an individual cannot put forward any logical argument in regards to how his/her ownership of certain land, coconut grove, galip [kangar] tree or breadfruit tree came to be, in relation to 'bihainim stori' [follow a story] or pathway, the big-man can easily disapprove of his identity of ownership and give the property to a person with a logical story. When these stories are told, usually more than one person knows about the same story, and such people should not be in the same village but in different villages so that they can give support to the person with the right of ownership.*

Hogbin did not write much about the *ro*, but in an article from 1939 he wrote extensively about land tenure and noted that membership in the local groups was 'determined less by birth than by inheritance of cultivation rights' (1939: 121). This is of central importance to the constitution of belonging and identity in Wogeo. Below I will present some of the stories the *ro* in Dab have followed, stories or pathways that make up what Gagin called 'logical reasons' for people to inherit a *ro*.

In Table 9.1 is an outline of the distribution of the Dab *ro* according to the stories that are mostly agreed upon, including who gave *vato* to each *ro* – and following the table are presented the detailed histories of the eight *ro* on the front of the house. I hardly ever got the same story about the *ro* from two different people, and many conflicts regarding power, position and origins surfaced when talking to people. I will therefore present all the different versions of the *ro* inheritance I was told about. This is at the cost of readability, as it involves many names and kinship relations, but it demonstrates the complexity and the multitude of possible directions the inheritance paths can take. I have also chosen to present the stories in this manner in order to avoid emphasizing one version or one person's political agenda at the cost of the others. The way these stories are used to argue for or against people's rights to *ro* and place will be the topic for the rest of this chapter.

Table 9.1: The *ro* of Singero in 1999. The eight *ro* on the front side of the house are regarded as the most important. The capital letters K, LL and MM indicates whether the *ro* belongs to Kajenamoa, Lukaluka or Moarmoar.

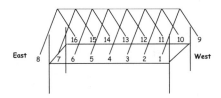

	Ro	Right holders	*Vato* contributed
K	1. Saoang Ngaud	Kumi and Gagin	• Oaiari of Kinaba – land • Tarere – land • Matarena – land
K	**2. Saboakai**	Saboakai	No vato contributed
K	**3. Saboaka/ Mangoari boe Gagin**	Unclear – Mangoari or/and Roger	• Iaman (Joboe) – *kangar* + breadfruit • Urmina (Joboe) – *kangar* • Bajimula (Joboe) – *kangar* + sago • Tarere – land • Three others should also have given
L	**4. Giririmba**	Maria	No *vato* contributed
M	**5. Tokodub**	Kulbobo	• Maloa (Joboe) – land • Oambo – *ib* (but has planted coconuts) • Ialoma – land
M	**6. Tarajimba**	Kulbobo or Boaiak	• Salam (Badiata) – land + *kangar* • Tangarua – *oeka* • Libaliba – land
M	**7. Itanefa Tamane/Boamera**	Matarena or Boaiak	No *vato* contributed
M	**8. Oambo**	Oambo (Tangina's FBS)	• Iaman – *kangar* • Four others should also have given
K	**9. Gagin**	Gagin	• Boarinya – *oasik* + breadfruit
M	**10. Koan Koajala**	Koan (and Sanakoa)	No *vato* contributed
L	**11. Kenang**	Oiab	No *vato* contributed

	Ro	**Right holders**	*Vato* **contributed**
L	**12. Moanuboa**	Maria	No *vato* contributed
M	**13. Kasiket boe Boara**	Kulbobo	No *vato* contributed
L	**14. Oiab/Kauni Saboau**	Bua or Oiab	No *vato* contributed
L	**15. Ialoma/ Kalosika**	Ialoma	• Oaiari (Kinaba) – breadfruit, *kangar*, sago • Iaman (Joboe) – breadfruit • Several others should also have given
M	**16. Oaring**	Libaliba	No *vato* contributed, but in 1994 Marifa named five people owing *vato* for *kangar*.

Ro 1. Saoang Ngaud

This *ro* is the most important one in Kajenamoa and should ideally be held by the leading *koakoale* in that part of the village. Consensus regarding the stories of inheritance of such important *ro* is crucial to maintain, and in this example we will see that Gagin in the 1990s had managed to maintain quite a solid consensus of his rights to the *ro* even though alternative pathways of inheritance could disturb this agreement. The story also involves political strategies concerning the distribution of power in the village.

In 1999 Gagin held the right to this *ro* together with Kumi, but he had not inherited the right from his father Dale. Dale had inherited his position and *ro* in Lukaluka from his *koakoale* father, Moarigum, who again had inherited his rights from his adoptive father Kenang. Gagin's position in Kajenamoa is the result of the efforts of Jaran, a great old *koakoale* in Kajenamoa/Lukaluka, to make Moarigum his heir, even though he was the son of Kenang and belonged to Lukaluka. According to Kulbobo, Jaran had 'kept pulling' Moarigum to Kajenamoa from the time when he was still a child, and in Hogbin's days, Moarigum actually spoke of Jaran as his father – although he was not acknowledged as his adoptive father (probably there was a kinship relation that prohibited an adoption). Jaran eventually chose Moarigum as *koakoale malala* in Kajenamoa/Lukaluka in favour of his eldest son Kedoboa (Hogbin 1940: 27).

Following the story of Jaran and Moarigum, Dale named his son Gagin after one of Jaran's sons and 'sent' him from Lukaluka to Kajenamoa so that he would have his *maleka* there: Gagin followed a path from Lukaluka to Kajenamoa. Saoang, Kedoboa's son, who many people claim should really have been the leading *koakoale* in Kajenamoa, died without sons of his own, and Gagin took the place in Kajenamoa that a son of Saoang would have had. He was also given the additional name Ngaud from the *ro* Saoang Ngaud.

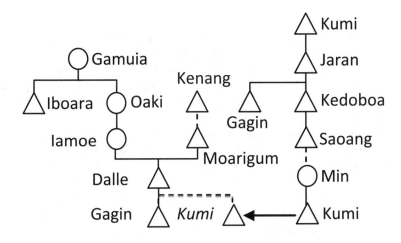

Figure 9.4. *Ro* 1. Saoang Ngaud – main *ro* in Kajenamoa

Min from Kajenamoa was Saoang's adopted daughter and was celebrated as a *moede* at her first *baras*. Her son was named Kumi after Jaran's father. Kumi's father died before Kumi was born, and Kumi remained in Kajenamoa, his mother's place. Gagin then adopted Kumi as a brother so that Kumi would get the proper rights in the *ro* Saoang Ngaud in Kajenamoa after his grandfather Saoang.[10] Gagin, as Ngaud, and Kumi were both given names and rights in this *ro* following these pathways and not through exclusive principles of patrifiliation.

Some said that Kumi was the *ngaro* of Gagin – his second-in-command – but others maintained that Kumi was the true *koakoale* of Kajenamoa. Should conflict arise between the two, these ambiguities could easily become problematic, but most likely Gagin's acknowledgement of Kumi's rights and the adoption of him as a brother will prevent such a situation from occurring. In addition, Kumi was of the Boaiak Bolova matrilineage, the long time allies of Gagin's lineage Boaiak Saumgum. Gagin has also said that Kumi will eventually get the principal right to this *ro* to pass on to his children. Both of the men had married women from the Moanoua family (arranged by their allies), and their sons would, thus, both have the proper matrilineal belonging to become powerful *koakoale* in Kajenamoa – a position that in the late 1990s seemed to belong to Gagin's son, Jaran – just like the old Jaran about a hundred years ago (as discussed in chapter 7). Kumi had, by 1999, no sons.[11] The *ro* is associated with the house Taregá Tabele.

Oaiari from Kinaba contributed *vato* for the use of land belonging to this *ro* – probably the same land that Hogbin (1939: 133) noted that Oaiari's father's adoptive father, Iboara, cultivated in 1934. Oaiari often participated in rituals and activities in Dab, on the Kajenamoa/Lukaluka side, and felt a strong connection to this place. Iboara was the mother's brother of the powerful *moede* Iamoe in Lukaluka/Kajenamoa.[12] There is also, independent of kinship, an enduring alliance between Oaiari's side of Kinaba and Kajenamoa/Lukaluka as places – the people from these two places may be spoken of as *dan ta*.[13]

Ro 2. Saboakai

The *ro* Saboakai is associated with a subsection (referred to as *kona*, 'corner' in Tok Pisin) of Kajenamoa called Kurita. It is one of two *ro* that are totally outside the control of Dab's leading *koakoale*. The stories told about this *ro* illustrate how the naming and the transference of rights in a *ro* are important, and how adoption is an important means to secure continuity as well as alliances, even though the origins of the path the adoptions follow remain hidden.

Saboakai inherited this *ro* from his adoptive father, Ulbaia, who died in January 1994 (see chapter 4). The name that he received from the *ro* had been given to several boys during the last century. Ulbaia's adoptive father, Boani, adopted one of Moarigum's sons and gave him the name Saboakai.[14] Alas, this Saboakai died when the great trading canoe Udemtarega was lost at sea in 1947 with fourteen of the young men of the district.[15] Boani then gave the name Saboakai to another adoptive son, but he also died young without children and there were, thus, no *ro* holders named Saboakai in that generation. Ulbaia did not have any children of his own, but he adopted the son of Jauon, Moarigum's youngest and dearest daughter, and gave him the name Saboakai. He is the present holder of the *ro*, and the adoption is spoken of as following a pathway, as repeating the actions of the predecessors of the people involved.

I have not heard anyone contest either Saboakai's position in the village or the history of this *ro*, an oddity when it comes to inheritance of *ro*. And this is the case even though Ulbaia was adopted (although this was denied by some), and even though I have not been able to find out anything about his birth parents. Likewise, I do not have any information on Boani's or Nyem's parents. Hogbin (1978: 100) wrote that Boani belonged to Bajor, but I have never heard that he did so. To the contrary, I was told that Ulbaia's mother, Nyem, was from Bajor. Nyem is a name belonging to Kajenamoa, and Ulbaia adopted a girl from Bajor and gave her the name Nyem. No doubt was there an important relationship between Ulbaia and Bajor – recall that his Bajor relatives wanted to bury him in Bajor (see chapter 5) – but I do not know the particularities of this connection. Saboakai himself takes great pride in his *maleka*, but usually emphasizes the direct connection to Moarigum in terms of descent through his birth mother and not his adoptive father.[16]

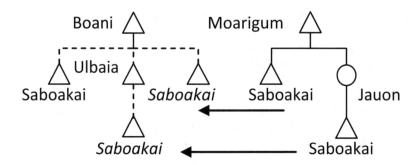

Figure 9.5. *Ro* 2. Saboakai – Kajenamoa

Ro 3. Saboaka/Mangoari boe Gagin

This *ro* provides an example of how different stories pointing to different paths of inheritance and descent are used to argue for one's right to a *ro* and how naming is a way of claiming these rights.

According to Kulbobo this *ro* in Kajenamoa was passed on from Jaran to his son, Saboaka. Saboaka did not have any children. Saboaka's sister's son, Bosa, then got the right. Bosa was the father of Kulbobo's mother, and Kulbobo claimed that his son Roger should have this *ro* and had given Roger the name Bosa from it. Roger was adopted by Maria and Tarere in Lukaluka/Kajenamoa and, thus, had an additional 'logical' history to follow in order to get the right to this *ro*. However, since it was said that Kulbobo was supposed to contribute *vato* for the use of land in this *ro*, he was acknowledged only partial rights in the *ro* and would, thus, gain support only for such a claim for Roger as well. Roger will most likely get the important *ro* Giririmba in Lukaluka.

In 1993 Gagin and Marifa told me a different story. They said that this *ro* was passed on from Jaran to his sons Mangoari and Gagin. None of them had children, and the *ro* was given to their brother Kedoboa's son, Saoang. Then Gagin inherited it, being 'sent' to Kajenamoa as Saoang's replacement. He got the name Gagin from this *ro*. I have not had the chance to ask Gagin about Kulbobo's story, but it seemed that his fellow villagers gave Gagin's version pre-eminence also in 1999. Gagin's second eldest son got the name Mangoari from this *ro*. In the 1990s it was Kumi who 'looked after' it.[17]

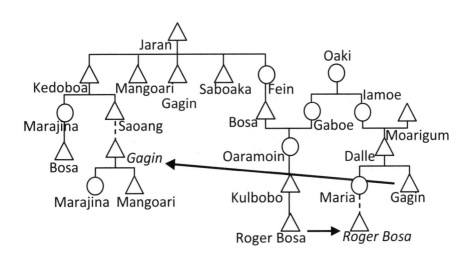

Figure 9.6. *Ro* 3. Saboaka/Mangoari boe Gagin – Kajenamoa

Ro 4. Giririmba

Giririmba is the main *ro* of the Lukaluka/Kajenamoa side of the village and is associated with the house Singero and the leadership of that part of the village. There were quite a lot of discussions regarding the paths people have followed to get rights in this *ro* when I interviewed people about it both in 1993 and 1999, but nobody really disputed the right the present day holder has to it.

I was told that Moarigum originally inherited this *ro* from his adoptive father Kenang. In 1993, Marifa said that this *ro* 'marked the clan of Jaran', using the term 'clan' to denote the side Kajenamoa/Lukaluka. In the 1990s Maria held the right in this *ro* and had inherited it from her father Dale. As stated in the introduction, people claimed that Dale decided on his deathbed that she was to take this place. Her adoptive son Roger, with the name Kasuk from this *ro*, is most likely next in line, although people said that this was not finally decided yet.

When Dale died, the old couple Tadanas from Badiata and Daboaia adopted Maria and looked after Dale's land. Daboaia was the daughter of Sua, Jaran's daughter's daughter. Like Moarigum, Sua was adopted by Kenang in Lukaluka, and Maria was also given the name Sua from this *ro*. Most people agreed about this version of the story, but several people have claimed that actually it was Mosua, the son of a matrilineal relative of Tadanas, who had the right in this *ro* and that Maria was merely looking after the *ro* and the house. Tadanas' mother, Moatakia, was from Lukaluka. Mosua lived in Rabaul, and people did not seem to believe that he would come back to Wogeo. Tadanas and Daboaia also adopted the boy Bua from Badiata, from Tadanas' brother Moiga, and he had the right to *ro* 14 in Lukaluka. This was one of the two *ro* that were outside of Gagin's control. [18] Bua gave his daughter the name Moatakia after Tadanas' mother. [19]

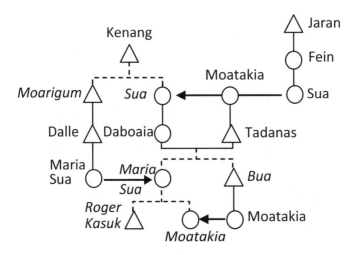

Figure 9.7. *Ro* 4. Giririmba – main *ro* in Lukaluk

Ro 5. Tokodub

Tokodub was the *ro* from which Singero's powerful basket (*jonga*) should hang, and it was associated with the *nyaboá* Bagura. It was also associated with the *Koakoale one* position – the leader of the male initiation rituals. Some of the genealogical connections in the history of the *ro* are unclear, but in this case names were used as proof that the path followed is a proper one. Kulbobo, who had this right in 1999, was also associated with the office of *Koakoale one*, but the last proper *Koakoale one* died in the early 1970s.

Kulbobo claimed that he had inherited the *ro* from his father, Bo, who in turn had inherited it from his father Kintabi (2). Kulbobo wanted his son, Kintabi (4), adopted by Matarena, to inherit it after him, but Matarena said that his adoptive son should have another *ro* (*ro* 7). In 1993 other people told me that Kulbobo got the rights in this *ro* from Itanefa. Itanefa had a brother with the name Kintabi (3) from this *ro*, but he was lost at sea in Udemtaregá, together with the above-mentioned Saboaka. According to Kulbobo, however, Kulbobo's grandfather had taken the place of the older Kintabi (1), Itanefa's grandfather, and it was this path he and the name of his son followed. It could be that if Kintabi (3) who was lost at sea had had a son, he might have received the right, but since history took its toll, Kulbobo's right to this *ro* is now undisputed. Probably Itanefa and Kintabi (2), shared rights in the *ro*.

Some people said that this *ro* did not have land, only power, but Kulbobo denied this energetically. Another story was that land from this *ro* was originally given to Kulbobo's father's mother, Makoa, by her father, Jaran, and, thus, that this land originally belonged to Kajenamoa/Lukaluka. This was also one of the reasons Kulbobo married Sanum from Lukaluka, some people said. According to this story, he could have lost the right to this land if he had not married Sanum,

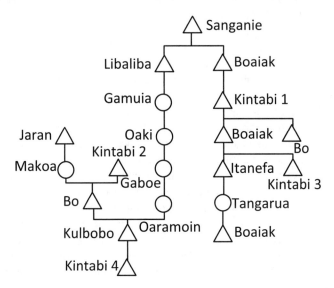

Figure 9.8. *Ro* 5. Tokodub – Moarmoar

something that might explain why some people said that the *ro* really did not have land. On the other hand, *vato* were given for partial rights in land from this *ro*, indicating that the land had now been established as belonging to this *ro* or, as Kulbobo said, the *ro* had its own land from the outset.

Some thought that Tokodub was fastened in the wrong place: Tarajimba and Giririmba should be placed next to each other. For some reason Tokodub had ended up in the middle several houses ago, perhaps because it was associated with the basket, the *nyaboá* and powerful knowledge. Kulbobo said that *ro* 13 on the back of the house was the *poroman* ('partner' or 'friend' in Tok Pisin) of Tokodub. In 1993 I learnt that this *ro* did not have land but was made for two men – Kasiket and Boara – who travelled around the island, staying for a while in all the villages (see Anderson 1996, 2003a). Kulbobo did not agree. These two men, Kasiket and Boara, had been given land from Tarajimba, the main *ro* in Moarmoar, and not from Tokodub's *poroman ro*; he, Kulbobo, had reclaimed this land, and their names were not supposed to be attached to any *ro* other than to Tarajimba or Moarmoar in general. His wife and others in Dab contradicted this when they pointed out that Kulbobo's son, Gimoro, had rights in *ro* 13 because he was adopted to Bajor, following a path between Bajor and Dab that was based on the story of the two men who eventually settled in Bajor.[20]

Ro 6. Tarajimba

This *ro* is the largest on the Moarmoar side of the village and should ideally belong to the *koakoale malala* in Moarmoar. Since Hogbin's day, there has not been a strong leader in Moarmoar, and the stories of this *ro* can be seen as a significant part of Kulbobo's efforts to establish his son as a proper *koakoale* in Moarmoar.

During my first fieldwork, most people said that the *ro* belonged to Boaiak, the son of Tangarua, Itanefa's daughter, *moede* and married to the *koakoale* Lala in Badiata. Marifa was looking after it since Boaiak did not live in Wogeo. Due to his illness, Kulbobo was not on the island in 1993/94, and then he was included only in the stories about Tokodub and Kasiket boe Boara. When I returned four years later, he worked hard to establish (or reclaim) his position as a leader in Moarmoar and claimed that this *ro* was his. He often sited the names of his father Bo and his father's father Kintabi to prove his position, but he did not go further back than Kintabi and never told me the names of Kintabi's parents. Hogbin (1938: 250; 1978: 67) wrote about a man called Bo (Bwo) as a younger brother of Boaiak and Bagasal's father, but the generation gap makes it impossible that this is Kulbobo's father. It does, however, show that the name Bo is repeatedly used in relation to this *ro*. Kulbobo's grandfather Kintabi is briefly mentioned in Hogbin's work (e.g. 1978: xi, 69) but he is not ascribed any place of importance.

In 1993/94 some people said that Kulbobo's grandfather, Kintabi, came from Badiata where he had the name Labim, and that he was adopted or following his wife to Dab. Kulbobo was really a *koakoale* of Badiata and a *ngaro* in Dab, they said. Hogbin (1939: 147) also mentioned a *koakoale* named Kulbobo in Badiata who could have been Kulbobo's predecessor there. Kulbobo was quite upset when I asked him about this and said that it was definitely incorrect. He did have some

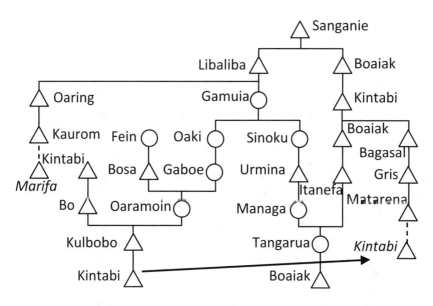

Figure 9.9. *Ro* 6. Tarajimba – main *ro* in Moarmoar

rights in Badiata, yes, and Kulbobo was a *koakoale* name from Badiata, but truly his grandfather Kintabi had been a *koakoale* from Moarmoar in Dab, as was Kulbobo himself. Hogbin described Kintabi as a member of 'Bagasal's group' (1978: 69). Kintabi was married to Moarigum's adoptive sister, Makoa, but I do not know which other paths he followed in Dab. What is certain is that Kintabi is a name that belongs to Moarmoar and that Kulbobo has a series of links back in time connecting him to Moarmoar. His mother was the daughter of Iamoe's sister, Gaboe. Iamoe's and Gaboe's mother, Oaki, was an important *moede* of the Moanoua matrilineage, and her mother, Gamuia, was said to have descended from an unbroken line of male leaders in Moarmoar. Oaki had five daughters, three of whom mothered leading *koakoale* in Dab, Joboe and Badiata. In addition, both Kulbobo's father's mother and his mother's father's mother were daughters of Jaran in Kajenamoa.

The father of Boaiak, the other often-cited holder of this *ro*, died when Boaiak was young, and his grandfather Itanefa had adopted him. Itanefa's patrilineal ancestors were three generations of men alternately called Boaiak and Kintabi, and Kulbobo's grandfather Kintabi most likely filled the same position as these earlier Boaiak and Kintabi. They were said to have descended patrilineally from Sanganie, the same *koakoale* from whom the above-mentioned Gamuia descended (see also the account of Tokodub). Boaiak, thus, had a more exclusive line of patrifiliation to strengthen his claim, but since he does not live on the island, Kulbobo could claim his position without too many protests. Kulbobo was not questioned about his claim in public while I was on the island, and he was respected by many as a *koakoale* in Moarmoar. What happened after his death I do not know. Undoubtedly Boaiak could claim this *ro* if he chose to return (something Kulbobo also acknowledged as Boaiak's right), but meanwhile Matarena would most probably have looked after the *ro* until his adoptive son Kintabi – Kulbobo's son by birth – was ready to take over.[21]

Ro 7. Itanefa Tamane

The story of this *ro* provides a rare example of a man that is apparently modest on his own behalf and favours someone other than his own son as heir to the more powerful position. But it could also be that he had a different agenda and gave pre-eminence to a patrilineal relative before his adoptive son.

Matarena saw his adoptive son Kintabi as the proper heir for this *ro*. Both Matarena's father Gris and his adoptive father, Damage, were the sons of Bagasal, *koakoale* in Moarmoar when Hogbin conducted fieldwork. As discussed in an earlier chapter, Bagasal had taken the place of his deceased brother Boaiak (2) until Boaiak's son Itanefa was old enough to take his place (cf. Hogbin 1939: 161). As Itanefa's replacement, Matarena thought that Boaiak (3), as the rightful *koakoale* in Moarmoar, should have Tarajimba and that his own adopted son, Kintabi, should have this less important *ro*. Matarena had also given his youngest adoptive son, Tamane, a name from this *ro*. No doubt both Kintabi and Tamane will have rightful claims to this *ro* – as will Boaiak (3). The disagreements concerning this *ro* and Tarajimba are really about who should be *koakoale* in Moarmoar. If Boaiak (3) does not return, Kintabi will probably take over Tarajimba, and Tamane take this *ro*, if they chose to live in Dab as adults.[22]

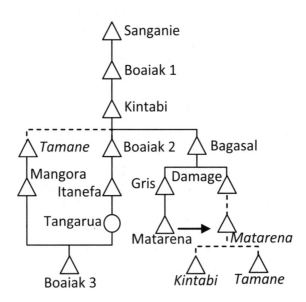

Figure 9.10. *Ro* 7. Itanefa Tamane – Moarmoar

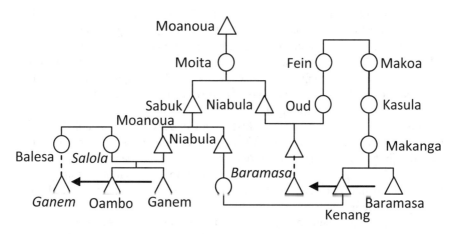

Figure 9.11. *Ro* 8. Oambo – Moarmoar

Ro 8. Oambo

This *ro* is, like Saboakai's *ro* in Kajenamoa, one of three *ro* in Dab that is not spoken of as having been passed on following pathways originating in the two great ancestors, Kumi in Kajenamoa and Sanganie in Moarmoar. Oambo, at present living in Wewak, inherited rights in this *ro* from his father, Moanoua. Moanoua's brother, Niabula, also had rights in the *ro*, and after his death in 1995 it has been Niabula's daughter Tangina who is cultivating this ground, since Oambo lived in Wewak.

The inheritance of this *ro* through the generations is generally agreed upon. But worthy of note is that a woman, Moita (Moanoua's and Niabula's paternal grandmother), had principal rights in the *ro*. Both of her sons, Sabuk and Niabula, passed on rights to this *ro*, and Sanganie, Niabula's cousin, also had rights in this *ro*. Some people said that Sanganie should have had primary rights in it, but for various reasons Niabula had taken the place as the head for this *ro*. Sanganie, who died in 1994, did not have any children but had adopted Baramasa, the son of Makanga whom Sanganie was very fond of and called 'sister'.[23] The adoption of Baramasa follows the same pathway that the marriage of Sanganie's parents did, and so also does Tangina's marriage to Kenang, Baramasa's brother. Gagin and Marifa said that the *ro* was called Karing but gave the same version of its history.[24]

* * *

For the rest of the *ro*, the stories are similarly complex and varied. As should be clear from these examples, it is impossible to identify a set of categorical and unquestionable rules for the inheritance of rights in the land of Dab. The sought-after continuity in Dab's social landscape is not created through exclusive principles of descent or in the shape of enduring groups in which members are replaced according to a set of indisputable criteria. Rather, the focus for continuity is the history of the place, that is, the people belonging to it, concretized in the *ro*. This does not mean that descent and kinship are insignificant in creating this continuity – all the paths of inheritance are in one way or another based on relations of filiation or descent – but that descent does not create clear-cut criteria for inheritance and belonging. As discussed in the last chapter, and as hopefully been made clear through the examples above, descent is as much a way of *speaking* about continuity as constituting it.

The stories about the *ro* elicit first of all endeavours to establish or keep important positions in Dab: who are the proper holders of the most important *ro* – Tarajimba and Giririmba in particular – and who are the true *koakoale* on the two sides. In doing this, people draw on histories about both mother's and father's sides, established alliances, pathways of marriage and adoption and, although usually not openly, matrilineal belonging.

The situation in Kajenamoa appears clearer than in Moarmoar, where Kulbobo's status was somewhat ambiguous. The absent Boaiak was, at least in 1993/94, seen as the more proper person to stand up as a *koakoale* and to have the right to the *ro* Tarajimba. Kulbobo had, however, many 'paths' or histories in Moarmoar, and his marriage to Sanum, as well as the adoption of Kintabi by Matarena, further secured his position – or, rather, his name and renown if his son's position in Moarmoar would keep on being recognized (both as a *koakoale* and as the holder of the *ro* Tarajimba). In Kajenamoa, the old Jaran's unfairness towards his son Kedoboa, when Moarigum was given the position of *koakoale malala* at the cost of Kedoboa, was still not forgotten. Gagin's diplomatic handling of the situation in relation to Kumi, Kedoboa's descendant, has, however, probably avoided a potential conflict. They both have good *ro* to pass on to their children. Through his sister, Maria, Gagin had also secured that his own sister's son will probably stand up as the leading man in Lukaluka, looking after Singero and the important *ro* Giririmba.

The more histories and connections people can point to, the more intertwined the network of relations reaches back in time, the more likely it is that a person will be able to secure his (or, in some cases, her) position, and that their name will be carried on as an important position to fill in the future – and, with the name, his or her renown. Names belonging to the *ro* are given to boys, and some girls, when they are young, but to ensure that they will keep being regarded as proper holders of the *ro*, a certain degree of consensus about the appropriateness of this ascription will need to be maintained.[25]

Flexibility and Perceived Permanence in the Dab Landscape

With Hogbin's detailed ethnography available, it should be possible to get an idea of the degree to which these paths of inheritance are relevant to the situation as described in Hogbin's work from the 1930s. According to the map Hogbin drew of Dab as it was in 1934 (Fig. 9.12) and the accompanying descriptions (e.g. 1978: 22), it is possible to recognize some of the names in the stories of the Dab *ro* presented here. From some of the people inhabiting Dab at that time (Sabuk, Bagasal, Moarigum, Boani and Saoang), the paths described above can be traced relatively unambiguously back in time: Maria's rights to Giririmba can be traced

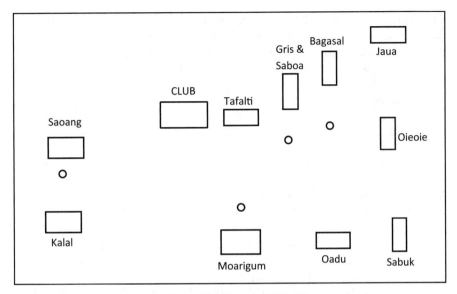

Figure 9.12: Dab in 1934 according to Hogbin (e.g. 1978:22)

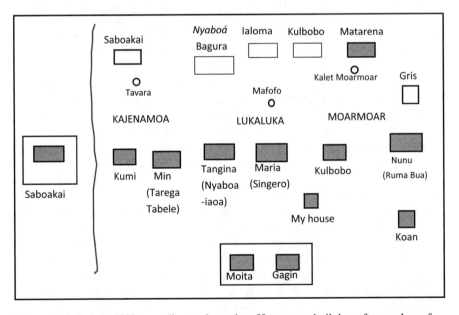

Figure 9.13: Dab in 1999 according to the author. Houses not built but often spoken of are without fill

from Moarigum through Dale, although Tadanas and Daboaia's adoption of Maria
played a part in this case and the path of inheritance thus took a turn away from
the line of descent. Tangina had her place from Sabuk through her father, Niabula,
although it was her cousin Oambo who was spoken of as having primary rights
in this *ro* and *maleka*. Matarena and Gris descended from Bagasal, their adoptive
father Damage's father who also was the father of Matarena's biological father.
Kumi had his position from Saoang through Saoang's adoptive daughter Min,
but the path had taken an extra turn through Gagin and his adoption of Kumi as
a brother.

According to the stories that I collected, there also seem to be several people
missing from Hogbin's descriptions that should have been there (e.g. Ulbaia and
Marifa). It is not uncommon in Wogeo to live in another place for some time
in connection with deaths of relatives or conflicts in the village, and if conflicts
prevail the absentees may even be spoken of as not belonging to the village
anymore. It could be that this was the case with these absentee inhabitants of Dab
in 1934, or their belonging in Dab may have become important only in retrospect.
It is also possible that there were hidden adoptions involved.

Hogbin did not use the names of the different parts of Dab but described them
as clusters of houses around the house of the two or three *koakoale*. He referred
to 'Moarigum's group' and 'Bagasal's group'. Could it be that the importance
assigned to the parts as named sides and not primarily as groups of people has
increased due to the absence of strong leaders? Or did Hogbin not regard the place
names and the placement of people as important data? Hogbin wrote:

> The position of the *niabwa* [*nyaboá*] is fixed, but a person likes to have his own house
> either alongside that of his parents or, in the event of his father being dead, on the
> identical spot where the old man dwelt. The matter is usually discussed with fellow
> villagers in an informal way, and their advice accepted should there be a sufficient
> reason for removal to another site. The *kokwal* [*koakoale*] interferes only if the place
> selected is likely to cause inconvenience to others (Hogbin 1939: 129).

To me Wogeos pointed to the places of the houses (*ruma maleka*) and claimed that
each had always been situated at the same spot. The names of these 'true' houses
were pointed out as significant knowledge, and people were eager to show me the
maleka of the houses and tell me their stories. The special designs and capacities
of the named houses also support the impression that the idea of houses as being
more significant than arbitrarily placed dwellings is not new. The discrepancy
between Hogbin's description and my data might, however, not be as substantial
as it might appear. People can build houses in places other than where the *ruma
maleka* is, but named houses have their particular place (*maleka*), whether
the house is actually built or not. Other houses are *haus nating* ('houses of no
importance' in Tok Pisin) – such as the house in which Kulbobo lived in 1999.
His real house was not built. Several of the houses built in 1934 were probably
also *haus nating*, perhaps explaining the absence of some of the houses that were
spoken of as always having been in Dab.

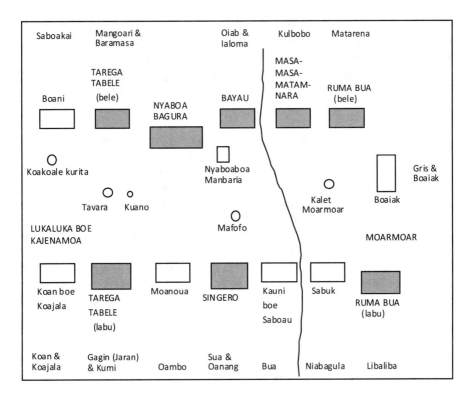

Figure 9.14: Dab according to Bernard Gagin Dale (copied by me from his drawing). The most important houses, houses with their own names and not the names of men, Gagin has coloured. The names of the houses are written directly below or above the houses – names of those who have the right to live in them are written further above or below.

Gagin, the *koakoale* of Kajenamoa/Lukaluka in the 1990s, has also drawn a map of the village (Fig. 9.14).[26] His main comments about the map concerned the histories of inheritance: the true holders of rights and power, and the true places of belonging according to *kastom*. Gagin took a great interest in Wogeo *kastom*, also in an academic sense, and he would probably be a better person to write the stories of inheritance than me. However, he was also a political actor in the Wogeo scene with a position to uphold and alliances to maintain, and his comments on my writings – including this map – must also be seen accordingly. The map does only partially correspond to the situation that I could observe and the stories I was told while in Wogeo, but since Gagin's agenda was different from those of my other main informants regarding these issues, and he was absent during most of the time I spent in Wogeo, this is not surprising.

As pointed out by Angèle Smith (2003) when discussing map making in Ireland: 'All maps are political. They control knowledge, claiming authorship and ownership of knowledge about landscapes, people and their past. Maps aim to dictate how to "see", "remember" and make sense of the world' (ibid.: 73). This is the case for Gagin's, Hogbin's and my own maps. Gagin is a political actor in Dab social life, and so his map supports his position in Dab as a political leader and as a keeper of knowledge. Hogbin on the other hand emphasized the social groupings around Bagasal and Moarigum, supporting an argument founded on discussions around descent and alliance. And my own maps emphasize place, spatial orientations and named houses and aim to explain the relation between experience and representations.

Gagin divided Dab into only two sides: Kajenamoa and Lukaluka to the west as one part (where he himself is the *koakoale*) and Moarmoar to the east. The houses are neatly placed in line, and his naming of the holders of the houses was presented as a definite and absolute version of the Dab social landscape: a perceived order and permanence in the village landscape, illustrating the importance Wogeos place in channelling and ordering the more disordered flow of people in time – as well as the importance for a leader to be able to define with authority the social landscape of a village. The village landscape as a map is an 'imagined landscape' (Smith 2003: 73) as opposed to the experienced landscape: it is an iconic representation of the distribution of people he sees as properly belonging to Dab. As long as he is able to maintain consensus about this map, it does not necessarily matter who actually lives in the village, who has built their named houses, or who lives in unnamed houses. If we see Gagin's map as a collection of multivocal signs – that is, names, *ro* and houses signifying various names and histories – it does not have to refer only to a definite limited number of people. Rather, the perceived order and permanence of the 'imagined landscape' allows flexibility in the actual landscape. A *ro* as a polysemic sign does not signify only one child or one history. It has the power to evoke histories about many relations and many people – some *ro* can elicit histories about nearly all the people belonging to a side of a village.[27] As such, the bestowal of a *ro* upon a child is seldom definite and absolute, even in retrospect, and it is this uncertainty that is the core of the politics of belonging in Wogeo.

Land Rights, Consensus and Corrugated Iron

Far from Wogeo, in Jordan, Andrew Shryock interviewed a Bedouin sheikh about the history of a certain tribe, something that commonly involved recitations of genealogies:

> Shaykh: 'What do you want with such talk? Do you want to sow discord among us?'
> Andrew: 'No. I don't want problems, I just want history.'
> Shaykh: 'Our history is all about problems. Do you want to write it down?'
> Andrew: 'Yes, but not as a troublemaker. I'm writing a dissertation on the history of tribes, so I can become a professor.'
> Shaykh: 'This is knowledge? God help you. Empty talk brings problems. Everyone recollects what he wants. Everyone makes his ancestor big; people lie and exaggerate, and the others get upset. By God, there is no benefit.' (Shryock 1997: 15).

The sheikh then continued by telling the 'truth': the history of his own lineage. In Wogeo his point of view would have been well understood – both his critical and reflexive comments as well as his insistence on still being able to tell the 'true story', even though he had just labelled such stories 'empty talk'. Shryock's book is about the transition from oral to written history in the construction of a 'national identity'. The conflicting versions of history that exist in the oral histories of the Bedouins represent the opposite of a unified national identity and 'as the tribes redefine their histories in opposition to textuality, a complex universe of thought, interest and action comes fully into view' (ibid.: 37). It is a similarly complex universe that comes into view in Wogeo when collecting and attempting to write down the stories of land rights, residence and inheritance. Wogeos had not started to write down their history, but they have had two anthropologists attempting to document their way of life, both with an interest in genealogies. The histories about land rights, inheritance, houses, pathways and alliances in Dab that I have presented in this book illustrate the complexity in the various ways of creating continuity and how these come into play, both in establishing a person's proper belonging and to ensure that a place is filled with the proper person. But this complexity is not necessarily how the Wogeos would like to represent their history if they were to write it themselves.

From neighbouring Kairiru, Smith writes how genealogical knowledge – what the Kairiru men now refer to as *straksa* (Tok Pisin for 'structure') – is the 'key to the village'. It is important to keep track of genealogies in order to maintain one's position and livelihood. *Straksa* is a highly charged topic, and Smith often had to promise not to write down what he had been told (Smith 2002: 112). In Wogeo, it is mainly matrilineal relations that are to be kept hidden, and mostly the stories presented above were told openly without cautions to be discrete. Nevertheless, different people in Dab would most likely object to several of the stories presented above, and arguments might arise if Wogeos were to sit down and read them carefully. Consensus about these histories is impossible to achieve, and if people are involved in conflicts, their platial belonging and matrilineal identity are easily brought up in discussions or gossip on the verandas at night. A woman once said to me that the root of all the problems in the village (*ol hevi bilong ples* in Tok Pisin, lit. 'all the heavy of the place') was that land was 'on the side of father' and blood and house 'on the side of mother'.

I have collected the stories from various people at different times, sometimes with several people – mostly men – present and sometimes with only one or two. When more people were present, they usually put great effort into reaching agreements upon one coherent story for each *ro*. But later on, one or more of them was likely to tell me that he disagreed with what they had told me. Also, when we discussed what others had said about the *ro*, people would usually state that the other's version was wrong, even if the story they presented themselves turned out to be quite similar. 'He does not have the knowledge,' they said. Everyone claims that there is *one* true story for each *ro*, and differences in opinion are, thus, commonly ascribed to 'not having knowledge'. On the other hand, everyone knows that they need to maintain consensus about their story in order to keep their position and that flexibility and negotiability is at the core of this 'politics of belonging'.

The ideas of matrilineal consubstantiality and solidarity, on the one hand, and the importance of patrifiliation to inheritance, on the other, seemed to have created a sort of 'systematic' disorder that people did not like to acknowledge. The emphasis on 'paths', 'histories' and other 'logical reasons' created order and continuity, whereas the tendency to stress simple and straightforward lines of descent when it came to land – patrilineal if possible – seemed to persist. That Wogeos felt somewhat dissatisfied with the flexibility and complexity that characterized the paths of inheritance and placement became particularly evident when I was invited to the completion of a new house in Moaroka in 1999. The new house was made of laboriously hand-carved, smooth plank, and it was to be completed with a corrugated iron roof. In most villages there was at least one such house, and many people wanted houses built in this fashion – both because they did not have to do the hard work of making *vato* and because it was modern and had 'style'. In Onevaro they had for some time discussed how all people could get the chance to live in such houses, and they wanted to convert the system of *ro* and *vato* into this new fashion of house building. The holder of a *ro* should contribute with one sheet of iron for the new house – that is, the carved *ro* were to be replaced by sheets of corrugated iron. The people who were obliged to give *vato* to a *ro* should contribute with money for the *ro* holder to buy the iron sheets. The house in Moaroka was the first to be built in accordance with these rules.

The men in Moaroka had held a meeting and written down the names of the *ro* holders. They were going to send this list to the appropriate authorities in Wewak so that they could register them as proper landowners. I was told to sit down with the young man who had made the list and record the names of the *ro* holders. In this way there would be no more confusion. Now they had distributed the land fairly to all the young men in the village. Before too many older men would control several *ro* whereas other, younger men would have none. From now on there would be no more discussions about who should inherit the *ro* – it was all written down and registered in Wewak. According to the stories I collected in Moaroka, the new distribution of the *ro* still followed paths of inheritance that approximately complied with the distribution prior to the construction of this house, but one or two men had now become principal *ro* holders instead of merely having the right to cultivate land on other people's *ro*.

Later I had several discussions with people about this change in tradition. The intention to register landowners in Wewak was seen as a positive initiative by most people. When it came to the intention of building all new houses with corrugated iron roofs, some were positive whereas others were more sceptical. Most people found the traditional houses, with their high and lofty ceilings and walls that allow the air to circulate properly, to be much more comfortable to live in. Unless the more 'modern' houses have proper ceilings and ventilation, they are terribly hot and noisy when it rains, people pointed out. But this did not outweigh the arguments of not having to make *vato* and the better 'style' of the new houses. The most substantial objection that was raised was that people did not necessarily have the cash to contribute to such houses. Not only did a couple have to raise money for building their own house, but also for buying corrugated iron for every new house that was built in the village, as well as smaller contributions to houses elsewhere, whereas traditionally one could contribute with a *vato* or two. People needed the money they made from selling copra and other cash crops for school fees, petrol for boat travels, medicines and other such necessities: money was already too scarce. But apart from the point about money, most people were satisfied that the conversion of *ro* and *vato* into iron sheets would serve the same purpose as the traditional way.

There were no *ro* in the sense of carved rafters in the new house. Wogeos take great pride in their *ro* and land right system and it seemed somewhat strange that people would stop making the *ro* so easily. Several times I raised the question of why they did not continue to fasten the actual *ro* in the new style houses. It was not necessary with these kinds of rafters in such houses, people said, and everyone still knows the system. They knew how the *ro* were replaced, and there was no need to make the *ro*.[26] It is, however, not unlikely that scarcity of money will make the building of modern style houses less common than people envisaged, and that old-fashioned houses with *ro* will continue to be built for a long time.

No more modern style houses were built while I was in Wogeo, and I do not know what has happened with the *ro* and their paths since then. It remains to be seen whether the intention to keep and register written records of landowners will be upheld and, if so, whether the written records of who has held the various *ro* will result in the system of inheritance becoming less flexible. One possible outcome is that patrifiliation could become more dominant than other paths of inheritance. But taking into account that matrilineal relations appear to be given increasingly more weight in some connections, and that there were no signs that the number of adoptions was decreasing, I doubt that this will be the result. It may not be as easy to create 'order' as the men of Moaroka envisaged when they decided to register the landowners of their village.

* * *

Hviding describes how the Marovo people of the Solomon Islands, whose paths of descent and kinship in relation to land rights are similarly complex and flexible as those of Wogeo, tried to create a simplified system of landownership in terms of kinship and descent in their encounter with an Australian mining company; a system 'simple enough to be understood by an Australian' (Hviding 1993: 813; see also J. Weiner and Glaskin 2007). This

> essentialization of tradition may be interpreted as a means of dealing with the outside world by attempting to present a uniform picture of one's own world, or as a means of addressing fundamental variabilities, or indeed perceived inconsistencies, in the Marovo world itself (Hviding 1993: 814).

To the Marovo, 'making sides' – for instance in terms of 'mother's and father's side' or other reciprocal relations (or 'halves') – is a central feature of their social organization (see also Hoëm 2003; Roalkvam 2003). In presenting a simplified and uniform picture of land rights in terms of unilineal descent, the Marovo were, in order to appear as a unified partner in the negotiations with the mining company, 'making reciprocal (political) sides', Hviding argues. This 'apparent "indigenous essentialism" may be seen rather as creative imitation, and even parody' (Hviding 1993: 820), of an 'anthropologically-derived ideal of well-defined customary land ownership based on unilineal descent' (ibid.; see also J. Weiner and Glaskin 2007). Also Wogeo experts' simplifications of the principles of inheritance as presented to Hogbin and me – as well as to authorities in Wewak – can be seen as a way of 'dealing with the outside world' in terms of 'side making', presenting pictures of a land right system 'simple enough for the anthropologist to understand'. To actually create a lasting agreement about the histories of the ro is difficult, if not impossible – as Hviding also notes for the Marovo (ibid.: 819). But more than being just a manner to deal with outsiders, it is the latter part of Hviding's interpretation that complies with my understanding of the Wogeo situation: the discontent that Wogeo men showed when I pointed out conflicting stories and inconsistencies, as well as the continuous disparagements of other people's representations of history, indicate that the competing stories of the ro are most of all part of internal political processes. Wogeos may be said, like the Kairiru, to 'fight with stories'.

However, the 'problem' of 'disorder' and flexibility in Wogeo principles of inheritance becomes apparent mainly when trying to present all the various pathways simultaneously. Apart from when talking to a visiting anthropologist, this happens when new houses are constructed: when the history of the villages is renegotiated and manifested in the shape of *ro*, *vato* or corrugated iron. Sometimes people could start fights at such occasions, I was told – although I never witnessed it myself. In Moaroka, they had finished the discussion prior to my visit and were not too eager to discuss their disagreements any further, but I know there had been some. In daily life, this 'disorder' was not a prevailing challenge. Like the Marovo contextual 'making of sides', Wogeos always know, according to the context, with whom they belong, on which side they should participate in exchanges and which paths they should follow. In the Wogeo relational world, social life is a constant movement from one relation to another, from one half (or side) paired with another (Strathern 1988: 14).

                                        *   *   *

In this last part of the book I have described how Wogeos follow histories or pathways in the constitution of their social landscapes, exemplified in the stories and people that were elicited during the construction of Singero in 1998. Representations of kinship and continuity appear as arguments in ongoing discussions about how to fill places with the proper people. As such, histories about places and people become the central focus for Wogeo politics, and, at the same time, these histories elicit the 'compositeness' of Wogeo persons and places. In the conclusion I will now summarize the discussions of experience and representation from the different parts of the book, showing how people through life are continuously engaged in the constitution and maintenance of their own and others' compositeness. As people wander through the Wogeo landscape, they create, cut and channel connections to people and their physical surroundings. By securing beneficial connections or flows with whatever and whoever they encounter, they look after their bodies as well as their relations. The experienced landscapes of houses, places and pathways are crucial in this work of relating: as loci for dwelling and movement and as images used to order and create a meaningful world.

Notes

1. Hogbin wrote that 'ownership of trees apart from ground, common elsewhere in Melanesia, is not customary' (1935a: 319). I am not sure how to interpret this: it could be that few of the Dab villagers had given away such rights at the time of his research and that he, thus, failed to document it, or it could be that such rights are a more recent invention (although I doubt the latter to be the case since people spoke about this as such an important part of Wogeo *kastom*).
2. Bagura was also the name of the *nyaboá* in Gole, the other 'middle place'.
3. In a letter dated August 2008, Gagin wrote that they had rebuilt the *nyaboá* in Dab and that the Prime Minister Sir Michael Somare was expected to come for the opening the following month. I was also invited, but received the letter eight months too late.
4. When we made the *vato* for my small house, I counted that we (six grown-ups) made twelve vato in one day. For a small house with about 120 pieces of thatch, six adults would thus need approximately nine days to make the *vato*.
5. There are exceptions though – Joboe for instance had fourteen *ro* in 1999.
6. I have also heard that Oanang, Jaran's (the *koakoale* prior to Moarigum) wife, of a Taregá lineage owned this house, but the most common version is that it is the Moanoua lineage that owns Singero.
7. Iaman died unexpectedly in June 1999.
8. Badiata did not participate for reasons not relevant here.
9. Also called Salagalaga.
10. Kumi has given his firstborn daughter the name Damalina after the old Kumi's daughter – Jaran's sister.
11. Gagin's wife is the oldest daughter of a great *koakoale* in Moaroka, and, since she is also married to a *koakoale* of equal standing, she is a true *moede*. She has many brothers who are important allies to Gagin and his children. They contribute by paying for Gagin's children's education and speak about them with great pride.
12. Gamuia, the mother of Iboara (and Iamoe's mother's mother) was from Moarmoar, and her descendants' affiliation to Kajenamoa these days is probably due to Iamoe's strong position in the Lukaluka/Kajenamoa side of Dab or another alliance between Iboara and Kajenamoa that I am unaware of. Leo Karang Seo (married to Gagin's wife's sister) also notes the connection between Gamuia and Dab when he writes about ownership to fishing magic in *Grassroots Research*: 'Gamuia from Moarmoar clan got married to Iboara of Kinaba. All the rituals and songs for fishing for the canoe Tagamot [a canoe now belonging to Kinaba] came with her' (Seo 1991: 29).
13. Tarere cultivated land belonging to this *ro* and contributed with *vato*. He had inherited this right from his adoptive mother, Kaite, Iamoe's sister. Matarena gave *vato* to this *ro* since he cultivated land belonging to the ro that was situated near his house in Moarmoar (see Fig. 9.1). This piece of land used to be Saoang's favourite spot in Dab's bush, but, since it was convenient for Matarena to have a garden here and nobody else needed it, he used it and gave *vato* for it.
14. After Boani died, Moarigum took his old widow, Nyem, as a third wife to keep his son close to him (cf. Hogbin 1935/36a: 31–32).

15. See e.g. Hogbin (1978: 100). After my first fieldwork I found a short article by Yoshiko H. Sinoto entitled *Drifting canoe prows* (1959), about a canoe prow that was found on the beach of a Micronesian island. The carvings on the prow looked familiar, and I sent a copy of the article to Gagin. He was sure that this was the prow from the Udemtaregá that was lost in 1947.

16. No *vato* were contributed to this ro and Saboakai did not say whether anyone should have given any. In 1993, Marifa said that Sanganie had rights to some trees belonging to this *ro*. Sanganie died in 1994, and his adoptive son, Baramasa, was not on the island when Singero was built. Marifa also said that he himself should give *vato* for a breadfruit tree belonging to this *ro*, but none of his children did so in 1998.

17. Tarere contributed with *vato* because Lukaluka and Kajenamoa made joint gardens on land belonging to it. Iaman, Saoang's sister's son from Joboe, gave *vato* for *kangar* and breadfruit trees. Urmina from Joboe gave *vato* for *kangar*, having relations to Kajenamoa through his mother and adoptive mother who were sisters of the above-mentioned Oaiari (see *ro* 1) and, thus, descended from Iboara. The same was the case for his adopted father, Talbul. Bajimula from Joboe gave *vato* for *kangar* and sago. Bajimula's mother's mother was also a daughter of Iboara, and thus there seems to be a particular connection between Iboara, his descendants and this *ro*. I did not hear anything about the particularities of this connection, but another reason for Bajimula's connection to this *ro* could be that his father, Bosa (the name Kulbobo gave to Roger) of Joboe was the son of Kedoboa's daughter, Marajina, after whom Gagin named his eldest daughter. Three others should also have given *vato* but did not do so, people said.

18. I have also been told that Tadanas's sister in Badiata was once expected to marry Moarigum's son Tafalti in Lukaluka – again pointing to the specific connection between Tadanas' matrilineage and Lukaluka. The name Roger had, Kasuk, was said to be the name of a famous ancestor through Iamoe and Oaki in Lukaluka. I have heard one man argue that only his matrilineage should give this name to a child, and that he did not agree with giving it to Roger, but I do not know of any further implications of this claim.

19. No *vato* were contributed to Giririmba. In 1994 Maria mentioned five people who should have given, all for *kangar*. Among them was a man from Badiata who had been given the rights to a *kangar* tree from this *ro* because he had helped Maria and Tarere a lot when he lived in Dab for a while, after marrying a girl in Moarmoar. He was also a descendant of Iamoe's sister. I asked Maria about this, and she said that he had not yet collected any nuts from this tree. I asked whether he would lose the rights since he did not contribute any *vato*, but she said it was all right – for the time being. As long as people do not utilize the right given, they also fail to establish a lasting tie to the place.

20. Maloa from Joboe gave *vato* for land belonging to this ro. Maloa was the daughter of Itanefa and got this right when she left Dab to be married to Labim in Joboe. Oambo from Moarmoar gave *vato* for *ib* (Tahitian chestnuts) to this *ro*, but he had planted coconuts on the spot instead. Ialoma, from Lukaluka, gave *vato* for the use of land belonging to Tokodub. Ialoma is Kulbobo's in-law, being the adoptive brother of Sanum.

21. Marifa had given names from the other branch descending from Sanganie to his children and grandchildren – among them, his son Libaliba (*ro* 16), his granddaughter Gamuia, and his grandsons Oaring and Kaurom. Salam from Badiata gave *vato* to this *ro* for a piece of land and a *kangar* tree. Kulbobo's grandfather in Moarmoar, Kintabi, had adopted Salam's mother, Makom. She was also the daughter of the above-mentioned Iboara. Tangarua, Itanefa's daughter and Boaiak's mother, gave *vato* for a *veka* tree – her connection to this *ro* has already been established. Libaliba, the son of Marifa, gave *vato* for land from this *ro*. Tarajimba is the *ro* with the most land in Moarmoar, and it is not unusual that other members of this part of the village are given land to use from such a *ro*.

In 1994 Marifa mentioned two more people who should have given *vato* to Tarajimba, a man and a woman whose mothers both came from Moarmoar.

22. Gagin and Marifa called this *ro* Boamera, the name of the older Tamane's son (see genealogy). They also said that there was a man called Boamera, living in Koil, who had rights in it. He was the grandson of the old Tamane. No one gave *vato* to this *ro*, but I have been told that two of the children of Tamane's daughter should have given for *kangar*.

23. She was his MMZDD, but of a different matrilineage, indicating that an adoption had taken place in at least one of the links.

24. Iaman of Joboe gave *vato* for *kangar* from this *ro*. I do not know any details of the relationship between Iaman and Niabula. As far as I know there are no close kin relations between them; possibly the alliance was based on Iaman being an in-law of Niabula through Niabula's first wife, Jambi, who died without children. When I spoke with Niabula about his *ro* in 1993, he told me that he wanted to build a new house, but nobody was supposed to give him *vato* for this *ro*. Since it requires much work to make vato, he would give away some trees to his *kandere* (sister's children) and in-laws. It could be that Iaman had been given rights to the *kangar* at that time. Tangina told me that four others should also have given *vato*, but did not do so.

25. The people who give *vato* for the various *ro* maintain their relations to Dab and to the various *maleka* in the villages: they keep their pathways open. Particularly Iboara's descendants appeared to see this as being worthwhile, and many of them took part in rituals and other important events in Dab – this was especially the case for Oaiari, *koakoale* of Kinaba. This particular alliance (or pathway) was established by Gamuia's marriage to Iboara in Kinaba. Kinaba, which is situated only five minutes walk from Dab, is a small village, and for Oaiari as koakoale in Kinaba it was – as it was for his predecessors – advantageous to maintain this alliance with Dab as a place of importance. The people from these places also have an enduring connection as *dan ta*.

26. After I completed my Cand. Polit. degree in 1996, Gagin read my thesis and commented upon it in letters. Unfortunately I did not get the chance to meet him during the last fieldwork, so I have to rely on what he has written.

27. Roxana Waterson (1997: 80) notes a similar flexibility among Tana Toraja in another place in the Austronesian world where fluidity rather than fixity characterizes questions about origin, genealogy and history.

28. I once asked Tarere how they expected their children or grandchildren to understand what a *ro* was when there was no actual *ro* in the house; did he not think the whole system would change as time went by and there were no more houses with the actual rafters? He gave it some thought and said that I had a point. He was going to demand that, at least in Dab, they would keep making the *ro* – even if they had no function in the actual structure.

Conclusion

The aim of this book has been to explore how experiences of dwelling in and moving through Wogeo landscapes shape and are shaped by the ways Wogeos constitute and give meaning to their world – in other words, to elicit how meaning is formed in a dialogical relation between embodied experience and representations.

Wogeos represent their way of life as 'steered' by stories from the past: stories about the doings of the mythical heroes as well as those about previous generations. I started out by presenting some of the heroes and their introduction of certain salient customs: first of all the large food festivals from the past (*oaraboa*). The first hero, Goleiangaianga, came to Gole and made this the first place of importance by arranging the first *oaraboa* and erecting the powerful *boaboaur* poles there. Later he travelled around the island and, with the name Onka, entered into a competitive relationship with the local hero Mafofo in Dab. The two of them each made their canoe and initiated the paths of trade to the mainland and the other islands. Dab became the 'middle place' on the front of the island, and here Onka instated the offices of *koakoale* leadership together with the associated sections of knowledge – spoken of as *moanuboa* plants standing on the beach, in the village and in the bush. 'Our *koakoale* is a reflection of Goleiangaianga,' Joe Kosman said. But Wogeos believe that much of the knowledge that Onka (Goleiangaianga) possessed was lost to them as he continued on to other places, and that their forefathers had been too stupid to listen. Other significant knowledge is regarded as lost in more recent times, and Wogeos appear quite pessimistic with regards to their wish to preserve the *kastom* ways. As such, the books of the old Wogeo anthropologist Ian Hogbin are seen as valuable documentation, and my own research has been influenced both by this nostalgia and by working 'in the shadow' of Hogbin. Accordingly, this text contains representations of customs lost as well as those that were salient in the 1990s.

Among the customs that point to continuity rather than change (or loss) are those pertaining to the most immediate concerns in Wogeo's being-in-the world: practices with the purpose of 'looking after' people's bodies, and this was the topic of the second part of the book. I described how various taboos mark out, and even create, connections between people and what and whom they encounter in the phenomenal world. Connections are made, channelled or cut according to the situation in order to secure and instigate what I described as beneficial flows. As people go about their daily tasks, connections are made to people they meet, pigs they feed, sweet potatoes they plant or fish they catch, and the states of people's bodies affect these pigs, fish, potatoes or other people – including beyond the direct contact. Germs, language and smells flow beyond the boundaries of the body and may also have an effect on other people or entities – like the *veka* fruit, certain mythical beings, the Palolo worms or a sick person in the village. They carry with them connections to things other than themselves – such as the world beyond Wogeo, dangerous contacts or breaches of innate flows of fertility. It is the ability these disembodied indices have to temporarily create such connections that give them their powerful potential, whether the connections are beneficial or malignant.

The more direct contact with dangerous corporal humors and substances – like the 'sick' menstruation blood or the coldness of a corpse – can cause illness and death unless proper cleansing procedures are carried out. The state of people's bodies represents the success people have had in leading a life according to *kastom*: the manner in which they have 'looked after' their bodies as well as their social relations, since people are not only responsible for their own wellbeing, but also for the other entities and persons they are connected to. To follow taboos establishes the self in relation to an external reality as intentional acts, Gell (1979: 133) argued. People are at all times immersed in networks of connections and their bodies should be looked after properly by avoiding threatening connections and facilitating beneficial ones. By doing so, these relations are also looked after. To 'sit good in one's place', one has to look after one's body and, through this, one's relations.

Some connections between people, and between people and the environment, are more enduring than others. As people grow up, they become attached to certain places. Children accompany their parents to their gardens and learn the history of every tree and piece of land, histories that will include themselves as they invest the land with their work and life history. Eventually the child itself, and the name it carries, will be associated with these places and histories. Places are filled with such names and histories, histories that tell people where they should belong, where they should 'sit down' or 'stand up' and with whom they should enter into and maintain certain relations. It is these histories that are at stake in what I called the politics of belonging.

In the third part of the book I described how the landscape provides images that Wogeos put to use in ordering the flow of sociality: relations are manifested as pathways that connect and shared belonging as sides that separate. People, food and houses follow pathways, and exchanges of food frequently take place between people based on platial belonging. *Koakoale* stand on each their side of the villages, but also on the beach, in the village and in the bush, each holding their *moanuboa* of knowledge associated with their parts of the village. The experience of the island landscape as a whole, and the movement of stars, the sun and the tide, creates the notions of sides, paths and directions as the 'Wogeo canoe' moves upwards and forwards in space-time, steered by stories from the past. Stories from the more recent past are added to the stories from the distant past, and this is the way Wogeos give meaning to their world. Onka becomes God, Hogbin becomes a *tilab* (a teacher), *ro* of wood become corrugated iron sheets and the charismatic movement brings the power of the place up in the clear.

Experience and Representation

In chapter 6 the Wogeo New Year celebration was presented as analogous to *baras* cleansings at female menstruation. The analogy is even clearer if we look at the celebrations for a girl's first menstruation. When the girl climbs through the liana, Wogeos say that her body becomes new or that it is emptied and has to be 'refilled' with good and strengthening food and medicine. Similarly, as the island is cleansed, it is 'changed' or becomes new. The night of the celebration is called 'the bridge between the two islands' – the old and the new. Strathern argued that 'Melanesians regard bodies as images of a kind, and, in the process of growing up, one kind of body has to be replaced by another' (1993: 44). One body (or image) is substituted by a new one. If we use the language of obviation, we can say that body as non-gendered child is obviated and body as adult gendered woman is evoked. Likewise, the island as an image of the movement of the *baras* stars across the sky and the pollution that has accumulated on the island through that time is obviated, and the island as imaging a new movement of the stars across the sky over an unpolluted place is created. In the same way as one body is substituted by a new body, the old polluted island is replaced by a new clean island. In the *baras* rituals, the *baras* blood runs downwards and is washed off in the sea. In the New Year rituals, the pollution of the island as a whole is chased downwards into the sea at the lowest end of the island. At each place the New Year was celebrated, the people washed on the beach, rubbed their bodies with *burenga*, the mixture of herbs, paint and oil, and then drank *kadaga* potion. Similarly, when the first time menstruating girl visited a place, she first climbed through a liana, then washed on the beach and got *burenga* rubbed on her body, and then she entered the village and was given food: her childish body was obviated and an adult one was created on each of the places that were salient parts of her sociality. Almost the same procedure was followed by the *manvara* mourners after a funeral as they visited the various places: they washed on the beach, rubbed their bodies with herbs, and were given food to eat – although *without* entering the village since their task was not to create or elicit relations but to finish them.

Washing can, thus, be seen as the point of obviation in 'anticipating and disposing of' the original effect and, through this, making a new one appear. Eating food (or drinking *kadaga*) becomes the completion or finishing of the 'work' (or a part of it) by establishing the new image. In the case of *baras* and *manvara*, the food eaten was a gift that elicited relations for the *baras* girl or finished relations for the deceased that the *manvara* represented. In order to engage in the relations elicited, the *baras* girl was made to 'stand up' in the place, making potential movement the result of the rituals. In contrast, the *manvara* were 'making the dead sit down' as they finished the relations of the deceased, evoking motionlessness as the outcome of their acts. The New Year celebration does not need to be completed by gifts or exchange in a similar way since the passage of the stars (or time) is not completed but is analogous to the cyclic menstruation of an adult woman.

Gendered analogies are also evident in the way houses are represented as more than mere dwellings, similar to what James Weiner (2001: 120) called enhousement – a parallel to embodiment. In a Wogeo named house, several types of relations may be said to be contained within it: the relations of the people actually living in it, following the relational history of the place; the matrilineal relations that constitute the owners of the house, founded in the salience of motherhood; and finally the relations that make up the social landscape of the village as a whole. These relations can partly, but not only, be seen as founded on a gendered pair of male and female qualities or potentialities: a male (ground) and a female (blood) side. When a named house is built, the matrilineage that owns it takes a special interest in its construction: at the construction of Singero, men of the Moanoua lineage were pointed out as important participants. The leading Moanoua men from each side of the village made and fastened the gables on the corresponding sides of the house, 'eclipsing' (Howell 2002; Strathern 1988: 155) the male (or ground) side and temporarily eliciting the house as signifying the matrilineage who owns it (the female side). At the same time the 'eclipse' also rendered apparent who were the leaders of the matrilineage, standing on each side of the village, and, through this, also the salience of sidedness.[1] When the *vato* were fastened, the emphasis changed and the house became predominantly a representation of the land of the village and the rights to the land: representations of male continuity eclipsed those of female continuity. At this stage of the ritual, conflicts regarding land rights and inheritance would often be brought to the fore: only at such occasions would the whole 'map' of the people and land of the village be brought together, made visible and negotiated.

When the house is completed, it is primarily a dwelling, providing shelter and protection for its inhabitants, but the imagery created through its construction is still inherent in it as powerful potentials. In some settings the house as a female icon of containment and safety can be made evident – for instance when someone dishonours the house or mischief happens within it. When Tafalti's money was stolen in Singero, it was Iamoe of the Moanoua lineage, rather than her husband, the head of the household, who became morally responsible: the qualities of safety and containment, associated with motherhood and the matrilineages were made dominant, and, in this context, Iamoe became the head of the female house. But houses may also be elicited as more 'male' forms – for instance when a *koakoale* calls for a meeting to discuss land rights on the veranda of his house and women's contextual subordination is made physically evident as she crawls behind their backs on her hands and knees when having to pass them. In the past, when the *nyaboá*, the male cult houses, were present in the villages, the shifting eclipsing of the male and female forms would have been even more evident: The *nyaboá* as a male cult house was certainly androgynous. The application of the term used for a mother who has just given birth – *boaruka* – to men who initiated the young boys and to those who tore down an old cult house all add further dimensions to the house as female. And when the *leoa* spirits were called to the village, the spirit that appeared first was a 'pregnant' one that went to the cult house and gave birth to the male *leoa*: the male cult house became a female birth hut (*boaruka*) (Hogbin 1970b: 61). But women were prohibited from entering the house, and, as such, the social context of the cult house was always male. Wogeo houses become, in this sense, similar to how Silverman described the Eastern Iatmul 'cosmos' as androgynous, 'combining a poetics of female fertility with the sociopolitic actions of men' (1996: 33).[2]

According to how Strathern has described Melanesian persons as 'composite', relations are also contained in persons. In the last part of the book I argued that rather than seeing people-sharing-place and people-sharing-blood as groups opposed to each other, the place side and blood side (or the male and female sides) can better be understood if we see them as embodied parts of every person. Which one is given salience depends on the situation. When Gagin's daughter Marajina menstruated for the first time and had her *baras* celebration, this was made quite explicit. The main rituals were focused on her status as a *moede* – a female leader – of the place: it was her father's sisters and other women of the place who were in charge of the rituals. Her mother did not participate, but instead prepared food for the visitors and for the final food exchange: her role was that of a nurturer. When Marajina went to visit another village, she and her followers walked through the bush, and only when she had entered through a split liana rooted in the ground of the village could she enter the village space. There she went directly to a female house where the women hilariously made a mockery of her future sexual life – a female *nibek*. Not until the final days of the celebration did she parade through Dab in all her finery as a gendered woman of her father's place. Prior to this, the *baras* girl is supposed to be pushed up and through the house to which she belongs – between the rafters and up through the roof thatch (the embodiments of the land of the village).[3] Considering the polysemy of the houses, and the roofs in particular, this symbolic birth out of the roof of the house into the place becomes a momentous, meaningful act, transforming the child into an adult gendered woman of the place – not only momentous in making evident the girl's (male) place side, but also in bringing to the fore the symbolic compositeness of the house as a whole. The following food exchange – the final 'work' of making her a *moede* of the place – can be seen as a predominantly male event, and it was her father who administered the distribution of food to the people of the district.

But the day before another ritual also took place. In the morning the women of Dab gathered on the beach to dance a particular dance. Taregá women stood in line on one side and Kilbong women on the other. In their hands they held taro blackened by fire and as they sang a simple song, they changed places with each other and back again. The first half of the song said 'Kilbong go and come back again', and the second half 'Taregá go and come back again'. A Taregá should marry a Kilbong and vice versa, and the relation between the two moieties should be one of respect and generosity and the taro cooked on fire symbolized the main task of women, namely cooking. Later the same day all the women of the district gathered on the beach. They each carried their plate and placed these in two rows – the plates of the Taregá women on one side and those of the Kilbong women on the other. The women sat down behind their plates, and the plates were then exchanged between them. This was the first exchange the young girls properly participated in – that is, they each had their plate that was exchanged in their own name and not in the name of their parents, place or lineage. In these events on the beach, the maternal side of the girl eclipsed her paternal side, and, at the same time, the rituals visualized some important aspects of womanhood: marriage, food and exchange. It was these two exchanges together – in a female form on the beach and in a male form in the village – that finally made her into a woman proper, responsible for herself maintaining the relations that constitute her as a social person.

Relations in the Landscape

Wogeo composite persons 'stand for' the relationships of their parents – a male and female side – but also the relationships that produced their parents and their parents again, as well as adoptions, marriages and other significant relations, are contained within the composite person (cf. Strathern 1988). It is the histories of these relations that Wogeos make relevant when they say that they 'follow a story', emphasizing trails through the various relational components – persons – back in time. The landscape of places and pathways is seen as structured and enduring, and personal names are embedded in the landscape as places to be filled if they are vacant. We can say that names as symbols or images (like houses and *ro*) refer only temporarily to individual persons. The primary reference of a name is its place in the village and the history of the people who have filled the name. It is as such a name that can be taken away from someone: then a person is removed from the history of the name and loses the rights associated with the name. When Gagin drew his map of Dab, it was the map of these positions he made manifest. It was adjusted to currently living people, but did not designate the composition of the village in terms of actual residents: it imaged the various positions in the village and some of the names associated with them. When a person is 'placed' in a name, he or she does so on the background of a certain congruence between the history of the person in terms of its compositeness and the history of the name, and the two collapse and become one – the history of the person is included in the history of the name and vice versa.

When wandering through the landscape, people carry within them, or embody, these histories. Some of the histories are spoken of as pathways in the landscape, opening for the quite concrete experience of the connectedness that the histories elicit when actually walking upon the paths. Following a pathway to another village, perhaps to take part in an exchange or merely to go and visit someone, thus becomes an act of relating both in space and time as well as manifesting an aspect of one's composite personhood and platial belonging. When a person dies, the *manvara* mourners take upon them to act out these relations of the deceased, embodying for the last time his or her composite personhood as they wander through the same landscape the person has filled with its life. Others gather in the place of the deceased, embodying the significant relations and histories that have constituted the social person through various kinds of connections – based on blood, place, marriage or other histories.

Through life, people are continuously engaged in the constitution and maintenance of their own and others' compositeness. In one context people may elicit a relation based on platial belonging, in another they may elicit a relation to the same person based on matrilineal ties. As people go about their daily tasks or participate in ritual activities, they secure beneficial connections or flows to whatever and whoever they encounter, looking after their bodies as well as their relations. Only in this manner can a person 'sit good' in one's place. The experienced landscapes of houses, places and pathways are crucial in this work of relating: as loci for dwelling and movement and as images used to order and give meaning to the Wogeo 'being-in-the-world'. As James Weiner has written about human sociality in PNG: it 'cannot be detached from its "ground", which is literally its earth, but also its historical grounding' (2001: 166).

Inspired by Merleau-Ponty (1962) and Bourdieu (1977), Csordas (1990) has suggested that 'embodiment' as a paradigm in anthropology will help us overcome the 'Cartesian split' between body and mind and bridge the gap between experience and representation, between practice and structure. Csordas saw the body as the 'existential ground of culture' (ibid.: 5) and defined embodiment as 'an indeterminate methodological field defined by perceptual experience and by mode of presence and engagement in the world' (1999: 182). In the case of the analysis of Wogeo sociality, and in accordance with my reading of Wagner, it seems important to also emphasize 'embodiment' as referring to the act of making 'concrete and perceptible' (Merriam Webster Collegiate Dictionary 2003): i.e. to how meaning is embodied (or made concrete) also in phenomena external to the body – for instance in houses, pathways, places or trees – although not 'external' in the sense of 'set apart from' since our perception of meaning is intrinsically a bodily matter. The knowledge of the *koakoale* is embodied in the *moanuboa*, fertility and growth in trees, relations between people in pathways, land rights in the rafters of houses, shared belonging in the sides of the village and the social composition of the villages in the named houses. In the concrete and experienced Wogeo landscapes, people's dwelling and movements are never merely just that: it is a continuous creation and manifestation of a meaningful world.

Postlude

An event that took place one Sunday in 1999 tellingly elicits the salience of place, pathways and the importance of 'looking after' people's bodies and relations in Wogeo sociality. It is also represents the way I like to remember Wogeo.

It was late Sunday morning in Dab. The women from Kajenamoa and Lukaluka had cooked pots of taro, sweet potatoes and bananas. *Oaila* herbs had been collected, and healing and soothing *kadaga* had been made. We were off to visit Kamagun and his family. His wife, Iangeine, and children had been quite sick for some time. They belonged to the side of Moaroka that was related to our side of Dab: they were *dan ta*. In addition, Iangeine was Tarere's niece and Kamagun was Gagin's brother-in-law. There were, thus, several relations that urged us to go and see the sick. Most people had gone to mass, and only Moita, Guria and I were left in Dab. The three of us took the pots on our heads and left the village towards Kinaba. Following the narrow pathway after one another, the forest provided a cooling shade from the hot sun as the warm pots weighed heavily on our heads. When we reached Kinaba and hurriedly walked over the hot pebbles covering the village space, a couple of people who had not gone to mass shouted to us from their verandas: 'Where are you going?' 'We are going to see Kamagun and Iangeine,' we answered, and they did not ask us to pause for a betel nut and a chat. Our destination and purpose was clear: Kamagun's family's condition was well-known and people were worried. As we continued towards Moaroka, the path trailed through several coconut groves and, eventually, along the beach just before Moaroka. In Moaroka we went straight through the village to Dan Ulú, which was 'our side' of Moaroka. The rest of the Lukaluka/Kajenamoa people were already there, and they had given the sick *kadaga* to drink. We took the bundles of *oaila* and rubbed the sweet smelling herbs on the skin of Iangeine and her three children. The *oaila* rendered their bodies fresh and cleansed, and, afterwards, the *oaila* were wrapped in a banana leaf and put aside. It was now polluted and should be thrown at sea.

The Dab women then served the food on plates and gave them to Kamagun and his family. Plates were given to the old people of the village as well – including Kulbobo who, in spite of his troubles breathing when walking too far, had made one of his rare visits outside of Dab. He was not sitting with us, though, but with the old *koakoale* Jangara in Lukaluka. Kulbobo was from Moarmoar and was not part of our work. Maloa from Jobae was also in Moaroka to visit the sick (she was a matrilineal relative of Iangeine's father), and, as we sat down to smoke and eat betel nuts, she came with plates of sago to us. The women of Moaroka had also started to cook – even Iangeine, who had been quite sick – and we were told to wait. The sun passed across the sky, and, in the shade on Kamagun's house, we consumed heaps of betel nuts and smoked many cigarettes. Eventually we were told to climb up onto the elevated veranda of Jabat's house, Omdara – the house associated with Mafofo that also had its place in Kajenamoa. There we were presented with an abundance of food. All the women of Moaroka had cooked. Two chickens had been slaughtered: one in the name of Moita and me, the other one in the name of Tarere and Mats (my linguist colleague). My friend, Medo, came with fried pork for Mats and me. All the plates were filled with delicacies – the obligatory taro, sweet potatoes and bananas, but also a type of edible liana, corn, fish, fruits and other sweet-tasting food. We were overwhelmed and ate until or stomachs nearly burst. Now we certainly would have to kill chickens for the Moaroka people when they came for the reciprocal visit, we agreed. After the meal, we were presented with betel nuts, tobacco and green coconuts. We shared this and the remainders of the food between us and carried it with us.

As the sun went down, we wandered along the pathway back to Dab. Our stomachs were full and heavy, but I could certainly understand the Wogeos' common claim in such situations: that they felt their bodies to be light. Walking along the path was easy. We had helped 'look after' the bodies of our Moaroka relatives, we had tied a rope of exchange, anticipating the return, and we had enjoyed the display of abundance of food. The Dab women would surely have to put some effort into reciprocating the hospitality and the grand gifts of food, but that was for later. It had indeed been a good day.

With the words Wogeos use when a story has been told to its end, at least for this time, I end this book: *Kabain nga. Kadok!* – That was all. Finished!

Notes

1. At the time of Hogbin's research, when the hiddenness of the matrilineages was more important than today, this was probably one of the few times the matrilineages were made manifest– although not to Hogbin who was probably not aware of the matrilineages and, thus, could not 'see' how the matrilineages were visualized.

2. David Lipset argues, inspired by Bakhtin, that the way Murik men play upon such images of motherhood in their ritual life can be described as a 'hidden dialogue' with a silent other (Lipset 1997).

3. An analogy to Nat Kadamoanga who was 'born' out of the ground can be made here.

References

Akin, D. 2004. 'Ancestral Vigilance and the Corrective Conscience: Kastom as Culture in Melanesia', *Anthropological Theory* 4(3): 299–324.

Allen, M. 1984. 'Elders, Chiefs, and Big Men: Authority Legitimation and Political Evolution in Melanesia', *American Ethnologist* 11(1): 20–41.

Anderson, A. 1996. 'Men Play Flutes, Women Bear Children. Sharing Places and Sharing Blood: Concepts of Belonging, Growth and Fertility in Wogeo, Papua New Guinea', Cand. Polit. thesis. University of Oslo, Oslo.

———. 1998. 'Sans av steder i Melanesia', *Norsk Antropologisk Tidsskrift* 9(1): 21–33.

———. 2001. 'Adopsjon og tilhørighet på Wogeo, Papua Ny-Guinea', *Norsk Antropologisk Tidsskrift* 12(3): 175–88.

———. 2003a. 'Landscapes of Sociality: Paths, Places and Belonging in Wogeo Island, Papua New Guinea', in I. Hoëm and S. Roalkvam (eds), *Oceanic Socialities and Cultural Forms: Ethnographies of Experience*. Oxford: Berghahn Books, pp. 51–70.

———. 2003b. 'Wogeo Landscapes: Places, Movement and the Politics of Belonging in Wogeo, Papua New Guinea', Dr. Polit. thesis. University of Oslo, Oslo.

———. 2004. 'Adoption and Belonging in Wogeo', in F. Bowie (ed.) *Cross-Cultural Approaches to Adoption*. London: Routledge, pp. 111–26.

Anderson, A. and M. Exter. 2005. *Wogeo Texts: Myths, Songs and Spells from Wogeo Island, Papua New Guinea*. Oslo: The Kon-Tiki Museum, Intitute for Pacific Archaeology and Cultural History.

Aufenanger, H. 1972. *The Passing Scene in North-East New-Guinea: (a Documentation)*. St. Augustin.

Bamford, S. 1998. 'To Eat for Another: Taboo and the Elicitation of Bodily Form among the Kamea of Papua New Guinea', in M. Lambek and A. Strathern (eds), *Bodies and Persons: Comparative Perspectives from Africa and Melanesia*. Cambridge: Cambridge University Press, pp. 158–72.

———. 2007. *Biology Unmoored: Melanesian Reflections on Life and Biotechnology*. Berkeley: University of California Press.

Barlow, K. 1985. 'The Role of Women in Intertribal Trade among the Murik of Papua New Guinea', *Research in Economic Anthropology: A Research Annual* 7: 95–122.

Barlow, K., D.M. Lipset and M.E. Meeker. 1986. 'Culture, Exchange, and Gender: Lessons from the Murik', *Cultural Anthropology* 1(1): 6–73.

Barnes, J.A. 1962. 'African Models in the New Guinea Highlands', *Man (N.S.)* 62(1): 5–9.

Barth, F. 1975. *Ritual and Knowledge among the Baktaman of New Guinea*. Oslo: Universitetsforlaget.

Battaglia, D. 1992. 'The Body in the Gift: Memory and Forgetting in Sabarl Mortuary Exchange', *American Ethnologist* 19(1): 3–18.

Beckett, J. 1989. *Conversations with Ian Hogbin*. Sydney: Oceania.

Bender, B. 1993. *Landscape: Politics and Perspectives*. Providence, R.I.: Berg.

———. 2006. 'Place and Landscape', in C. Tilley, W. Keane, S. Küchler, M. Rowlands and P. Spyer (eds), *Handbook of Material Culture*. London: Sage, pp. 303–14.

Berkaak, O.A. 1991. 'Samtidskultur som påbegynt virkelighet: noen tolkningsproblemer', *Norsk Antropologisk Tidsskrift* 1(1): 62–77.

Biersack, A. 1991. 'Introduction: History and Theory in Anthropology', in A. Biersack (ed.) *Clio in Oceania: Toward a Historical Anthropology*. Washington: Smithsonian Institution Press, pp. 1–36.

Bourdieu, P. 1977. *Outline of a Theory of Practice*. Cambridge: Cambridge University Press.

Brady, I. 1976. *Transactions in Kinship: Adoption and Fosterage in Oceania*. Honolulu: The University Press of Hawaii.

Brown, P. 1980. 'Ian Hogbin's Ethnography of Wogeo', *Reviews in Anthropology* 7(1): 131–39.

Bulbeck, C. 2002. *Australian Women in Papua New Guinea: Colonial Passages 1920–1960*. Cambridge: Cambridge University Press.

Busse, M. 2005. 'Wandering Hero Stories in the Southern Lowlands of New Guinea: Culture Areas, Comparison, and History', *Cultural Anthropology* 20(4): 443–73.

Carrier, A.H. and J.G. Carrier. 1991. *Structure and Process in a Melanesian Society: Ponam's Progress in the Twentieth Century*. Chur: Harwood Academic Publishers.

Carroll, V. (ed.). 1970. *Adoption in Eastern Oceania*. Honolulu: University of Hawai'i Press.

Carsten, J. and S. Hugh-Jones (eds). 1995. *About the House: Lévi-Strauss and Beyond*. Cambridge: Cambridge University Press.

Casey, E.S. 1996. 'How to Get from Space to Place in a Fairly Short Stretch of Time: Phenomenological Prolegomena', in K.H. Basso and S. Feld (eds), *Senses of Place*. Santa Fe, New Mexico: School of American Research Press, pp. 13–52.

Counts, D.R., T.G. Harding and A. Pomponio. 1991. 'Children of Kilibob: Creation, Cosmos, and Culture in Northeast New Guinea', *Pacific Studies* 17(4 (special issue)).

Csordas, T.J. 1990. 'Embodiment as a Paradigm for Anthropology', *Ethos* 18(1): 5–47.

———. 1999. 'The Body's Career in Anthropology', in H. Moore (ed.) *Anthropological Theory Today*. Cambridge: Polity Press, pp. 172–205.

Dalle, B.G., T. Fandim and H.I. Hogbin. 1972. 'Wogeo Notes', *Oceania* 42(1): 25–32.

De Lepervanche, M. 1967/68. 'Descent, Residence and Leadership in the New Guinea Highlands', *Oceania* 38(2,3): 134–58, 163–89.

Douglas, M. 1966. *Purity and Danger: An Analysis of Concepts of Pollution and Taboo*. London: Routledge.

Elden, S. 2002. *Mapping the Present: Heidegger, Foucault and the Project of a Spatial History*. London: Continuum International Publishing.

Encyclopædia Britannica Online. 2002. *'Pleiades'*. Retrieved February 6, 2002 from <http://search.eb.com/bol/topic?eu=61925&sctn=1>.

Englund, H. and J. Leach. 2000. 'Ethnography and the Meta-Narratives of Modernity', *Current Anthropology* 41(2): 225–48.

Errington, F. and D. Gewertz. 2001. 'On the Generification of Culture: From Blow Fish to Melanesian', *Journal of the Royal Anthropological Institute* 7(3): 509–25.

Evans-Pritchard, E.E. 1937. *Witchcraft, Oracles, and Magic among the Azande* Oxford: Clarendon Press.

Eves, R. 1997. 'Seating the Place: Tropes of the Body, Movement and Space for the People of Lelet Plateau, New Ireland (Papua New Guinea)', in J.J. Fox (ed.) *The Poetic Power of Place: Comparative Perspectives on Austronesian Ideas of Locality*. Canberra: Research School of Pacific and Asian Studies, ANU, pp. 174–96.

———. 1998. *The Magical Body: Power, Fame and Meaning in a Melanesian Society*. Amsterdam: Harwood Academic Publishers.

Exter, M. 2003. *Phonetik und Phonologie des Wogeo*. Köln: University of Cologne.

Feld, S. 1990. *Sound and Sentiment: Birds, Weeping, Poetics and Song in Kaluli Expression*. Philadelphia: University of Pennsylvania Press.

Firth, R. 1957. 'A Note on Descent Groups in Polynesia', *Man* 57(2): 4–8.

Fox, J.J. 1995. 'Austronesian Societies and Their Transformations', in J.J. Fox, P. Belwood and D. Tryon (eds), *The Austronesians: Historical and Comparative Perspectives*. Canberra: Research School of Pacific and Asian Studies, ANU, pp. 229–44.

———. 1997a. 'Genealogy and Topogeny: Towards an Ethnography of Rotinese Ritual Place Names', in J.J. Fox (ed.) *The Poetic Power of Place: Comparative Perspectives on Austronesian Ideas of Locality*. Canberra: Research School of Pacific and Asian Studies, ANU, pp. 89–100.

———. 1997b. 'Place and Landscape in Comparative Austronesian Society', in J.J. Fox (ed.) *The Poetic Power of Place: Comparative Perspectives on Austronesian Ideas of Locality*. Canberra: Research School of Pacific and Asian Studies, ANU, pp. 1–20.

Fox, R. 1967. *Kinship and Marriage: An Anthropological Perspective*. Harmondsworth: Penguin Books.

Freeman, J.D. 1961. 'On the Concept of Kindred', *The Journal of the Royal Anthropological Institute* 91(2): 192–220.

———. 1962. 'The Family System of the Iban of Borneo', in J. Goody (ed.) *The Developmental Cycle in Domestic Groups*. Cambridge: Cambridge University Press, pp. 15–52.

Gell, A. 1977. 'Magic, Perfume, Dream …', in I. Lewis (ed.) *Symbols and Sentiment*. London: Academic Press, pp. 25–38.

———. 1979. 'Reflections on a Cut Finger: Taboo in the Umeda Conception of the Self', in R.H. Hook and G. Devereux (eds), *Fantasy and Symbol: Studies in Anthropological Interpretation*. London: Academic Press, pp. 133–48.

———. 1999. 'Strathernograms, or, the Semiotics of Mixed Metaphors', in E. Hirsch (ed.) *The Art of Anthropology: Essays and Diagrams*. London: The Athlone press, pp. 29–75.

Gillison, G. 1980. 'Images of Nature in Gimi Thought', in C. MacCormack and M. Strathern (eds), *Nature, Culture and Gender*. Cambridge: Cambridge University Press, pp. 143–73.

Godelier, M. 1986. *The Making of Great Men: Male Domination and Power among the New Guinea Baruya*. Cambridge: Cambridge University Press.

Godelier, M. and M. Strathern. 1991. *Big Men and Great Men: Personifications of Power in Melanesia*. Cambridge: Cambridge University Press.

Goodenough, W.H. 1955. 'A Problem in Malayo-Polynesian Social Organisation', *American Anthropologist* 57(1): 71–83.

Gregor, T.A. and D.F. Tuzin. 2001. *Gender in Amazonia and Melanesia: An Exploration of the Comparative Method*. Berkeley: University of California Press.

Harrison, S. 1989. 'Magical and Material Politics in Melanesia', *Man (N.S.)* 24(1): 1–20.

———. 1990. *Stealing People's Names: History and Politics in a Sepik River Cosmology*. Cambridge: Cambridge University Press.

———. 2000. 'From Prestige Goods to Legacies: Property and the Objectification of Culture in Melanesia', *Comparative Studies in Society and History* 42(3): 662–79.

Heidegger, M. 1962. *Being and Time*. Oxford: Blackwell.

———. 1993[1954]. 'Building Dwelling Thinking', in D.F. Krell (ed.) *Basic Writings: From Being and Time (1927) to the Task of Thinking (1964)*. New York: Harper Collins, pp. 343–64.

Herdt, G.H. 1982. 'Fetish and Fantasy in Sambia Initiation', in G.H. Herdt (ed.) *Rituals of Manhood: Male Initiation in Papua New Guinea*. Berkeley: University of California Press, pp. 44–98.

Hirsch, E. 1995. 'Introduction', in E. Hirsch and M. O'Hanlon (eds), *The Anthropology of Landscape: Perspectives on Place and Space*. Oxford: Clarendon Press, pp. 1–30.

Hirsch, E. and M. O'Hanlon (eds). 1995. *The Anthropology of Landscape: Perspectives on Place and Space*. Oxford: Clarendon Press.

Hoëm, I. 1995. 'A Sense of Place: The Politics of Identity and Representation', Ph.D. thesis. University of Oslo, Oslo.

———. 2003. 'Making Sides: On the Relationship between Contexts and Difference in Tokelau', in I. Hoëm and S. Roalkvam (eds), *Oceanic Socialities and Cultural Forms: Ethnographies of Experience*. Oxford: Berghahn Books, pp. 137–56.

Hoëm, I. and S. Roalkvam (eds). 2003. *Oceanic Socialities and Cultural Forms: Ethnographies of Experience*. Oxford: Berghahn Books.

Hogbin, H.I. 1935a. 'Native Culture of Wogeo', *Oceania* 5(3): 308–37.

——. 1935b. 'Trading Expeditions in Northern New Guinea', *Oceania* 5(4): 375–407.

——. 1935/36a. 'Adoption in Wogeo, New Guinea', *Journal of the Polynesian Society* 44,45(4,1): 208–15, 217–38.

——. 1935/36b. 'Sorcery and Administration', *Oceania* 6(1): 1–32.

——. 1936. 'Mana', *Oceania* 6(3): 241–74.

——. 1938. 'Social Reaction to Crime: Law and Morals in the Schouten Islands, New Guinea', *The Journal of the Royal Anthropological Institute* 68(Jan.–Jun.): 223–65.

——. 1938/39. 'Tillage and Collection: A New Guinea Economy', *Oceania* 9(2,3): 127–51, 286–325.

——. 1939. 'Native Land Tenure in New Guinea', *Oceania* 10(2): 113–65

——. 1940. 'The Father Chooses His Heir: A Family Dispute over Succession in Wogeo', *Oceania* 11(1): 1–40.

——. 1943. 'A New Guinea Infancy: From Conception to Weaning in Wogeo', *Oceania* 13(4): 285–309.

——. 1945a. 'Marriage in Wogeo', *Oceania* 15(4): 324–52.

——. 1945b. *Peoples of the Southwest Pacific*. New York: The John Day Company.

——. 1946a. 'A New Guinea Childhood: From Weaning to the Eight Year in Wogeo', *Oceania* 16(4): 275–96.

——. 1946b. 'Puberty to Marriage: A Study of the Sexual Life of the Natives of Wogeo', *Oceania* 16(3): 185–209.

——. 1952/53. 'Sorcery and Succession in Wogeo', *Oceania* 23(2): 133–36.

——. 1961. *Law and Order in Polynesia: A Study of Primitive Legal Institutions*. Hamden: The Shoe String Press.

——. 1964. 'Wogeo Kinship Terminology', *Oceania* 34(4): 308–9.

——. 1970a. 'Food Festivals and Politics in Wogeo', *Oceania* 40(4): 304–28.

——. 1970b. *The Island of Menstruating Men: Religion in Wogeo, New Guinea*. Scranton: Chandler.

——. 1971. 'A New Guinea Childhood from Conception to the Eighth Year', in L.L. Langness and J.C. Weschler (eds), *Melanesia: Readings on a Culture Area*. Scranton: Chandler, pp. 173–213.

——. 1978. *The Leaders and the Led: Social Control in Wogeo, New Guinea*. Melbourne: Melbourne University Press.

Hogbin, H.I. and A. McGrath. 1983. 'Interview with Ian Hogbin', in *National Australian Library oral history project*. Sydney: National Australian Library.

Holy, L. 1996. *Anthropological Perspectives on Kinship*. London: Pluto Press.

Howell, S. 1986. 'Formal Speech Acts as One Discourse', *Man (N.S.)* 21: 79–101.

——. 2001. '«En vanlig familie»: utenlandsadopsjon i Norge, et stadig voksende fenomen', in S.L. Howell and M. Melhuus (eds), *Blod – tykkere enn vann? Betydninger av slektskap i Norge*. Bergen: Fagbokforlaget, pp. 73–98.

——. 2002. 'Nesting, Eclipsing and Hierarchy: Processes of Gendered Values among Lio', *Social Anthropology* 10(2): 159–72.

———. 2006. *The Kinning of Foreigners: Transnational Adoption in a Global Perspective*. New York and Oxford: Berghahn Books.

Hugh-Jones, S. 2001. 'The Gender of Amazonian Gifts: An Experiment with an Experiment', in T.A. Gregor and D. Tuzin (eds), *Gender in Amazonia and Melanesia: An Exploration of the Comparative Method*. Berkeley: University of California Press, pp. 245–78.

Hviding, E. 1993. 'Indigenous Essentialism? "Simplifying" Customary Land Ownership in New Georgia, Solomon Islands', in T.v. Meijl and P.v.d. Grijp (eds), *Politics, Tradition and Change in the Pacific*, pp. 802–24.

———. 1996. *Guardians of Marovo Lagoon: Practise, Place and Politics in Maritime Melanesia*. Honolulu: University of Hawai'i Press.

———. 2003. 'Disentangling the *Butubutu* of New Georgia: Cognatic Kinship in Thought and Practice', in I. Hoëm and S. Roalkvam (eds), *Oceanic Socialities and Cultural Forms: Ethnographies of Experience*. New York and Oxford: Berghahn Books, pp. 71–114.

Ingold, T. 2000. *The Perception of the Environment: Essays on Livelihood, Dwelling and Skill*. London: Routledge.

Iteanu, A. 1995. 'Rituals and Ancestors', in D. de Coppet and A. Iteanu (eds), *Cosmos and Society in Oceania*. Oxford: Berg Publishers, pp. 135–64.

Jebens, H. 2005. *Pathways to Heaven: Contesting Mainline and Fundamentalist Christianity in Papua New Guinea*. New York and Oxford: Berghahn Books.

Jeudy-Ballini, M. 2002. 'To Help and to "Hold": Forms of Cooperation among the Sulka, New Britain', in M. Jeudy-Ballini and B. Juillerat (eds), *People and Things: Social Mediations in Oceania*. Durham: Carolina Academic Press, pp. 185–210.

Keesing, R.M. 1981. *Cultural Anthropology: A Contemporary Perspective*. New York: Holt, Rinehart and Winston.

———. 1982. 'Introduction', in G.H. Herdt (ed.) *Rituals of Manhood: Male Initiation in Papua New Guinea*. Berkeley: University of California Press, pp. 1–43.

———. 1992. *Custom and Confrontation: The Kwaio Struggle for Cultural Autonomy*. Chicago: The University of Chicago Press.

———. 1993a. '"Earth" and "Path" as Complex Categories: Semantics and Symbolism in Kwaio Culture', in P. Boyer (ed.) *Cognitive Aspects of Religious Symbolism*. Cambridge: Cambridge University Press, pp. 93–110.

———. 1993b. 'Kastom Re-Examined', in G.M. White and L. Lindstrom (eds), *Custom Today*, pp. 587–96.

Krell, D.F. 1993. 'General Introduction: The Question of Being', in D.F. Krell (ed.) *Basic Writings: From Being and Time (1927) to the Task of Thinking (1964)*. New York: Harper Collins, pp. 3–36.

Lawrence, P. 1971[1964]. *Road Belong Cargo: A Study of the Cargo Movement in the Southern Madang District, New Guinea*. Manchester: Manchester University Press.

Leach, J. 2000. 'Situated Connections: Rights and Intellectual Resources in Rai Coast Society', *Social Anthropology* 8(2): 163–80.

————. 2003. *Creative Land: Place and Procreation on the Rai Coast of Papua New Guinea*. New York and Oxford: Berghahn Books.

————. 2009. 'Knowledge as Kinship: Mutable Essence and the Significance of Transmission on the Rai Coast of Papua New Guinea', in J. Leach and S. Bamford (eds), *Kinship and Beyond: The Genealogical Model Reconsidered*. New York and Oxford: Berghahn Books, pp. 175–92.

Leavitt, S.C. 2001. 'The Psychology of Consensus in a Papua New Guinea Christian Revival Movement', in C.C. Moore and H.F. Mathews (eds), *The Psychology of Cultural Experience*. Cambridge: Cambridge University Press, pp. 151–72.

Lévi-Strauss, C. 1983. 'The Social Organization of the Kwakiutl', *The Way of the Masks*. Seattle: University of Washington Press, pp. 163–87.

Liep, J. 1991. 'Great Man, Big Man, Chief: A Triangulation of the Massim', in M. Godelier and M. Strathern (eds), *Big Men and Great Men: Personifications of Power in Melanesia*. Cambridge: Cambridge University Press, pp. 28–46.

Lindstrom, L. 1984. 'Doctor, Lawyer, Wise Man, Priest: Big-Men and Knowledge in Melanesia', *Man* 19: 291–309.

Lipset, D.M. 1985. 'Seafaring Sepiks: Ecology, Warfare, and Prestige in Murik Trade', *Research in Economic Anthropology: a Research Annual* 7: 67–94.

————. 1997. *Mangrove Man: Dialogics of Culture in the Sepik Estuary*. Cambridge: Cambridge University Press.

Lutkehaus, N.C. 1990. 'Manam Hierarchy and "Heroic Society"', *Oceania* 60(3): 179–98.

————. 1995a. 'Gender Metaphors: Female Rituals as Cultural Models in Manam', in N.C. Lutkehaus and P.B. Roscoe (eds), *Gender Rituals: Female Initiation in Melanesia*. New York: Routledge, pp. 183–204.

————. 1995b. *Zaria's Fire: Engendered Moments in Manam Ethnography*. Durham: Carolina Academic Press.

McCarthy, G.J. 1993. *Hogbin, Herbert Ian Priestley (1904–1989): Bright Sparcs Biographical Entry*. Retrieved February 10, 2006 from http://www.asap. unimelb.edu.au/bsparcs/biogs/P002068b.htm.

McGregor, A.M. 2005. Diversification into High-Value Export Products: Case Study of the Papua New Guinea Vanilla Industry, Food and Agriculture Organization (UN), Rome.

McKinnon, S. 1991. *From a Shattered Sun: Hierarchy, Gender and Alliance in Tanimbar Islands*. Madison: The University of Wisconsin Press.

————. 1995. 'Houses and Hierarchy: A South Moluccan Society', in J. Carsten and S. Hugh-Jones (eds), *About the House: Lévi-Strauss and Beyond*. Cambridge: Cambridge University Press, pp. 170–88.

McWilliam, A. 1997. 'Mapping with Metaphor: Cultural Topographies in West Timor', in J.J. Fox (ed.) *The Poetic Power of Place: Comparative Perspectives on Austronesian Ideas of Locality*. Canberra: Research School of Pacific and Asian Studies, ANU, pp. 101–13.

Meigs, A.S. 1984. *Food, Sex and Pollution - a New Guinea Religion*. New Jersey: Rutgers University Press.

Mels, T. 2005. 'Between "platial" Imaginations and Spatial Rationalities: Navigating Justice and Law in the Low Countries', *Landscape Research* 30(3): 321–335.

Merleau-Ponty, M. 1962. *Phenomenology of Perception*. London: Routledge.

Merriam-Webster Collegiate Dictionary. 2003. *Embodies*. Retrieved January 20, 2003 from <http://search.eb.com/dictionary>.

Mihalic, F. 1971. *The Jacaranda Dictionary and Grammar of Melanesian Pidgin*. Port Moresby: The Jacaranda Press.

Mosko, M. 1991. 'Great Men and Total Systems: North Mekeo Hereditary Authority and Social Reproduction', in M. Godelier and M. Strathern (eds), *Big Men and Great Men: Personifications of Power in Melanesia*. Cambridge: Cambridge University Press, pp. 97–114.

Munn, N.D. 1973. *Walbiri Iconography: Graphic Representation and Cultural Symbolism in a Central Australian Society*. Ithaca: Cornell University Press.

Myers, F.R. 1986. *Pintupi Country, Pintupi Self Sentiment, Place and Politics among Western Desert Aborigines*. Washington, D. C.: Smithsonian Institution Press.

van Oosterhout, D. 2001. 'The Scent of Sweat: Notions of Witchcraft and Morality in Inanwatan', in A. Strathern and P.J. Stewart (eds), *Humors and Substances: Ideas of the Body in New Guinea*. Westport, Conn.: Bergin & Garvey, pp. 23–50.

Paijmans, K. (ed.). 1976. *New Guinea Vegetation*. Amsterdam: Elsevier Scientific Publishing Company.

Parmentier, R.J. 1987. *The Sacred Remains: Myth, History, and Polity in Belau*. Chicago: University of Chicago Press.

Paulsen, R. 1992. 'Symbolic Dimensions in the Analysis of Social Organization: A Case Study of Food Taboos among the May River Iwam, Papua New Guinea', Cand. Polit. thesis. University of Oslo, Oslo.

Richards, A.I. 1950. 'Some Types of Family Structure Amongst the Central Bantu', in A.R. Radcliffe-Brown and D. Forde (eds), *African Systems of Kinship and Marriage*. London: Oxford University Press, pp. 207–51.

Rival, L. 1998. 'Trees, from Symbols of Life and Regeneration to Political Artefacts', in L. Rival (ed.) *The Social Life of Trees: Anthropological Perspectives on Tree Symbolism*. Oxford: Berg, pp. 1–36.

Roalkvam, S. 1997. 'Pathways to Hardness: Values of Body, Gender and Place in Onotoan Social Life', Ph.D. thesis. University of Oslo, Oslo.

———. 2003. 'Pathway and Side: An Essay on Onotoan Notions of Relatedness', in I. Hoëm and S. Roalkvam (eds), *Oceanic Socialities and Cultural Forms: Ethnographies of Experience*. Oxford: Berghahn Books, pp. 115–36.

Robbins, J. 2004. *Becoming Sinners: Christianity and Moral Torment in a Papua New Guinea Society*. Berkeley, Calif.: University of California Press.

———. 2007. 'Continuity Thinking and the Problem of Christian Culture – Belief, Time, and the Anthropology of Christianity', *Current Anthropology* 48(1): 5–38.

Sack, P.G. 1975. 'Mythology and Land Rights in Wogeo', *Oceania* 46(1): 40–52.

Sahlins, M. 1963. 'Poor Man, Rich Man, Big Man, Chief: Political Types in Melanesia and Polynesia', *Comparative Studies in Society and History* 5(3): 285–303.

———. 1985. *Islands of History*. Chicago: University of Chicago Press.

Scheffler, H.W. 1965. *Choiseul Island Social Structure*. Berkeley: University of California Press.

———. 1985. 'Filiation and Affiliation', *Man (N.S.)* 20(1): 1–21.

Schneider, D.M. 1984. *A Critique of the Study of Kinship*. Ann Arbor: The University of Michigan Press.

Scott, M.W. 2007a. 'Neither "New Melanesian History" nor "New Melanesian Ethnography": Recovering Emplaced Matrilineages in South-East Solomon Islands', *Oceania* 77(3): 337–54.

———. 2007b. *The Severed Snake: Matrilineages, Making Place, and a Melanesian Christianity in Southeast Solomon Islands*. Durham, N.C.: Carolina Academic Press.

Seo, L. 1991. 'Fishing on Vokeo Island', *Grassroots Research Bulletin* 1(2): 27–31.

Shryock, A. 1997. *Nationalism and the Genealogical Imagination: Oral History and Textual Authority in Tribal Jordan*. Berkeley: University of California Press.

Silverman, E.K. 1996. 'The Gender of the Cosmos: Totemism, Society and Embodiment in the Sepik River', *Oceania* 67(1): 30–47.

Sinoto, Y.H. 1959. 'Drifting Canoe Prows', *Journal of the Polynesian Society* 68(4): 354–56.

Smith, A. 2003. 'Landscape Representation: Place and Identity in Ninteenth-Century Ordnance Survey Maps of Ireland', in P.J. Stewart and A. Strathern (eds), *Landscape, Memory and History: Anthropological Perspectives*. London: Pluto Press, pp. 71–88.

Smith, M.F. 1994. *Hard Times on Kairiru Island: Poverty, Development, and Morality in a Papua New Guinea Village*. Honolulu: University of Hawaii Press.

———. 2002. *Village on the Edge: Changing Times in Papua New Guinea*. Honolulu: University of Hawai'i Press.

Sperber, D. 1975. 'The Symbolic Mechanism (Chapter 5)', *Rethinking Symbolism*. London: Cambridge University Press.

Strathern, A. 1991. 'Struggles for Meaning', in A. Biersack (ed.) *Clio in Oceania: Toward a Historical Anthropology*. Washington: Smithsonian Institution Press, pp. 205–30.

Strathern, M. 1988. *Gender of the Gift: Problems with Women, Problems with Society in Melanesia*. Berkeley: University of California Press.

———. 1991. 'Introduction', in M. Godelier and M. Strathern (eds), *Big Men and Great Men: Personifications of Power in Melanesia*. Cambridge: Cambridge University Press, pp. 1–4.

———. 1992. 'Parts and Wholes: Refiguring Relationships in a Post-Plural World', in A. Kuper (ed.) *Conceptualising Society*. London: Routledge, pp. 75–106.

————. 1993. 'Making Incomplete', in V. Broch-Due, I. Rudie and T. Bleie (eds), *Carved Flesh, Cast Selves: Gendered Symbols and Social Practices*. Oxford: Oxford University Press, pp. 41–82.

————. 1994. 'Parts and Wholes: Refiguring Relationships', in R. Borofsky (ed.) *Assessing Cultural Anthropology*. New York: McGraw-Hill, pp. 204–17.

————. 1996. 'Cutting the Network', *Journal of the Royal Anthropological Institute* 2(3): 517–35.

Swadling, P. 1980. 'Traditional Settlement Histories and Early Historical Accounts of the Schouten Islands, East Sepik Province', *Oral History* 8(2): 91–100.

Sørum, A. 2003. 'Sociality as Figure: Bedamini Perceptions of Social Relationships', in I. Hoëm and S. Roalkvam (eds), *Oceanic Socialities and Cultural Forms: Ethnographies of Experience*. Oxford. Berghahn Books, pp. 13–28.

Tiesler, F. 1969–70. 'Die Intertribalen Beziehungen an Der Nordküste Neuguineas Im Gebeit Der Kleinen Schouten-Inseln', *Abhandlungen und Berichte des Staatlichen Museums für Völkerkunde Dresden* 30–31: 118–23.

Tilley, C. 1994. *A Phenomenology of Landscape: Places, Paths and Monuments*. Oxford: Berg Publishers.

Tuan, Y.-F. 1977. *Space and Place: The Perspective of Experience*. Minneapolis: University of Minnesota Press.

Turner, V. 1967. *The Forest of Symbols: Aspects of Ndembu Ritual*. Ithaca and London: Cornell University Press.

Tuzin, D.F. 1982. 'Ritual Violence among the Ilahita Arapesh: The Dynamics of Moral and Religious Uncertainty', in G.H. Herdt (ed.) *Rituals of Manhood: Male Initiation in Papua New Guinea*. Berkeley: University of California Press, pp. 321–56.

————. 1991. 'The Cryptic Brotherhood of Big Men and Great Men in Ilahita', in M. Godelier and M. Strathern (eds), *Big Men and Great Men: Personifications of Power in Melanesia*. Cambridge: Cambridge University Press, pp. 115–29.

————. 1997. *The Cassowary's Revenge: The Life and Death of Masculinity in a New Guinea Society*. Chicago: The University of Chicago Press.

Vorman, F. [1901]1980. 'A Journey to the Schouten Islands in May 1901', in P. Swadling (ed.) *Traditional Settlement Histories & Early Historical Accounts of the Schouten Islands, East Sepik Province. Oral History 8(2), Special Edition*, pp. 91–100.

Wagner, R. 1974. 'Are There Social Groups in the New Guinea Highlands', in M.J. Leaf (ed.) *Frontiers of Anthropology: An Introduction to Anthropological Thinking*. New York: D. van Nostrand, pp. 95–122.

————. 1977a. 'Analogic Kinship: A Daribi Example', *American Ethnologist* 4(4): 623–42.

————. 1977b. 'Scientific and Indigenous Papuan Conceptualization of the Innate: A Semiotic Critique of the Ecological Perspective', in R.G. Feachem and T.P. Bayliss-Smith (eds), *Subsistence and Survival: Rural Ecology in the Pacific*. London: Academic Press, pp. 385–410.

————. 1978. *Lethal Speech: Daribi Myth as Symbolic Obviation*. Ithaca: Cornell University Press.

———. 1981. *The Invention of Culture*. Chicago and London: University of Chicago Press.

———. 1986a. *Asiwinarong: Ethos, Image, and Social Power among the Usen Barok of New Ireland*. Princeton, N.J.: Princeton University Press.

———. 1986b. *Symbols That Stand for Themselves*. Chicago: The University of Chicago Press.

———. 1988. 'Visible Sociality: The Daribi Community', in J.F. Weiner (ed.) *Mountain Papuans: Historical and Comparative Perspectives from New Guinea Fringe Highlands Societies*. Ann Arbor: The University of Michigan Press, pp. 39–72.

Waterson, R. 1997. 'The Contested Landscapes of Myth and History in Tana Toraja', in J.J. Fox (ed.) *The Poetic Power of Place: Comparative Perspectives on Austronesian Ideas of Locality*. Canberra: Research School of Pacific and Asian Studies, ANU, pp. 63–90.

Weiner, A.B. 1976. *Women of Value, Men of Renown: New Perspectives in Trobriand Exchange*. Austin: University of Texas Press.

———. 1988. *The Trobrianders of Papua New Guinea*. New York: Holt Rinehart and Winston.

Weiner, J.F. 1991. *The Empty Place. Poetry, Space, and Being among the Foi of Papua New Guinea*. Bloomington: Indiana University Press.

———. 2001. *Tree Leaf Talk: A Heideggerian Anthropology*. Oxford: Berg.

Weiner, J.F. and K. Glaskin. 2007. 'Customary Land Tenure and Registration in Papua New Guinea and Australia: Anthropological Perspectives', in J.F. Weiner and K. Glaskin (eds), *Customary Land Tenure and Registration in Australia and Papua New Guinea*. Canberra: ANU E Press, pp. 1–14.

Westmark, G. 2001. 'Anthropology and Administration: Colonial Ethnography in the Papua New Guinea Eastern Highlands', in N.M. McPherson (ed.) *In Colonial New Guinea: Anthropological Perspectives*. Pittsburgh: University of Pittsburgh Press, pp. 45–63.

Glossary

Wogeo	English
bag	bed, platform, partner (exchange partner within the island, can also be used for overseas exchange partners)
baga	mainland
baikó	body (3rd pers. sg. poss.)
baj	carry (on shoulder)
bale	to tell
baras	menstruation, menstruating woman, female initiands, the Pleiades (stars), one year
bija	down
binga	power (ability) of producing/bringing forth in abundance
bitanga	big
boab	protective magic (malignant), mark
boabou	bad smell
boasa	magical spell
boasava	to leave someone alone, to the effect that the spirit of the person who has left remains and spoils the efforts of the person who stays behind
bobo	butterfly, *koakoale's* 'spy'
boeka	to hang
boka	salt, ocean
boro	pig
bua	betel nut
bulum	mountain
bum	grandparent/grandchild – reciprocal term of address
bunga	white
burenga	aromatic mixture of herbs, coconut oil and red ground/*Bixa orrelana* seeds, used to cleanse people's bodies
buti	small
dan	water, term designating people belong to, or are associated with, the same place
dara	blood
dol	to finish
dualí	affines in same generation – reciprocal term of reference (3rd pers. sg. poss.)
faraik	to cut (into halves)
farík	to cut (off)
fíle	to say (something), speak
filava	statement

filava sangarar	metaphor, 'picture talk'
gina	light green
gira	edible greens
giramoa	wooden slit gong, *garamut* (TP)
goate	basket
gongon	to play, dance
ia	him, her or it
iaboua	sorcery
iamaiama	thought (also in the sense of wisdom), feeling
iamuna	male initiands
ianá	affines in parent/child generation – reciprocal term of reference (3rd pers. sg. poss.)
iaoá	spouse – reciprocal term of reference (3rd pers. sg. poss.)
iata	up
ib	Tahitian chestnut (lat. *Inocarpus fagifer*)
ié	tree with fruits containing red seeds used as body decoration (lat. *bixa orrelana*)
ika	fish
iko	you
ila	side towards sea
iló	inside
itakaoa	to fall down
itú	star
ival	to refuse, avoid
jala	path
jala osar	to clear a path
jer	ground
jim	black, rain cloud, ashes
jiraboa	container
jonga	circular boar's tusk, basket of power
ka	tree
kaba	garden, delimited place
kabain	like this
kaboaram	type of *oaila*
kadaga	drink made from coconut water and various ingredients, such as herbs or bark from trees (used for medical purposes)
kadok	finished, enough
kaiuk	bridge
kaoera	yellow
kalaoá	mother's brother/sister's child – reciprocal term of reference (3rd pers. sg. poss.)
kalet	back (side)
kaleva	moon
kalingó	good
kaloga	plate
kalogaloga	exchange of food on plates

kamá	fish, *fusilier* of the *Caesionidae* family
kamina	large basket
kangar	*canarium* almond (*galip* in Tok Pisin)
kanyik	relish (equivalent to the Tok Pisin *abus* for food added to the staple – like fish, meat and greens – see also *ngada*)
kat	canoe
ke	dog
kenken	palm spathe
kiam	cold
kiamiam	gathering of mourners after a death (something similar to, or related to, cold)
klgrlg	girl
kilbong	flying fox
kita	we
kitarú	the two of us
koab	forest
koadem	banana
koakoale	chief
kura	fish, rock cods and groupers of the *Serranidae* family
kurita	octopus
kus ta	one skin
kusí	skin (3rd pers. sg. poss.), also used synonymous with body
lako	to go, walk
langana	disease from contact with menstrual blood, sexual fluids and similar
lele	to lean over
leoa	mask, mask spirit
lona	outer reef
loso	to wash
lu	opposite-sex sibling – reciprocal term of reference (3rd pers. sg. poss.)
lugu	to put
luma	smell of sex
lung	rollers for launching canoes
maian	steel, used for anything 'of the white man'
malala	village, cleared area
maleka	something's or someone's place
malekatí	to stand up in one's predecessor's place
maleva	knowledge, competence
malmalí	breath (life, lung) (3rd pers. sg. poss.)
mama	father – term of address
manif	to work (verb and noun)
manuan	palolo worm (*Eunice viridis*), the moon of the palolo worm
manvara	those who have touched a dead body
maoir	type of *kadaga* made after a death
masaoa	empty

mariaboa	spirit, ghost
maun	cross-cousin, reciprocal term added to the relevant sibling term
meme	tongue, language
moang	good
moanuboa	*cordyline*, symbol of *koakoale* positions and the associated knowledge
moanyako	food
moado	to sit
moede	*koakoale's* wife/daughter
mos	pregnant
muj	poisin
nanaranga	mythical beings; histories about mythical beings
nanarani	teach
nanasa	(n) history or myth, (v) to tell a story
nanau	to instruct
nanauva	instruction
nat	boy, child
natú	child – term of reference (3rd pers. sg. poss.)
nga	only
ngabir	giant taro (lat. *Alocasia macrorrhiza*)
ngada	relish (equivalent to the Tok Pisin *abus* for food added to the staple – like fish, meat and greens – see also *kanyik*)
ngadur	a type of *burenga* used at the New Year celebration
ngaro	teeth, the second-in-command to the *koakoale*
nges	ginger
ni	coconut
ni tongatonga	species of coconut (red)
nibek	ceremonial flute, flute spirit, also used to refer to things associated with the male cult
nigi	oil
nigira	soup
nyaboá	male cult house
nyonyo	breast, milk, reciprocal term of address for mother/child and aunt/niece/nephew
oagare	stinging nettle (lat. *Laportea*)
oaila	aromatic herbs
oanga	sweet potato
oaoa	mother's brother/sister's child (reciprocal term of address)
oala	to adopt
oalisi	to empty
oaraboa	display and exchange of food
oaro	liana, rope, wine
oarooaro	kindred
oasá	bird of paradise
oasaboai	pair of boys initiated together

oasek	okari nut (lat. *Terminalia kaernabachii*)
oatala	type of nut
olage	inter-village ceremonial exchange of food (in someone's name)
one	beach
ramata	human being, man, person
raoa	beach
rekareka	dirty, bad, polluted
ruma	house
singara	rudder, law, customary way
singare	to steer
somoa	sick, disease
tabo	no, not
tabul	to turn
tafas	to arrive
tamá	father – term of reference (3rd pers. sg. poss.)
tangboal	genre of dance and song
taregá	eagle
taur	conch shell
tavá	companion, partner, also used for boys initiated together (3rd pers. sg. poss.)
teí	younger same-sex sibling – term of reference (3rd pers. sg. poss.)
tilab	teacher
tiná	mother – term of reference (3rd pers. sg. poss.)
titi	type of banana with yellow meat
toká	elder same-sex sibling – term of reference (3rd pers. sg. poss.)
tubú	grandparent/grandchild – reciprocal term of reference (3rd pers. sg. poss.)
tuga	indeed, very
udem	bandicoot
ulú	on top of
uta	side towards bush
vabel	potential malignant connections with *nanaranga* or work associated with *nanaranga* (said to be equivalent to 'germs')
vama (vam)	outrigger (*vama* is the proper Wogeo term, *vam* is the Koil 'shortened' term)
van	to give
vanua	island, country, village, place of belonging
vanunu	shadow, ghost
var	fence
vatak	to show
vato	roof thatch
vava	name
vaine	woman
veka	type of fruit said to grow only in Wogeo, possibly *Casimiroa Edulis* (White Sapote).

Index